Y0-BOE-987

# Personal Relationships

# Personal Relationships

## An Interdisciplinary Approach

DALE E. WRIGHT
**Juniata College**

Mayfield Publishing Company
Mountain View, California
London • Toronto

Copyright © 1999 by Mayfield Publishing Company

All rights reserved. No portion of this book may be reproduced in any form or by any means without written permission of the publisher.

*Library of Congress Cataloging-in-Publication Data*

Wright, Dale E.
    Personal relationships : an interdisciplinary approach / Dale E. Wright.
        p.   cm.
    Includes bibliographical references and index.
    ISBN 1-55934-952-2
    1. Interpersonal relations.   I. Title.
HM132.W73   1998
302—dc21                                                                98-30174
                                                                        CIP

Manufactured in the United States of America

10   9   8   7   6   5   4   3   2

Mayfield Publishing Company
1280 Villa Street
Mountain View, California 94041

Sponsoring editor, Franklin C. Graham; developmental editor, Barbara Armentrout; production editor, Linda Ward; copy editor, Judith Brown; design manager, Jean Mailander; cover designer, Claudia Smeltzer; art editor, Amy Folden; illustrator, Anne Eldredge; photo researcher, Brian Pecko; manufacturing manager, Randy Hurst. The text was set in 10/12 Sabon by UG/GGS Information Services and printed on 50# Finch Opaque by R. R. Donnelley & Sons Company.

Cover image: Judith Dunworth, untitled, 1997. Mixed media. 30″ × 30″. Photo by Judith Dunworth © 1997.

Text and photo credits appear on page 355, which constitutes a continuation of the copyright page.

# Brief Contents

Preface xvii
Introduction 1

PART I RELATIONSHIP PROCESSES
Chapter 1 The Evolutionary Perspective 7
Chapter 2 Relationship Development 26
Chapter 3 Relationship Maintenance 44

PART II RELATIONSHIP GOALS
Chapter 4 Personal Relationships and Well-Being 62
Chapter 5 Coping With Loneliness 84

PART III FRIENDSHIP
Chapter 6 Children's Friendships 104
Chapter 7 Adolescent Friendships 122
Chapter 8 Adult Friendships 141
Chapter 9 Stigma and Disability 160

PART IV INTIMACY PROCESSES
Chapter 10 Liking and Loving 175
Chapter 11 Physical Attractiveness 197
Chapter 12 Self and Other 215
Chapter 13 Commitment 233

PART V CHALLENGES AND ISSUES
Chapter 14 Power 250
Chapter 15 Jealousy 268
Chapter 16 Conflict 288

Bibliography 305
Credits 355
Index 357

# Contents

Preface    xvii
Introduction    1

## Part 1 Relationship Processes

### CHAPTER 1    THE EVOLUTIONARY PERSPECTIVE    7

Origins of Social Behavior    8
  *Four Characteristics of Relationship*    8
Affiliation    9
  *Disadvantages of Affiliation*    9
  *Advantages of Affiliation*    10
Attachment    11
  *Disruption of Normal Attachment*    12
  *Early Attachment and Later Adjustment in Humans*    13
  *From Attachment to Altruism*    15
Altruism    16
  *Kin Selection*    17
  *From Kin Selection to Reciprocal Altruism*    18
  *Human Emotion and Cooperation*    19
Sexuality    22
  *In a Different Key: Where Have All the Shakers Gone?*    23
Conclusion    23
Suggestions for Further Reading    24

## CHAPTER 2   RELATIONSHIP DEVELOPMENT   26

Stage Theories   26
  *Murstein's S-V-R Theory*   27
  *Critique of the Stage Approach*   28
Incremental Approaches   28
  *Social Penetration Theory*   28
  *Critique of Social Penetration Theory*   31
Issues in Communicating Interest   33
  *Uncertainty Reduction*   33
  *Receptivity Signals*   33
  *Affinity Testing*   34
The Question of "Early Decision"   36
  *Going Beyond the Normative*   39
  *Nonengagement*   40
Conclusion   40
  *In a Different Key: Friendship in Fuenmayer*   41
Suggestions for Further Reading   42

## CHAPTER 3   RELATIONSHIP MAINTENANCE   44

Exchange Theory   45
  *Basic Concepts of Exchange Theory*   45
  *Critique of Exchange Theory*   47
  *Exchange in Friendships, Dating, and Marriage*   48
  *In a Different Key: Friendship in Andalusia*   49
  *The Emergence of Norms*   50
  *Equity Theory*   50
  *The Role of Attribution*   52
Relationship Definition   53
  *Mutuality of Relationship Definition*   54
  *Mutuality of Control*   55
  *Consensus Concerning Influence Potential*   55
The Shift From Flattery to Authenticity   56
  *The Emergence of Authenticity*   56
The Social Context of Personal Relationships   58
  *The Dyadic Withdrawal Hypothesis*   59
  *Dyadic Realignment*   59
Conclusion   60
Suggestions for Further Reading   61

# Part II Relationship Goals

CHAPTER 4 PERSONAL RELATIONSHIPS AND
WELL-BEING 62

*In a Different Key:* Social Support Among the Hutterites 63

Types of Support 64

*Instrumental Support* 64

*Financial Resources* 64

*Validational Support* 65

*Emotional Support* 65

*Companionship* 65

*Social Identity* 66

Epidemiological Research Into the Health Effects of Social Support 66

*Social Connectedness and Health* 66

*Community Cohesiveness and Heart Disease* 69

*Social Support, Stress, and Complications During Pregnancy* 71

*Church Attendance and Health* 72

*Social Connection and Mortality Among Members of a Health
Maintenance Organization* 72

*Social Connection and Cancer* 72

*Rehabilitation and Recovery* 73

*The Role of Confidants* 73

*In a Different Key:* Thomas Adeoye Lambo 74

Effects of Partner Loss on Health 75

*Bereavement and Mental Health* 75

*Bereavement and Physical Health* 76

*Bereavement and Mortality Rate* 76

*Causes of Death Among the Bereaved* 77

*Health Consequences of Separation/Divorce* 78

*Preliminary Conclusions on Partner Loss and Health* 79

How Social Support Affects Health 79

*The Behavioral Route: Social Support for Healthy Behaviors* 80

*The Physiological Route: Stress and the Suppression of Immune
Function* 81

Conclusion 82

Suggestions for Further Reading 82

**CHAPTER 5   COPING WITH LONELINESS   84**

Descriptions of Loneliness   85
  *Types of Loneliness   85*
  *Measuring Loneliness   87*
  *The Statistical Picture   87*
Loneliness Over the Life Span   89
  *Loneliness in Children   89*
  *Loneliness During Adolescence   90*
  *Loneliness in Adulthood   91*
Gender Differences in Loneliness   93
Social Interactions and Loneliness   94
  *What Do Lonely People Do?   95*
  *Quality Versus Quantity of Relationships   95*
  *In a Different Key: Shunning Among the Amish   96*
  *Changes in Status of Relationships   97*
Personality Factors and Loneliness   97
  *Shyness   98*
  *Self-Esteem   98*
  *Social Skills   99*
  *How Others Perceive the Lonely   100*
Intervention   101
Conclusion   102
Suggestions for Further Reading   102

## Part III Friendship

**CHAPTER 6   CHILDREN'S FRIENDSHIPS   104**

The Child's Concept of Friendship   104
  *Stage Theories   105*
The Theme of Reciprocity   107
  *Tit-for-Tat Exchange   107*
  *Preschoolers and the Emergence of Shared Meaning   107*
  *Reciprocity: From Practice to Principle   108*
  *Friendship as an Accomplishment   109*
Selected Areas of Research in Children's Friendships   110
  *Siblings and Friends   110*
  *Similarity   111*
  *Gender   111*

*Race   112*
*Stability in Children's Friendships   112*
*Sociometric Status   112*
*Friendship and Popularity   115*
Children at Risk   116
*Correlates of Early Peer Rejection   116*
*Intervention   118*
*In a Different Key: Arranged Friendships   119*
Conclusion   121
Suggestions for Further Reading   121


**CHAPTER 7   ADOLESCENT FRIENDSHIPS   122**
The Significance of Friends in Adolescence   123
Girls' Friendships in Early, Middle, and Late Adolescence   123
Adolescent Culture   125
*Cliques and Crowds as a Way of Establishing Identity   125*
*Crowds as the Context for Friendship   129*
*How Important Are Cliques and Crowds?   131*
The Stability of Adolescent Friendships   131
*In a Different Key: Camaradia   132*
*Best Friends   133*
*Conflict   133*
Correlates of Adolescent Friendships   133
*Friendship and Family Background   133*
*Friendship and Similarity   134*
*Friendship and Gender   135*
*Opposite-Sex Friendships   136*
*Friendship and Race   137*
*Friendship and Popularity   137*
*Friendship and Conformity   138*
*Friendship and Social Adjustment   138*
Conclusion   139
Suggestions for Further Reading   139


**CHAPTER 8   ADULT FRIENDSHIPS   141**
Issues in Friendship During Adulthood   141
*Defining and Measuring Friendship in Adulthood   142*
*Close Friends and Friendly Relationships   142*
*Special-Interest Friendships   144*

*Gender Differences in Friendships*   144

*In a Different Key: Women in Rural Taiwan*   145

*Friendships and the Workplace*   147

Adult Friendships Across the Age Range   148

*Friendships Among Young Adults*   149

*Friendship During Maturity and Middle Age*   151

*Friendships Among Adults 65 and Over*   153

Is There a Downside to Friendship in Adulthood?   157

Conclusion   158

Suggestions for Further Reading   158


**CHAPTER 9   STIGMA AND DISABILITY   160**

Effects of Stigma   161

*The "Marked" Versus the "Markable"*   161

*"Passing"*   161

*In a Different Key: Stigma and Obesity*   162

*Deviance Disavowal*   164

*Choice of Friends*   164

The Problem of Norm Ambiguity and Ambivalence   165

Stigma Across the Age Range   166

*Children and Their Peers*   167

*Adolescents and Their Peers*   167

*Personal Relationships and the Stigmatized Adult*   169

Degree of Impairment and Social Adjustment   171

*Adaptation Over Time*   171

*Relationships With Spouse and Family*   172

*Intimate Relationships*   172

Conclusion   173

Suggestions for Further Reading   173


*Part IV Intimacy Processes*

**CHAPTER 10   LIKING AND LOVING   175**

Rubin's Liking and Love Scales   176

*Correlates of Liking and Love Scores*   176

Different Types of Love   177

*Passionate Versus Companionate Love*   178

*Friendship as a Component of Love*   180

*Preliminary Conclusions*   181

More Comprehensive Models of Love   181

*Lee's Typology   181*

*In a Different Key:* Arranged Marriage   *183*

*Sternberg's Triangular Theory   184*

*Love as a Prototype   187*

*Love as Attachment   192*

Conclusion   195

Suggestions for Further Reading   196

**CHAPTER 11   PHYSICAL ATTRACTIVENESS   197**

Why Physical Attractiveness?   198

Measuring Physical Attractiveness   199

*In a Different Key:* Is an Appreciation for Beauty Built Into Our
Biology?   *200*

Physical Attractiveness and Gender   200

*The Evolutionary Account   201*

*The Sociocultural Account   202*

Physical Attractiveness and Attributions   203

*Social Consequences of Physical Attractiveness   204*

*Physical Attractiveness and Occupational Success   204*

*Physical Attractiveness and "Legal" Settings   204*

*Physical Attractiveness and Mental Health   205*

*Physical Attractiveness and Personality   205*

Physical Attractiveness Over the Life Span   206

*Physical Attractiveness and Children   206*

*Physical Attractiveness and Romantic Relationships   207*

*Physical Attractiveness and Social Mobility   209*

*Physical Attractiveness and Same-Sex Friendships   210*

*Physical Attractiveness and Marriage   211*

*Does Physical Attractiveness Have a Downside?   212*

Conclusion   213

Suggestions for Further Reading   213

**CHAPTER 12   SELF AND OTHER   215**

Identity Negotiation   216

*The Self-Verification Process   216*

*Routine Self-Verification   219*

*The Role of Friends in Self-Verification   219*

*Preliminary Conclusions   221*

Complementarity   222

*The Early Work on Complementarity   222*

*Similarity and Complementarity*  222
Interpersonal Theory  223
Self-Evaluation Maintenance  223
  *Relevance*  225
  *Closeness*  225
  *The Dynamics of SEM*  225
Transactive Memory  227
  *Experimental Evidence for Transactive Memory*  228
  *The Generation Effect*  230
  *Implications of Transactive Memory*  230
Conclusion  231
Suggestions for Further Reading  231

**CHAPTER 13   COMMITMENT  233**
Personal and Structural Commitment  234
Dissonance Theory and the Commitment Process  235
  *How Costs Increase Perceived Value*  235
  *Ambivalence and Personal Relationships*  238
Rusbult's Investment Model  240
  *Satisfaction Versus Commitment*  240
  *In a Different Key:* Commitment Among Lesbians and Gay
    Males  243
  *Commitment and Relationship Maintenance Strategies*  244
  *Sacrifice and Attribution*  245
  *Commitment Testing*  247
Individual Differences in Commitment  247
  *In a Different Key:* Till Death Do Us Part  248
Conclusion  248
Suggestions for Further Reading  249

*Part V Challenges and Issues*

**CHAPTER 14   POWER  250**
The Dynamics of Power  251
  *Power as a Double-Edged Sword*  251
  *Liking as a Source of Power*  252
  *Power and Friendship*  253
  *The Principle of Least Interest*  254
  *Power and the Availability of Alternative Relationships*  254

Power and Gender    256
   *Power Tactics    257*
   *The Boston Couples Study    257*
   *Other Research Findings on Power and Gender    258*
   *In a Different Key: Whom Does a Princess Marry?    262*
   *Gender, Careers, and Personal Relationships    262*
Power and Individual Differences    264
   *Need for Power    264*
   *Power and Aversion to Conflict    265*
   *Strong Versus Weak Tactics    265*
Conclusion    266
Suggestions for Further Reading    266


**CHAPTER 15    JEALOUSY    268**
Types of Jealousy    268
What Provokes Jealousy?    269
   *Jealousy as a Prototype    270*
   *In a Different Key: What Provokes Jealousy Cross Culturally?    274*
Jealousy and Individual Differences    275
   *Measuring Jealousy    275*
   *Jealousy and Self-Concept    277*
   *Jealousy and Self-Esteem    277*
   *Jealousy and Attachment Style    278*
   *Jealousy and Self-Evaluation Maintenance    279*
Gender Differences in Jealousy    279
   *In a Different Key: Polyandry    280*
Jealousy and Violence    281
Jealousy and the Nature of the Relationship    282
   *Relationship Status    282*
   *Attribution and Jealousy    283*
   *Equity Theory and Jealousy    284*
   *Jealousy, Attitudes, and Alternate Lifestyles    285*
Conclusion    286
Suggestions for Further Reading    287


**CHAPTER 16    CONFLICT    288**
Conflict Between Friends    288
Conflict and Romantic Relationships    289
   *Areas of Conflict    289*
   *Precipitating Events    290*

Conflict and Relationship Development    290
    *Conflict and Successful Relationships    290*
    *Conflict and Unsuccessful Relationships    292*
    *Confronting Versus Avoiding Conflict    293*
The Role of Attribution in Conflict    295
    *Levels of Interdependence    295*
    *Attributions Among Distressed Versus Nondistressed Couples    296*
Other Issues in the Study of Conflict    298
    *The Demand-Withdraw Pattern    298*
    *Conflict Over Values, Beliefs, and Goals    298*
    *Marital Conflict and Duration of Marriage    299*
    *What About Couples Who Never Fight?    300*
Conflict Resolution    300
    *Negotiation    300*
    *In a Different Key:* Conflict Resolution Among the Nzema    301
    *Escalation    301*
    *Conciliation    302*
    *Integrative Agreements    302*
Conclusion    303
Suggestions for Further Reading    304

Bibliography    305
Credits    355
Index    357

# Preface

Research in the area of personal relationships has grown dramatically in recent years. What has been particularly interesting about this development is its interdisciplinary nature. Researchers from fields as diverse as evolutionary biology, social psychology, sociology, marriage and family studies, developmental psychology, communication, leisure studies, gerontology, and anthropology have all made contributions. This book is an effort to bring this research together into something resembling a coherent whole. It's only fair to note, however, that my own background is in psychology, and no doubt, the book reflects this point of view. It's possible—even likely—that other writers would have emphasized different issues.

Since I first began offering a seminar on friendship, a dozen or more years ago, I have been fortunate in having the contributions of many curious and highly motivated students, who somehow could never limit their focus to platonic relationships. Their interests always spilled over into romantic relationships. After seeing this happen year after year, I became convinced not only that a broader approach to the area of personal relationships was advisable, but also that the study of friendship helped to shed light on romantic relationships and vice versa.

This book is intended for undergraduates. I have tried to avoid jargon as much as possible, and when it has been necessary to use technical terms, I have tried to define and illustrate them in ways that make the underlying concepts clear.

The approach throughout is primarily descriptive. Such theories as we find (perhaps *themes* would be a better term) are exchange (or interdependence) theory and its several variations. Exchange of some sort appears to be a cross-cultural universal in human interactions, but, as students will see, its application to the area of personal relationships leaves many questions unanswered. A second theme in the research literature is the generation of models, or prototypes. With experience in the business of relating, we come to anticipate what others are likely to do in various situations. This, in turn, leads us to expect certain things of others and to understand that they expect certain things of us in return. Over time these prototypical cases tend to take on a prescriptive quality and, as a consequence, come to play a powerful role in determining satisfaction or dissatisfaction with our personal relationships.

Based on these expectations, we tend to make attributions concerning the other person's abilities, interests, and motives in relating. This is the third theoretical thread found in the research on personal relationships. It is in the departures (both positive and negative) from our expectations that attributions of such qualities as caring and trust (or their opposites, such as exploitation and betrayal) are likely to be made and acted upon.

I would like to express my thanks to the administration and trustees of Juniata College for granting me a sabbatical, during which the lion's share of the work on the manuscript was completed. I have also been fortunate in having the comments, criticisms, and suggestions of several anonymous reviewers early in the manuscript's development. I count myself especially lucky to have had the suggestions and assistance of Barbara Armentrout, Judith Brown, Frank Graham, and Linda Ward, editors at Mayfield Publishing Company, whose efforts on my behalf have been far above and beyond the call of duty.

Finally, I would like to dedicate this work to my wife Helen and our daughter Cathy who allowed me to monopolize the family room while the project was under way.

*Dale E. Wright*
*May 1998*

# Introduction

None of us needs to be convinced of the importance of personal relationships. Our songs, our films, our literature, our everyday conversation, and our own experience all testify to their significance. Relationships, especially close personal relationships, provide much of the meaning of life for most of us (Klinger, 1977). They account for many of our joys when they go well and many of our sorrows when they do not (Argyle, 1987).

With so much riding on personal relationships, one might think we would know more about them, but, somewhat surprisingly, the scientific study of personal relationships is a relatively recent undertaking. Many of the findings in the area are quite tentative. Some are common sense, some are anti-intuitive, some are conflicting, and many questions remain.

## What Do We Mean by Personal Relationships?

There are many definitions of personal relationships, but what they all seem to have in common is some reference to such things as interdependence, need fulfillment, emotional bonding, and commitment. By *interdependence,* we mean that people associate with one another; their lives are in some sense intertwined; what each one does affects the other; and their interactions are frequent, important, diverse, and enduring (Berscheid & Peplau, 1983).

But interdependence can occur without leading to a personal relationship. For example, politicians often form coalitions simply because they "need" each other, without this implying much in the way of caring, sharing, or heartfelt emotion. What else distinguishes those relationships we call "personal" from those we don't? Such things as the need for intimacy, the need for social integration, the need to nurture, the need to belong, and the need to receive assistance and reassurance have all been mentioned as important (Baumeister

1

& Leary, 1995; Weiss, 1969). In healthy personal relationships, such needs are met.

In addition, emotional bonding seems to be a fundamental part of personal relationships. Clearly, the way others make us feel about ourselves is important to friendship (Lea, 1989), and the same can be said for romantic relationships.

Finally, personal relationships include an element of commitment. The other person is seen as important for his or her own sake rather than for any instrumental value he or she might have (Wright, 1984), and this is true in good times and bad.

## The Focus of the Book

In this book we focus on relationships that are for the most part voluntary. We will not be concerned about relationships between parents and children, nor will we be concerned about (nonvoluntary) relationships between relatives, except as they shed light on other types of personal relationships. Relationships between relatives tend to involve somewhat different issues.

We will focus on what the person on the street would call friendship and love in the romantic sense. Where possible we will look at research that deals with real people in real relationships. When this is not possible, we will turn to laboratory experiments, simulations, questionnaire studies, and the like. In any case, we are interested here in the empirical study of personal relationships rather than the speculations we sometimes find in the popular literature.

## Overview

Chapter 1 begins with a brief look at the literature on relationships among nonhuman animals in an effort to discover something in the evolutionary record that might suggest a biological basis for the nature and function of personal relationships. Here we explore the themes of affiliation, attachment, altruism, and sexuality.

Clear evidence for each of these themes is present in the evolutionary record long before humankind came upon the scene. In the tendency to live in groups, characteristic of so many species, we see an indication of the advantages and disadvantages of togetherness. In attachment, especially as it exists in the mother-infant bond, we see the evolution of a behavior whereby the young are nurtured and protected against the various threats that the environment poses. Reciprocal altruism (or mutual aid) has been documented in nonhuman animals (for example, see Packer, 1977) and seems to provide a basis for acting in the interest of others—sometimes to one's own disadvantage—which is so much a part of close personal relationships. Finally, closeness, as it is expressed in sexuality, provides a way of passing these tendencies (to affiliate, to bond, and to help others) to future generations.

What is the effect of this heritage? For one thing, it seems to have endowed us with an interest in associating with others, getting to know them, and letting them get to know us. And so we turn next to a consideration of the ways in which initial tentative interactions evolve into stable relationships, as we look at relationship development and relationship maintenance.

In Chapter 2 we explore such notions as stage theories, incremental exchange, self-disclosure, uncertainty reduction, signals of receptivity, affinity testing, cooling-off signals, early decision, and nonengagement. Each of these topics touches on different aspects of the processes involved in the early phases of relationship development.

Chapter 3, on relationship maintenance, begins with a consideration of exchange theory, the emergence of norms, and equity. From there we turn to the attributions people make when their relationships live up to expectations or fail to do so. Next we consider the issue of mutuality in relationship definition and control, and consensus concerning influence potential. Rounding out the chapter, we note the shift from flattery to authenticity as relationships deepen and mature. The chapter ends with a discussion of the role that social context plays in supporting and validating personal relationships.

In Chapter 4 the focus is on personal relationships and well-being. Research in this area suggests clear therapeutic advantages associated with close personal relationships, for both mental and physical health, and clear costs in terms of mental and physical well-being associated with separation, loss, and isolation.

In Chapter 5, on coping with loneliness, we note first that there seem to be different types of loneliness. In particular, research suggests a distinction between the kind of loneliness experienced in the absence of a close dyadic relationship (such as a romantic relationship) and that experienced in the absence of a wider network of friends. People can be perfectly happy with a close dyadic relationship and still feel isolated socially and vice versa. On the other hand, there seems to be surprisingly little relationship between the number of people in one's social network and feelings of loneliness. Some people have a seemingly insatiable appetite for socializing, while others are content with one or two close friends. Further, we find that loneliness can affect people differently over the life span. Older people tend to experience less loneliness, even in the face of reduced social interactions. The chapter closes with a discussion of personality characteristics associated with loneliness and with intervention: Evidence suggests that such things as social skills training are effective in helping people overcome problems of loneliness.

Chapters 6 through 9 cover friendships during childhood, adolescence, and adulthood, and the effects of stigma and disability on personal relationships. Chapter 6 explores changes that occur in the concept of friendship as children grow from preschool age to preadolescence; the role of reciprocity;

and the implications of peer acceptance, neglect, and rejection. Then we look at some of the long-term consequences of peer rejection during childhood, followed by the work on intervention in cases where children have problems making and keeping friends.

Adolescent friendships are of particular interest, both because of the subjective importance they seem to have and the role they play in the emancipation process. Thus, in Chapter 7 we explore the role of cliques and crowds as the context for friendship, the distinction between popularity and friendship, gender differences in adolescent friendships, and some of the implications of peer orientation and conformity during the teen years.

In Chapter 8 we distinguish between three kinds of friendships: close, casual, and "special interest" (friendships that revolve around a particular activity). And we note the changing role of friendships associated with three major periods of adult life: the shift from "singlehood" to "couplehood" during the early adult years, a second shift toward a more family-centered social life with the arrival of children, and a third shift when children leave home, or the "empty nest." In addition, we consider gender differences, opposite-sex friendships, and the influence that socioeconomic status has on the nature of adult friendships.

Chapter 9 covers some of the effects that stigmatizing conditions, such as obesity and physical disability, have on personal relationships. Here we focus on the visibility of a stigmatizing condition, deviance disavowal, adapting to an acquired physical disability, social adjustment, and the self-esteem of the stigmatized.

In Chapter 10 we turn to liking and loving. Here we consider such topics as *passionate* versus *companionate* love, and *friendship as a component of love*. Next, we consider four of the more comprehensive approaches to love as represented in John Lee's work on love styles, Robert Sternberg's triangular theory, Beverley Fehr's treatment of love from the perspective of prototype theory, and love considered from the perspective of *attachment theory*.

Chapter 11 addresses the issue of physical attractiveness. We find that physical attractiveness has a far more pervasive influence in relationships than most of us realize or care to admit. For example, the influence of physical attractiveness is evident in the interactions of very young children, of both the same and opposite sex. It is one of the major issues in dating and relating among adolescents and young adults. It also plays an important role in relationship satisfaction among committed couples. And although males and females seem to differ somewhat in the emphasis they place on physical attractiveness, both friends and romantic partners tend to be surprisingly well matched on physical attractiveness. We also touch briefly on certain correlates of physical attractiveness in real-world situations, such as job interviews and judicial settings, and on some of the problems associated with physical attractiveness.

In Chapter 12 we explore some of the research focusing on self and other. We begin with the work of William Swann and his associates on identity negotiation. Then we turn to the concept of complementarity as exemplified in the work of Arthur Aron and Elaine Aron on "inclusion of other in self," "interpersonal theory," the application of the self-evaluation maintenance (SEM) model to personal relationships by Abraham Tesser and his associates, and the work of Daniel Wegner and his associates on transactive memory.

In Chapter 13, on commitment, we note that stable long-term friendships and romantic relationships offer an advantage not offered by relationships that easily fragment and dissolve. We focus first on the dynamics of the commitment process as suggested by Philip Brickman (1987). Then we turn to a consideration of some of the ways this process plays out, as demonstrated in Caryl Rusbult's investment model.

The final three chapters of the book look at some of the more problematic aspects of personal relationships, as we consider such issues as power, jealousy, and conflict.

We begin in Chapter 14 by noting that in the day-to-day business of relating, those who make a superior contribution, over time, can generate a "surplus." When this happens, such individuals are in a position to command a certain amount of respect, status, or admiration, or else they are likely to look elsewhere for a better return on their "investment." So it is that differences in abilities, effort, talent, or contribution translate into differences in influence and power in personal relationships. The principle of least interest, playing hard to get, gender issues, female dominance, and individual differences in need for power are some of the topics touched on in Chapter 14.

In Chapter 15 we look at jealousy and find that it seems to be closely tied to self-esteem. We explore the work on prototypes as they have been applied to various jealousy-provoking situations. We find that certain personality characteristics and certain alternative lifestyles tend to be associated with jealousy. We also note that jealousy is strongly influenced by culture. Behavior that is jealousy provoking in one culture may be entirely acceptable in another.

A certain amount of conflict seems to be a normal part of relating. Yet, we find very little research devoted to the issue of conflict between friends. Accordingly, most of our treatment of conflict in Chapter 16 focuses on the problems experienced by couples involved in romantic relationships. Here we find clear differences between relationships that are generally satisfying and those that are "distressed." Studies comparing distressed and nondistressed couples show that they tend to make very different attributions concerning their partner's behavior in the face of positive and negative interactions.

We cannot leave the area of personal relationships however, without some coverage of the diversity of findings in the area. Accordingly, boxed text with the heading "In a Different Key" appears at various points in each chapter. The purpose of these elements is to remind us that the traditional Western mindset is only one of many ways to look at personal relationships. People differ in the way they conceive of, and express, personal relationships.

## In a Different Key
### Personal Relationships in Perspective

Even a brief review of the cross-cultural literature suggests that traditional Western ideas about personal relationships are in many ways the exception (Buunk & Hupka, 1986, 1987). For example, a Vietnamese American received permission to emigrate to the United States but was only allowed to bring either his mother or his wife and child. He chose his mother. Later he managed to convince the authorities to allow his wife and child to emigrate as well (Triandis, 1994). In New Guinea, part of the process of establishing and maintaining a trading partner is to "fall in love" with the partner. In parts of Melanesia, a man marries a woman, not out of any feelings of affection for her, but for the express purpose of having her brother as his best friend. And in Ghana, same-sex friends who love each other "marry," with one acting as the husband and paying the "bridewealth" to the friend's parents (Brain, 1976). For the Karaki of New Guinea, a male who has not engaged in homosexual activity before his marriage is considered abnormal (Triandis, 1994).

With this look at the landscape, then, we turn to our subject matter in more depth, always keeping in mind the goal of trying to understand what it is that we can do to cultivate more satisfying, enduring, and fulfilling personal relationships for ourselves and those around us.

# CHAPTER 1

## ⚭ *The Evolutionary Perspective*

*Chimpanzees cannot swim, and because of this, when they are in captivity, they are sometimes kept on islands where they can then be left to roam free. Washoe was one of a colony of chimps kept in this fashion. One day, it seems, a young female chimp, Cindy, somehow crossed over an electric fence, fell into the water below, splashed wildly, and sank. Seeing this, Washoe jumped the electric fence, gained a footing on a small strip of ground between the fence and the water, and, holding onto a clump of grass, grabbed Cindy as she resurfaced. Why would Washoe risk such danger to rescue another chimp? She was not related to Cindy, nor had the two been together very long. (Personal communication by R. Fouts and D. Fouts as cited in Goodall, 1986a)*

The publication of Charles Darwin's *On the Origin of Species by Means of Natural Selection* in 1859 was one of the most significant events in the history of science. In this book Darwin presented his theory of evolution and supported it with extensive research. He began with the simple fact that there is variation among members of the various species, and in the continuing struggle to survive, those that adapt successfully to their environment—the fittest—survive and others do not.

Darwin developed the notion of survival by means of natural selection after reading Thomas Malthus's *Essay on the Principle of Population*, written in 1789. Malthus reasoned that although the human population increases geometrically, the food supply only increases arithmetically. As a result, humans would inevitably face a scarcity of food, and some would survive while others would not. Darwin expanded upon this principle, arguing that it applied to all living things, and formulated the concept of natural selection: Those life forms that succeed in the struggle to survive tend to pass on to their offspring the same characteristics that led to their survival, and over many generations this has resulted in changes so extensive that it accounts for (the origin of) various species (Schultz & Schultz, 1995).

What is the importance of evolutionary theory for a consideration of personal relationships? In the evolutionary scheme of things, we—Homo sapiens—arrived rather "late in the movie." Such things as the tendency to be social, to form attachments, and to come to the aid of others in times of need, together with the role of sexual reproduction in passing these tendencies on to future generations, were all firmly established in the social behavior of primates long before we came on the scene. And importantly, for our purposes, these characteristics also laid the foundation for our tendency to form and maintain personal relationships.

In this chapter we will explore some of the similarities between the interactions of nonhuman animals and the personal relationships of humans. We begin with a broad look at social behavior.

## Origins of Social Behavior

The basic assumption of contemporary evolutionary theory is that all forms of life have undergone (and continue to undergo) a process of **differential reproduction** and **natural selection.** From an evolutionary perspective, what we think of as "traits," "tendencies," "sensitivities," "emotions," and the like, have all been fashioned and survive in the gene pool because they have contributed to the survival of various species (including our own) over many generations.

Similarly, such notions as pleasure, preference, and reinforcement are best understood by placing them within a broader context. For example, when we ask why humans today have a taste for sweets and fats, the answer in evolutionary terms is that our ancestors who had a taste for the ripest (sweetest) and most nutritional fruits, or were good hunters and "brought home the bacon," were more likely to survive, reproduce, and rear offspring successfully than were those who did not. A taste for sweets and fats, then, has had survival value, and this remains with us today in the form of taste preferences.

The same line of reasoning applies to other preferences and behavior tendencies, such as the tendency to be social and affiliate with others. For example, the notion that the strongest, most aggressive individuals would somehow have an advantage in the struggle to survive has a certain ring of common sense to it. It seems intuitively obvious that the ability to win in a battle over scarce resources would be an advantage. But if survival has depended only on being the most competitive, aggressive, and self-serving, how did social behavior evolve in the first place? How has it been maintained over many, many generations, and how does it affect our own interest in personal relationships?

### Four Characteristics of Relationship

An interest in personal relationships is expressed in our tendency to affiliate with others, to form attachments, to behave in ways that are altruistic—such as coming to the aid of others in time of need—and in our sexual drives and behaviors. These characteristics will be viewed here in quite general terms and will serve as examples of the way our evolutionary past influences our present motivations and behaviors.

It would be hard, for example, to imagine a personal relationship that did not involve some sort of togetherness or **affiliation.** However, affiliation is just the tip of the relationship iceberg. It may be necessary for a personal relationship, but it is not sufficient.

Similarly, **attachment,** we will assume, evolved initially to ensure the care and nurturing of offspring, especially in the form of the mother-infant bond, perhaps the strongest of the caring relationships. And although it would theoretically be possible to have **altruism** without some kind of attachment, the reverse wouldn't make a lot of sense. What would possibly be accomplished, in the evolutionary scheme of things, by selecting for attachment without its involving some sort of advantage in the form of aid, protection, or caring?

Finally, as we will see in this chapter, affiliation, attachment, altruism, and **sexuality** are closely linked, especially in primates, whose early experiences in the form of mother-offspring and/or peer relationships provide the basis for normal adult sexual behavior (Harlow, 1971).

We will consider these four classes of behavior from an evolutionary perspective, in an effort to establish a foundation in biology for humans' interest in forming and maintaining personal relationships.

## Affiliation

The advantages of group living seem so obvious to us that we seldom see any reason to question it. Most of us live in cities and towns. Most of us work and socialize with others on a routine basis, without giving it much thought. But from an evolutionary perspective, affiliation has disadvantages as well as advantages. Let's begin with a look at some of the disadvantages.

### Disadvantages of Affiliation

The resources necessary for day-to-day survival, such as food, water, and shelter, are often scarce and widely scattered in a state of nature. Living in groups inevitably leads to competition for these resources, especially during hard times (Alexander, 1979a). A subordinate male baboon is essentially made sterile around a dominant male. The female nesting bird in a colony is unlikely to get much attention from the father of her young when there are other females nearby. And group living increases the risk of exposure to disease (Eibl-Eibesfeldt, 1979).

Why then, we may ask, beyond the bare minimum necessary for mating and raising offspring, is there such a strong tendency to affiliate? For clearly there is. Note, for example, the number of words in our language that refer to groups of animals. Birds and sheep come in flocks, fish in schools, wolves in packs, deer and elk in herds, monkeys in colonies, and lions in prides. And we sometimes hear of a gaggle of geese, a covey of partridges, a bevy of quail, or a set of swan as well (Etkin, 1967). So the tendency to affiliate is evident in a wide variety of species.

This tendency suggests that although affiliation carries with it certain disadvantages, there must have been certain advantages that outweighed these, or we would not see species gather together in groups as much as we do. What are the advantages?

## Advantages of Affiliation

Charles Darwin's cousin Francis Galton first called attention to the tendency to affiliate in a way that was consistent with evolutionary thought. Galton published an article in 1871 entitled "Gregariousness in Cattle and in Man," based on his observations in Africa. It seems the main predators of cattle in the region were lions, and they showed a preference for attacking animals that were either on the outside of the herd or isolated. In light of this, Galton wrote as follows:

> Yet although the ox has so little affection for or interest in, his fellows, he cannot endure even a momentary severance from the herd. If he be separated from it by stratagem or force, he exhibits every sign of mental agony and when he succeeds he plunges into its middle, to bathe his whole body with the comfort of closest companionship. (Galton, 1871, as cited in Hamilton, 1971, p. 148)

Suppose that an animal senses the presence of a lion and moves toward the middle of the herd. In so doing it decreases its exposure, or its domain of danger. Over time, the tendency to "approach your nearest neighbor" becomes highly adaptive. Avoidance of predators by using the group as a cover, then, is one of the benefits of affiliation, but it is not the only one.

Groups sometimes have an advantage in locating and exploiting food sources, as in the case of wolves (Mech, 1970), or in locating scattered food sources, as in the case of vultures (Alexander, 1979a). Certain resources, such as water holes, sleeping cliffs, and islands, are localized so various species may simply gather where they can feed and rear their young in relative safety and reduce their vulnerability to attack through group defense (Alexander, 1979a; Kummer, 1968; Smuts, 1985; Strum, 1987). Other advantages of affiliation include sharing food, driving competitors from food sources, finding a mate, warning of possible danger, and caretaking when a member of the group is sick or wounded (Alexander, 1979a; Goodall, 1986a, 1990; Trivers, 1985).

We can conclude that affiliation carries with it both advantages and disadvantages, and for a given species, time, and circumstance, one may outweigh the other. But, clearly, our ancestors need not have acted alone as they responded over the years to various environmental challenges and opportunities, and those that had a tendency to affiliate with others often had an advantage in the struggle to survive.

## Attachment

The term *affiliation* is typically used to refer to the tendency to associate with others in general, while the term *attachment* is used to refer to a bond between specific individuals. From an evolutionary point of view, attachment seems to have evolved in higher animals as a mechanism to guarantee caregiving (mothering) and to provide a buffer between the relatively vulnerable offspring and an environment that is not always hospitable (see, e.g., Bowlby, 1969, 1973). Mothers in most mammalian species protect their infants from any treatment that might seem threatening. Some do not even allow others near their young.

Note, however, that attachment is a two-way process. The predisposition to caregiving on the part of the mother is complemented by crying, gesturing, and clinging on the part of the infant. The infant's part in this process was vividly demonstrated some years ago in a series of experiments by Harry Harlow. His interest at the time was in studying the consequences of abnormal mothering among infant monkeys.

In his experiment Harlow used four surrogate (dummy) mothers, none of them very good mothers. One mother shook violently, so that when the infants hugged "her," their teeth chattered and they had to hold on for dear life. One mother blew compressed air in the face of the infants with such force that it nearly took their fur with it. A third was equipped with a spring frame that popped out and knocked the infant off the mother. And the fourth had spikes

It is thought that attachment evolved to ensure care and nurturing of offspring, especially between mother and infant, the strongest of caring relationships. This infant monkey clings to the cloth mother, which is warm, rather than to the wire mother, which provides food. Even "monster mothers" represent love and security to the "adopted" young.

that emerged, periodically, from her body. As abominable as they were in these respects, however, the mothers were all covered with cuddly soft cloth, and the infant monkeys clearly became attached to them. Rather than making the infants let go, the shaking and the blasts of air only made them cling. In the case of the other two mothers, the infants had no choice except to "leave," but as the frame retracted in one and the spikes retracted in the other, the crying and protesting infants returned with their hugs. All was forgiven.

The experiments failed completely in their original aim, which was to see whether "poor mothering" would produce psychological abnormalities in infant monkeys. No such abnormalities developed. But no experiment has more clearly demonstrated the power of attachment bonds in infant primates. Even these "monster mothers" represented love and security to their "adopted" young (Harlow, 1971).

We can see that there seem to be two complementary forms of attachment—the attachment of the mother to the infant and the attachment of the infant to the mother (Harlow et al., 1963). In most primate species, including humans, for an infant to be left alone in a strange situation is intrinsically fear producing. The situation need not be associated with any negative consequences (Ainsworth & Bell, 1970). Historically, being left alone in a strange situation has indeed been dangerous for the young. Infants who were frightened when isolated, and cried and protested, were more likely to receive the aid of caretakers and as a consequence more likely to survive.

In addition, opportunities for learning through modeling and imitation are available to infants who remain close at hand but not to those who wander off. In this way the "attachment package" not only provides the protection of the mother-infant bond but also serves as a foundation in higher species upon which social learning can build, and as a result, the social adaptations of one generation can be passed on to the next (Bruner, 1972; Charlesworth, 1988). The phrase "monkey-see-monkey-do" actually refers to a highly adaptive process.

## Disruption of Normal Attachment

The crucial role of early attachment is demonstrated most clearly when it is absent. An example of this was shown in the mother-deprivation experiments of Harlow and his colleagues.

In their classic series of studies, Harry Harlow and Margaret Harlow (1969) separated macaque monkeys from their mothers for the first six months of life. This early mother deprivation led to profound disturbances in later behavior, including such things as indifference to others, vacant staring, stereotypical movements, self-clutching, suicidal aggression against older monkeys, and most importantly for our purposes, difficulty in mating later in life. Further, when females who had been "mother deprived" became mothers themselves, they tended to neglect and abuse their own infants.

What we must conclude from such examples is that among the primate species studied, both mothers and their offspring normally show strong attachment bonds. They go to extraordinary lengths to maintain these bonds, both in the lab and in naturalistic settings. Indeed, such attachments are so powerful that in several primate species, such as chimpanzees, gorillas, baboons, and rhesus monkeys, mothers have been observed to carry the body of an infant for days after it had died (Goodall, 1986a; Mellen, 1981). When separated from their mothers in the wild, infant, juvenile, and even young adult primates show searching, whining, and crying. And finally, early disruption of attachment behavior in some (but not all) primates leads to disastrous consequences for social and sexual adjustment later in life.

### Early Attachment and Later Adjustment in Humans

As shown in Figure 1-1, the evolutionary line that eventually led to Homo sapiens branched off from the ape lines approximately 15 million years ago. Accordingly, we must be careful about generalizing too freely from nonhuman primates to man (Mellen, 1981).

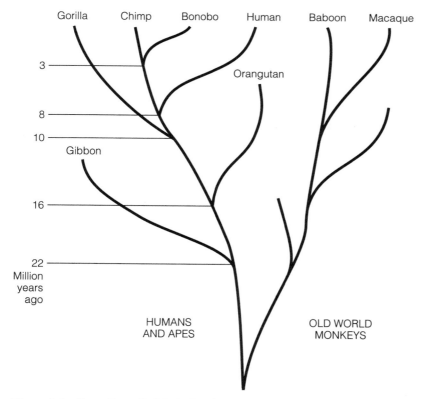

**Figure 1-1**   From Frans B. M. de Waal (1992). *Peacemaking among Primates*. Cambridge, MA: Harvard University Press. Copyright © by Frans B. M. de Waal. Reprinted by permission of author and publisher.

The development of attachment between parents and children, Dr. T. Berry Brazelton believes, has a major influence on the children's emotional and behavioral development, perhaps for a lifetime.

Many species showing infant-mother attachment show no other particularly close ties. For example, monogamy based on a male-female pair bond—an extension of the attachment theme—does occur in other primates, but it is not common. Still, the effects of certain types of early experiences in nonhuman primates do have important parallels in humans.

For ethical reasons, experiments on the effects of mother deprivation cannot be done deliberately on humans, but some "naturalistic experiments" provide important parallels. Included in these are early loss of mother, orphanage rearing, and extended hospitalization (MacDonald, 1988).

*Early Loss of Mother*   Separation from or loss of their mothers in early childhood has been shown to be associated with depression in a population of working-class women in Great Britain. Even when things were apparently going well, and the women seemed in midlife to have gotten over the effects of their early loss, the fact that they showed increased risk of depression later suggests that they continued to live with the scars (Brown & Harris, 1978).

*Orphanage Rearing and Attachment*   Children who had been admitted to an orphanage before the age of 6 months were compared with those who had been admitted after the age of 6 months (Goldfarb, 1947). All of the children were later adopted at about 3 years of age. Follow-up studies indicated that adjustment for those admitted before the age of 6 months (those who experienced disrupted attachment earlier) proved to be much more problematic. For example, 11 out of 15 of them had severe behavioral problems as adolescents, while only 4 out of 15 of those admitted after the age of 6 months experienced such problems.

Even more compelling is a study of the effects of rearing in a "stimulating" institutional environment—but one that had a great deal of employee turnover and a policy of discouraging close attachments between the children and the staff (Tizard, 1978). By the age of 24 months, for example, the average child in this study had been looked after by approximately 24 different caretakers!

After adoption between the ages of 2 and 4 years, a follow-up was conducted when the children were 8 years old. At this point, half of these children showed behavioral abnormalities such as restlessness, irritability, quarrelsomeness, lying, resentfulness when corrected, and indiscriminate showing of affection. As a group they tended to have fewer friends than normal, to be less popular and more aggressive toward their peers. They also tended to show an exaggerated friendliness or else shyness in the company of adults and strangers. And they were rated by teachers as being poor in social development. These results occurred despite every effort on the part of the adoptive parents to spend more time with the adoptees than did the parents in a comparison group (Tizard, 1978).

*Extended Hospitalization*   Extended hospitalization provides the third type of evidence bearing on the importance of early attachment in humans. Extended hospitalization, especially between the ages of 6 months and 3 years, seems to be particularly disruptive and has been correlated with problem behavior, delinquency, and unstable job performance during adolescence (Douglas, 1975; Quinton & Rutter, 1976).

It's important to add, however, that not all children who experience orphanage rearing or undergo extended hospitalization are adversely affected. About one third of the children in Tizard's study had no significant problems in later adjustment, for example. When a child has a close, warm relationship with an adult or an older child, starting life in an institution in itself does not necessarily lead to poor adjustment. And later positive relationships can help compensate for the effects of disrupted early attachment (Pringle & Bossio, 1960; Wolins, 1970).

## From Attachment to Altruism

Although it would be folly to underestimate the role of mothering in the rearing of offspring, apparently some degree of substitution is possible, both in the form of adoption and in the form of peer play. For example, Harry Harlow

As children play, they begin to form stable social relationships with their peers. And although it is play, it is serious play, for it acquaints the young with the rules of give and take as well as the sense of well-being that comes from affiliating with others.

(1959) has shown that although macaque monkeys raised with wire mesh mothers or terry cloth mother substitutes are more backward than infants raised normally, when they are allowed to play with age mates for as little as 20 minutes a day, they behave essentially the same as those who received normal mothering.

Ordinarily the influence of peers begins with transient interactions among the young. Acceptance of contact transfers gradually from its beginnings in the intimate mother-infant relationship, and it is out of these interactions that mutual contact among peers becomes less threatening. As they venture away from their mothers, juveniles and adolescents begin to form relatively stable social relationships with their peers. We call much of this early interaction *play,* but, as we shall see, it is very serious play.

What does such play accomplish? Play acquaints the young with the rules of give and take in the relationship game, the consequences of operating within the rules, and the consequences of violating them.

Early mother-infant attachment serves as the foundation upon which peer socialization is to be built. Thus, although attachment seems to have evolved initially to ensure the care of the young, it also provides the basis for the development of other social behaviors and is best seen as part of a larger picture.

## Altruism

Now the point of our opening paragraph about Washoe and Cindy should be clear. One of the most significant aspects in this larger picture of social behavior is the development of sensitivity to others and the emergence of altruism. *Altruism* is defined as engaging in any behavior that benefits another at some cost, or potential cost, to the altruist. Here we find the same behaviors that are typically associated with mothering—caring, sharing, nurturing, protection and aid in time of need—now extended beyond the mother-infant bond (Goodall, 1986a). Providing another with food in times of hunger, help in times of injury, protection in times of danger, comfort in the face of loss—all of these are possible examples of altruism.

There are, for our purposes, two ways of measuring costs. First there are the **immediate costs.** These are measured in terms of the direct consequences of an act, such as the wounds received in a fight or the loss of a valued resource. Second, there are **ultimate costs.** These are costs that affect one's representation in the gene pool. It's possible to experience immediate costs and still be adaptive in ultimate terms. One can lose the battle and still win the war. How?

## Kin Selection

As it turns out, it is possible to be represented genetically without making a direct contribution to the gene pool. Specifically, one can contribute to the reproductive success of close relatives. The classic expression of this notion came in William Hamilton's (1964) paper, "The Evolution of Social Behavior."

Hamilton's position was that the (then current) account of natural selection had to be expanded. Rather than focus on the individual and his or her reproductive success, theorists had to focus on *genetically similar* individuals. His reasoning was as follows: Suppose an individual exhibits behavior that is altruistic to the point of being self-sacrificing. The resulting loss of such an individual and her or his reproductive potential can be compensated for if those that benefit are genetically similar, that is, if the sacrifice benefits close relatives. In short, the notion of "fitness" had to be recast in terms of one's genetic representation in future generations. And genetic representation in future generations is not necessarily dependent upon individual survival or on making a direct contribution to the gene pool.

The worker honeybee that dies in defense of the hive, for example, is sterile but is represented genetically by the queen and fertile drones, and thus the tendency to self-sacrifice is passed on. Similarly, when Uncle Ned, who has remained a bachelor all his life, takes an interest in his nephew and helps him financially so he can get through college, he is, in fact, helping to ensure that genetically similar individuals will be represented in future generations. Nephews who are college graduates are more likely to attract mates and have control over the resources necessary to raise offspring to maturity.

A genetic predisposition toward altruistic behavior can be adaptive in ultimate terms, even when it is not in immediate terms. Therefore, genetically, it makes sense to come to the aid of our close relatives. Now let's take the next step.

### From Kin Selection to Reciprocal Altruism

The logic underlying the concept of reciprocal altruism (Trivers, 1971) is similar in many ways to the principle underlying the notion of kin selection, but reciprocal altruism applies to kin and nonkin alike. Conceptually, reciprocal altruism rests on the assumption that an act of sacrifice, caring, aid, or generosity establishes a (personal) relationship. And this relationship, at some future time, will be of direct (or indirect) benefit to the altruist. In comparison to kin selection, the notion of reciprocal altruism simply substitutes a psychological relationship for a biological one.

Reciprocal altruism, consistent with genetic theory, seems to apply most clearly to humans, whose long memory allows them to keep track of the costs and rewards of a given relationship (Wilson, 1975). But it has been documented in some nonhuman species as well.

*Reciprocal Altruism in Nonhuman Species*    Craig Packer (1977) reported **reciprocal altruism** in 13 different pairs of male olive baboons. Each male in the pair tended to give and receive aid from the other. Out of 140 solicitations for help, 97 resulted in aid. Twenty of these involved females in estrus, and in 14 of these cases, the female ended up with the male who received help from a second male—sort of the baboon equivalent of a best man. By contrast, 6 other cases were noted in which females were lost by a male acting alone in conflict with *two* challengers. In short, males working cooperatively in pairs were more likely to get females and, as a consequence, increase their reproductive success.

Similarly, in her study of baboon friendships, Barbara Smuts (1985) noted that male baboon "friends"—defined as those who helped a female with her offspring and defended her and her young against threats—received favorable treatment in the form of increased sexual access when the female later came into estrus. The average male could double his chances of forming a consortship (the baboon equivalent of a honeymoon) with a female by being her friend. Far from being the most aggressive males, these friends tended to be the most helpful and caring. So again we see a genetic payoff in return for some sort of aid. Who says nice guys finish last?

*The Problem of Cheating*    The problem with the notion of reciprocal altruism, comes in the possibility of cheating. Theoretically, it would be possible for individuals to quit while they were ahead in a given exchange and as a result maximize their own gains without helping in return. So any account of altruistic behavior based on the principle of reciprocity depends on cheating somehow being discouraged, and the evidence suggests that it is. For example, Frans de Waal (1982) cites a case in which Puist, an adult female chimpanzee, supported the male Luit against a young challenger. Later, however, when another male threatened Puist, she solicited Luit's support, and he did not respond. At this point Puist turned on Luit, chased him across the compound and hit him. Such a response seems to be a clear case of moralistic aggression directed toward Luit for his failure to return favor for favor. From this example, we see that among chimps there can be costs in failing to reciprocate an altruistic act in time of need. Even nonhuman primates are capable of understanding the rights and obligations that go along with relationships.

Thus, although altruism may have evolved, initially, in a context where altruistic acts were directed primarily toward one's close relatives, in the case of higher social animals, who have long memories, who recognize one another, and whose behavior is largely governed by learning, attitudes toward kin and nonkin alike are likely to be the result of the outcomes of the interactions the individuals have with one another. So we see that altruistic relationships have moved beyond the circle of immediate relatives. Among higher animals who formed enduring relationships, those who helped another in time of need, those who came to another's defense in time of threat, and those who supported others in distress could expect help in return. Reciprocal altruism, so considered, became an investment in a relationship.

Accordingly, we would expect that natural selection might have favored certain capacities (such as caring), sensitivities (such as empathy), and dispositions associated with altruistic behavior, and this is what we find. In general, reciprocal altruism is important because it generates cooperation between individuals, and the significance of this for personal relationships in humans is demonstrated in the next section.

## Human Emotion and Cooperation

Whatever else survival in humans has depended upon over the generations, it has always been closely associated with interactions with others. And cooperation and reciprocity have been central issues in these interactions. Accordingly, we would expect that certain positive and negative emotional states should be routinely associated with different interaction outcomes such as cooperation (or lack of cooperation) and support (or lack of support). Such an assumption has led investigators to study the emotional states associated with the various outcomes in what is known as the prisoner's dilemma game.

The **prisoner's dilemma game** (Luce & Raiffa, 1957) features a hypothetical situation in which two men are arrested on suspicion of robbery. The district attorney, who needs further evidence to make a case strong enough to get a conviction, talks with each prisoner separately. Their options are simple: to squeal on their partner or not to squeal on their partner. If neither squeals, both will face a lesser charge (of, say, illegal possession of firearms). If A squeals, he will get off easy, and B will serve 20 years. If B squeals, he will get off easy, and A will serve 20 years. You see the dilemma? Both prisoners are better off if they remain silent, but each is worse off if he remains silent and the other squeals. In short, the basic issue in the prisoner's dilemma game is this: Can the other person be trusted to come through when the going gets rough?

|  | [Other] support | [Other] betray |
|---|---|---|
| {Self} support | {[trust, friendship, love, pride, obligation]} | {anxiety, guilt} [anger] |
| {Self} betray | [anger] | {[rejection, hate]} |

**Figure 1-2**   Adapted from Gleitman, H. (1991). *Psychology* (3rd ed., p. 526). New York: Norton; and Neese, R. M. (1990). Evolutionary explanations of emotion. *Human Nature, 1,* (3), p. 275. New York: Aldine de Gruyter. Copyright © Walter de Gruyter, Inc.

Insofar as this model reflects fundamental issues in personal relationships, we would predict that certain emotional states would have evolved that correspond to each of the four possible outcomes represented in the game. And this is what we find. The emotions associated with the four major outcomes of the prisoner's dilemma game are shown in Figure 1-2.

*Trust, Friendship, and Love*   When two people cooperate and support each other over many interactions, feelings such as trust, friendship, and love increase. These are positive emotional states that serve to generate and maintain stable relationships.

But feelings of trust, friendship, and love go more deeply than mere cooperation, which after all can be limited to tit-for-tat reciprocity (Axelrod & Hamilton, 1981). Why, we might ask, would strict exchange not do? What particular advantage has occurred over the generations in selecting for emotional states that take us beyond tit-for-tat reciprocity?

Emotional states generated by positive outcomes take us beyond the exchange per se and lead us to focus on the relationship itself. Positive feelings about a relationship make us want to preserve it. Those who have an illogical willingness to cooperate, to share, and to help in time of need are more likely to form and maintain relationships than are those whose relationships depend on some immediate payoff, or who leave a relationship as soon as better prospects come along. People involved in the former type of relationships have an advantage over those whose relationships dissolve more easily.

*Anger*   In interpersonal situations, betrayal (for example, not coming to the aid of someone in need) or cheating (providing less than one's fair share) generates anger (Sprecher, 1986). Anger as an emotion supports both abandoning a relationship and spite (harm to the other even at some cost to the one who is angry). Note, however, that anger is not a reasoned, logical response. Why don't we just abandon the relationship and have done with it? How can such an emotion be adaptive? The answer seems to lie in the fact that relationships are worth preserving for their own sake, even at considerable cost.

Moralistic aggression such as that noted earlier in the case of Puist and Luit signals to others that cheating and betrayal will not be tolerated and, as a consequence, provides (or has provided historically) something of a guarantee against exploitation. Those who are angry act in unpredictable ways. The betrayed, the jilted, and the insulted all have an ally in anger. The tendency to retaliate has presumably been fashioned in evolutionary wisdom to serve notice and to bring would-be cheaters and betrayers into line. It constitutes a force that supports stability in relationships.

From this perspective, the spats that take place from time to time in developing relationships may be viewed as screening devices, which test commitment to the relationship. These tests serve to separate "friends in deed" from "fair-weather" friends, and serious romantic partners from those who are counterfeit.

*Conscience and Guilt*   Turning the question of betrayal and cheating around, we note that others are not the only ones that trouble us in our relationships. Sometimes we trouble ourselves. *We* are sometimes tempted to cheat. *We* are sometimes tempted to betray. Should we stay with our tried-and-true friend, or should we try our chances with someone new and possibly more interesting? Should we remain in a troubled marriage, or could we do better if we were free to look for a new mate?

Anytime we are tempted not to live up to the obligations implicit in a close personal relationship, we are likely to experience anxiety and guilt. These serve as a kind of early warning system telling us that to act on our immediate impulses could be dangerous. As such, anxiety and guilt support stability in relationships even at times when remaining in relationships is inconvenient.

By assuming that the value of keeping relationships intact is important, the seeming paradox is resolved. Anxiety and guilt in would-be cheaters are mechanisms that support the integrity of relationships. They are "advocates" of the long term over the immediate and the expedient in relationships.

*Pride and Obligation*   When we forego the attractive alternative, an internal mechanism—pride—kicks in to tell us what a good little boy or girl we are and that the alternative relationship really isn't all that great (sour grapes). This allows us to gloat in our sense of responsibility and obligation. When we betray, on the other hand, guilt is always waiting in the wings to make sure we don't enjoy the fruits of our defection, and this serves (possibly) to keep us from repeating our offense (Neese, 1990; Neese & Lloyd, 1992).

Those who have the capacity for conscience in such matters are more likely to follow the rules of relationships when they are tempted not to. By and large, the relationships that result are stronger and more dependable and offer an advantage over those that are easily fragmented by cheating and betrayal.

*Self-Interest*    The notion that the genes are ultimately selfish has often led theorists to conclude that friendship and love must somehow also be selfish—that when push comes to shove, in the struggle to survive, it's looking out for number one that counts. But self-interest may indeed be served by taking another's interests into account. In personal relationships, when one person wins, the other does not necessarily lose. Personal relationships can be win-win situations. They can offer individual advantage as well as joint or collective advantage, but only so long as they remain intact. Positive emotions provide the glue that helps keep our relationships together even during the hard times, and this presumably has been their adaptive function over the generations.

For much of our history as a species, we lived in small bands that involved face-to-face (personal) relationships. There was no Medicare, no health insurance, no refrigeration for storing and preserving food, no police, and no professional army. Our ancestors had to depend on one another in time of need. Under such circumstances, no one would have wanted to be considered untrustworthy or uncooperative. Those who cheated or betrayed would not only eat last when food was scarce, they would also lose status and the respect of others. And loss of status and respect was likely to result in decreased opportunities for reproductive success (Alexander, 1979a). And so we arrive (conveniently) at the final main topic of this chapter—sexuality.

## Sexuality

The pattern of male-female relationships that accompanies sexual activity is quite varied among primates. The two extremes are monogamy, on the one hand, and promiscuity, on the other. Monogamous relationships have been reported in gibbons and siamangs (or black gibbons) of southeastern Asia and Indonesia, and also among one or two groups of monkeys. But as primate sexual behavior goes, monogamy is representative of only about 18% of the cases (Hrdy, 1981). A male and his harem are just as common. On the other hand, complete promiscuity is not common either, although bonnet macaques of southern India apparently come pretty close (Mellen, 1981). The majority of primates fall somewhere in between. Perhaps the most common pattern involves clear signs of preferences based largely on status.

For example, Caroline Tutin (1979) noted two distinct mating patterns among the chimpanzees of Gombe. One pattern consisted of a male whose rank allowed him to keep other males away, persistently attending to a female in estrus. The second pattern was that of consortships, in which a male and female pair separated from the rest for a "honeymoon." These lasted an average of 10 days. In one case the same male-female pair went into consortship

> ## Box 1-1 In a Different Key
> ## Where Have All the Shakers Gone?
>
> The Shakers are members of a religious sect that traces its history back to 18th-century England when Mother Ann Lee led a break with the Quakers in 1774. They settled initially in New York State and for a time were of significance in the early history of the United States. They lived together in communal groups (affiliation). They gave aid to the poor and the needy (altruism). And we are safe in assuming that they also "bonded" with each other from time to time (attachment). Yet we are likely to have heard of them today (if at all) because of their association with Shaker-style furniture. Shaker communities that a century ago numbered their members in the thousands have virtually disappeared. Today the last seven remaining Shakers live in Sabbathday Lake, Maine. All the other Shaker communities have either closed or been converted to museums. Why? Their beliefs required that they remain celibate. And there is a moral there somewhere (Larson, 1997).

every time the female came into estrus. Such consortships have also been reported among rhesus macaques, savanna baboons, and bonnet macaques, and they probably occur in other species as well.

Consistent with Smuts's (1985) findings (noted earlier) females in Tutin's study showed a clear preference for males who spent the most time with them grooming and sharing food. Although such consortships accounted for a minority of the copulations that Tutin observed, because of their timing, they accounted for at least half of the pregnancies.

There is a logic to the progression that we have taken from (less intimate) affiliation to (more intimate) sexuality. In most primates, it is in the affiliation, attachments, and early peer exchanges of the young that the foundations for normal sexual behavior are laid down. Sexual behavior tends to be hopelessly inept if the groundwork for increasing levels of intimacy has not been experienced in the form of early mothering, supported by expressions of mutual caring in social interactions and peer play. Affiliation, attachment, altruism, sexuality—one, two, three, four, "Bingo."

Whatever the immediate consequences of our interactions with others, in the long term (genetically) all is lost unless these translate (directly or indirectly) into reproductive success. From the genes' point of view, everything else is merely prelude. The significance of this is illustrated in Box 1-1.

## Conclusion

By exploring the evolutionary roots of the behavior tendencies that seem so basic to personal relationships, this opening chapter has provided the vantage point from which we may come to better understand personal relationships in the broader scheme of things. Specifically, the discussion has emphasized parallels in the need for affiliation, in the role of early attachments, and in peer play and altruism in determining social and sexual competence and success.

If what has been said to this point has any validity, then our evolutionary heritage should have left us with certain preferences, certain tendencies, certain sensitivities, and certain "gut feelings" associated with our interactions with others. What is referred to as affiliation in our nonhuman ancestors translates into the human need to be with others, to belong, and to be accepted by others (Baumeister & Leary, 1995). Attachment translates into the special bonds we feel for those we call "loved ones" (Hazan & Shaver, 1987). Reciprocal altruism translates into cooperation, caring, sharing, and trust (Holmes & Rempel, 1989). And sexuality translates into attraction and passion.

When these tendencies are thwarted, they are likely to be expressed in terms of competition (power struggles), conflict, jealousy, and loneliness. With this in mind, we turn to explore the ways these wellsprings play out in everyday personal relationships.

## Suggestions for Further Reading

Alexander, R. D. (1979). Natural selection and social exchange. In R. L. Burgess & T. L. Huston (Eds.), *Social exchange in developing relationships*. New York: Academic. An advanced presentation by one of the leading authorities in the field. Spells out the link between kin selection and social exchange.

Buss, D. M. (1994). *The evolution of desire: Strategies of human mating*. New York: Basic. A short, highly readable paperback in which one of the pioneers of evolutionary psychology presents his controversial case.

de Waal, F. B. M. (1982). *Chimpanzee politics: Power and sex among apes*. New York: Harper & Row.

de Waal, F. B. M. (1989). *Peacemaking among primates*. Cambridge, MA: Harvard University Press. Both volumes by de Waal present highly accessible accounts of the advantages of coalition formation as illustrated in the life of a chimpanzee colony.

Goodall, J. (1986). *The chimpanzees of Gombe: Patterns of behavior*. Cambridge, MA: Belknap Press. Jane Goodall's classic overview of her life's work at Gombe. A well-written and extensively illustrated volume. Chapter 13, "Friendly Behavior," is especially recommended.

Harlow, H. F. (1971). *Learning to love*. San Francisco: Albion. This out-of-print work is worth tracking down in the library. Here the motherless-monkey studies are described by the master himself. No one before or since makes the case for the importance of attachment with such compelling authority coupled with such poetic writing.

MacDonald, K. B. (1988). *Social and personality development: An evolutionary synthesis*. New York: Plenum. An excellent presentation of the bridge between animal and human research, focusing especially on the attachment theme.

Smuts, B. (1985). *Sex and friendship in baboons.* New York: Aldine de Gruyter. The author notes that baboon friendships can have a genetic payoff.

Wilson, E. O. (1975). *Sociobiology: The new synthesis.* Cambridge, MA: Belknap Press. The classic work by the one who started it all.

Wright, R. (1994). *The moral animal.* New York: Pantheon. A well-written and authoritative overview of evolutionary psychology. Makes extensive reference to the life of Charles Darwin.

# CHAPTER 2

## ⚵⚵ *Relationship Development*

*"When I first met Jay,* I really didn't like him. He was so arrogant. He was obnoxious. He used to come into my office and bum cigarettes off of me all the time. I hated that. Then he came in and bummed coffee. And my mother didn't like him because he wasn't Catholic. When we decided to get married in the church, you know what he did? He told the priest he didn't believe in God. I could've killed him. We almost didn't get married because of that."* (Female colleague, mother of two, recounting 25 years of marriage. *Name has been changed. Used by permission.)*

Many approaches have been taken to the study of the development of personal relationships (see, for example, Perlman & Fehr, 1987). One approach views relationships as progressing through a series of separate and distinct stages. Another emphasizes gradual increases in the level of intimacy or involvement as relationships mature. And a third approach focuses on the signals that people send to each other (verbal and nonverbal) indicating their relative interest or lack of interest in pursuing a relationship further. In this chapter we will explore examples of these approaches, pointing out some of the strengths and weaknesses of each.

## Stage Theories

We begin with stage theories because they were popular in the early study of personal relationships, and the idea of developmental stages is common in theories of human development generally. Stage theories assume that developing relationships proceed in a stepwise fashion, moving from one stage to the next only after the requirements of the previous stage have been satisfied.

We begin with an examination of one of the better known of these—
Murstein's S-V-R theory.

### Murstein's S-V-R Theory

According to S-V-R (stimulus-value-role) theory (Murstein, 1970, 1976a,
1986, 1987), people are likely to be attracted to each other initially based on
easily observable characteristics, such as physical appearance, dress, and manner. Accordingly, the first stage of relationship development is called the **stimulus stage.**

If a developing relationship survives the first stage, it still faces a second
hurdle, the **value stage,** in which the potential friends or romantic partners
explore matters of substance and arrive (possibly) at value consensus. Finally,
in the **role stage,** new acquaintances face the specifics of relating in more or
less concrete ways in the give-and-take of everyday life.

S-V-R theory has an intuitive appeal; indeed, at one level, it is a truism.
In the early stages of relating, we do not usually have much to go on except
the obvious physical stimulus information, and attraction has to be based on
whatever information is available. Values can only be conveyed and picked
up over time (Rokeach, Smith, & Evans, 1960). New acquaintances are likely
to put their best foot forward in an effort at "self-presentation" (Goffman,
1959), sometimes making it difficult, in the short term, to separate form from
substance. Deciphering the values underlying the appearances, then, is the task
of the second stage.

Similarly, in the third stage, new acquaintances have to negotiate their
respective roles over time. A potential friend or romantic partner can both
look good and sound good but still not deliver where it counts. Bernard Murstein's stage theory is represented graphically in Figure 2-1.

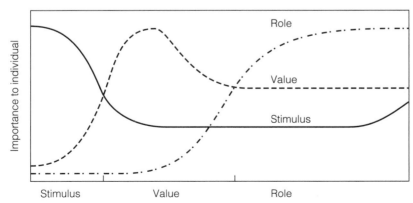

**Figure 2-1**   From Murstein, B. I. (1977). The stimulus-value-role (S-V-R)
theory of dyadic relationships. In S. Duck (Ed.), *Theory and Practice in
Interpersonal Attraction.* London: Academic Press. Reprinted by permission
of author and publisher.

**Critique of the Stage Approach**

Murstein's data have generally supported and fit well with the commonsense view that different issues tend to be important at different points in a developing relationship (Murstein, 1970, 1976a, 1976b, 1986, 1987). But, generally, the evidence for a stable sequence of qualitatively separate stages in developing relationships is simply not compelling. The fact that stage theorists themselves do not agree on the number or characteristics of the stages in relationship development is the best evidence that support for a fixed sequence is not strong, and critics have been quick to point this out (see Cate & Lloyd, 1992, Chapter 3, for a review).

For example, in a study in which newlyweds gave accounts of the way their relationships had developed over time, Catherine Surra and Ted Huston (1987) found little evidence that progress toward committed relationships fell neatly into a predictable sequence of stages. The word *phases* might be more appropriate, but these phases seem to occur at various points, last varying lengths of time, and depend very much on the individuals involved. Not surprisingly, then, some theorists have considered other ways of looking at relationship development as more promising. Among these have been the incremental approaches.

## *Incremental Approaches*

Incremental approaches to the study of relationships represent the major theoretical alternative to stage theories. In general, the incremental approaches have in common the assumption that personal relationships tend to develop gradually. For incremental theorists, there is no substitute for repeated interactions over a period of time. According to this view, relationships tend to develop their own internal economy, fueled by such things as shared experiences, mutual self-disclosure, and mutual help in time of need. This is the position of several theorists (for example, Altman & Taylor, 1973; Levinger, 1983, 1988; Levinger & Snoek, 1972).

Incremental theorists note that when we meet others for the first time, we have little knowledge of them and no common pool of resources to draw upon. There is no real way of knowing that the new acquaintance will pursue a budding relationship in a sensitive and responsible way. As a consequence, upon first meeting, we tend to keep our initial investments relatively low and distribute the costs and rewards of the relationship rather evenly, moving gradually (perhaps) to deeper involvement over time. One of the better known of the incremental approaches is called social penetration theory.

**Social Penetration Theory**

Social penetration theory was initially proposed by Irwin Altman and Dalmas Taylor (1973) and has subsequently been modified and elaborated several times (Altman, 1974; Altman et al., 1981; Morton et al., 1976). Although

Single people have the same basic desire for intimacy as married people have, but first encounters tend to be low in expectations, perhaps because of the impersonal nature of public settings.

Altman and his colleagues refer to stages of relationship development, the heart of the theory pictures developing relationships as moving from less intimate to more intimate involvement over time. This process has been described using an onion analogy (Altman, 1974), in which deeper and deeper aspects of the self are portrayed as layers that are made available to the other as a relationship progresses.

"Depth" represents a dimension reaching from the outermost to the innermost or central core of personality. According to social penetration theory, progressing inward involves more fundamental, and (ordinarily) less accessible, "layers" of the personality that are more and more unique to the individual. (Similar notions may be found in the writings of Fromm, 1956; Newcomb, 1961; Rogers, 1958a, 1958b; Rokeach, 1960, 1968.)

"Breadth" is used in the everyday sense of the term. It refers to information about a broad range of topics, such as one's family, career, religion, politics, and the like. Thus, relationships may be seen as broad or narrow, and shallow or deep, in any combination.

Figure 2-2 illustrates four prototypical relationships portraying depth and breadth dimensions using the onion analogy. Quadrant 1 represents the case of a narrow and shallow relationship, for example, an initial acquaintance or a superficial relationship. In such relationships only the outermost layers of the personality are exposed, and the range of topics shared is limited.

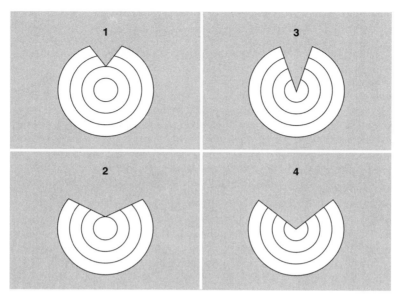

**Figure 2-2**    Adapted from Altman, I. (1974). The communication of interpersonal attitudes: An ecological approach. In T. Huston (Ed.), *Foundations of Interpersonal Attraction.* New York: Academic Press.

Quadrant 2 shows a case of low accessibility but openness across a number of topics. This might be representative of a casual acquaintance in which the individuals share several areas of their lives but at a superficial level. In quadrant 3 we have an example of a relationship that might be typified by the summer romance, the quickie marriage, or the instant intimacy sometimes encouraged in encounter groups, where people probe rapidly to the depths of one another's personalities but with little breadth. Quadrant 4 represents a broad-based relationship in which there has been considerable information exchange across many areas of mutual interest and at considerable depth. A friendship or marriage of long duration is an example of this type of relationship.

According to social penetration theory, in the early phases of a developing relationship, we are likely to proceed with caution, discuss less intimate topics, monitor conversations for signs of reciprocity, and move gradually to more intimate disclosures, until we know enough about each other that there is little left to hide and little to be gained by trying to keep up false appearances.

The early phases of relationship development tend to be characterized by low-stakes exchanges. During this time we are likely to send out trial balloons ("Do you like to ski?"), make tentative overtures ("If you'd like some help with your calc, I have some time tomorrow night"), and perhaps offer invitations suggesting increased involvement ("Some of us are getting together for dinner Friday, nothing formal, you understand. Would you be interested in joining us?"). But things are likely to be kept rather noncommittal at the beginning. This is considered a period of testing, during which we evaluate the costs and rewards of a potential relationship and make forecasts concerning its (likely) future.

*Self-Disclosure*    Social penetration theory has focused especially on self-disclosure as an indication of the state of a developing relationship (Altman & Haythorn, 1965; Hays, 1985; Morton, 1978; Taylor, 1968; Taylor et al., 1969). For example, in an investigation of relationship development among college roommates, Dalmas Taylor (1968) found that their relationships tended to progress gradually over time, with early exchanges dealing with more superficial matters ("So, what did you do this summer?") and those involving more intimate areas coming later ("I think you should know I'm diabetic. It's pretty much under control, but, just in case, I carry this can of orange juice with me").

*Beyond Self-Disclosure*    So it is that in the early phases of acquainting, the range of interaction is likely to be somewhat restricted. We tend to think of certain topics as off-limits until we have enough information about the other person to have some idea of how she or he is likely to respond. To indicate a strongly held opinion on a topic near and dear to our heart may meet with rejection right off the bat ("These animal-rights kooks are trying to get the lab shut down. Can you imagine that? How do they think medicines are supposed to get tested for crying out loud?" "I happen to support animal rights, and I do not consider myself a kook. I am interested in seeing that animals are treated humanely that's all"). As a consequence, the relationship would be nipped in the bud. Direct questioning runs the risk of touching on a sore spot ("Are you prolife or prochoice?"). And self-disclosure that comes too early and is too intimate is likely to carry with it a sense of desperation (Duck, 1977).

There is a certain wisdom to the small talk that we typically use when we meet people for the first time. Topics such as the weather and sports run little risk of alienating anyone ("Have you been following the playoffs?"). They have the advantage of being common-denominator issues, and opinions on them are not likely to be very consequential one way or the other.

## Critique of Social Penetration Theory

Social penetration theory is one of the most comprehensive, detailed, and extensively researched accounts of relationship development. Its broad framework incorporates many of the research findings that have focused on more specific issues. It is basically an incremental exchange theory in which the (anticipated) rewards and costs of a developing relationship are the primary concern.

It pictures individuals in a developing relationship as actively seeking information from samples of each other's behavior and using the information to infer underlying stabilities. It also acknowledges that matters of importance change as a relationship progresses, and such factors as individual differences in liking, power, and status can influence relationship development. Further, social penetration theory sees developing relationships as being embedded in broader cultural settings, which respond with support or withhold support, depending on how the relationships work in the eyes of others.

Support for social penetration theory comes from the well-documented findings that intimacy tends to increase as relationships develop over time, and the norm of reciprocity tends to characterize interactions, at least in the early phases of relationship building. The theory has an intuitive appeal. It applies to different types of developing relationships, such as friendships and budding romantic interests. It is easy to understand and seems to ring true to personal experience.

Roommates who meet for the first time in college often indicate that they get to know each other by sharing small talk, exchanging small favors, and the like. Starting slowly, they disclose more and more about themselves and become more involved over time. Much the same can be said for developing romantic relationships.

Still, there are limitations to social penetration theory. The smooth progress that it assumes may characterize some developing relationships but not all (a point conceded by Altman et al., 1981). Beyond the individual difference measures, which have sometimes been used, we still have little insight into why some relationships proceed smoothly and others do not. Social penetration theory has little to say here. Other than the notions of gradualism and reciprocity, the dynamics of self-disclosure are not particularly well spelled out, and certain aspects of self-disclosure are left begging for explanation. Why, for example, do we disclose more frequently to total strangers than to our spouses (Morton, 1978) or our friends? (Derlega et al., 1976).

Some researchers have suggested that when we receive self-disclosures from someone new, we tend to make an inference about that person (for example, how informed, interesting, discriminating, and trustworthy she or he might be). This, in turn, determines whether we trust and like the person (Jones & Archer, 1976). In short, we seem to be actively seeking information and assessing possibilities in the early phases of relating. But if we evaluate developing relationships and form expectations in light of our evaluations (Miell et al., 1979), can our expectations change? Something like this seems to have happened in the relationship pictured in the opening paragraph of this chapter. This relationship apparently got off to a rocky start and yet developed into one that has lasted for years. How does this fit with the prediction that relationships develop gradually?

When Dorothy Miell and Steve Duck (1986) investigated the cues that people give off in the course of early relationship development (that is, what is considered appropriate and what is not), they found that during initial interactions, people tend to be polite. Conversations tend to be topical, and the subject matter tends to be of a general nature. During these early interactions, people are not likely to reveal too much about themselves. All of this is consistent with social penetration theory.

At the same time, people tend to seek information about each other and observe each other's reactions (Bell & Daly, 1984). It is apparently during these early exchanges that people make a decision (not necessarily consciously) either to restrict the relationship to the "normative" and keep the topic of conversation general or to converse at a deeper level, explore a wider range of topics, and make an effort to pursue the relationship further. Such efforts seem to be calculated to match the responsiveness of the other person and depend on whether or not she or he seems interested in pursuing the relationship as well.

## *Issues in Communicating Interest*

Three issues that seem to be important as new acquaintances explore the possibility of a relationship developing further are **uncertainty reduction, receptivity signals,** and **affinity testing.** In the following sections we look briefly at each of these.

### Uncertainty Reduction

The early phases of a budding relationship are likely to be full of uncertainty (Berger & Calabrese, 1975). Initial conversations often take the form of gathering background information, which can then be used to predict attitudes that the other has not yet disclosed (Berger, 1975). Early interactions tend to involve information exchanges, such as hometown, occupation, and family characteristics, which help reduce uncertainty and provide for more predictable communication (Berger, 1987). When we learn that someone lives 30 miles from our hometown, it gives us useful information. (We might want to share a ride sometime.) When we learn that someone spent the summer traveling throughout Europe, this tells us a great deal about that person. (She doesn't have to work summers to put herself through school.) But this kind of information is just one aspect of early relationship development.

### Receptivity Signals

People interested in pursuing a new relationship further apparently indicate their interest by giving certain cues. When we look closely, we find that the initial phases of developing relationships tend to be characterized by efforts to convey certain things about oneself. For example, we might hear such comments as "When I was in the Navy . . ." or "We were recently involved in a messy custody case at the office and . . ." or "When you were brought up on a farm like I was . . .". These are ways of leaking information that might seem incidental to the conversation at the time but helps locate the person in the broader scheme of things and provides perspective that each person considers important for the other to know (Duck, 1991).

In this process of exchange we make the other person a party to unique information. Stereotypes are dispelled, and we come to know each other as

In communicating interest, a person entering a relationship is likely to show how he or she feels by giving receptivity signals through looks and touch. How the other reacts will either reduce uncertainty or confirm that the other person is not as interested in developing the relationship further.

individuals, rather than members of a class. This suggests that a much more active process is at work in the early phases of relationship development than stage and incremental approaches imply. One of the best examples of the active nature of this process can be seen in the case of affinity testing.

### Affinity Testing

Affinity testing refers to strategies we sometimes use early in the relationship-building process to determine whether the other person is interested in developing a relationship further or is just being polite (Douglas, 1987). Such simple things as pausing to see whether the other person picks up on the conversation or lets it die are examples of affinity testing.

Along these same lines are "secret tests" that provide an indication of the other's interest (or lack of interest) in pursuing a relationship further (Baxter & Wilmot, 1984). A question ("I understand you went abroad your junior year. Where did you go?") may be treated as an expression of interest and responded to personally or treated in a matter-of-fact way and dismissed. In the case of romantic partners, when someone says, "I'd like you to meet my folks," he or she is issuing an invitation to mark a milestone in the relationship. Announcing a relationship to others, even informally, is one indication that it is becoming serious.

Not surprisingly, affinity testing seems to have its counterpart in "affinity seeking" (Bell & Daly, 1984). In affinity seeking, we use certain strategies such as offering assistance, adhering to the rules of polite conversation, showing an interest in the topic of conversation, and treating others as equals in an effort to get them to like us. Figuratively speaking, we place the ball in the other's court and wait for and evaluate the return. Such processes are never one-way. They depend on, and are guided by, the responsiveness on the part of the other (Duck, 1991).

*Turning Points*   Do we take certain responses on the part of others as especially important indications of the state of the relationship? Apparently we do. In a study of accounts of important times in romantic relationships, Leslie Baxter and Connie Bullis (1986) noted that partners agreed 54% of the time on what the researchers referred to as turning points. Turning points are events seen as having serious implications (either positive or negative) for the relationship, and they vary somewhat depending on the level of intimacy of the relationship at the time.

In the early phases of relationship building, we are hesitant to refer to the relationship directly. At this point, we seem to feel we have no right to raise certain relationship issues. But after making a certain investment, we feel that we have more of a right to raise questions about the long-term viability of the relationship, and "relationship talk" becomes more common. So when Joe decides to spend spring break at home rather than accept the invitation from Mary and her family to join them at the shore, it may be interpreted one way if the relationship is relatively new, but the same decision later in the relationship may raise questions about Joe's priorities, how serious he is about Mary, and his commitment to the relationship. The way these issues are resolved will later be seen as turning points.

There seems to be little in the way of deliberate planning involved in turning points. For example, in a study by Connie Bullis and her colleagues (1993), couples indicated *intending* that an issue or event be a significant turning point in only about 35% of the cases. Such a finding raises the question of whether relationship development proceeds according to a series of strategic decisions or whether things tend to "just happen." There is some evidence that relationship development involves more of a combination of intention and spontaneity than is generally appreciated (Duck & Sants, 1983).

Most significantly, however, the greater the number of turning points reported in a relationship, the *lower* the relationship satisfaction tends to be (Bullis et al., 1993). One way of interpreting this finding is that turning points grow out of uncertainty. Relationships that are characterized by steady, predictable growth presumably involve less uncertainty, have fewer turning points, and as a consequence are considered more satisfactory than those that are characterized by many turning points—many ups and downs.

Such findings are inconsistent with the suggestion that relationship development is best characterized by clear-cut stages, or moves gradually from less intimacy to greater intimacy in a smooth progression, and is more in line with the approach that emphasizes the importance of uncertainty reduction (Berger, 1988; Berger & Calabrese, 1975).

***Cooling-Off Signals***   Looking at the other side of the coin for a moment, we sometimes feel that a relationship is moving too fast or is approaching a level we would just as soon not encourage. When this happens, we may find it necessary to send cooling-off signals and to distance ourselves from a particular relationship. Sometimes this can be done subtly, but not always. The advantage of subtle hints, at this point, is that the other person (who is presumably pressing for greater involvement) saves face, confrontation is avoided, and some semblance of a relationship can remain intact.

The author once attended a workshop devoted to the strategic use of hints ("Well, I have to run now, I'd like to talk with you sometime") and benign neglect in creating distance in relationships that were becoming uncomfortable. Corporations sometimes give their executives and the executives' wives "cram courses" on how to downgrade old relationships that have become incompatible with their new status, without offending. Comments such as "Well, I mustn't keep you" provide the necessary exit cues to most people. One woman even told of how she kept a coat handy and started to put it on every time she answered the door. If the person at the door was somebody she wanted to see, she said she was just coming in. If it was somebody she didn't particularly want to see, she said she was just on her way out!

## The Question of "Early Decision"

Do you believe in love at first sight? What about friendship at first sight? Increasingly, evidence shows that decisions about whether or not to pursue a particular relationship may be made quite early in a relationship (Berg & Clark, 1986). Measures taken early in the acquaintance process predict the course of developing relationships just about as well as measures taken somewhat later. For example, in his study of developing friendships in college, Robert Hays (1984, 1985) asked students early in the school year to name two same-sex others whom they thought might make good friends. The only requirement was that they had not known each other prior to coming to school. Then, at three-week intervals, the students were asked to indicate the amount and kind of interaction they had with these potential friends. Measures were taken in four general areas: companionship, consideration, communication, and affection. The students were then asked to give an indication of how close they felt to their new prospective friends. And what were the results?

Consistent with the predictions of social penetration theory, these budding friendships tended to develop gradually over time, with initial exchanges involving more superficial levels of interaction (for example, joking about someone they both knew; going to a party together) and progressing to more intimate levels of interaction later on (for example, discussing family problems or seeking each other out when one or the other was feeling depressed). But, overall, progress was not as gradual as expected.

Those who eventually became friends were involved in more interactions each time measures were taken over the six months of the study. And, interestingly enough, the most obvious differences between those who later became friends and those who did not occurred between the third and sixth week. Successfully developing friendships showed increases in interaction during this time, while nonprogressing relationships showed declines.

During the third to sixth week, friend-making seemed to involve a flurry of activity, which eventually leveled off and then declined somewhat as the school year progressed. But even in the face of decreasing interactions later in the school year, successful pairs indicated increases in positive attitudes toward their friendship. This suggests that over time the status of the relationships became less dependent on the frequency of interactions. For example, after three-weeks' acquaintance, the number of interactions and friendship ratings were highly correlated; however, as the relationships progressed, the number of interactions became less important, and indications of intimacy

Over time, successful relationships are characterized by spending time together in enjoyable activities, mutual consideration, and self-disclosure, and, when called for, helping each other.

level emerged as equally important (and in some cases more important) in the friendship ratings.

Over the course of six months, successful friendships showed a general increase in each of the four measures taken (examples of which were spending time together in enjoyable activities, consideration given to each other, mutual self-disclosure, and mutual aid). No single measure was a better predictor of friendship status than the others. As the relationships developed, a broad range of interactions was more likely (Hays, 1984). But, significantly, many of the indicators that eventually differentiated close friends from nonfriends were apparent two weeks into the relationship. Therefore, consciously or unconsciously, new acquaintances seemed to make decisions about the nature of their relationship's future and act on those decisions quite early.

Similarly, in his studies of dating couples and college roommates, John Berg (1983, 1984) found that measures taken early in the relationship were as accurate (or nearly so) in predicting relationship outcomes as measures taken later. In relationships that lasted, partners communicated more about their relationship, were more likely to change their behavior in order to resolve conflicts, gave and received more in the way of self-disclosure, considered their relationships superior to other possible relationships, and considered their relationships to have exceeded their own expectations. And this was true for roommates (same-sex friendships) and for romantic relationships alike.

Both the Berg and Hays studies focused on relationships that were in progress. In neither case were participants studied the first time they met. Both focused on individuals who had indicated that a relationship of some sort was possible and even likely. They were either dating (Berg, 1983), had indicated that certain individuals might become friends (Hays 1984, 1985), or were roommates (Berg, 1984). Accordingly, those who became friends or continued as dating partners may have been selected in a way that those in a more typical first meeting would not be.

In fact, research suggests that we make decisions about potential relationships almost immediately upon meeting, and these early decisions lead to significant differences in the way we behave toward each other from the first. For example, Margaret Clark and Judson Mills (1979) led participants in their study to believe that a friendly, attractive accomplice (someone who was part of the experiment), either the same or the opposite sex, was new to the university and interested in meeting people, or (alternatively) had been at the university for some time and was not particularly interested in meeting others.

Clark and Mills hypothesized that these simple differences in "introductions" would lead the participants to follow either an exchange (meaning merely a friendly) strategy or a communal (meaning a more personal) course of action. And this is what they found. New acquaintances tended to be treated quite differently if they were presented as being likely candidates for either friendship or possible roommates, rather than as someone likely to be interested only in a more casual relationship. In this study the differences were apparent in the first hour.

Many of the same practices seem to hold true for prospective romantic relationships. In fact, there is some evidence that in dating the relationship is seen as either promising or not in the first 30 seconds of meeting (Berg & Piner, 1990). Early decision indeed!

We have to be careful of what we make of these two studies on new relationships; initial attraction is not the same as developing a relationship. Still, it is clear that we cannot dismiss the importance of the early phases of acquaintance.

## Going Beyond the Normative

Let's take a closer look at what is going on in the early phases of relationship development. Apparently, we are confronted with two general issues: (1) deciding what type of relationship we would like to pursue (if any) and (2) conveying our interest (or lack of interest) to the other person. To be effective in signaling what our interests might be, we must try to avoid ambiguity. At the same time, being too obvious in expressing our interest could mean running the risk of seeming desperate, or of being rejected and humiliated, should the other(s) not be interested.

Accordingly, when the decision to pursue a relationship further is favorable and mutual, the early phases of relating seem to be characterized by certain "intent signals" in which each person gives subtle indications of his or her interest in moving toward a closer relationship, and this is reflected very early in the acquaintance process. How?

John Berg and Margaret Clark (1986) offered the following analysis of the process at work. We accentuate relationship-type cues in the early phases of a (prospective) friendship or a romantic relationship by signaling that we are interested in something more than a garden-variety acquaintance. In order to do this, we must let the other person know of our interest by going beyond the normative (Duck, 1991; Kurth, 1970). Newly acquainting pairs, interested in pursuing a relationship further, conspire to let each other know that they consider the relationship special.

In newly forming relationships, people show an initial flurry of interaction that later tends to subside (Hays, 1985). Robert Hays refers to this as "the relationship-building phase." Furthermore, while interactions later decline, friendship ratings still tend to increase. Once the relationship is progressing well, intent signals are apparently no longer necessary, and the relationship returns to a state characterized by more relaxed interactions.

Consistent with this, researchers have found that immediate reciprocity of self-disclosure tends to be greater between strangers than between friends (Derlega, et al., 1976; Won-Doornik, 1979) or between married couples (Morton, 1978). One way of accounting for such findings is that newly acquainting individuals feel they must demonstrate their interest by responding immediately, while in relationships of longer duration, interest and intent is already clear, and an immediate response is no longer necessary (Miller & Berg, 1984). Budding friendships, or prospective romantic interests, then, seem to be distinctive. And, apparently, rather specific scripts are followed (Ableson, 1981).

Developing a friendship or a romantic relationship involves sending and receiving signals that are qualitatively different rather than simply engaging in more of the standard acquaintance recipe. Engaging a different script, then, serves to convey intent. Once such scripts are under way, they have an all-or-nothing quality about them. Thus, upon making a decision (even a tentative one) to pursue a potential friendship or romantic relationship, certain rules come into play. For example, interpersonal attraction tends to increase as the content of a reply to the other person is more "responsive," either indicating concern for the other or addressing a similar line of conversation that the other has suggested (Berg & Archer, 1980, 1982). However, as we see in Box 2-1, the rules governing relationships differ from one culture to the next.

**Nonengagement**

When we look at potential relationships from the other direction and ask whether we know quite early what type of relationships are *not* of interest, again the answer seems to be yes. We are quite sensitive to cues (for example, age and wedding rings) that indicate what type of relationship might be undesirable or inappropriate. This was demonstrated by Mariam Rodin (1982) and is known as "positive disregard." For example, a young professional woman might show positive disregard for a middle-aged man as a romantic interest but attend closely to such an individual in an academic context (such as a lecture). When we respond to someone with positive disregard, we tend not to remember much about them, such as what they wore or what they said. For certain purposes, they become "invisible."

## *Conclusion*

What can we say about the early phases of relationship development? First, there seems to be little support for the notion that progress in developing relationships is characterized by a sequence of clear-cut stages. In getting acquainted, we tend to start slowly and keep our investments small until we are sure (or somewhat sure) of the other's interest.

On the other hand, when we are interested in pursuing a new relationship, we are faced with the issue of communicating our interest to the other person. This presents us with the dilemma of how best to express our interest, without appearing desperate and risking rejection. As a consequence, we are likely to give subtle signals of our own interest and intent while looking for signals of receptivity from the other person. This is why the early phases of relating are so important and so full of information. The fate of a budding relationship can rest with a single smile, a nod appropriately timed, a yawn, or a glance across the room.

Further, when certain cues (such as age) are available, we know immediately what types of relationships are (and are not) appropriate. As much as we may wish it were otherwise, first impressions do seem to account for a great deal in relationship development.

*Box 2-1 In a Different Key*
**Friendship in Fuenmayer**

In Fuenmayer, a rural village in southwestern Spain, three types of friendships are commonly distinguished. *Amistad* is a casual friendship, *compromiso* is a committed friendship, and *amistad de confianza* is a friendship of trust and confidence.

Here public and private lives are kept separated. In the *casa* (home), for example, only family are allowed. Outsiders (other than kin) are given limited access only during certain rites of passage. Public spaces—such as streets, plazas, and places of business, particularly bars, taverns, and casinos—are the sites of socializing among the men. These are the places where *amistad* is played out. Camaraderie in public places is almost entirely male. They interact nightly, or nearly so, among "good friends" and acquaintances. The conviviality is governed by reciprocal exchange. For example, it is considered a breach of etiquette to accept more than one or two drinks without "inviting" one's hosts in return.

These casual friendships are not intimate, however, and they do not generate much in the way of obligations beyond the immediate circumstances. Such friends, for example, would not ask one another for money or the loan of tools. Nor would they open up to each other in terms of self-disclosure. To do this would be considered indiscreet and risky.

As friendships deepen and those involved come to accept each other as well intentioned, the value and frequency of exchanges increase. Such friends may help each other find work or offer aid to families, and in these cases the focus moves from the local bar to the home. Such a move transforms the relationship to a higher level of obligation, one that is passed from one generation to the next. Households so bound are said to have a *compromiso* relationship, and they express their friendship in certain prescribed ways. One must go to the bedside of an ill *amigo* with whom one has a *compromiso* relationship, for example, and attend funeral services and wakes of family members and express deeply felt sympathy.

Should the *compromiso* relationship be violated, the relationship is seen immediately as exploitive, and the tie degenerates into *lio*, a state of unbearable tension. If the violation is not dealt with immediately, the relationship is broken off and replaced by one of spite. It is the risk of generating a *lios* that guarantees reciprocity among the Fuenmayorenos. Anyone who is deceitful is known as a *lioso* and is shunned.

The relationship of *compromiso* is known to be a fragile thing, and there is vigilance between friends who share it. Even such friends, it seems, still have something to fear from one another. It is only in the *confianza* relationship that friends share confidences and trust. Confianza comes about only when one opens his heart to another. Such relationships are then called *amigo de confianza*, and in such a relationship one is assured that his friend will keep confidences (Gilmore, 1975).

So much for getting relationships started. How do we keep them going? The next chapter will address ways of maintaining relationships.

## Suggestions for Further Reading

Altman, I., & Taylor, D. A. (1973). *Social penetration: The development of interpersonal relationships*. New York: Holt, Rinehart & Winston. Although somewhat dated now, this volume offers a comprehensive treatment of social penetration theory.

Berscheid, E. (1994). Interpersonal relationships. In L. W. Porter & M. R. Rosenzweig (Eds.), *Annual review of psychology* (Vol. 45). Palo Alto, CA: Annual Reviews. An overview of the area of interpersonal relationships by one of the leading authorities.

Cappella, J. N., & Palmer, M. T. (1992). The effect of partner's conversation on the association between attitude similarity and attraction. *Communication Monographs, 59,* 180–189. A discussion of the role of attitude similarity in interpersonal attraction.

Chapdelaine, A., Kenny, D. A., & LaFontana, K. M. (1994). Matchmaker, matchmaker, can you make me a match? Predicting liking between two unacquainted persons. *Journal of Personality and Social Psychology, 67,* 83–91. Before we get too smug about what we know in the area of interpersonal attraction, we should note that it is hard to predict who will become friends.

Festinger, L., Schachter, S., & Back, K. (1950). *Social pressures in informal groups: A study of human factors in housing*. New York: Harper. The classic study on the power of proximity in friendship formation.

Hays, R. B. (1988). Friendship. In S. Duck (Ed.), *Handbook of personal relationships: Theory, research and intervention* (pp. 391–408). New York: Wiley. An excellent overview of research on developing friendships.

Hill, C. T., Rubin, Z., & Peplau, L. A. (1976). Breakups before marriage. The end of 103 affairs. *Journal of Social Issues, 32,* 147–168. A classic study of breakups among romantically involved student couples.

Kalbfleisch, P. J. (Ed.). (1993). *Interpersonal communication: Evolving interpersonal relationships*. Hillsdale, NJ: Erlbaum. An edited volume of representative works by leading researchers in the area of interpersonal communication.

Moreland, R. L., & Beach, S. R. (1992). Exposure effects in the classroom: The development of affinity among students. *Journal of Experimental Social Psychology, 28,* 255–276. Present the first part of this study to your classmates, and see if they can predict the results.

Newcomb, T. M. (1961). *The acquaintance process*. New York: Holt, Rinehart & Winston. The classic work on the acquaintance process.

Rindfuss, R. R., & Stephen, E. H. (1990). Marital noncohabitation: Separation does not make the heart grow fonder. *Journal of Marriage and the Family, 52,* 259–270. A timely article, which outlines the problems associated with long-distance relationships.

Rodin, M. J. (1982). Nonengagement, failure to engage, and disengagement. In S. W. Duck (Ed.), *Personal relationships 4: Dissolving personal relationships* (pp. 31–

50). London: Academic. In reading this chapter you will be surprised at how instantly we assess and dismiss certain people as ineligible for a personal relationship.

Sunnafrank, M. (1992). On debunking the attitude similarity myth. *Communication Monographs, 59,* 164–179. Sunnafrank's challenge to the importance of attitude similarity in interpersonal attraction. Should be read along with Cappella and Palmer (noted earlier).

Wright, R. A., & Contrada, R. J. (1986). Dating selectivity and interpersonal attractiveness: Toward a better understanding of the "elusive phenomenon." *Journal of Social and Personal Relationships, 3,* 131–148. Does it pay to play hard to get? Here's what the research has to say.

# CHAPTER 3

# Relationship Maintenance

The case of Dr. and Mrs. Blair: *Being president of the college had been his lifelong dream, but when his wife became seriously ill, Dr. Blair submitted his resignation, stating that he would have to devote more time to taking care of her. Rather than accept his resignation, however, the members of the board indicated their interest in finding ways for him to continue. When Dr. Blair asked his wife what she thought of the idea, she agreed, and so he stayed on. People watched, first out of curiosity, then in disbelief, and finally in awe as the Blairs moved to a house on campus. Quietly and inconspicuously, wheelchair ramps were installed all around campus, because everyone knew that where Dr. Blair went, his wife went. She kept track of appointments, reminded him of peoples' names, took notes, wrote letters, and, all in all, they made a remarkable team. And so it was until her death 14 years later. Today Dr. Blair still holds the record as the longest serving president in the history of the college.*

Like a garden, personal relationships require a certain amount of maintenance, or they can lapse into disrepair (Canary & Stafford, 1992; Harvey & Omarzu, 1997). In this chapter we will consider those aspects of relating that contribute to the stability and integrity of relationships and serve to keep them intact. Some of the theoretical approaches that have tried to characterize this process have emphasized such things as exchange (or interdependence), equity, mutuality of relationship definition, the importance of authenticity, and the role of a wider network of others in validating and supporting personal relationships. We will consider examples of each of these, beginning with exchange theory.

## Exchange Theory

Exchange theory rests on the assumption that the same principles that govern our behavior in most other areas of life (for example, rewards and costs) apply to our personal and social relationships as well (Blau, 1964; Homans, 1961, 1974; Thibaut & Kelley, 1959).

According to **exchange theory,** whatever our feelings may be, however pure and admirable our motives may seem, however genuine our devotion may appear, we pursue relationships with others only so long as they are satisfying in terms of the (overall) rewards and costs. In exchange theory, then, we have an approach in which (voluntary) personal and social relationships are viewed in terms of their actual (or anticipated) outcomes (Thibaut & Kelley, 1959).

### Basic Concepts of Exchange Theory

One of the better known versions of exchange theory comes from John Thibaut and Harold Kelley (1959). Their approach features four basic concepts: (1) reward, (2) cost, (3) outcome, and (4) comparison level.

Richard Cline © 1994 from The New Yorker Collection. All Rights Reserved.

*"If you leave me, you know, you'll never see this kind of rent again."*

A **reward** is anything that a person wants and will respond to in a positive way. Rewards are sometimes tangible, but in the case of personal relationships they are just as likely to come in the form of support, smiles, compliments, and verbal expressions, such as "I love you."

**Costs** are essentially the opposite of rewards. In personal relationships, costs usually involve behaviors on the part of one person that affect the other in a negative way. Uncertainty about where one stands, conflicts, arrogance, demandingness, inequities, and lack of consideration are all examples of possible costs. Costs may also be measured in terms of forsaken opportunities. For example, just as Maria's decision to go into accounting can mean giving up a promising career as a singer, so it is that marrying Juan can mean giving up the company of Tony. The cost of forgoing alternative possibilities is particularly important in certain types of personal relationships, notably those that have an element of exclusivity about them, such as courtship and marriage.

Both rewards and costs can be established empirically. Rewards are those things that increase the probability of a given behavior. In the case of Maria's relationship with Juan, for example, rewards would be those aspects of Juan's behavior that increased Maria's tendency to interact with him. Costs would be those aspects of his behavior that had the opposite effect.

**Outcomes** are defined as rewards minus costs. Interactions are said to yield a profit when rewards outweigh costs and are said to yield a loss when costs outweigh rewards.

*Comparison Level (CL)*    In addition, Thibaut and Kelley (1959) noted that in order to predict how satisfied an individual is likely to be with a given relationship, it is necessary to take his or her expectations into account. They referred to one measure of these expectations as **comparison level (CL)**. Comparison level is defined as the kinds of outcomes people have come to expect based on their relationships in the past and their observations of the relationship outcomes of similar others. For Maria to be satisfied with her relationship with Juan, the outcomes must match or exceed her comparison level. If her past experience has led her to expect a lot from her personal and social relationships, she would be characterized as having a high CL. If her past experience has led her to expect little, she would be characterized as having a low CL. The same level of outcomes that might be acceptable to one person, then, would not necessarily be acceptable to another.

*Comparison Level for Alternatives (CLalt)*    In addition to our past experience, we have information from our immediate social environment to draw upon. Included in this would be others in our neighborhood, school, or workplace. These, for Thibaut and Kelley, provided the basis for a second type of comparison level, a **comparison level for alternatives (CLalt)**. CLalt is similar to CL, except that CLalt is based on our perception of the readily available alternative to our present relationship(s).

If we receive more from our present relationships than from any readily available alternative relationships (or from being alone), we are said to be dependent upon our present relationships, even if they are not particularly satisfying. If, on the other hand, the outcomes of our current relationships are perceived to be lower than those that are likely to come from readily available alternative relationships, then, other things being equal, we will be inclined to transfer our interests to the relationships that promise better outcomes.

So, whereas CL translates into satisfaction or dissatisfaction with our present relationships, CLalt translates into dependence or independence. If we perceive the rewards of other readily available relationships to be greater than our present ones, we are less dependent upon our present relationships (Berg, 1984; Berg & McQuinn, 1986; Green & Sporakowski, 1983).

Suppose, for example, that Maria and Juan are married and live and work around a large number of unmarried men and women about the same age. Would this influence the stability of their relationship? The concept of CLalt suggests that it might. And, indeed, researchers have found increased levels of separation and divorce among young couples who live and work in areas where there are large numbers of unmarried men and women (South & Lloyd, 1995). Other "available" men and women apparently increase the likelihood of their perceiving that an alternative relationship might be more attractive than their present one. On the other hand, when people see themselves as having no better alternatives outside their present relationships, they are likely to remain in them even though they do not find them particularly satisfying (Rusbult & Martz, 1995).

## Critique of Exchange Theory

Exchange theory has been criticized for painting a picture of personal and social relationships in terms of rewards and costs. Such an approach doesn't seem to explain why people do things to help others at considerable cost to themselves. For example, firemen risk their lives to return to a burning building in an effort to save one last victim. Soldiers throw themselves on grenades to save their buddies. Businessmen volunteer to ring the bell for the Salvation Army at Christmas time. While the costs of these actions are clear enough, where are the rewards?

Exchange theorists recognize the problem and deal with it simply by referring to different kinds of profit (Homans, 1974). Profit depends on what people value. Not everybody values money, possessions, or power. When people act in an altruistic way, they can profit as much as anyone else; they simply take their profits in a different coin. By such an account, the Mother Teresas and Albert Schweitzers of the world are profiteers as much as the Rockefellers and the Vanderbilts. They may amass their "fortunes" in terms of honor, respect, admiration, or "eternal blessings," but they are profiteers nonetheless.

When we speak of exchange in personal and social relationships, then, any number of things can be valued and exchanged. Goods and services can

If relationships are based on personal and social exchange, what intangibles are involved between friends who come from different ethnic or cultural backgrounds? Respect and admiration may be "goals" that serve to cement many such relationships.

be valued and exchanged, but so too can intangibles, such as indications of affection, sympathy, concern, respect, love, esteem, and status.

### Exchange in Friendships, Dating, and Marriage

In terms of exchange theory, friendships would seem to be rewarding by definition. When the costs of a friendship outweigh the benefits, over a period of time, the relationship is likely to be abandoned in favor of another that is more rewarding. It's possible to imagine someone being "trapped" in a loveless marriage or a shotgun wedding. But, for most of us, the notion of being trapped in an unrewarding friendship doesn't make a lot of sense.

Yet, when we look closely, we are likely to see two very different, but complementary, themes in the literature on friendship. One is the general theme of exchange and feelings of obligation to return favor for favor. The second theme assumes that friends are important in their own right and that friends take the good with the bad. As soon as one person becomes a means rather than an end, there is very little possibility of friendship.

Thus, conventional wisdom has it that a fundamental difference separates friendships (and close personal relationships generally) from more casual types

*Box 3-1 In a Different Key*
**Friendship in Andalusia**

In the small agricultural village of Alcalá in Andalusia, the villagers are bound by friendships as strong as any kinship ties. Here friendship is considered sacred, and, with the exception of the parent-child bond, more meaningful than ties between kin. Friendship is expressed in terms of mutual respect and underlies all social behavior. The worst thing that could happen to a man is to be without friends (Pitt-Rivers, 1954/1963).

Nightlife in Andalusia consists largely of males congregating in bars, sharing cigarettes, and buying each other drinks. The casual observer might interpret such practices as idleness, hedonism, or a fondness for strong drink. But when we look more closely, we find there are very practical reasons for the men to while away the evening hours among their friends in this way. The bars serve as unofficial labor exchanges for farmworkers. And in an area plagued by chronic unemployment, this is where the hiring tends to be done for the next day. So it is that laborers spend their evenings in bars where they can hear of work opportunities. This is the hidden agenda behind friendship in the bars of Andalusia (Gilmore, 1991).

of relationships. Friendships are typically viewed as intrinsically rewarding and as ends in themselves (Blau, 1964). Those in close personal relationships are seen to be responsive to the needs of the other, while those in relationships that are not particularly close are more likely to base their behavior on past rewards or on some expected future reward in a tit-for-tat fashion (Clark & Mills, 1979; Kelley, 1979; Mills & Clark, 1982).

In fact, though we may want to believe that we give selflessly and with little or no thought of receiving, a tacit agreement of reciprocity exists (Tedeschi, 1974). What distinguishes friendships and other close personal relationships from garden-variety friendly relationships seems to be the degree of obligation felt. So it seems that in friendship we have an example of reciprocal altruism described in Chapter 1. That is, in striking up a friendship, however intrinsically rewarding it may seem, we are also investing in a relationship that at some time and place will prove to be to our advantage. And this is not only true in the United States but also in other societies. According to anthropologists, the norm of reciprocity (the obligation to repay favor for favor) is a cross-cultural universal (Gouldner, 1960). An example appears in Box 3-1.

Much the same principle seems to apply to dating relationships. Sally Lloyd, Rodney Cate, and June Henton (1984), for example, reported that among dating couples, those who showed higher levels of "rewardingness" in their interactions with each other were more likely to have remained together seven months later.

Studies of happy versus unhappy married couples have shown the same thing. Happy couples seem to behave toward each other in ways that are more rewarding (and less costly) than do less happy couples, and such rewardingness tends to be reciprocal, need based, and more or less stable (Gottman, 1979; Jacobson et al., 1982). How is this achieved?

## The Emergence of Norms

It is common in personal relationships of some duration to see norms emerge that essentially constitute rules of the relationship. These are not necessarily formalized, contractual, openly stated, or for that matter even conscious. They may be as mundane as a husband and wife agreeing: "You wash and I'll dry" or "You do the yard work and I'll take care of the housework." Or they may have a more generic quality about them, such as who is dominant or who sets the agenda and in what area. In any case, the more accepted and "agreed upon" the norms, the greater the ratio of rewards to costs is likely to be and, in sociological terms, the more "cohesive" the relationship (dyad or group). Why do agreed-upon norms make for better relationships?

Norms substitute for direct confrontations and the more obvious shows of power. They allow decisions to be made in terms of "policy" rather than influence tactics. Without such norms, every new issue would require negotiation and renegotiation, and this would increase the costs of relating. Indeed, the reason that norms are adopted is largely because they facilitate interaction and reduce the costs of relating.

One of the ways that people maintain their friendships and romantic relationships, then, is to adhere to the rules of the relationship with regard to such things as exchange, equity, intimacy, relationships with third parties, and coordination of interactions. And one of the reasons that relationships fail is because of ignorance of, or disregard for, the rules of the relationship, or the inability to carry them out owing to a lack of social skills (Argyle & Henderson, 1984; Burleson, 1995).

One of the most fundamental norms governing relationships, particularly close personal relationships, has to do with the issue of perceived fairness. Typically, fairness in personal relationships is not consciously calculated in terms of scorekeeping, but is more likely to be seen in terms of a pattern over the long term (McClintock et al., 1984). This makes fairness in personal relationships a particularly interesting and subtle issue, because close friends and loved ones are in a position to verify the contributions (and the costs) that one brings to a relationship. Posturing and pretense continually run up against the facts, and over the long term, intimates are not easily fooled (Swann et al., 1994).

## Equity Theory

Perceived fairness has been the particular focus of one version of exchange theory called **equity theory** (Walster et al., 1978). Like exchange theory, equity theory is based on certain assumptions:

1. Individuals in personal relationships are trying to maximize their outcomes.

2. Individuals may form groups of two or more people to maximize their joint (or collective) outcomes, and in so doing, they develop systems (norms) for the equitable distribution of resources, rewards, and costs among the members.

3. When individuals find themselves in inequitable relationships, they experience distress, and the degree of distress increases in proportion to the perceived inequity.

4. When individuals experience such distress, they will attempt to restore equity.

In contrast to Thibaut and Kelley's (1959) theory, which says information for generating CL (that is, what is expected or considered fair) comes either from one's past experience or from observations of similar others (or both), equity theory focuses on the relative contributions and outcomes of the partners. Accordingly, the relevant information for determining what is considered fair comes from *within* the relationship. Those who make more of a contribution to the relationship should expect to get more out of it. Those who contribute less should expect to get less.

Consider two partners in business together. One invests $100,000 and the other $50,000. You wouldn't expect them to have equal say in running the business and split the profits equally, would you? The one who puts the most into the partnership should have the most to say in running it and get the most out of it. Similarly, in a traditional marriage, for example, both a husband and wife might agree that the husband plays a dominant role in the marriage because of his contribution as the sole wage earner. According to equity theory, a relationship may be asymmetrical in some respects and still be considered equitable.

Equity theorists assume that this general principle applies to all healthy relationships, from the most casual to the most intimate, and that people are likely to be attracted to, and satisfied in, relationships in which the outcomes are perceived as equitable (Walster et al., 1978).

***The Overbenefited and the Underbenefited***   The terms *overbenefited* and *underbenefited* are used to characterize people in inequitable relationships. Equity theorists hold that both overbenefited and underbenefited individuals should feel a sense of distress, and this distress should lead to a desire to restore equity.

When we turn to the research on personal relationships, we find that it is at least partially supportive of equity theory. For example, Elaine Hatfield and her colleagues (1979) asked 537 college males and females, who were dating either casually or regularly, to indicate how equitable their relationships were. Based on their perceptions of what they put into the relationship and what they got out of it, the participants were classified as either equitably treated, overbenefited, or underbenefited. Generally, the students indicated that they were more satisfied with their relationships when they considered them to be equitable. Those who saw themselves as underbenefited were likely to report feeling angry, and those who saw themselves as overbenefited tended to report feeling guilty.

Additionally, those who were in equitable relationships were more likely to see the relationship as moving toward more serious involvement, including sexual intimacy. They were also more likely to see their relationships as lasting. Those who felt overbenefited or underbenefited were not so confident, and for good reason. In a follow-up 14 weeks later, they were more likely to have broken up.

***Restoring Equity***   Equity theory also predicts that should either party in, say, a romantic relationship change status significantly, there would be a shift in what was then considered equitable. For example, when Maria inherits a sizable fortune from her grandmother, her contribution to the relationship is likely to change relative to Juan's, who is still working (let us say) as deliveryman at the local dry cleaners. Following such a shift, negotiation is necessary in order to recalibrate the balance of costs and benefits in light of the changed relative contributions of the two partners. In so doing, one person may try to restore equity by increasing or decreasing his or her contribution or insisting on more or less in terms of benefits (Berscheid & Walster, 1978).

## The Role of Attribution

Friends and romantic partners do not spend most of their time exchanging goods and services. Exchange, in personal relationships, is more likely to involve such things as emotional support, consideration, respect, and indications of affection. How, then, do people determine the equivalence of what is exchanged? How is equity between friends (or romantic partners) determined? At first, this would seem to be the Achilles heel of exchange theory and its many variations. But we can turn this embarrassment into an advantage simply by noting that equivalence is not calculated very carefully.

Indeed, as momentary imbalances make it harder to keep a tit-for-tat accounting, personal (or dispositional) attributions come into play. Sometimes the attribution is one of exploitation, and efforts are made to restore some semblance of balance. At other times, the attribution is one of acceptance, respect, caring, consideration, love, and affection, and this becomes part of the way the relationship itself is perceived (Harvey & Omarzu, 1997). Over the long term, personal relationships are likely to become more and more forgiving of momentary imbalances, and scorekeeping gives way to a sense of trust. Indeed, this shift is what in large part defines a relationship as close and "personal."

Much of what takes place in the early stages of friendship and romantic relationships seems to involve a process of transforming the feelings of uncer-

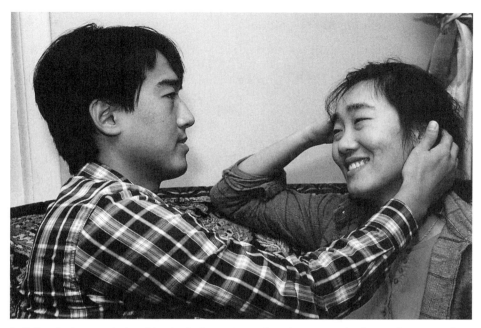

Building intimate relationships includes reciprocal exchanges in the form of emotional support, consideration, respect, and shows of affection.

tainty and ambivalence that come with dependency and vulnerability to a more secure sense of trust and interdependence. Several researchers have suggested that such a transformation is necessary if a relationship is to develop into a lasting one (Berscheid & Fei, 1977; Braiker & Kelley, 1979; Dion & Dion, 1976; Harvey & Omarzu, 1997; Holmes & Rempel, 1989; Swann et al., 1994).

Indications of faithfulness and "just being there" carry a secondary message of caring (Argyle & Henderson, 1984; Stafford & Canary, 1991). And since reciprocity tends to be the rule in close personal relationships (Burggraf & Sillars, 1987), positivity, trust, and caring are likely to be contagious and generate a climate that is more and more rewarding and satisfying.

## Relationship Definition

The closer the relationship, the more interdependence is likely to be expressed over a wide range of issues. Indeed, it is the extent and diversity of influence that distinguish close personal relationships (Kelley et al., 1983). Among the more important issues that are likely to emerge in such relationships are **mutuality of relationship definition, mutuality of control,** and **consensus about influence potential** (Morton et al., 1976). We will look at each of these in turn.

## Mutuality of Relationship Definition

Why do some relationships last through very difficult times, while others seem to crumble over the most trivial matters? The difference, according to Teru Morton and colleagues (1976) is to be found, not so much in the events per se, but in the fact that mutuality of relationship definition at a higher level can absorb a number of imbalances at a lower level. In other words, having agreed upon a framework, people can agree to disagree about certain specifics and still get on with the business of relating.

From this perspective, Maria and Juan's relationship may be defined as one that is dominated by Juan, one that is dominated by Maria, one in which both partners have equal say, or one in which they agree upon specific areas of responsibility. *Relationship definition,* then, is something of an umbrella term for those aspects of relating that are important to the stability and viability of a relationship. These may be made explicit, but just as often they are simply "understood." For example, a teenager may meekly request the use of the family car or boldly assert that she is taking the car. The content in both cases is much the same, but the implied relationship is quite different. If the parents respond by saying "Have fun!" they are not only agreeing that the teenager can take the car but also tacitly accepting the implied relationship. On the other hand, when a parent responds, "Have you done the dishes?" not only is agreement conditional but also a particular definition of the relationship is assumed.

Mutuality of relationship definition, then, implies that certain tacitly agreed-upon rules and modes of communication contribute to relationship stability. But it also assumes that relationships have an integrity of their own that is more than the separate contributions of the individuals who make them up. And those whose relationships are satisfying have a vested interest in maintaining the relationship definition (Canary & Stafford, 1993).

Relationship definition may be conveyed in many different ways. The use of self-disclosure, touched on in Chapter 2, has received a great deal of attention in the research literature, but it represents only one way of indicating the desired nature of a relationship. Newly acquainting pairs appear to depend on a tit-for-tat form of reciprocity in self-disclosure, in part because their relationship is in the process of being defined. Those in relationships of long duration tend to show greater latitude of acceptance across a wide range of behaviors and are still able to maintain their relationships.

On the other hand, nonmutuality of relationship definition generates crises in a relationship (Morton et al., 1976). The way this nonmutuality is expressed may vary from simple misunderstandings (Courtright et al., 1979) to coercion (Falbo & Peplau, 1980) to reciprocal escalation of disagreement (Canary et al., 1991) and serious conflict. In any case, the fundamental issue is always one of unilateral decision making or influence versus mutuality, and the task at hand is always one of restoring mutuality. This can occur in any one of several ways. One of the parties may simply give in, both may compromise a little, or they may renegotiate the definition of the relationship. But if mutuality of relationship definition is not restored, the relationship is not likely to be satisfying.

## Mutuality of Control

In addition to mutuality of definition, close relationships require mutuality of control in order to remain viable (Morton et al., 1976). Mutuality of control implies bilateral influence (Falbo & Peplau, 1980), leading (it is hoped) to bilateral acceptance and general agreement on issues of mutual interest and concern (Canary et al., 1991).

As two people become increasingly interdependent, and able to understand and predict each other's behavior, interactions tend to become increasingly synchronized, and their relationship is characterized by mutuality of control. In mature relationships, decisions are made more and more by consensus, and mutuality of control is likely to characterize interactions in many areas.

So considered, mutuality of control means that both partners agree, not only with the specific decisions made but also with the way decisions are made. As an example, let's look at the case of Carol and Brenda.

Carol and Brenda had been friends since childhood. They grew up in houses across the street from each other; one was virtually never seen without the other. What could possibly come between them? It was a silly thing really. One day on their way to high school they stopped for some gas. The gas station was having a promotion, and they received two raffle tickets to win a new Oldsmobile. Carol, who was driving, paid for the gas, laughed jovially, kept one of the tickets and gave one to Brenda. The time for the drawing came, and, wouldn't you know it, Brenda won that new Oldsmobile, and Carol didn't know anything about it until she saw the notice in the paper. That night Carol went over to Brenda's house and said that she had paid for the gas and it was her ticket and she really should get the car, or they should each get half. But Brenda said that Carol had given her the ticket, and it was her car. And that was the end of the friendship.

In the case of Dr. and Mrs. Blair, described in the opening of this chapter, we see an example of mutuality of relationship definition and mutuality of control being restored after a crisis threatened to disrupt the balance in the relationship. But in the case of Carol and Brenda, mutuality was never restored. The two never spoke again.

## Consensus Concerning Influence Potential

Finally, agreement as to influence potential is fundamental in defining the nature of a relationship (Morton et al., 1976). The meaning of influence potential is best conveyed by an example. Two people in a car pool and a couple in a marriage of long duration may both be in long-term relationships, both be in complete agreement on the definition of their relationships, and achieve mutuality of control. But there is a clear difference between the two, which

Teru Morton and colleagues (1976) refer to as "influence potential." Two people in a car pool are likely to have a relationship that is limited in influence potential. Because it affects only a small part of their lives, the relationship may involve very little in the way of emotional bonding. A married couple, on the other hand, affect each other's lives in many ways, and the level of emotional bonding is likely to be high.

Mutual understanding and acceptance of the degree and distribution of influence potential are important characteristics of any personal relationship. Concepts such as costs, benefits, power, and similar notions are all useful, but these must be translated into a **relational context** in which there is both mutual involvement and mutual acceptance.

For example, when both the husband and wife in a traditional marriage agree that the husband should have more influence, the relationship can be a stable one (Peplau et al., 1993). If the traditional wife becomes an ardent feminist, however, the relationship is likely to undergo a crisis of nonmutuality in definition. The point is that neither a symmetrical nor an asymmetrical distribution of power and influence in a relationship guarantees that a relationship will remain viable. Relationship viability depends on mutuality—mutuality of relationship definition, mutuality of control, and consensus concerning the distribution of influence potential.

Still, mutuality of relationship definition, control, and influence potential are no guarantee that the relationship will be an adaptive one in the real world—no guarantee that two people will not choose to live their lives in a fool's paradise. But this is not likely to happen, because as personal relationships develop, a subtle change typically takes place. Partners in healthy relationships tend to help one another keep their feet firmly on the ground by giving honest, straightforward feedback. And it is to this issue that we turn next.

## The Shift From Flattery to Authenticity

People involved in close personal relationships are in a unique position to gather information and to provide sustained, credible feedback that serves to validate one another's views of themselves (Harvey & Omarzu, 1997; Swann et al., 1994). They tend to be honest with each other rather than to flatter each other. Such a climate of authenticity helps bring order and coherence to close personal relationships (Swann, 1983, 1987, 1992; Swann et al., 1994). Authenticity tends to be characteristic of both friendships and romantic relationships, but its role is most clear-cut in the case of romantic relationships.

### The Emergence of Authenticity

Assuming that individuals start their journey toward couplehood by "putting their best foot forward" in the dating and rating game, how do they arrive at a relationship characterized by authenticity rather than flattery? Honesty rather than diplomacy? William Swann and his colleagues (1994) see courtship (in the United States) as similar to an audition, in which each partner indulges in a good deal of positive self-presentation. So it is that the mode of relating during the early stages of courtship is likely to be more evaluative than com- mittal, and this may account for the volatility of some courtships.

For couples in long-term relationships, on the other hand, the mode of relating is primarily one of commitment. Once two individuals become a cou- ple, they are more likely to define their goals and purposes together. And we find trust playing a pivotal role in this process. In trusting, one assumes that the other partner is positively disposed and well intended (Holmes & Rempel, 1989; Johnson-George & Swap, 1982), has the interest of the relationship at heart, and is willing and able to live up to his or her promises and obligations, both expressed and implied. In short, **trust** refers to the degree to which one person is willing to risk investment in the other, and, as such, it is fundamental to any personal relationship (Rempel et al., 1985). Trust, so considered, has been shown to be associated with measures of love (Larzelere & Huston, 1980), confidence in the other (Johnson-George & Swap, 1982), quality of the relationship (Canary & Cupach, 1988), and positivity. Those who are cheerful and who avoid criticism of each other tend to have more stable re- lationships (Canary & Stafford, 1992; Stafford & Canary, 1991). Positivity

In time, couples come to prefer authenticity to flattery. Relationship maintenance can be understood as an ongoing process of increasing mutual influence and interdependence.

is important in relationship stability not only because it is rewarding (although it is), but also because it is related to trust.

Not surprisingly, lack of trust tends to undermine relationships (Argyle & Henderson, 1984; Larzelere & Huston 1980; Van Yperen & Buunk, 1990). Accordingly, although we would expect dating relationships to be characterized by efforts that promote positive evaluation, marriage should be characterized more by a "warts and all" authenticity. And this is what we typically find.

Why do couples, over time, come to prefer authenticity to flattery and honesty to diplomacy? As we mature, our concept of self becomes more and more important in bringing coherence to our experience, and as a consequence, it becomes important for others, especially close others, to verify our self-concept—the good, the bad, the beautiful, the ugly (Swann, 1983, 1987).

Once the decision is made to join forces, there is little to be gained by trying to keep up a facade, because it will eventually be exposed anyway. Once their fates are joined, a couple typically focuses less on impressions and more on substance. As a consequence, they prefer that their partner sees both their strengths and their weaknesses. Interestingly enough, romantic partners are not alone in this task. As their social network begins to recognize their relationship, they also get "a little help from their friends."

## The Social Context of Personal Relationships

Until recently, little attention has been devoted to the broader social context in which friendships and romantic relationships take place. However, the broader social network can have a strong influence on the course of a developing relationship. A shared network serves as a basis of support and provides a staging area for increasing interdependence to play itself out. We may not let our friends tell us who we should and should not take a liking to, but neither do we ignore them. There is a link between shared networks and liking among romantic couples (Canary & Stafford, 1993).

When Mark and Lisa first go out together, not much is likely to be made of it. Most social networks tend to be quite accepting of casual relationships. When things get more serious, however, evaluation from a wider network of friends is likely to follow, and when a relationship "goes public," the social milieu responds with its own assessment and either supports the relationship or discourages it (Ridley & Avery, 1979). A wider social network of friends, relatives, and acquaintances, then, seems important in providing the context within which our close personal relationships develop and are validated (Huston & Levinger, 1978; Huston et al., 1981; Levinger, 1983; Lewis, 1975; Milardo, 1986; Milardo & Lewis, 1985; Parks & Eggert, 1991; Ridley & Avery, 1979). For example, among dating couples, the relative number of *mutual* friends tends to increase as the relationship progresses (Milardo, 1986). And as we see in the next section, the pattern of events is most interesting.

## The Dyadic Withdrawal Hypothesis

The **dyadic withdrawal hypothesis** minimizes the influence of others in developing romantic relationships. Here the idea is that romantic couples retreat into their own world to carve out the form that their developing relationship will take, largely unfettered by the opinions of others.

Ted Huston and his colleagues (1981), for example, noted that during courtship, couples tended to devote more of their leisure time to each other and less to their respective social networks. Catherine Surra (1985) found that the more "exclusive" couples recalled their courtships to have been, the more rapidly things tended to progress toward engagement and marriage. Finally, when Michael Johnson and Leigh Leslie (1982) compared couples at different stages in the courtship process—occasional dating, regular dating, exclusive dating, engaged and married—they found that those who were engaged or married had *fewer* friends, tended to place somewhat less importance on the opinion of both friends and relatives, and disclosed somewhat less to friends and relatives than did those in the earlier stages of courtship. All of these findings are consistent with the notion of dyadic withdrawal among romantically involved couples.

But when Robert Milardo, Michael Johnson, and Ted Huston (1983) asked individuals who were in developing relationships to record their interactions of 10 minutes or more over a 10-day period and to repeat the same thing 3 months later, they found that withdrawal (when it occurred) took place primarily with regard to those on the fringe of their social network—acquaintances and intermediate friends rather than close friends and relatives. In other words, although the researchers found some evidence for withdrawal, it tended to be selective withdrawal.

## Dyadic Realignment

The notion of dyadic withdrawal seems to be more illusory than real, with much of the effect coming from the decision to devote more time to the partner, and establishing new priorities with regard to social obligations, now that two sets of friends, acquaintances, and relatives must be taken into account (Johnson & Leslie, 1982). Put another way, what has been seen as dyadic withdrawal may really be a process of realigning what had been two separate social networks into one (Parks & Eggert, 1991; Parks et al., 1983).

From this perspective, relationship development may be seen as a process of increasing the mutual influence and interdependence of partners, and this dyadic interdependence extends to the partners' networks as well. Indeed, Robert Milardo (1982) found in the later stages of courtship that couples, on average, have approximately twice as many mutual friends as they did in the early stages of courtship.

Several studies have documented the correlation between relationship development and support from family and friends. Robert Lewis (1973), for example, in a study of 316 couples before their marriage, noted that over a 10-week period, those who indicated having the greatest support of friends and family also indicated the most commitment and progress in the relationship (see Krain, 1977; Leslie et al., 1986, for similar findings).

Further, the information exchanged between partners and their social networks serves to increase the partners' ability to interpret each other's feelings and behavior. Friends and relatives act as sounding boards for the couples' attitudes, expectations, and plans. And experiences of others can provide "recipes for success" and lead to uncertainty reduction (for example, "We both worked while we were in school, and so can you").

As a couple's new social network stabilizes, it offers a reservoir of supportive relationships, many of which would be lost if their relationship were to end. Indeed, the evidence suggests that access to a given social network and its resources can help to facilitate interpersonal attraction in the first place (Eggert & Parks, 1987; Parks & Adelman, 1983; Parks et al., 1983). For example, before prospective partners meet, they have typically already developed some connection with the other's existing social network (Parks & Eggert, 1991). It is as if the group acts as something of a launch pad for the new relationship.

Conversely, when romantically involved pairs saw their relationships as receiving lower levels of support from their social network, researchers have been able to predict with approximately 90% accuracy that the relationship was going to deteriorate (Parks & Adelman, 1983).

Further, when partners experience conflict, they are likely to consider their position as more or less legitimate depending on how much support they receive from their respective, *and each other's,* social networks (Klein & Milardo, 1995).

In general, then, research suggests that the development of same-sex friendships and romantic relationships is strongly (positively) linked to the perceived level of support from their wider social network (Milardo, 1982; Parks & Eggert, 1991). Those in close personal relationships are not only interdependent to the extent that they interact, cooperate, and share in one another's lives, they are also interdependent in the relationships that they have in common with other members of their social network (Milardo, 1983, 1986).

## Conclusion

The many aspects of maintaining personal relationships are captured to some extent within the framework of exchange theory and its several variations, such as equity theory, but as relationships develop and mature, relationship maintenance is likely to be expressed more and more in terms of agreed-upon rules. Such rules, and the practices they generate, tend to have a distinctive quality about them. They are custom tailored to fit the relationship, if you will.

Accordingly, as relationships become more intimate, the evidence suggests that mutuality of relationship definition, control, and influence potential become increasingly significant in maintaining stability and satisfaction of personal relationships. And one of the things that we expect of close others is to offer us good, honest feedback, even when it hurts.

Relationships that have achieved some maturity tend to be more stable and satisfying, and departures from tit-for-tat reciprocity are likely to generate attributions of trust and caring. These attributions serve to carry friends and romantic couples over the rough spots and momentary imbalances.

Finally, just as "no man is an island," research is now beginning to show that no relationship is an island. Complementing the contributions of the particular individuals involved in developing friendships and romantic relationships is the validation and support that comes from their wider network of friends and relatives.

## Suggestions for Further Reading

Argyle, M., & Henderson, M. (1984). The rules of friendship. *Journal of Social and Personal Relationships, 1,* 211–237. A look at what we assume on the part of our friends and what they assume of us.

Canary, D. J., & Stafford, L. (1993). Preservation of relational characteristics: Maintenance strategies, equity and locus of control. In P. J. Kalbfleisch (Ed.), *Interpersonal communication: Evolving interpersonal relationships.* Hillsdale, NJ: Erlbaum. Strategies of relationship maintenance from the perspective of communication research.

Harvey, J. H., & Omarzu, J. (1997). Minding the close relationship. *Personality and Social Psychology Review, 1,* 224–240. An excellent theoretical article on relationship maintenance, with a focus on romantic relationships.

Milardo, R. M. (1986). Personal choice and social constraint in close relationships: Application of network analysis. In V. J. Derlega & B. A. Winstead (Eds.), *Friendship and social interaction* (pp. 146–166). New York: Springer-Verlag. The influence of our social network on our close relationships.

Morton, T. L., Alexander, J. F., & Altman, I. (1976). Communication and relationship definition. In G. R. Miller (Ed.), *Explorations in interpersonal communication.* Beverly Hills, CA: Sage. Despite its being somewhat dated, this chapter remains a highly relevant statement on relationship definition.

Parks, M. R., & Eggert, L. L. (1991). The role of social context in the dynamics of personal relationships. In W. H. Jones & D. Perlman (Eds.), *Advances in personal relationships* (Vol. 2, pp. 1–34). London: Kingsley. When friends don't think romantic partners are a good match, it doesn't bode well for the relationship.

South, S. J., & Lloyd, K. M. (1995). Social alternatives and marital dissolution. *American Sociological Review, 60,* 21–35. Young marrieds should choose their neighborhood and work setting carefully. There are spouse snatchers lurking about.

Swann, W. B., Jr., De La Ronda, C., & Hixon, J. G. (1994). Authenticity and positivity strivings in marriage and courtship. *Journal of Personality and Social Psychology, 66,* 857–869. An overview of the rationale behind the shift from flattery to authenticity as relationships develop and mature.

# CHAPTER 4

## Personal Relationships and Well-Being

*After their ship sank off the coast of Tasmania, seven crew members drifted in the Pacific Ocean for nine days in an inflated life raft. They experienced rough seas and had only a limited supply of drinking water and some biscuits. One man died while on the life raft, and two others died shortly after they reached shore. In interviews following the ordeal, the survivors were asked what helped them cope. Here are some of their comments:*

*"We kept our hands occupied with rowing and talking about our wives. I said, 'Well, this is it. I'm never going to see anyone again.' I felt sorry for my mother. . . ."*

*"She [his wife] was always at the back of my mind, and my son was at the back of my mind, but I didn't want to think of them too much . . . that was what I had to get back for."*

*"We were thinking about our families. I just kept thinking about my wife and family—that was all I had to live for."*

*"Every night I could see my wife's face. Every time I closed my eyes I could see my wife there." (When asked what helped him most) "Well, I suppose a picture of my wife and kids. . . . I thought about them all the time. . . . I was worried about the boys' school and my daughter's future at school, and whatnot, and what would happen to my wife."*

*"We chatted about our families."*

*"We all talked about our families. It does pass through your mind, 'Will she be all right?'" (Henderson & Bostock, 1975, p. 222)*

For most of human history, there were no doctors, no hospitals, and no insurance. In times of need, people depended on one another, and to be isolated or ostracized was like a death sentence. We should not be surprised, then, to find an association between personal relationships and well-being. In this

## Box 4-1 In a Different Key
## Social Support Among the Hutterites

The Hutterites are a religious sect whose members live primarily in Canada. They make their living by farming. They dress simply. Jewelry, art, and other decorations are considered frivolous. Contacts with "the outside" are kept to a minimum. Radios and movies are forbidden, and Hutterite children typically go to school only through the eighth grade.

Life among the Hutterites is simple and harmonious. For example, in their study, Joseph Eaton and Robert Weil (1955) noted that there were no murders, no arsons, no serious physical assaults, no sex crimes, no drug addiction, no alcoholism, and no syphilis among the Hutterites. Divorce, separation, and desertion were rare. Only five marriages had been known to fail since 1875 (Eaton & Weil, 1953).

Particularly relevant for our purposes is the Hutterite system of mutual aid and caring. Any misfortune to anyone in the community is responded to by the group. This applies to the ill, the infirm, the retarded, the aged, widows, orphans, and the mentally ill as well. And apparently it works. A report to the Manitoba Provincial Legislature in 1947, for example, indicated that the way of life in the Hutterite community resulted in a complete absence of mental illness (Eaton & Weil, 1953). And at the time of Eaton and Weil's study, there were no Hutterites in mental hospitals, nor was anyone a patient in formal psychotherapy or the subject of psychiatric casework.

On closer scrutiny, however, Eaton and Weil concluded that the Hutterites were not completely free from mental illness. In the Hutterite community, signs of mental illness were typically seen as the result of "working too hard." And the "patients" were treated by integrating them as fully as possible into community life. They were never isolated. They stayed in their homes in familiar surroundings. They were encouraged to participate in normal family life. They continued to work as they could at what interested them. A mentor relationship was often arranged, and they were praised for signs of improvement. Compassion was shown for those who were depressed. And because of the potential for suicide, such individuals were given special care. Sexual relations continued for married adults, and some continued to have children even when they were mentally ill. Even psychotics were not stigmatized, and when they recovered, they could assume any role in the community.

In a word, the Hutterites were plain people. They brought no medical insights or specialized training to the problems of the mentally ill; they followed their inclinations, and they cared for their own with remarkable results. Schizophrenia was rare. Only a few cases were identified in Eaton and Weil's study. And, overall, the rate of psychosis was approximately a third of what it was for the state of New York at the time.

chapter we will explore the effects of personal relationships on both mental and physical health. The term **social support** is often used in this context; it refers to the availability of others who care about us, value us, and love us (Sarason & Sarason, 1984). Social support is an umbrella term for friends, neighbors, husbands, wives, and others who can be called upon in time of need (Cutrona et al., 1990). An example of the power and significance of social support can be seen in Box 4-1.

A considerable body of research documents the relationship between social support and mental and physical health. Some studies have focused on the impact of social support on risk factors and the *onset* of illness. Other studies have focused on social support as it affects *coping* and *recovery* after the individual is ill or otherwise incapacitated. Both approaches show similar patterns. People who are isolated or suffer the loss of their spouse or other loved ones or who experience the death or absence of parents in early childhood, are at increased risk for mental and physical illness and show higher mortality rates as well (Berkman, 1985, 1986; Brown & Harris, 1978; Burman & Margolin, 1992; Cohen, 1988, 1989; Cohen & Syme, 1985; Schwarzer & Leppin, 1991; Stroebe & Stroebe, 1986, 1987, 1992).

## Types of Support

Social support comes in various forms and, like many things in life, is most keenly felt when it is absent. The following sections discuss types of support noted by Wolfgang and Margaret Stroebe (1986).

### Instrumental Support

Our effectiveness in coping with the demands of everyday life rests on the resources at our disposal, including the knowledge, abilities, and skills of those close to us. The loss of a particularly close other, such as one's marriage partner, is likely to decrease the demands of day-to-day living very little, if at all; but it is likely to reduce the availability of resources a great deal. A couple who have been married many years, for example, have typically established a routine division of labor for household chores, raising children, and the like. Consequently, divorce or the death of a spouse leaves a vacuum at a practical level. The remaining partner must now be responsible for the tasks that the other once assumed. The less flexible and less skilled in these various areas an individual is, or the more difficult it is to find substitutes, the more difficulty she or he is likely to have in adjusting.

### Financial Resources

Much the same logic that applies to instrumental support applies to financial resources. Even the most resourceful individual is likely to have areas in which she or he must call upon others for help. The widowed or divorced partner who is able to pay for help in the area of child care, for example, is in a better position to cope with other issues. The problems of coping on our own are greatly increased when we must also curtail social and other activities in an effort to make ends meet. However, to some extent, relatives in our social support network often compensate for low financial resources (Walker et al., 1977).

### Validational Support

Coping is not just a matter of having skills and financial resources. In times of stress we are likely to turn to others for validation. In the case of marriage and the symbiotic relationship it represents (Lewis & Spanier, 1979), it is likely that partners will have figured greatly in the creation and validation of each other's social reality. Left with no one to serve in this role, the widowed, separated, or divorced partner is confronted with more situations that are especially stressful. For example, in one study approximately 40% of the bereaved reported being concerned about losing their sanity (Glick et al., 1974). The case of Cora and Ed illustrates this point.

When his wife died, Ed felt his whole world had collapsed. Now that the children were grown and on their own, he and Cora had planned on retiring in a few years and maybe moving to Florida. Ed even took up woodworking as a hobby to pass the idle hours, but now all that seemed pointless. At one point Ed visited his brother and his family in Colorado, but he felt he was intruding. They had their own lives to live. The minister called and told him that he should get more involved in church, but Ed just didn't feel comfortable going to church without Cora. He became more and more depressed as the months passed. Life just didn't seem worth living somehow.

### Emotional Support

Of the many sources of stress that one can experience, the loss of emotional support (empathy, caring, love, and trust) seems to be the most important. A study of working-class women who were at risk for depression, for example, noted the special significance of having a confidant. Those who had someone close to confide in were far less vulnerable. Of the women in the study who experienced high levels of stress, only 4% of those who had an intimate relationship with a husband or boyfriend developed psychological problems (Brown et al., 1975).

### Companionship

Although there are wide variations in how dependent people are on each other, partner loss can be devastating to the widowed or divorced for whom substitutes are not readily available. When faced with loss, those who have a social support network typically have an easier time adjusting (Brown et al., 1975; Lewis & Spanier, 1979).

## Social Identity

The informal groups to which we belong and on which we depend for social sustenance are the basis of our social identity. Having lost the status of friend, confidant, or life partner, the individual is now likely to be faced with the task of renegotiating an identity (Stroebe & Stroebe, 1986). In a study of 132 widows, 13 months following partner loss, researchers noted that where the outcomes were less positive, the widows tended to see their other personal/social relationships as less supportive than did the widowed who had more positive outcomes (Maddison & Walker, 1967).

Perhaps Thomas Matarazzo put it best:

> More psychotherapy is accomplished between good friends at coffee every morning at 10 o'clock than all day long in psychologists' and physicians' offices. A good talk with a close friend can help solve problems or at least put them in perspective before they become overpowering. One of the problems faced by today's mobile society is the scarcity of good friends.[1]

In sum, various types of social support seem to have an influence on our mental and physical health. Investigations into this relationship have taken place on many different levels and have involved many different methods. We turn next to a look at the broad statistical picture.

# Epidemiological Research Into the Health Effects of Social Support

**Epidemiology** is the study of health-related matters, illness, and mortality, at the statistical level. The following sections discuss a sample of studies comparing various groups on such things as heart disease, cancer, and complications during pregnancy. In general, the studies show that morbidity (disease) and mortality (death) rates are lower for those who have social supports than for those who do not (see Atkins et al., 1991; House et al., 1988, for reviews).

## Social Connectedness and Health

Victor Fuchs (1974) compared health statistics in Nevada and Utah, two states that were similar in many ways. Their educational and income levels were similar. They had about the same distribution of people living in urban versus rural areas, similar levels of health care facilities, and about the same number of doctors per 1,000 population. Yet in 1960, for white males and females

---

1. From Matarazzo, J. D. (1979). A good friend: One of mankind's most effective and inexpensive psychotherapists. *Journal of Clinical Psychology, 35,* 231–232. Copyright © 1979. Reprinted by permission of John Wiley & Sons, Inc.

ages 25 to 64, Nevada had by far the highest mortality rate in the United States, while Utah had one of the lowest. Why?

Most people in Utah are Mormons. One of the reasons for their good health may be that Mormons do not smoke or drink alcoholic beverages. Other reasons, however, may be that they tend to be family oriented, they tend to have stable marriages, and they tend to stay put. At the time of the study, for example, 63% of the residents of Utah had been born there. By contrast, 90% of Nevadans (middle aged) had come from out of state. Over 20% of the males aged 35–64 in Nevada were either single, widowed, divorced, or otherwise separated from their wives. Of those who were married, over a third had been divorced or widowed. Comparable figures for the state of Utah suggested much more in the way of marital stability (Fuchs, 1974).

Similar findings emerged from the research of Lisa Berkman and Leonard Syme (1979), who investigated the relationship between social and community ties and mortality rates for a sample of 4,725 men and women (ages 30–69) in Alameda County, California. The indicators of social support in this study included such things as whether or not the individual was married, degree of satisfaction in marriage, contacts with extended family and close friends, church attendance, and involvement in other formal and informal groups. From these indicators, Berkman and Syme derived an index of "social connectedness." As we see in Figure 4-1, social connectedness was clearly associated with mortality rate. Overall, males who were more socially connected

Participation in groups, even informal groups, can have a positive overall effect on one's general health.

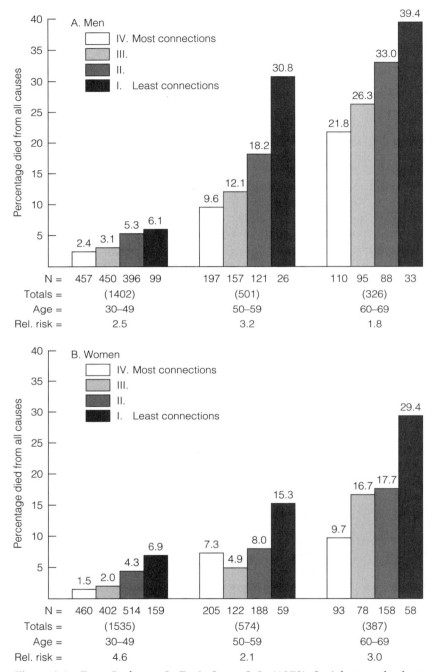

**Figure 4-1**  From Berkman, L. F., & Syme, S. L. (1979). Social networks, host resistance, and mortality: A 9-year follow-up study of Alameda County residents. *American Journal of Epidemiology, 103*, 186–204.

were 2.3 times, and females were 2.8 times, more likely to have survived 9 years later than were their less socially connected counterparts.

Not only was social connectedness associated with the mortality rate in general, but it was also associated with specific health-related problems, such as ischemic heart disease, cerebrovascular and circulatory diseases, diseases of the digestive and respiratory systems, accidents, and suicide. Those who were married, both males and females, had lower mortality rates than did those who were separated, widowed, single, or divorced (Berkman & Syme, 1979).

In addition, the Berkman and Syme study found evidence for a degree of "substitutability" of various forms of social connectedness. For example, those who were not married but had a network of friends and relatives had much the same mortality rates as married couples who had few contacts with friends and relatives. It was only in the absence of any source of social connectedness that people were at increased risk over the 9-year period.

## Community Cohesiveness and Heart Disease

Stewart Wolf (Wolf, 1992; Wolf & Bruhn, 1993) has conducted a long-term study of Roseto, Pennsylvania. What had initially caught his attention in the 1960s was that the residents of Roseto (primarily Italian Americans) enjoyed a diet that was rich in the kinds of foods ordinarily associated with heart disease. Their daily caloric intake was above the national average, and their cholesterol levels were similar to those of people living in nearby towns. Yet this small town of 1,630 inhabitants had one third the rate of heart attacks of neighboring communities.

One possible explanation was that Rosetans might have come from particularly sturdy stock, with a lower susceptibility to heart disease, but this seemed unlikely. When people from Roseto moved away, they had the same rate of heart disease as those in the surrounding communities.

Looking for the reason behind this relative immunity from heart disease, Wolf noted that the way of life in Roseto differed from that of its neighbors in important ways. It involved cooperation and mutual support instead of individualism and competition. The entire town seemed to radiate a cooperative spirit. People celebrated holidays, birthdays, graduations, and festivals together. The family unit, which often involved three generations in the same household, was central to community life (Wolf, 1992).

Over time, however, a change took place in the social fabric of Roseto, especially among the young people. Interviews began to suggest that they were likely to abandon the old ways. And so the once traditional town began to look more and more like the towns around it (Bruhn & Wolf, 1978). By 1985 three-generation households had all but disappeared. Interviews indicated that commitment to traditional religious values and practices was on the decline, and the community seemed to become less cohesive, more materialistic, and more like the rest of the United States (Wolf, 1992). And as we see in Figure 4-2, along with these changes came an increase in heart disease.

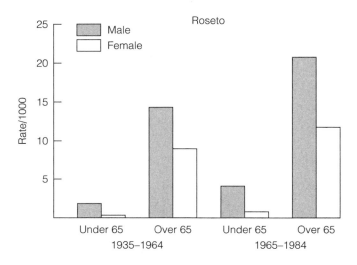

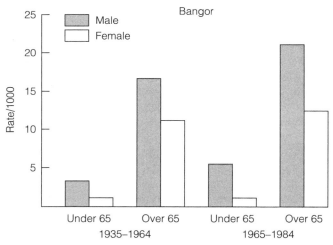

**Figure 4-2**   Mortality rates/1000 from myocardial infarction. Statistical Significance (Chi-Square): For Rosetans (male & female) under 65; 1935–64 vs. 1965–84: $p > 0.01$. For Rosetans (male & female) over 65; 1935–64 vs. 1965–84:ns. For Bangorians (male & female) under 65; 1935–64 vs. 1965–84:ns. For Bangorians (male & female) over 65; 1935–64 vs. 1965–84:ns. For all subjects, all years; under age 65 vs. over age 65: $p > 0.01$. From Wolf, S. (1992). Predictors of myocardial infarction over a span of 30 years in Roseto, Pennsylvania. *Integrative Physiology and Behavioral Science, 27,* 249. Copyright © 1992 Transaction Publishers; all rights reserved. Reprinted by permission.

One of the ironies of the Roseto findings was that, during the course of the study, Rosetans, like the rest of Americans, had generally changed their eating habits in keeping with the recommendations of the American Heart Association: The increase in death from heart disease was accompanied by what was thought to be a more prudent diet containing significantly less lard, butter, and eggs.

### Social Support, Stress, and Complications During Pregnancy

The effects of social support seem to extend to many different aspects of health. Katherine Nuckolls and her colleagues (1972) investigated the relationship between social support and complications during pregnancy. In this study, expectant mothers were assessed for the extent and severity of recent stressful life events and levels of social support. The results showed that those who had high levels of social support had significantly fewer complications during pregnancy than those with lower levels of social support, particularly among those who had recently experienced high levels of stress. Ninety-one percent of the women who were high in levels of recent life stress and low in social support experienced complications during pregnancy. The comparable figure for those high in social support was only 33%.

Neither stress nor the lack of social support by itself was associated with complications during pregnancy; it was only when the two occurred together.

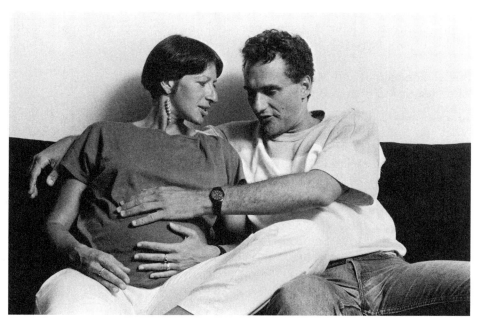

Pregnancy can be stressful and affect one's overall health. Stable relationships and support, however, have been shown to lessen the chances of health complications.

The combination of high levels of stress and low levels of social support was associated with a variety of health complications during pregnancy (Nuckolls et al., 1972).

### Church Attendance and Health

In their study of Washington County, Maryland, George Comstock and Kay Partridge (Comstock, 1971; Comstock & Partridge, 1972) found that church attendance was also related to a variety of health consequences. Even after such factors as smoking and socioeconomic status were taken into account, Comstock (1971) found that the risk of death from heart disease among white males who attended church at least once a week was 60% of that for infrequent attenders. Results from a study of women showed a similar pattern (Comstock & Partridge, 1972). Indeed, church attendance was correlated with a number of health consequences. But because the association was so wide ranging, it's fair to say that the effects are nonspecific—that is, church attendance seems to be associated with lower risk of health-related problems in general.

There are two ways of interpreting the Comstock and Partridge findings. One interpretation would be that the association was due to the effects of church attendance upon health; the other would be that the association was due to the effects of health upon church attendance (that is, sick people stay away from church). This latter interpretation is unlikely, however. If the association between church attendance and health were due to people wanting to make peace with their maker, we would expect the association to be in the opposite direction (church attendance would be associated with more health problems, not fewer).

### Social Connection and Mortality Among Members of a Health Maintenance Organization

In a study of 2,600 members of a health maintenance organization, Thomas Vogt and colleagues reported a link between social connections and mortality. Over a period of 15 years, those who reported greater numbers in, and involvement with, their social networks showed lower mortality rates.

In a later analysis of the same data, Judith Hibbard and Clyde Pope (1993) focused specifically on social support in the workplace and marriage. They found no relationship between social support and health for men, but for married women, those who reported more equality in decision making in their marriage showed lower mortality rates. Those who indicated having greater social support in the workplace also showed lower mortality rates and lower risk of stroke over a 15-year period.

### Social Connection and Cancer

In a study extending over 17 years, Peggy Reynolds and George Kaplan (1990) reported a relationship between social connections and risk of cancer for women. Social isolation, such as having few contacts with friends and relatives, lack of church membership, and feelings of loneliness, were associated with an increased risk of cancer generally, and particularly an increased mortality from hormone-related cancers. Findings consistent with these have been reported by others as well, for both men and women (Atkins et al., 1991; Orth-Gomer et al., 1993).

## Rehabilitation and Recovery

Not only does social support seem to affect the onset of various health-related problems, but it also plays a role in the rehabilitation and recovery process. For example, it has been found that the adjustment of schizophrenics following their discharge from the hospital is significantly better when friends and neighbors are available to offer social support (Lyon & Zucker, 1974). And in a major cross-cultural study involving 10 countries, sponsored by the World Health Organization, researchers have noted that patients with schizophrenia from developing countries show far better outcomes over time than do those from industrialized nations. For example, 63% of those in developing countries showed remission over a 2-year follow-up, while the comparable figure for developed countries, such as the United States, was 37% (Jablensky et al., 1992; Sartorious, et al., 1986). Presumably the differences are due to the more accepting attitudes and support of family and friends in developing countries for those who have had schizophrenia. A case in point appears in Box 4-2.

Similarly, in a study of 22,323 male heart attack survivors (myocardial infarction) between the ages of 30 and 69, a group of researchers found that indices of stress and social isolation were both related to mortality over a 3-year period, with those experiencing high levels of stress *and* isolation showing 4–5 times greater risk (Ruberman et al., 1984).

Much the same findings have been reported in the case of support groups for women with breast cancer (Spiegel, 1991). Over a period of 10 years, the average survival rate for the support group members was 36.6 months, compared with 18.9 months for a control group receiving only routine care (Spiegel, et al., 1989; see also Richardson et al., 1990).

From the statistical picture, we see that the association between personal relationships (by whatever name) and health-related matters appears to be a significant one. And, as researchers have looked more closely, the role played by confidants seems to be especially important in this picture.

## The Role of Confidants

James Pennebaker (1989) has noted that how one adjusts to various traumatic events seems to be associated with confiding in others. "Survivors" who talk with others close to them following a traumatic event, such as the accidental death of a spouse, seem to be healthier and less obsessed with the trauma a year later. On the other hand, adults who have experienced some type of

### Box 4-2  *In a Different Key*
## Thomas Adeoye Lambo

Thomas Adeoye Lambo was born in Nigeria. He studied medicine at Birmingham University (UK) and took advanced training in psychiatry at the University of London Institute of Psychiatry. He was employed by the Nigerian government to study mental illness among African students studying abroad, and his observations led him to note that despite their Ph.D.s and designer suits, the students' illnesses took them back to their native Africa. Their delusions were expressed in terms of witchcraft. These investigations led to his becoming a pioneer in *ethnopsychiatry*.

Returning to Africa to become director of Nigeria's new mental hospital at Aro, Lambo found himself waiting for construction to be completed. During this time he hired a dozen traditional African practitioners to work alongside his clinical staff. Patients were lodged in nearby villages. Hosts were chosen because they were tolerant of the guests and their illness. And the patient's entire family was incorporated into the therapy sessions.

As the program evolved, studies were conducted in which schizophrenics were placed randomly either in hospital treatment or in "village treatment." Patients in both hospital settings and village treatment received structured therapy sessions, but the social dynamics were different. What soon became apparent was that village life itself was therapeutic. Everyone in the traditional villages was considered a brother or sister, and this facilitated extended care and modeling. In traditional treatment the "healer" spent a lot of time with the patient and the patient's family and got to know them. The results indicated that village treatment was more effective, led to more rapid "cures," fewer relapses, and cost one fifth the amount of standard hospital treatment (Bass, 1993).

childhood trauma, but have never discussed it with anyone, are more likely to experience health problems ranging from hypertension, influenza, and diarrhea, to cancer (Pennebaker & Susman, 1988).

Much the same findings have been noted for college populations as well (Pennebaker et al., 1988). Even when other measures of social support, such as number of friends, was taken into account, the relationship between confiding and illness remained (Pennebaker, 1989). In other words, confiding in someone seems to be important, even when other forms of social support are available. Those who experienced some sort of trauma but did not confide in someone were more likely to be ill later. This is shown in Figure 4-3.

The role of social supports in buffering the stresses of everyday life, then, may be due in part to the presence or absence of close others in whom we can confide. And, conversely, those who lose a confidant are especially at risk for negative health consequences. This connection is shown most clearly in the research that has focused on the health consequences of partner loss.

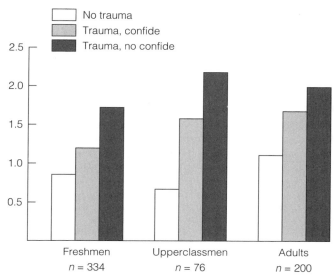

**Figure 4-3** Illness measures among subjects who reported experiencing no traumatic experiences, traumatic experiences that were all confided, or traumas that were not confided. In the freshmen sample, the y-axis refers to actual number of health center visits in the 4 months following completion of the trauma questionnaire. For the upperclassmen sample, the y-axis refers to number of self-reported visits to a physician in the 6 months preceding the completion of the trauma questionnaire. The y-axis for the adult sample reflects number of self-reported major and minor illnesses in the previous year. From Pennebaker, J. W. (1989). Confession, inhibition, and disease. In L. Berkowitz (Ed.), *Advances in Experimental Social Psychology, 22,* 211–244. New York: Academic Press.

## Effects of Partner Loss on Health

Research indicates that the widowed, especially in the first year of bereavement, have many more complaints about their health, more mental and physical symptoms, and an increased mortality risk (Stroebe & Stroebe, 1986, 1987). Such effects are not due to the selection processes of marriage itself (that is, that the less healthy do not marry) (Berkman & Syme, 1979) or to differences in such factors as serum cholesterol, blood pressure, or obesity (Weis, 1973).

### Bereavement and Mental Health

Several studies have focused on the relationship between bereavement and depression. For example, in a survey of widows who had lost their husbands

16–18 months earlier, researchers found that 36% of the widowed group indicated having high levels of depression, while only 2.8% of a comparison group of married, single, and divorced women did so (van Rooijen, 1979). Others have reported similar findings (see Stroebe & Stroebe, 1986, for a review).

Consistent with this, the bereaved, both widows and widowers, tend to be overrepresented in the psychiatric population. For example, Colin Parkes (1964a, 1964b), in an analysis of the records of patients entering Bethlehem Royal and Maudsley Hospitals in London, found that those who had recently been widowed were six times more likely to be represented among patients seeking psychiatric treatment than were their nonwidowed counterparts.

## Bereavement and Physical Health

Those who are widowed also run a greater risk of physical illness than do comparable marrieds (National Center for Health Statistics, 1970). And, again, this seems to be especially true for those who are recently bereaved (Thompson et al., 1984).

One of the most important studies along these lines was based on interview data from the National Hospice Study (Greer et al., 1983). This study involved 1,447 "primary care persons" (not necessarily the spouse) of terminally ill patients. When compared with national averages, these "bereaved" had a higher number of visits to physicians. This fact alone can be interpreted in different ways, however. For example, these caretakers may have neglected their own routine health care while they were involved in the care of terminally ill patients. But Janice Kiecolt-Glaser (1993) has reported that hospice caretakers who were bereaved showed continued signs of weak immune response 2–4 years after loss. So the effects of bereavement seem to extend to various caretakers who are involved in the care of terminally ill patients, and this includes those who are not particularly close relatives.

## Bereavement and Mortality Rate

Over a century ago, William Farr (1858/1975) noted the difference in mortality rates between marrieds and singles and the even greater difference in the mortality rates between marrieds and the widowed. Since then, such differences have been reported many times in the literature (Kraus & Lilienfeld, 1959; Stroebe et al., 1982). Other things being equal, married people, both males and females, show lower mortality rates than do those who are not married. Younger widowed people show the highest *relative* mortality rate among various age groups. And when compared to the mortality rate for married men and women, the mortality rate is greater for widowers than it is for widows. This general pattern is characteristic of mortality rates for many different countries and has shown considerable stability over time (Stroebe & Stroebe, 1987).

For example, Michael Young and his colleagues (1963) studied the mortality rate among 4,486 widowers, age 55 and over, who had lost their wives in 1957. This group was then compared to married men of similar age. The mortality rate was 40% greater for the widowed group in the first 6 months of bereavement. In a follow-up of the same population, Colin Parkes and his associates (1969) found that after 6 months, the mortality rates remained essentially at or below the rates for married males. The primary causes of death were heart problems (for example, myocardial infarction) and other complications of atherosclerosis. Other researchers have reported similar findings (Cottington et al., 1980; Helsing et al., 1981; but see Clayton, 1979).

## Causes of Death Among the Bereaved

The problem with global statistical data is that it gives little or no indication of the specific factors at work. The death of one partner followed by the death of another could be due to a common third factor, such as contagious disease, accidents such as fire, or environmental contaminants, as might be the case in a household of heavy smokers, for example (Stroebe et al., 1982).

***Do the Widowed Die of a Broken Heart?***   James Lynch (1977) has suggested that those who have been bereaved or otherwise isolated and alone are especially at risk for coronary heart disease and related problems. Indeed, when

For the aged, friendships and companionship do affect overall health and are possibly even a factor in enhancing the function of the immune system.

the National Center for Health Statistics (1970) published a report on causes of death for individuals according to marital status, the major causes of death were coronary heart disease, stroke, and cancer, in that order. But this was true for the widowed and the married alike.

When we compare the mortality rates of the widowed to married, we find that it is violent deaths (accidents, suicides, and homicides) that differentiate the widows from married females. And homicides, cirrhosis of the liver, suicide, accidents, tuberculosis, followed by cancer differentiate widowers from married males (Stroebe et al., 1982). For example, the suicide rate for divorced or widowed men age 65 and older, between 1980 and 1992, was 2.7 times the rate for married men, and the rate for divorced or widowed women was 1.8 times that for married women. Indeed, one of the risk factors for suicide among older adults is social isolation in general (Center for Disease Control, 1996). On the other hand, as noted earlier, Parkes and colleagues (1969) found that two thirds of the increased mortality rate during the first 6 months of bereavement was due to some sort of disease of the circulatory system. What's going on here?

The reason for the confusion is probably the different methodologies involved in various studies. Next to accidents and violent deaths, heart attack is likely to be a faster cause of death than are diseases such as tuberculosis, cirrhosis of the liver, or cancer. Accordingly, following bereavement, we would expect the effects of heart disease to show up earlier in the statistics as a cause of death, while health problems that take longer to cause death are not likely to show up unless measures are taken over a longer period of time (Stroebe & Stroebe, 1986, 1987).

*Bereavement and Cancer*    As part of a study of 110 male patients with subacute or chronic pulmonary (lung) lesions, various psychosocial factors were assessed using semistructured interviews (Horne & Picard, 1979). The men who later developed cancer were found to have experienced higher levels of stress as identified by a host of indicators, including lack of stability in childhood, jobs, and marriage; lack of plans for the future; and recent loss of a loved one.

Based on such indicators, the researchers were able to predict 61% of the cases in which the patients later developed cancer and 80% of the cases that turned out to be benign. They noted in their conclusions that although smoking has been clearly associated with increased risk of coronary heart disease and lung cancer, in this study the psychosocial factors were one to two times as important in predicting cancer.

## Health Consequences of Separation/Divorce

Although the plight of the widowed parallels that of the separated/divorced in many ways, the evidence suggests that compared with their widowed counterparts, the separated/divorced are especially vulnerable to problems of mental and physical illness. Reviews of the relationship between mental illness and separation/divorce (for example, Crago, 1972; Gove, 1972) indicate not only that separation and divorce are associated with an increased risk for mental and emotional problems, but also that their impact seems to be greater than the impact of bereavement.

In a survey of 88,000 households in the United States, by the National Center for Health Statistics (1970), individuals who were divorced showed higher than average rates of illness and disability on all measures taken. In terms of days of restricted activity, limitations of activity due to chronic conditions, and number of visits to the doctor, the separated and divorced were similar to the bereaved, while in terms of acute conditions, they showed more problems than the bereaved (Verbrugge, 1979).

### Preliminary Conclusions on Partner Loss and Health

Taken as a whole, the statistical evidence is compelling enough that we are safe in concluding that the bereaved, the separated, and the divorced are at increased risk for problems of mental and physical health. This conclusion is based on several studies involving different populations, using a variety of approaches and methodologies, and focusing on various types of mental and physical problems (Helsing & Szklo, 1981; Stroebe & Stroebe, 1986, 1992; van Rooijen, 1979). This still leaves us with the question of the mechanism(s) at work: How do personal relationships affect health? And it is to that issue that we turn next.

## How Social Support Affects Health

Although research findings show a relationship between social support and health, how the presence of social support protects against disease or facilitates recovery is not well understood. In general, there seem to be three possible links between personal relationships and health. The first is that illness leads to disruption of social support. Caretakers may "burn out," and friends and neighbors may stop visiting. Illness can repulse (Wortman & Dunkel-Schetter, 1979). In addition, physical disability may interfere with certain social activities, such as hiking or dancing, and thus decrease contacts with potential sources of support. However, all things considered, such factors do not seem to play a major role in accounting for the relationship between illness and social support (Atkins et al., 1991).

A second possibility is that both illness and level of social support may be related to a third factor. For example, socioeconomic status (especially poverty) is related to mortality rate from coronary heart disease (Kaplan, 1985). There are any number of reasons why this might be the case. Work among the lower classes tends to be unstable, unrewarding, physically demanding, and something the individuals feel they have little control over. Such factors are associated with coronary heart disease (Karasek et al., 1981). In addition, lower income families are exposed to more dangerous levels of environmental contaminants, such as lead (Mahaffey et al., 1982).

On the other hand, there is no indication that the poor lack for social support. For example, both James House and colleagues (1982) and Victor Schoenbach and colleagues (1986) found that low-income blacks were well integrated into stable rural communities. Their social support levels were high. Yet, even when socioeconomic status was taken into account, the researchers still found that lower levels of social support were associated with higher mortality rates.

A third possible link between health and social support is that those who have poor health habits (for example, not watching their diet, not getting enough exercise) may also be those who have few social supports, and those who have high levels of social supports may be encouraged by others close to them to follow regimens that involve better health habits. But again, when health habits have been taken into account, there is still a relationship between personal relationships and mortality rate (Belloc & Breslow, 1972). Thus, although it is always possible that other factors may be at work, there is little evidence that they explain away the relationship between personal relationships and illness or mortality rates.

Most compelling in this picture, perhaps, is the temporal sequence; disruptions in personal relationships tend to *precede* such problems as heart attacks. Equally important is the fact that both animal research (Manuck et al., 1988) and human studies (Kiecolt-Glaser et al., 1984) have demonstrated the effects of isolation on disruption of immune function.

What does this suggest? How do stressful life events affect health? There would seem to be two general ways. One is a behavioral route and the other physiological.

### The Behavioral Route: Social Support for Healthy Behaviors

In interviews, those who experience the loss of a loved one often say, especially early in bereavement, they feel that life is no longer worth living. The increased suicide rate immediately after partner loss lends credence to such statements. Under such conditions, people are less likely to take the steps necessary to ensure their own health and safety. For example, increased rates of cirrhosis of the liver result largely from consumption of alcohol and malnutrition. Because even advanced cases of cirrhosis of the liver can be improved or virtually cured by abstaining from alcohol and watching one's diet, such deaths are best considered self-inflicted (Stroebe & Stroebe, 1986).

A similar argument applies in the case of tuberculosis. Because tuberculosis can be arrested and even cured with the right treatment, the increased death rate from tuberculosis among the bereaved suggests that treatment has not been pursued. Poor nutrition is also a likely contributing factor, since the bacteria that cause tuberculosis thrive under conditions of malnutrition.

When we look closely, some of the best evidence for the importance of social support in encouraging positive health-related behaviors comes in the area of recovery, rehabilitation, and adaptation. For example, in a review of the literature on the relationships between social support and health, Robert Kaplan and Michelle Toshima (1990) noted that the studies were sometimes conflicting. But those studies that reported a clear connection tended to focus on specific behaviors, such as compliance with health-related regimens (medications, diet, exercise) or health-related habits, such as not smoking (Dubbert & Wilson, 1984).

In addition, health-related practices tend to run in families (Patterson et al., 1987), and the effect tends to be rather specific, correlating with such things as exercise and diet (Sallis et al., 1987) rather than with support in general (Schafer et al., 1986). Social support, then, may be too general a notion to tell us very much about specifics. One's friends may be health-food advocates or drinking buddies, and this could make a difference in times of stress.

### The Physiological Route: Stress and the Suppression of Immune Function

Any number of factors increase or decrease an individual's susceptibility to various diseases (for example, prior exposure, nutrition, and genetic endowment), and one of the most important is stress. It is now generally accepted that stress can affect the immune system (Kiecolt-Glaser, 1993; Kiecolt-Glaser et al., 1984, 1987, 1988). Such findings are consistent with our everyday experience that under prolonged exposure to stressful events, we become more susceptible to colds and flu, for example. And, of course, one of the causes of stress is disruption, loss of, or problems in personal relationships.

For example, Roger Bartrop and his colleagues (1977) found that cellular immunity was significantly suppressed among widows 6 weeks after bereavement. And Steven Schleifer and colleagues (1983) reported evidence for the suppression of lymphocyte stimulation response in a group of men whose wives were terminally ill from breast cancer.

However, it is in the work of Janice Kiecolt-Glaser and her associates that we find the most compelling evidence for a link between the state of one's personal relationships and immune function. Kiecolt-Glaser and colleagues (1987) gathered data from 38 married and 38 separated or divorced women, matched on such variables as socioeconomic status, age, educational level, and number of children. The women underwent extensive psychological testing, and blood samples were taken and analyzed for indications of stress response. Among the findings of this study were that women in the separated/divorced group showed significantly lower percentages of helper T lymphocytes than did those in the married group. This difference was especially marked among the separated or divorced women who remained psychologically attached to their ex-husbands. There were also significantly lower levels of natural killer (NK) cells among the recently (1 year or less) separated or divorced women, compared with the married women, as well as differences in antibody activity and depression.

Even among the married group, indications of marital quality were strong predictors of both depression and immune function response. And, finally, those who initiated the separation or divorce (suggesting a measure of control) tended to show less suppression of immune function than those who did not (Kiecolt-Glaser et al., 1988).

In short, there is evidence for a relationship between psychosocial stress, suppression of immune function, and susceptibility to infectious disease. Such findings have important implications for the health of those who experience partner loss, whether through bereavement, separation, or divorce. The experience of loss seems to be associated with impairment of immune function and lower resistance to disease.

## Conclusion

The association between the state of one's personal relationships and mental health is compelling enough that any reasonable person would accept it. Because of the relationships between bereavement, separation or divorce, and mortality rate, the connection between personal relationships and physical health seems to be compelling as well. The role of confidants, together with the influence of friends and family, in promoting good health habits seems to be important in this regard. And especially significant in this picture is the link between partner loss and immune function.

## Suggestions for Further Reading

Atkins, C. J., Kaplan, R. M., & Toshima, M. T. (1991). Close relationships in the epidemiology of cardiovascular disease. In W. H. Jones & D. Perlman (Eds.), *Advances in personal relationships* (Vol. 3, pp. 207–231). London: Kingsley. An authoritative overview of the association between personal relationships and heart disease.

Berkman, L. F., & Syme, S. L. (1979). Social networks, host resistance and mortality: A nine-year follow-up of Alameda County residents. *American Journal of Epidemiology, 109,* 186–204. A classic study documenting the association between social connection and health.

Brown, G. W., & Harris, T. (1978). *Social origins of depression: A study of psychiatric disorder in women.* New York: Free Press. Documents the role of social-personal relationships in depression among women.

Burman, B., & Margolin, G. (1992). Analysis of the association between marital relationships and health problems: An interactional perspective. *Psychological Bulletin, 112,* 39–63. An excellent (and comprehensive) overview.

Comstock, G. W., & Partridge, K. B. (1972). Church attendance and health. *Journal of Chronic Diseases, 25,* 665–672. Frequent church attenders are less at risk for a variety of illnesses. Our grandmothers may have been onto something.

Kiecolt-Glaser, J. K., Fisher, L. D., Ogrocki, P., Stout, J. C., Speicher, C. E., & Glaser, R. (1987). Marital quality, marital disruption and immune function. *Psychosomatic Medicine, 49,* 13–34. Hard data on the association between marital disruption and suppression of immune function.

Nuckels, K. B., Cassel, J., & Kaplan, B. H. (1972). Psychosocial assets, life crises and the prognosis of pregnancy. *American Journal of Epidemiology, 95,* 431–441. Women who experience high levels of life stress and have low social supports are much more likely to have complications during pregnancy.

Orth-Gomer, K., Rosengren, A., & Wilhelmsen, L. (1993). Lack of social support and incidence of coronary heart disease in middle-aged Swedish men. *Psychosomatic Medicine, 55,* 37–43. A major study documenting the association between social support and heart disease in males.

Pennebaker, J. W. (1989). Confession, inhibition and disease. In L. Berkowitz (Ed.), *Advances in experimental social psychology* (Vol. 22, pp. 211–244). Confession is not just good for the soul. It's also good for the body.

Reynolds, P., & Kaplan, G. A. (1990). Social connections and risk of cancer: Prospective evidence from the Alameda County Study. *Behavioral Medicine, 9,* 101–110. Lack of social connection increases cancer risk.

Stroebe, W., & Stroebe, M. S. (1987). *Bereavement and health: The psychological and physical consequences of partner loss.* New York: Cambridge University Press. A comprehensive review of the relationship between bereavement and health.

Stroebe, W., & Stroebe, M. S. (1992). Bereavement and health: Processes of adjusting to the loss of partner. In L. Montada, S. Filipp, & M. J. Lerner (Eds.), *Life crises and experiences of loss in adulthood.* Hillsdale, NJ: Erlbaum. Here Wolfgang and Margaret Stroebe update their 1987 position.

## CHAPTER 5

# Coping With Loneliness

*The dorm was nearly empty this particular night. It was the weekend, and I was on duty. About 11 o'clock, a piece of paper came sliding under my door. On it was a message in red felt pen. It read: "It's no use." I didn't think too much about it. Someone on the floor was always doing something crazy. The next night, about the same time, another sheet of paper came sliding under my door. Again there was a message in red felt pen: "I'm not kidding." I showed the paper to the dorm director, and almost immediately someone who overheard us talking mentioned that a student on his floor hadn't unpacked yet. (It was about a week or so after term break.) The two of us bounded up the stairs and knocked on his door. There was no answer. We let ourselves in. There he was stretched out on the bed, unconscious but still alive. A high school yearbook was open beside him, and a half-empty bottle of sleeping pills lay nearby. On his desk was a note, again in red felt pen. It read: "No one even knows I exist."*

Loneliness is the emotion we feel when our social network, our intimate relationships, or both are less satisfying than we would prefer (Jones, 1985). This way of characterizing loneliness addresses two of the major issues in the literature. People differ considerably in their appetites for socializing and intimacy, and perhaps as a consequence, there is little correspondence between absolute numbers in one's network of personal and social relationships and feelings of loneliness (Stokes, 1985). Loneliness seems to be very much an individual matter. We can be alone without feeling lonely. We can feel lonely in a crowd or when we are with someone we cannot "reach" (Bernikow, 1982). We may seek *solitude,* even prefer it, but we do not seek loneliness. Loneliness, by definition, is unpleasant (Perlman, 1988).

Most of us don't need to be convinced of this. We are quite aware that our happiness is intimately tied to our relationships with those who are close to us (Argyle, 1987). And yet loneliness is a matter of increasing concern in the United States as well as many other industrialized countries. It is at the root of many social and personal problems. It is one of the primary reasons why people turn to psychotherapy, and it is related in important ways to health problems as well (Jones, 1985).

## Descriptions of Loneliness

In describing the experience of loneliness, writers have used such terms as "anxiety" (Moustakas, 1961); "boredom" (Weiss, 1973); "interpersonal hostility" (Sermat, 1980); feeling "angry," "self-enclosed," "empty," and "awkward" (Russell et al., 1978).

Harry Sullivan (1953) saw the anguish associated with loneliness as a motivating force that served to compel the lonely to seek interactions with others, and Frieda Fromm-Reichman (1959) spoke of the "paralyzing hopelessness" associated with loneliness. Robert Weiss (1973) noted that for the lonely person, tasks tend to lose their meaning. Suzanne Gordon (1976) indicated that to be lonely simply means that one has failed. And when Carin Rubenstein and Philip Shaver (1980) asked lonely people to describe their feelings, such things as depression, sadness, boredom, self-pity, and longing for one special person were all mentioned.

What are we to make of such varied descriptions of loneliness? How can the same state be both boring and frightening? How can one be apathetic and hostile at the same time? Are there different kinds of loneliness? Some writers suggest that there are.

### Types of Loneliness

Different typologies have been suggested for distinguishing between various kinds of loneliness. One approach deals with the difference between loneliness as a *state* and loneliness as a *trait*. **State loneliness** is perhaps best characterized as the feeling an individual has when she or he is new to a community. An initial period of adjustment is common, but feelings of loneliness are typically viewed as due to circumstances and something that anyone would experience in a similar situation. We would expect this type of loneliness to pass as the person settles in socially, and the evidence suggests that it usually does (Cutrona, 1982; De Jong-Gierveld & Raadschelders, 1982; Hanley-Dunn et al., 1985; Rook, 1988; Shaver et al., 1985).

In contrast, **trait loneliness** seems to involve deficits in such social skills as taking the initiative, self-disclosure, assertiveness, and the ability to interpret nonverbal behavior (Gerson & Perlman, 1979; Rook, 1988). People who are trait lonely often anticipate failure going into social situations and show a preference for passive responses to feelings of loneliness, such as overeating, watching TV, or taking drugs.

Researchers are finding that there are different types of loneliness, and the various types can be distinguished.

A second typology, proposed by Robert Weiss (1973), distinguishes between *emotional* and *social* loneliness. **Emotional loneliness**, according to Weiss, is characterized by feelings of anxiety and isolation stemming from the lack of an intimate relationship. **Social loneliness**, on the other hand, is characterized by feelings of boredom and aimlessness and is associated with the absence of a network of others with whom one identifies and shares common interests and activities.

Weiss suggested that these two types of loneliness stem from quite different interpersonal needs—needs that are met by different kinds of relationships. For example, individuals experiencing the end of a serious romantic interest, separation, divorce, or the death of a spouse are likely to experience emotional loneliness and to seek an intimate relationship in response. Social loneliness, on the other hand, is more likely to be experienced by those who are housebound, those who are new arrivals to a community, or those who have gone away to college for the first time. According to Weiss, emotional loneliness is likely to be felt as more aversive.

One type of loneliness, however, does not fall into any of the above categories. Some individuals lack both intimacy and social connection yet seem resigned to their fate, making little or no effort to change things. Such individuals are *adapted* in the sense that they see their condition as inevitable and seem to accept it with a sense of fatalism (De Jong-Gierveld & Raadschelders, 1982). This is the type of loneliness we see in the case of Rosa.

Rosa is a middle-aged woman. She works as a domestic. She lives alone and has been single all her life. Her only relatives, a brother and his family, visit from time to time. She used to attend church regularly, but she has now stopped. She makes little effort to take in social functions. The last time she dressed up was about 6 months ago, when her brother asked her to join him and his family for a family photograph. But after waiting at the studio for almost an hour, she left, indicating that she didn't like having her picture taken. Her days are taken up with work. In the evenings, she watches soap operas that she has taped during the day.

### Measuring Loneliness

A number of scales have been developed to measure loneliness. The UCLA Loneliness Scale (Russell, 1996; Russell et al., 1980), now in its third revision, has become a standard in the area. It focuses primarily on measuring loneliness as a state—that is, a temporary condition due to circumstances rather than an enduring personality trait. An early version of the scale appears in Table 5-1.

A considerable amount of research has been done using the UCLA scale. Its validity has been demonstrated on a number of at-risk groups. The recently divorced, prison inmates, and individuals seeking help in social skills classes all tend to show relatively high scores on the UCLA scale (Russell et al., 1980).

Other scales include the New York University Loneliness Scale (Rubenstein & Shaver, 1982), which was developed to measure loneliness as a (relatively stable) personality trait. The Differential Loneliness Scale (DLS) (Schmidt & Sermat, 1983) is aimed at differentiating between various subtypes of loneliness—a "general family" component, romantic/sexual loneliness, loneliness due to the state of one's friendships, and loneliness due to the lack of relationships with the larger community. For example, a group of recent immigrants may be satisfied with their family, friendships, and romantic relationships and still feel a lack of belonging to the larger community. Finally, the Social and Emotional Loneliness Scale for Adults (SELSA) (DiTommaso & Spinner, 1993) was developed to confirm and expand upon Weiss's distinction between social and emotional loneliness. Using the SELSA, Enrico DiTommaso and Barry Spinner (1997) have shown that emotional loneliness can be further broken down into romantic emotional loneliness and family emotional loneliness components.

We should keep in mind that all of these scales are "self-report," and this raises an important issue. Some types of loneliness may be beyond the usual psychometric measures. The neo-Freudian tradition, for example, suggests that it's possible for someone to experience loneliness and not be aware of it. This type of loneliness is not likely to be picked up on standard loneliness scales (Marangoni & Ickes, 1989).

### The Statistical Picture

Several studies have tried to estimate how common loneliness is in the general population. Robert Weiss (1973) reported that approximately 25% of those

**Table 5-1   UCLA Loneliness Scale**

Indicate how often each of the statements below is descriptive of you. Circle one letter for each statement:

O indicates "I often feel this way"

S indicates "I sometimes feel this way"

R indicates "I rarely feel this way"

N indicates "I never feel this way"

| | |
|---|---|
| 1. How often do you feel unhappy doing so many things alone | O  S  R  N |
| 2. How often do you feel you have nobody to talk to | O  S  R  N |
| 3. How often do you feel you cannot tolerate being so alone | O  S  R  N |
| 4. How often do you feel as if nobody really understands you | O  S  R  N |
| 5. How often do you find yourself waiting for people to call or write | O  S  R  N |
| 6. How often do you feel completely alone | O  S  R  N |
| 7. How often do you feel you are unable to reach out and communicate with those around you | O  S  R  N |
| 8. How often do you feel starved for company | O  S  R  N |
| 9. How often do you feel it is difficult for you to make friends | O  S  R  N |
| 10. How often do you feel shut out and excluded by others | O  S  R  N |

Scoring: For each question, give yourself 1 point if you responded "never" (N), 2 points if you responded "rarely" (R), 3 points if you responded "sometimes" (S), and 4 points if you responded "often" (O). Your total loneliness score is computed by adding your score on each of the ten questions together.

**Normative Data for the UCLA Loneliness Scale**

| (Ten Item Version) | |
|---|---|
| Group | Average Score |
| College Students | 20 |
| Nurses | 20 |
| Public School Teachers | 19 |
| Elderly | 16 |

Based on these normative data, a score above 30 on this version of the scale would indicate that the person is experiencing severe levels of loneliness.

Courtesy of Daniel W. Russell. Used by permission.

in his study indicated they had recently felt lonely or "remote" from others. Carin Rubenstein and Philip Shaver (1980) circulated a questionnaire on loneliness in the Sunday supplements of the New York *Daily News* and the Worcester (Massachusetts) *Telegram*. About 15% of their respondents reported being lonely most of the time, and only 6% said they were never lonely.

In a study conducted in Sweden, Lars Tornstam (1992) found that 40% of marrieds reported being lonely "often" or "sometimes." Sixteen percent indicated feeling lonely even when they were with others. And 7% said they were lonely at the time. In the same study, however, very few people reported having no friends at all.

So, depending on the population sampled and the method used, statistics on loneliness vary widely. Still, there are some general patterns, and we see these most clearly when we look at loneliness over the life span.

## Loneliness Over the Life Span

Loneliness seems to take on a different cast from age group to age group. As children grow older, loneliness tends to be of increasing concern, typically reaching a peak during adolescence and then declining somewhat after that.

### Loneliness in Children

It is hard to say when children first experience loneliness. Zick Rubin (1982) suggested that children could experience loneliness by the age of 3, but this is somewhat speculative. Differentiating between loneliness and separation anxiety in young children is problematic. On the other hand, children can take

Young schoolchildren who are rejected or isolated are likely to indicate that they are lonely. Vulnerability to feelings of loneliness may persist into adulthood.

scales assessing loneliness by the age of 7 or 8 (Asher et al., 1984), and when they do, their scores correspond closely to other types of measures. Children who are rejected or isolated based on peer ratings, for example, are also likely to indicate that they are lonely (Perlman, 1988).

***The Role of Early Experience***    Does loneliness have its origins in childhood? There is some evidence that it does or at least that it can. Carin Rubenstein and Philip Shaver (1980) suggested that insecure attachment during childhood is reflected in vulnerability to feelings of loneliness. Specifically, they found that children who experience the separation, divorce, or threat of divorce of their parents tend to show increased loneliness later in life. Further, the younger the children were at the time of separation or divorce, the more severely affected they tend to be. Those who were under 6 years of age at the time tend to be the loneliest as adults (Rubenstein et al., 1979).

Other researchers have taken a broader view of the parent-child relationship and its effect on loneliness. For example, in a study of university women, Judith Lobdell and Daniel Perlman (1986) found that lack of parental involvement early in life was associated with increased loneliness. Still others have noted that the lonely tend to remember having less nurturant parents who were remote, less trustworthy, and less agreeable (Franzoi & Davis, 1985). Those who remember their parents as being helpful report less loneliness than those who remember their parents as unhelpful. When relationships with parents were conflicted and unpredictable, moderate levels of loneliness are reported; the highest degree of loneliness is reported when one parent has been absent (Rubenstein & Shaver, 1980).

These are disturbing findings in view of the projections for future generations of children. It is estimated that about half of the children growing up today will live with both of their biological parents through both childhood and adolescence (Jacobson, 1987). It's important to note, however, that the death of a parent, whether occurring during childhood, adolescence, or adulthood, does not seem to have the same effect as separation or divorce on feelings of loneliness later in life. Apparently, it is not the absence of a parent per se but the perception that such a separation was a matter of choice (which is interpreted as rejection) that is important.

## Loneliness During Adolescence

As suggested in this chapter's opening paragraph, loneliness in our society tends to be greater among adolescents than any other age group (Parlee, 1979; Rubenstein et al., 1979; Rubenstein & Shaver, 1982). Several factors come together to make this so. Adolescent culture focuses on popularity and other indications of social success. At the same time, adolescents' social skills tend to be limited. Their role in our society is somewhat ambiguous, and the sense of marginality that this can generate no doubt contributes to the feeling of not fitting in. Meanwhile, ties to parents are being severed, which takes some getting used to, and romantic relationships are looming on the horizon. All of these factors set the stage for increased feelings of loneliness (Brennon, 1982).

The way this combination of pressures on adolescents plays out was illustrated in a study using paging devices to monitor the activities and feelings of high school students over time. When the records were analyzed, they showed that students tended to feel the most lonely on Friday and Saturday nights. If they were alone during the day, it didn't seem to bother them so much, but Friday and Saturday nights were times when they felt they were *not supposed to be alone* (Larson et al., 1982).

Philip Shaver and colleagues (1985) gathered information on students during the summer before they went away to college and then again in the fall, winter, and spring of their first year. The researchers found that loneliness was greatest during the fall, and by spring most of the students had recovered from loneliness. They also noted that loneliness was greater among males than among females, but individuals differed widely. Those whose social skills were good, especially in terms of relationship initiation, were likely to avoid many of the pangs of loneliness associated with going away to college for the first time.

The changing nature of loneliness between adolescence and young adulthood was further demonstrated in a study by Daniel Russell and colleagues (1981), who compared loneliness among 18- and 19-year-olds and among those 24 and older. For the younger group, loneliness was associated with satisfaction (or lack of satisfaction) with their friendships, whereas for the older group, loneliness was associated with satisfaction (or lack of satisfaction) with their romantic relationships.

## Loneliness in Adulthood

Intuitively, we would expect to find a relationship between marriage and loneliness among adults, and for the most part, this is the case. Married adults report being less lonely than the divorced and the widowed (Weiss, 1973). But when those who are not married are further divided into various subgroups, there are significant differences among them. Single parents seem to be especially vulnerable to feelings of loneliness. For example, Jenny De Jong-Gierveld (1986a) noted that 50% of adults living alone and 60% of parents without partners mentioned feelings of loneliness, but only 13% of those who were living with a partner did so. Consider the case of Kim.

For most of her life, Kim never gave much thought to loneliness. She had always had lots of friends. Just after the birth of their second child, however, her husband became involved with another woman, and Kim soon found herself divorced, working full time, and raising two small children on her own. Money was a problem. Finding baby-sitters was a problem, but the thing that she was totally unprepared for was being deserted by her friends. The small town in which she lived was almost completely family oriented. There was no "swinging singles" scene. Every other weekend, when the children were with their father, Kim visited her mother in a nearby town. A divorced friend of her ex-husband asked her out once. That was the only "date" she had since her divorce. She wanted to go to more social events with friends, but that meant finding someone to go with. She felt awkward going out alone, so she spent most of her free time reading and watching TV. Sometimes she ached just to have someone to share things with.

Somewhat surprisingly, adults who never marry tend to be less lonely than either the divorced or widowed. Indeed, there is some indication that loneliness is not significantly greater among adults who have never married than it is among marrieds (Gubrium, 1974).

Loneliness can occur within marriage as well, and again there is a pattern (Rubenstein & Shaver, 1982; Tornstam, 1992; Weiss, 1973). Husbands of lonely wives tend to be less self-disclosing. Wives of lonely husbands tend to feel less liking for, and less intimacy with, their husbands (Sadava & Matejcic, 1987). Circumstances surrounding the marriage also play a part. For example, women who are homemakers are twice as likely to indicate feeling lonely as are those employed outside the home (Grove & Geerken, 1977). And, not surprisingly, the level of marital satisfaction for marrieds who feel lonely tends to be low (Perlman et al., 1978).

Age also seems to be a factor in feelings of loneliness during adulthood. On the whole, older adults seem to be *less* lonely than younger adults. Even though the number of social contacts tends to decline with age (Larson et al., 1985), older adults do not necessarily feel more lonely (Lowenthal et al., 1975; Rosow, 1967; but see Barretta et al., 1995, for contradictory findings). Older adults also tend to be more satisfied with their friendships and consider their friends to be closer (Rubenstein et al., 1979; Schultz & Moore, 1988). The relationship between age and loneliness in one study is shown in Figure 5-1.

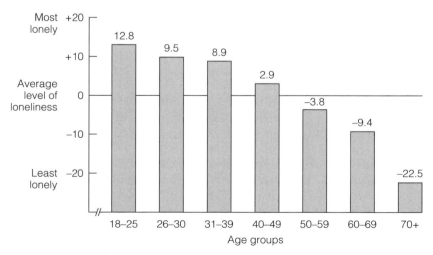

**Figure 5-1**  Loneliness scores by age groups. From Rubinstein, C., Shaver, P., & Peplau, L. A. (1979). Loneliness. *Human Nature* (February), 58–65. Used by permission of authors.

## Gender Differences in Loneliness

When people are asked about loneliness directly, women are more likely to indicate feeling lonely than are men (Borys & Perlman, 1985; Tornstam, 1992). But in their review, Shelley Borys and Daniel Perlman (1985) found that 24 of the 28 studies in which the UCLA Loneliness Scale was used reported no gender differences. And in a large-scale study in Sweden, Lars Tornstam (1992) found that, as a group, unmarrieds reported more loneliness than marrieds, but there were no differences between males and females in this respect. On the other hand, there were gender differences in loneliness among marrieds. As we see in Figure 5-2, married women between the ages of 20 and 49 indicated being more lonely than men.

One way of accounting for gender differences has been to suggest that women may simply be more willing to admit to feelings of loneliness. If this were the case, however, we would expect to find gender differences across the entire age range. But this is not what Tornstam found. Even after controlling for the fact that some of the women remained at home with small children, the sex differences remained (Tornstam, 1992).

Other findings suggest that the picture on gender differences in loneliness is more complex. For males, the issue of loneliness tends to revolve around one intimate relationship, but for females, loneliness seems to depend much more on the state of their social networks (De Jong-Gierveld, 1986b).

Other researchers have found that loneliness among females is correlated

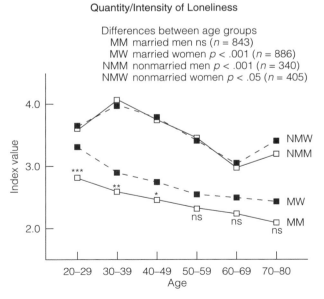

Figure 5-2   From Tornstam, L. (1992). Loneliness in marriage. *Journal of Social and Personal Relationships, 9,* 197–217. Copyright © 1992 Sage Publications Ltd. Reprinted by permission of Sage Publications, Ltd.

Differences between married men and women within age groups:
***$p < .001$; **$p < .01$; *$p < .05$; ns not significant

with a lack of self-disclosure to peers (Berg & Peplau, 1982; Davis & Franzoi, 1986; Solano et al., 1982), and loneliness in males is related to the density of the social network (the number of relationships between network members and the extent of closeness/confiding among them) and participation in organized groups—a finding somewhat at odds with De Jong-Gierveld's, noted above (see also Wheeler et al., 1983).

To complicate the picture still further, one of the most interesting findings in the literature is the *negative* relationship between loneliness and androgyny (Berg & Peplau, 1982; Wittenberg & Reis, 1986). Those who show *both* masculine and feminine traits tend to be less at risk for loneliness. Such findings suggest that a combination of both masculine and feminine traits is advantageous in personal and social relationships. Masculinity is associated with relationship initiation and skills in dating, and femininity is associated with the development of intimate behaviors, such as self-disclosure (Shaver & Buhrmester, 1983).

## Social Interactions and Loneliness

There is some indication that the lonely have less in the way of social interactions than those who are not lonely. For example, loneliness among adolescents is associated with participating less in intramural sports and other social activities at school, spending less time with peers or parents, and dating less (Brennan & Auslander, 1979). Lonely adolescents do not appear to be "joiners." The case of Jerry illustrates this point.

Jerry's parents divorced when he was in middle school. He lived with his father at first, but then his father changed jobs and had to travel a great deal, so Jerry went to live with his mother. From then on nothing seems to have gone right. He is in a new high school in a strange town. His mother works evenings in a restaurant, and they see little of each other. His face has started breaking out, and he has gained weight. He hates gym because he is embarrassed to shower. His peers call him "two ton." When he signed up to work on the yearbook after school, the rest of the staff ignored him. He has started skipping school, and his grades are slipping. He talks to people, but he feels he has no real friends. He's never had a real date. He'd like to go to the teen dances on the weekends, but he's shy about asking anybody out because he's afraid of being turned down. He has never been on a team or in a club at school. He studies by himself. He spends most of his evenings in front of the television.

When we turn to the college population, the picture is much the same as for adolescents (Russell et al., 1980). For example, when Warren Jones (1981) had college students record their interactions over a two-day period, he found no evidence that loneliness is associated with either length or frequency of interactions, relative number of interactions with the opposite sex, or even the perceived intimacy of those interactions. However, he did find that loneliness is associated with the *diversity* of interactions. Lonely college students have about the same number of interactions as nonlonely ones, but they have them with fewer people. More of their interactions are with strangers and casual acquaintances, and fewer are with friends and family.

In the case of adults, lonely widows and the divorced or separated also report being less involved in social activities (Jones et al., 1980). And the same finding has been reported for the elderly (Perlman et al., 1978). So when we look at the number and type of social contacts, we find that the lonely seem to differ from the nonlonely.

Consistent with this, Joseph Stokes (1985) found no relationship between network size and loneliness but did find a relationship between loneliness and network *density* (that is, how many of one's friends were friends with each other). Those with higher network density tended to be less lonely.

This suggests a hypothesis. Kin networks tend to be dense by definition. Relatives tend to know each other. Accordingly, we would predict that those who are more family oriented in their social networks would be less lonely. And, indeed, evidence suggests that this is the case. People who interact more with family members tend to be less lonely (Jones, 1981).

### What Do Lonely People Do?

What do people do when they are feeling lonely? Carin Rubenstein and Philip Shaver (1980) found that watching TV was the most common response to loneliness. Listening to music came next, followed by calling a friend. When the results of their study were analyzed further, four kinds of responses were evident. The first they referred to as "sad passivity." This type of response was most characteristic of the chronic, long-term lonely. The other three types of responses were more characteristic of those whose loneliness was intermittent. Rubenstein and Shaver called these responses "active solitude," in which individuals were involved in an interesting activity or hobby that they could pursue alone, "spending money," and "social contact."

### Quality Versus Quantity of Relationships

Many studies have examined the relationship between loneliness and various kinds of personal/social relationships (e.g., Cutrona, 1982; Rook, 1987; Russell et al., 1984; Shaver & Buhrmester, 1983; Weiss, 1973; Wheeler et al., 1983). A consistent finding has been that for adults, the absence of a mate or prospective mate is associated with loneliness (Tornstam, 1992). Jenny De Jong-Gierveld (1986a) focused specifically on the role that confidants play in determining loneliness. She noted that 89% of those with a partner mentioned their partner as a confidant. Relatives were mentioned 59% of the time, while friends or neighbors were mentioned only 6% of the time. For those who were living alone, the picture was quite different. Only 3% of these mentioned a partner as a confidant, 54% mentioned a close relative, 25% a friend, and 18% mentioned neighbors and colleagues.

## Box 5-1 In a Different Key
### Shunning Among the Amish

Loneliness can result from sanctions imposed upon someone by the wider society. Those who are in prison have the company of other prisoners, and yet they still experience loneliness and isolation because they are separated from loved ones. Soldiers stationed in a foreign country may be surrounded by people and still feel lonely because they are away from home. Loneliness under such circumstances is "situational" in the sense that when one's circumstances change, the feelings of loneliness are likely to be lifted. Some cases of situational loneliness are quite different, however. One of these is the traditional practice of shunning among the Amish.

The Amish of Pennsylvania and Ohio make their living by farming. They are known primarily for their rejection of modern ways. They dress in plain clothing. They get about by horse and buggy, farm with plow horses, and interact with outsiders as little as possible. Amish children typically go to school only through the eighth grade.

In traditional Amish societies, members of the community who depart from acceptable ways are formally declared "out of fellowship" and "shunned."

Shunning is a serious matter for the Amish. For those raised in the Amish tradition, separation from the community is a wrenching experience. Those who are shunned become nonpersons in the eyes of the community. Families are split. Wives are not permitted to talk to their own husbands. Sons no longer speak to their own fathers. Longtime friends are totally alienated from one another. Livelihoods are taken away, as the community refuses to patronize certain businesses. Oftentimes those who are shunned have nowhere to turn. Their background has prepared them for the Amish way of life, and there is little they can do in the outside world. And so they remain in their community surrounded by former friends and loved ones, yet completely alone psychologically.

Shunning is less common today than it has been historically. One of the reasons for the decline of shunning, ironically, is its success. Over time, those who were declared out of fellowship banded together and formed their own community. Today in central Pennsylvania, there are several different Amish-Mennonite communities in the same region (Hostetler, 1993).

For college students, dates, steady boy/girlfriends, and friends seem to play the role that mates do for adults. For example, students who have never had a steady boyfriend or girlfriend report being more lonely than those who have (Jones et al., 1980).

Still, loneliness does not seem to be just a matter of having (or not having) one particular kind of relationship. This was shown in a study by Carolyn Cutrona (1982), which focused on relationship satisfaction among college freshmen in three general areas (friendships, dating relationships, and family relationships). Her findings indicated that all three types of relationships were important in determining loneliness. Lack of satisfaction with friendships, dating partners, and family relationships was a better predictor of loneliness than were measures of the frequency of interaction alone. But in this study, the most important factor seemed to be satisfaction with friendships. At this point in their lives, at least, romantic relationships did not seem to play a particularly crucial role in determining loneliness. (Keep in mind these were freshmen.)

It seems, then, that both quantity and quality of personal relationships play a role in loneliness, but absolute numbers appear to be less important than how closely relationships have achieved some desired level. For adults, having an intimate relationship with someone they can confide in seems especially important, but friends and family and the way they interact with one another also seem to play a role.

### Changes in Status of Relationships

From what has been said so far, we would predict that the end of a close personal relationship should be a time when people are likely to feel lonely, and generally this is what we find. Weiss (1973) spoke of relationship loss as being felt most acutely. Charles Hill and colleagues (1976) found that "breaking up" among dating couples was associated with feelings of loneliness and depression. And Helena Lopata (1969) noted that 40% of the urban widows in her study considered loneliness to be a major problem, while 22% mentioned loneliness along with something else.

Approximately 60% of divorced men consider loneliness a major problem (Bloom et al., 1979). Women seem to be particularly affected when they feel stigmatized, when they have financial problems, or when they want to participate in some activity and feel they aren't able to (Woodward et al., 1980). And, as we see in Box 5-1, loneliness has sometimes been imposed by the larger society.

## Personality Factors and Loneliness

Personal limitations, real or imagined, which make establishing and maintaining relationships difficult, increase one's chances of being lonely. Shyness, self-consciousness, depression, a negative self-concept, inhibited sociability, and lack of assertiveness have all been found to be associated with loneliness (Anderson et al., 1983; Horowitz & French, 1979; Jones et al., 1981; Rubenstein & Shaver, 1980; Russell et al., 1978, 1980; Schmidt & Sermat, 1983; Stokes, 1985). But are these causes or consequences of loneliness?

It's difficult, given the present state of our knowledge, to disentangle the factors that lead to loneliness from those that happen to be correlated with loneliness, and strategies that people use in coping with loneliness. For example, people who have a history of social rejection, who see themselves as responsible for this rejection, and who feel there is little or nothing they can do to change things may simply maintain a low social profile in order to avoid further rejection and humiliation (Mehrabian & Ksionzky, 1974). This low social involvement can lead to a self-fulfilling prophecy. Such people are not likely to take the social risks necessary to generate additional friendships even when they would like to have more friends (Duck, 1991).

Lonely people tend to see themselves as being poor at communication (Solano & Koester, 1989), and they see others as lacking in communication skills as well (Spitzberg & Canary, 1985). And when we look closely at the interactions of the lonely, we find that they tend to express a disproportionate amount of negativism and cynicism in their conversations, and they are also likely to react quite strongly to criticism (Check et al., 1985). It's easy to see how such characteristics might scare others away.

### Shyness

Not surprisingly, shyness is associated with loneliness (Zimbardo, 1977). Those who are shy are less likely to take the initiative in encouraging social interactions (Pilkonis, 1977; Pilkonis & Zimbardo, 1979). Lonely college students, for example, tend to be introverted and lacking in assertiveness (Cutrona, 1982). Those who report being lonely score lower on measures of social risk taking (Sermat, 1980) and often describe themselves as shy and self-conscious (Cheek & Busch, 1981; Jones, 1985; Jones et al., 1981; Solano et al., 1982). This is true of the young and old alike (Perlman et al., 1978).

### Self-Esteem

Low self-esteem also seems to go hand in hand with loneliness (Cutrona, 1982). Not only does the feedback that we get from others affect our self-esteem, but our self-esteem affects the way we interpret feedback. This was vividly demonstrated by Wolfgang Stroebe (1977). In this study, confederates (people who were part of the experiment) gave either complimentary or critical feedback to individuals who were either high or low in self-esteem. The task of the participants was to indicate whether they thought the comments were the confederate's true opinion or the result of instructions from the experimenter. The results were clear and dramatic. Those who were high in self-esteem generally viewed the complimentary remarks as "true opinions" and the critical remarks as due to instructions from the experimenter. Those who were low in self-esteem showed exactly the opposite pattern. For them, criticisms were judged to be "true opinions," and compliments were seen as due to the experimenter's instruction.

One of the roles that friends play, both directly and indirectly, is to help maintain our self-esteem. This takes place in many different ways, but the very fact that others choose or do not choose to spend time with us sends a message that they value (or do not value) our company. Personal relationships provide us with feedback for our feelings, opinions, and beliefs (Swann et al., 1994). Isolation tends to deprive us of this "private culture," and as a consequence, the lonely are left "at sea," unanchored in the social scheme of things and without opportunities for comparing their reactions, beliefs, and values with others.

What we see, then, is a picture in which the very feelings of low self-esteem that lead to loneliness in the first place can also be a consequence of loneliness. This may be why loneliness is such a persistent problem for some. Once set in motion, the behaviors associated with loneliness seem to generate a chain of events that leads to still further isolation (Marangoni & Ickes, 1989).

Consistent with this, we find that adolescents who are lonely also tend to be depressed, and this in turn is associated with the ability of the family to cope with the everyday stresses of life, and the level of communication between the mother and adolescent (Brage et al., 1993).

## Social Skills

Studies show that the lonely have deficits in social skills (Vitkus & Horowitz, 1987), are seen by others as having such deficits (Spitzberg & Canary, 1985), and are aware of this themselves (Horowitz et al., 1982; Wheeler et al., 1983; Wittenberg & Reis, 1986). In addition, a significant anxiety component seems to be associated with their assessment (Solano & Koester, 1989).

These deficits apparently create a self-perpetuating cycle in which avoidance of anxiety-provoking situations (social interactions in this case) becomes reinforcing for the lonely. This, in turn, tends to limit their experience in the

Everyone feels dejected or lonely at times, but pervasive feelings of depression and loneliness may signal deeper emotional problems and the need to seek professional help.

kinds of situations that might help them to sharpen their social skills and alleviate loneliness.

Support for this hypothesis has come in a number of studies. For example, Reed Larson and his associates (1982) used a time-sampling technique to determine how individuals felt when they were alone and when they were with others. The researchers found that the lonely reported feeling more positive when they were by themselves and the most uncomfortable when they were with others. Along these same lines, college students who have a more positive view of their social skills are likely to engage in social activities when they feel lonely, and those who have a less positive view of their social skills tend to engage in diversionary activities, such as reading, busywork, drinking, and taking drugs (Paloutzian & Ellison, 1979).

Lonely students indicate having problems introducing themselves, participating in small talk, enjoying themselves in informal settings, initiating social activities, and being friendly (Horowitz et al., 1982). Their attempts to influence others tend to be coercive, which is sometimes effective in the short run but typically proves counterproductive in the long run (Gerson, 1978). Philip Shaver and his colleagues (1985) have referred to such problems as a deficiency in relationship initiation skills.

Relationship initiation is not the entire picture, however. Mitchell Wittenberg and Harry Reis (1986) studied loneliness in relation to such factors as self-disclosure, dating skills, giving advice and guidance, assertiveness, and conflict resolution. Their findings suggested that in addition to skills in initiating relationships, *relationship-deepening* skills were also important in predicting loneliness. Once relationships are initiated, we must have something to offer by way of maintaining and nurturing them.

Indeed, when we look at specific social behaviors, we find that the lonely show consistent deficiencies in the kinds of social skills that serve to maintain and nourish personal and social relationships (Jones et al., 1981; Russell et al., 1980; Solano et al., 1982; Williams & Solano, 1983). For example, in a study of conversations among college students, Warren Jones and his associates (1982) noted that lonely students tend to focus the conversation on themselves, inquire less about those they are talking to, and change the topic of conversation more frequently then do their nonlonely peers.

Possibly as a consequence of being more self-focused, the lonely are less attentive to the feelings and concerns of others, because, interestingly enough, after interactions are over, they tend to have lower recall of the others' communications than do the nonlonely (Bell, 1985).

### How Others Perceive the Lonely

There is some indication that people view the lonely less positively than the nonlonely, but findings have been somewhat mixed. For example, Cecilia Solano and her colleagues (1982) found that lonely individuals, when compared with the nonlonely, show significantly different patterns of self-disclosure, and such differences tend to be noticed by others. Studies show that both their best friends (Williams & Solano, 1983) and strangers (Bell, 1985) perceived lonely individuals as being less attentive and less interested in developing relationships further.

On the other hand, when friends and strangers view the same behavior, they give different evaluations of those who are shy or socially withdrawn. Strangers tend to interpret the behavior as hostile, while friends do not (Burgoon & Koper, 1984). Consistent with this, Cecilia Solano and Phillip Batten (1979) found initially that lonely individuals were rated as more difficult to get to know, but when the same ratings were repeated at the end of the semester, there were no longer any differences between the ratings for the lonely and the nonlonely students.

Similarly, Steve Duck and his colleagues (1994) reported that when others evaluated lonely individuals, they noted an occasional negative characteristic but otherwise viewed them much the same as they viewed anyone else. Meanwhile, the lonely themselves did not necessarily rate their conversations negatively, even though they tended to evaluate their relationships with others more negatively overall.

So, although the lonely seem to expect rejection from others, the evidence that others evaluate the lonely any differently than they do the nonlonely has been weak and inconsistent. It may be that it simply takes time to get to know some people.

## Intervention

The language of relating has many different accents and many degrees of fluency, and like other things in life, some people are better at these than others. For some, initiating and maintaining relationships seems to come quite naturally. For others, relationships require a good deal of effort. But the evidence is that the elements of relating can be worked at, polished, and refined like any other complex skill (Baxter & Dindia, 1990; W. H. Jones et al., 1982, 1984). It's easy, for example, to be unaware of one's own role in perpetuating or overcoming loneliness (Rubenstein et al., 1979).

In a study of the relationship between social skills and loneliness, Warren Jones and his colleagues (1982) assigned lonely males to one of three conditions: treatment, assessment only, and no-contact control. Those in the treatment condition were given training designed to focus their attention on the other person's feelings, beliefs, and behavior. Not only did such training yield significant changes in the patterns of interactions with others, but it also led to a reduction in loneliness on self-report measures. Most people, however, are not used to thinking in such terms, and as a consequence, we sometimes find surprising resistance to intervention programs.

Changing one's standards—that is, reducing the threshold of acceptability of others—is another approach to intervention that has been suggested. For example, in her study of lonely college students, Carolyn Cutrona (1982) found that overcoming loneliness had little to do with the strategies used. No single technique seemed to work best. What distinguished those who overcame their loneliness from those who did not was whether (or not) they increased their number of friends. Those who did were less lonely. Those who didn't remained lonely.

## Conclusion

We see from our brief review that loneliness is not a unitary phenomenon. It means different things to different people. To one person, loneliness refers to a state of longing for one special person; to someone else, it means being bored; to a third, it means feeling alienated and not belonging anywhere.

Estimates of loneliness in the United States vary widely, but some patterns are clear. Isolation from their peers is correlated with loneliness among schoolchildren. Adolescence seems to be a time when loneliness is especially a problem for some. And in adulthood the separated and the divorced (especially single parents) report being lonely more often than do those who are "partnered." Interestingly enough, older adults report feeling less lonely than other adults even in the face of reduced opportunities for socialization.

Research findings on the relationship between gender and loneliness have been somewhat mixed. When asked directly, however, women are more likely to report being lonely than are men. For men, loneliness tends to be associated with the absence of an intimate relationship. For women, it is more likely to be associated with the lack of a supportive social network.

As a group, the lonely tend to be less involved in social activities than are the nonlonely. However, overall, the quality of relationships seems to be more important than the quantity in determining loneliness. And, finally, certain personality characteristics such as shyness, low self-esteem, and lack of social skills are associated with loneliness.

There is not likely to be a single remedy for loneliness that works for everyone. Encouraging results have been reported for intervention programs focusing on social skills training, but the best match between various types of loneliness and various types of intervention has yet to be determined. And those aspects of loneliness that reflect deeper and more pervasive ills of society rather than personal inadequacies will take more than individual efforts if we are to address them successfully (Rubenstein & Shaver, 1980).

## Suggestions for Further Reading

De Jong-Gierveld, J. (1986). Loneliness and the degree of intimacy in personal relationships. In R. Gilmour & S. W. Duck (Eds.), *The emerging field of personal relationships* (pp. 241–249). Hillsdale, NJ: Erlbaum. An overview of the loneliness literature by one of the leading authorities in the area.

DiTommaso, E., & Spinner, B. (1997). Social and emotional loneliness: A re-examination of Weiss's typology of loneliness. *Personality and Individual Differences, 22,* 417–427. A recent test and expansion of Weiss's distinction between social and emotional loneliness.

Duck, S. W., Pond, K., & Leatham, G. (1994). Loneliness and the evaluation of relational events. *Journal of Social and Personal Relationships, 11,* 253–276. A study noting the way lonely individuals see their relationships.

Jones, W. H. (1985). The psychology of loneliness: Some personality issues in the study of social support. In I. G. Sarason & B. R. Sarason (Eds.), *Social support: Theory, research and application* (pp. 225–241). The Hague: Martinus Nijhoff. One of the leading researchers in the area focuses on personality correlates of loneliness.

Marangoni, C., & Ickes, W. (1989). Loneliness: A theoretical review with implications for measurement. *Journal of Social and Personal Relationships, 6,* 93–128. In this article the authors ask whether some people may be lonely and not realize it.

Peplau, L. A., & Perlman, D. (Eds.). (1982). *Loneliness: A sourcebook of theory, research and therapy.* New York: Wiley. Despite its age, this volume is a gold mine of information in the area of loneliness.

Rook, K. S. (1988). Toward a more differentiated view of loneliness. In S. W. Duck (Ed.), *Handbook of personal relationships.* New York: Wiley. An overview of loneliness considered from several perspectives.

Rubenstein, C., & Shaver, P. (1974). *In search of intimacy.* New York: Delacorte Press. A popularly written account of the authors' study of loneliness and peoples' search for intimacy in two eastern cities.

Tornstam, L. (1992). Loneliness in marriage. *Journal of Social and Personal Relationships, 9,* 197–217. Report of a major study in Sweden focusing on loneliness in marriage.

Weiss, R. S. (1973). *Loneliness: The experience of emotional and social isolation.* Cambridge, MA: MIT Press. In this book the author presents his classic distinction between emotional and social loneliness.

CHAPTER 6

# Children's Friendships

*If you will look very closely at one of your children when he finally finds a chum . . . you will discover something very different in the relationship— namely, that your child begins to develop a new sensitivity to what matters to another person. And this is not in the sense of "what should I do to get what I want," but instead "what should I do to contribute to the happiness or to support the prestige and feeling of worth-whileness of my chum" . . . This change represents the beginning of something very like full-blown psychiatrically defined love.[1]*

Researchers have focused on several different areas in their studies of children's friendships. Among these have been the changing nature of children's concept of friendship as they get older; the role of reciprocity in children's friendships; similarity; gender differences; friendship and race; stability in children's friendships; the significance of peer acceptance, rejection and neglect; and intervention in cases where children have problems making or keeping friends. In this chapter we will sample something from each of these areas. We begin with the child's concept of friendship.

## The Child's Concept of Friendship

The ways that children describe their friends and the expectations they have of them undergo systematic change with age. Preschoolers, for example, are rather limited in their concept of friendship. When preschoolers refer to

---

1. From *The Interpersonal Theory of Psychiatry* by Harry Stack Sullivan. Copyright © 1953 by the William Alanson White Psychiatric Foundation. Reprinted by permission of W. W. Norton & Company, Inc.

friends, they are really talking about playmates. For example, when interviewers asked a 4-year-old if making friends was hard or easy, the child replied that it was hard, because sometimes when he waved, the other child might not see him. When the interviewer asked what would happen if the other child saw him, the child responded that then it was easy (Selman & Jaquette, 1977b).

As children get older, their concept of friendship becomes progressively richer, more sophisticated, and more subtle. For example, when Brian Bigelow and John La Gaipa (1975) analyzed essays on friendship by children in grades one through eight, they noted the emergence of certain themes:

- References to friends as helpers in time of need and to common activities tend to appear by the second grade.

- References to propinquity (or proximity) and evaluation (the good and the bad) appear about the third grade.

- The themes of acceptance, admiration, and increasing interaction appear about the fourth grade.

- Concepts such as loyalty and commitment appear about the fifth grade.

- Genuineness and authenticity are mentioned by about the sixth grade.

- Intimacy and common interests are not typically mentioned until about the seventh grade.

Other researchers have found that references to intimacy in friendships increased significantly from childhood to adolescence (Berndt & Perry, 1986). This trend is shown graphically in Figure 6-1.

### Stage Theories

Changes in the concept and expectations of friendship among children have led some researchers to posit stages of development in the case of friendship

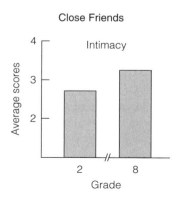

**Figure 6-1**  Reported intimacy among close friends increases from second to eighth grade. Berndt, T. J., & Perry, T. B. (1986). Children's perceptions of friendships as supportive relationships. *Developmental Psychology, 22,* 640–648.

Within the family, infants experience the intimacy and loyalty necessary for forming friendships.

along much the same lines as we see in Jean Piaget's stages of cognitive development and Lawrence Kohlberg's (1969) stages of moral development (Selman, 1980; Selman & Jaquette, 1977a; Selman & Schultz, 1990).

However, when attempts have been made to demonstrate the existence of stages or to show a relationship between the level of cognitive development and the behavior of friends, success has been limited (Berndt, 1979). For example, in Thomas Berndt's (1981) study of children in kindergarten, grade 3, and grade 6, all of the children considered sharing and helping as more characteristic of friends than acquaintances. The most significant change that Berndt found with age came in an increased emphasis on intimacy and loyalty, particularly among girls. But, although the children could verbalize such notions as sharing and helping, they often failed to show them in terms of behavior.

In short, there seems to be little compelling evidence for anything resembling a predictable progression from lower to higher stages of reasoning about friendship. Nor does there seem to be a close relationship between the level of cognitive functioning as it relates to friendship and actual behavior (Rubin, 1980). As a consequence, researchers have turned to other approaches, and a particularly promising theme is reciprocity. This approach assumes that differences in the way friendship is conceived and expressed, as the child matures, do not reflect changes in cognitive development so much as they reflect changes in the concept of reciprocity.

# The Theme of Reciprocity

For James Youniss (1980, 1986), **reciprocity** is the major defining feature of friendship. In one study, for example, Youniss (1980) interviewed more than 300 children and adolescents ages 6–14 concerning their ideas about what led to friendship, what norms governed friendship, and what constituted violations of friendship. He noted that the theme of reciprocity was characteristic of friendship expectations quite early in childhood and remained so through adolescence. But the way that reciprocity was conceived became progressively richer and more sophisticated with age.

## Tit-for-Tat Exchange

Among 6–8-year-olds, specific exchanges were seen as supporting friendship, and lack of reciprocity drove friends apart. For example, when children in the first grade were asked to define friendship, they typically gave examples such as "We share things"; "I go over to his house and watch TV, and he comes over to my house and watches TV." However, the same was true of those who were definitely not friends, that is, those who had negative exchanges, such as "He stuck his tongue out at me, so I stuck my tongue out at him."

There appeared, in other words, to be an appreciation on the part of young children of tit-for-tat exchange. They defined friends as anyone with whom they had positive exchanges. Such friendships tended to be easy to make and easy to break, because those who did not reciprocate favor-for-favor were no longer friends. But as we see in the next section, there is more to friendship than just tit-for-tat reciprocity, even among the very young.

## Preschoolers and the Emergence of Shared Meaning

When we look closely at the interactions between preschoolers, we find something more than just tit-for-tat reciprocity at work. Preschoolers clearly show preferences for particular peers, and it is at this point that we would be tempted to call such associations friendships (McCandless & Marshall, 1957). Friends often develop themes in common, with one initiating a theme and the other extending and elaborating upon it.

In one study, for example, Jenny Cook-Gumperz and William Corsaro (1977) analyzed verbatim conversations from the naturally occurring interactions of preschool children. They noted a common theme across the transcripts in which preschoolers arrived at a sense of shared meaning. The children delegated roles, asked questions, criticized, clarified, and negotiated. There were two levels of "co-construction" in these interactions, according to Cook-Gumperz and Corsaro. The first was shown in the conversations themselves, and the second was in the topics or references of the conversations, such as the creation of fantasy situations, taking on imaginary roles, and referring to objects whose only basis in reality was in the conversations themselves. Consider the case of Danny and Scott.

DANNY: (Climbing on the jungle gym) "Hey Scott, look, I'm Batman."

SCOTT: (Looking up from the floor where he is playing with a truck) "No you're not, you're a poophead."

DANNY: (Crying)

SCOTT: (Tries to comfort Danny) "You're Batman and I'm Robin, OK?"

Such behavior typically increases significantly in the second and third years of life. These relationships are fundamentally interactive, so not only do we see an elementary form of reciprocity in the interactions, but in the process, a new "reality" is created.

## Reciprocity: From Practice to Principle

Children's friendships are unlikely to last if they are based on tit-for-tat reciprocity alone. This is apparent from the children's own accounts. A positive act by one child may be reciprocated by another, but so too will a negative act lead to a negative response. "She didn't ask me to her birthday party, so I'm not asking her to mine." There is not much direction to tit-for-tat reciprocity. It doesn't go anywhere.

However, about age 9–10, something very different emerges in children's accounts of their friendships. At this point, friends tend to be viewed as equals,

It is in the give and take of relative equals that children feel they can "be themselves."

friendships are viewed as expressions of voluntary preferences for one person rather than another, and they involve certain rights and obligations.

As noted in the opening statement of this chapter, the emergence of this "psychological dimension" is a hallmark of the child's developing friendships. For example, when asked to describe a situation in which one person showed kindness to a friend, preadolescents typically described a problem, such as illness, loss, or difficulty studying, with kindness directed toward alleviating the problem in some way, or the friend's offering support and sympathy. However, when asked what the friend could do in return, they indicated that there was *nothing the friend could or should do until the other had a need as well* (Youniss, 1986).

Conversely, an unkind act was often characterized as knowing that a friend was in need and doing nothing. Clearly, in such a situation, preadolescents were assuming that some sort of obligation had occurred and had gone unmet. Consider the case of Debbie, who put it this way: "Like when we were selling magazines for school, I helped her sell in her neighborhood, and she said she would go around with me. Then she went over to Marty's, and I had to go around by myself—some friend." Here we see an example of the *principle* of reciprocity replacing the *practice* of reciprocity.

## Friendship as an Accomplishment

A further transformation in the concept of friendship typically takes place around puberty. It stems from the realization of the fact that relationships can endure only if they are nurtured—that is, friendship is an accomplishment. This is seen most clearly in acts of self-disclosure and indications of mutual understanding. We see an example of this in the case of Carlos and Fred— two boyhood friends. Carlos was clearly feeling down one day, and Fred asked him what the problem was. He said his dad had been laid off, but he wasn't supposed to tell anybody. Later in the week, when Fred noticed that Carlos started bringing a bag lunch instead of buying his usual "hot lunch" in the cafeteria, Fred started bringing a bag lunch too.

What is interesting about these acts is that the children know that in opening up to their friends, they are taking risks and revealing weaknesses. They acknowledge this vulnerability, but they are also confident that their friends will not use this information to embarrass them. Part of the reason is that they have a good deal of personal information about their friends as well. (For example, Carlos knew that Fred couldn't swim.) Like partners in crime, they feel that they have enough on each other to guarantee that the other will not "squeal" (Youniss, 1986).

So, we find evidence for reciprocity as one of the major defining features of friendship among children from about 2 years of age to 13 and beyond. This is characterized by a developmental trend in which children move from a concrete tit-for-tat sense of exchange to a more abstract principle of reciprocity involving caring and sharing.

By about the age of 9 or 10, close friends tend to see their relationships as more or less enduring and stable. Scorekeeping is seen as less and less necessary on a day-to-day basis; reciprocity is not necessarily immediate; and indeed some pride is taken in the fact that they "trust" each other. When reciprocity does occur, it tends to be tailored to the particular needs of the individual, and this helps to define, confirm, and maintain the relationship.

## *Selected Areas of Research in Children's Friendships*

In the following sections we look at several issues associated with children's friendships that have received attention in the research literature. Some of the most often noted are siblings versus friends, similarity, gender, race, relationship stability, sociometric status, and friendship versus popularity.

### Siblings and Friends

Older siblings are not always happy at the arrival of a new baby in the home. Parents are now likely to pay less attention to older brothers and sisters, and as a consequence, siblings sometimes feel neglected. They tend to resent the loss of attention and show ambivalent feelings toward the new sibling, sometimes becoming demanding and problematic—possibly hitting or otherwise hurting the baby.

This **sibling rivalry** (or jealousy) can sometimes be reduced if the parents devote more time to the older children or get them to help with the baby, being careful not to neglect them any more than is necessary. But the evidence suggests a fine line between too much and too little attention to older siblings under such circumstances. For example, Judy Dunn and Carol Kendrick (1982) found that when parents gave older daughters increased attention after the arrival of a new baby, the daughters tended to be more negative, not less, toward the baby 14 months later. Older siblings who were not permitted to respond negatively toward the baby, on the other hand, were more likely to show more positive behaviors (14 months and 6 years) later (Dunn, 1984). In general, siblings are likely to be less conflicted when parents treat children equally and with sensitivity rather than favoritism (Brody et al., 1994; Dunn, 1993).

Later in childhood, most children adjust quite well to a new family member, but even under the best of circumstances there are likely to be conflicts between siblings. For example, altercations between young siblings sometimes run as high as 56 an hour (Dunn, 1993). But, generally, research suggests that relationships between siblings are more likely to be positive than negative, with older siblings being more dominant and younger siblings being more submissive. There is something of a paradox in the findings, however. When siblings are similar in age, they tend to be closer, but at the same time they have more conflicts (Furman & Buhrmester, 1985a, 1985b). For example, during grade school, sibling relationships are considered both more important and more reliable than relationships with friends, but at the same time they are considered less satisfying.

## Similarity

During childhood, friends tend to be similar in age, attitudes, personality, size, level of intelligence, activities, and physical maturity (Kupersmidt et al., 1995; Rubin, 1980). But there is some evidence that the kinds of similarities that are important change with age. As children get older, for example, the importance of similarity in age and physical appearance tends to decrease, while the importance of similarity in tastes, interests, and attitudes tends to increase (Berndt, 1982; Furman & Bierman, 1983; Ladd & Emerson, 1984; McGuire & Weisz, 1982). Still, friends are typically more similar than nonfriends in terms of race, age, sex (Berndt, 1982), and social status (Clark & Drewry, 1985) on into early adolescence and beyond.

For example, in their study of friendship patterns of third and fourth graders, Janis Kupersmidt and her colleagues (1995) noted that the more similar children were, in terms of demographic variables, behavior, and academics, the more likely they were to be friends. The friends of children from low-income backgrounds also tended to be from low-income backgrounds; the friends of children from the middle class tended to be middle class. There is also some indication that problems associated with deviance, such as delinquency and dropping out of school, may have their roots in childhood. Aggressive, low-income, and low-achieving children tend to associate with each other.

## Gender

There is general agreement among researchers that although preschoolers often have cross-sex friendships, children in elementary school and middle school do so very infrequently (Maccoby, 1990). Generally speaking, boys associate with boys, and girls associate with girls, right through elementary school.

In a questionnaire study involving children in the second, fifth, and eighth grades, Duane Buhrmester and Wyndol Furman (1984) found that the amount of time spent with same-sex friends and opposite-sex friends increased while time spent with mother and father decreased. But neither second nor fifth graders spend much time with the opposite sex (Asher et al., 1977). And, indeed, in their sample of 554 third and fourth graders, Kupersmidt and colleagues (1995) did not find a single cross-sex, same-class, best-friendship pair.

In part, the separation of the sexes at this age seems to be due to a preference on the part of boys for rough-and-tumble play, which girls tend to dislike (Maccoby, 1990). But there are more subtle differences in the friendships of boys and girls as well. For example, girls tend to express more intimacy in their friendships and characterize their friendships as closer, more caring, more secure, and more validating (Foot et al., 1977; Parker & Asher,

1993). This is true not only of descriptions of what the "ideal" friendship should be (Berndt, 1981; Bigelow & La Gaipa, 1980) but also of actual friendships (Sharabany et al., 1981).

Buhrmester and Furman (1984) asked children to indicate how much they talked to or shared their private thoughts and feelings with various others. At age 7, boys and girls did not differ significantly, but by the fifth grade, girls rated their friendships as more intimate than boys did, and by the eighth grade, the difference was substantial (Buhrmester & Furman, 1986). Girls in the fourth and fifth grades talk to each other more than do fourth- and fifth-grade boys (Thorne & Luria, 1986). In the fifth through ninth grades girls spend more than twice as much time talking with their friends as do boys (Raffaelli & Duckett, 1989). Girls, age 11, consider help and support more important in friendship than do boys (Bukowski et al., 1987).

There is also some evidence that girls' friendships tend to be more exclusive. Donna Eder and Maureen Hallinan (1978), for example, studied sex differences in friendships among fifth and sixth graders. They found that girls showed a preference for smaller groups. And when comparisons were made in friendship choices over time, two girls in a close friendship were significantly less likely than two boys to welcome a third person.

## Race

Race does not seem to be a strong predictor of friendships in young children, but it becomes increasingly important as children get older. And while interracial friendships are not common among children (Hallinan & Kubitschek, 1990; Kupersmidt et al., 1995; Singleton & Asher, 1979), the percentage of such friendships actually decreases with age (Steinberg, 1985). This is true of both blacks and whites.

## Stability in Children's Friendships

Some children's friendships are quite stable, especially when children live close to each other and/or attend the same school or day care (Howes, 1988). There have also been reports of friendships between two children that endured despite long periods of separation (Gottman, 1983), but these are probably rare.

Children whose friendships are more stable tend to show greater social competence than do those whose friendships come and go. They are more likely to be popular and generous with their peers, they are seldom lonely, and they also tend to have high self-esteem (McGuire & Weisz, 1982). In light of such findings, a number of researchers have explored the relationship between friendship and sociometric status.

## Sociometric Status

Sociometric status is typically determined by asking children (for example, in a classroom setting) to indicate who they like. These are called **positive nom-**

**inations.** They may also be asked to indicate others who they do not like, or who they like least. These are called **negative nominations.**

Using such techniques, researchers are able to classify children as high in sociometric status, or **popular** (those receiving a large number of positive nominations and few if any negative ones), **rejected** (those receiving a large number of negative nominations and few positive ones), or **neglected** (those receiving few positive or negative nominations). In addition, the positive and negative nominations are sometimes added, yielding a *social impact score*. Those who receive a large number of both positive and negative nominations are called **controversial.** Most of the research has focused on children who are popular, rejected, or neglected. Typically, only a small percentage of children are classified as controversial (Kupersmidt et al., 1990).

*Popular Children*   Although there are important distinctions between popularity and friendship (which are discussed a bit later in the chapter), popular children seem able to achieve a fair degree of success in both areas. They tend to be well liked by the larger group as well as by their friends. They show assertiveness and aggressiveness when necessary, but their interactions with others are made up primarily of socially skilled behaviors and generally lead to positive outcomes. Popular children seem to have skills that are central to enjoyable social interactions with their peers. These serve to maintain their friendships as well as their status among their peers. They are sought out, in part, because their behavior tends to bring out the best in others (Newcomb et al., 1993).

*Rejected Children*   Rejected children tend to show essentially the opposite behavior patterns of popular children. They tend to be more aggressive, and their aggression is more likely to be unprovoked. They are less cognitively skilled and less sociable than average. They tend to be disruptive and inattentive in school, make lower grades, and have lower test scores (Berndt, 1992). They also lack the positive social behaviors that might serve to balance out their aggressive tendencies. And they are sometimes victimized, both physically and verbally, by their peers (Ray et al., 1997).

Rejected children typically have a social network (Cairns et al., 1988), but even within their network they tend to be neglected. Other children simply seem to close ranks and leave rejected children isolated, despite the efforts of the rejected child (Hymel et al., 1990). Indeed, rejected children tend to show more social withdrawal than do neglected children.

The problems of the rejected in social situations seem to be recognized by both their peers and themselves. For example, when Charlotte Patterson and her associates (1990) asked third and fourth graders to respond to questions concerning their own social competencies and relationships, rejected children indicated having the least supportive relationships with their fathers, the least love and affection from their fathers, and the most conflict with their friends. Still, when compared with the ratings of their peers, rejected children tend to overestimate their social competence, while neglected children do not.

What purpose such "denial" serves is not clear. In the short run it might make rejected children feel better about themselves (Alvares & Adelman, 1986; Boivin & Begin, 1989). On the other hand, to the extent that such defenses are successful, they are likely to decrease the motivation to change and as a consequence set in motion the need for ever more defensive measures (Patterson et al., 1990). Let's look at the case of Donny.

Donny is in the third grade and is totally rejected by his peers, and it is not hard to understand why. He is big. He stands nearly a foot taller and weighs almost twice as much as most of his classmates. At the same time, however, he is immature, impulsive, inattentive, and loud. During organized, supervised play, he is sometimes cooperative, but as soon as the teacher is no longer around, he becomes demanding and aggressive. His mother, a single parent, has sought professional help. He was recently moved to a private school and seems to be somewhat better. But the other boys and girls still reject him. Even the fourth and fifth graders steer clear of him.

Evidence suggests that rejected children are at risk for adjustment problems later in life. What is less clear is whether early rejection is a cause of later problems or merely an early indication of some underlying deficit that is responsible for the behavior that leads to rejection by peers and later adjustment problems as well (Newcomb et al., 1993).

*Neglected Children*    Neglected children (those who are neither popular nor rejected) tend to be shy. They spend more time alone than do other children, but there is no evidence that they lack social skills (Rubin & Krasnor, 1986), nor is there any indication that they develop social problems later in life.

Andrew Newcomb, William Bukowski, and Linda Pattee (1993), for example, found that neglected children were similar to average children in terms of positive social behaviors and friendship. And although they are less aggressive, less disruptive, and less sociable than average, they also tend to be less depressed.

So there seem to be only limited differences between neglected and "normal" children. Neglected children are likely to have a best friend in later childhood, and their sociometric status (as neglected) does not necessarily remain stable over time (Coie et al., 1982; Newcomb & Bukowski, 1983). Further, adults do not necessarily see neglected children as different in terms of aggression, sociability, or withdrawal, although their peers do. Even their peers see neglected children as relatively likable (Newcomb et al., 1993). On the other hand, neglected children are more likely to indicate that they feel the least socially competent with their peers, and they also indicate having the least companionship from their best friends (Patterson et al., 1990).

*Controversial Children*    Controversial children (those who are liked by some of their peers and disliked by others) are similar to rejected children in that they show high levels of aggression (in fact, they tend to be more aggressive than rejected children). On the other hand, controversial children are similar to popular children in that they show high levels of sociability. As a group, they tend to be highly verbal and to have significantly better cognitive and social abilities than do rejected children. They can show a talent for leadership and have a sense of humor, but their behavior is not as stable or dependable as that of more popular children. In addition, they tend to be more temperamental, all of which apparently leads to something of a love-hate relationship on the part of their peers.

Controversial children are not seen as either particularly aggressive nor particularly social by adults. This suggests that these children may be adept at discriminating between situations in which adults are present and those where only their peers are present, and adjusting their behavior accordingly. Another explanation for why their behavior may be controversial among peers, but not necessarily seen that way by adults, is that they may simply be overengaged (become too involved) in social situations (Newcomb et al., 1993).

***Stability in Sociometric Status***    How stable is sociometric status? John Coie and Kenneth Dodge (1983) studied the sociometric status of third and fifth graders over a period of 5 years. Their findings indicated that there is a tendency for children who started out rejected to remain rejected, and the same tended to be true to a lesser extent for neglected children. Children who move to a different town, for example, tend to assume, for good or ill, much the same place in the social scheme of things in their new school as they had in their old one (Bukowski & Newcomb, 1984; Coie & Dodge, 1983). As much as we may wish it were otherwise, even children seem to have a hard time leaving their past behind them.

This does not mean that sociometric status is carved in stone. In Coie and Dodge's (1983) study, only about one third of the children who were rejected in the initial stage were still rejected 4 years later. Taken together, then, the findings suggest that although there is a measure of stability in the social status of children, children can and do change their social standing with their peers.

## Friendship and Popularity

What is the relationship between friendship and popularity? Do efforts to encourage children to be more popular serve the purposes of friendship, or is popularity more akin to a superficial congeniality that has little to do with friendship? The answer to this seems to depend on the type of measure used. For example, one study of 10,000 children found a low *negative* correlation between peer (or sociometric) status and those whom children designated as "most liked" (Roff & Sells, 1967). In other words, the higher the sociometric status, the less liked! Such a finding raises many questions about what measures of popularity really mean.

Conceptually, the notion of popularity suggests a glibness that friendship does not. Indeed, researchers have often gone to great lengths to distinguish between popularity and friendship, by asking children specifically who their friends are in their class. It is possible that personal friendship and popularity at the group level involve somewhat different skills and serve somewhat different functions (Hartup, 1983; Price & Ladd, 1986).

Anthony Mannarino (1976, 1978) undertook a study of friendship, in contrast to popularity, in two groups of preadolescents. In this study, the groups were matched on popularity but differed as to the stability of their friendship patterns. Preadolescents with a stable pattern of close friendships were higher both in terms of self-reported altruism and altruism as assessed in the laboratory than were those without such close friendships. Another study found that those with close friends showed a greater number of altruistic responses and were better at taking the other person's point of view than were those without close friends (McGuire & Weisz, 1982). Sociometric status (for example, popularity), on the other hand, was found to be unrelated to either altruism or perspective taking.

Along these same lines, a study of Italian children, ages 9–10, found that those who had reciprocal friendships were viewed by teachers as being more prosocial than were those who had no such friendships (Menesini, 1997).

The research suggests, then, that there are differences between popularity and friendship, and children seem to be quite capable of distinguishing between the two.

## Children at Risk

Peer rejection during childhood is associated with negative consequences later in life (Parker & Asher, 1987). Because these patterns develop early and have a tendency to remain stable, they have given rise to the concept of children at risk. By **children at risk,** we mean children who are not accepted and who have difficulty either making or keeping friends, and thus are likely to develop social or emotional problems later in life.

### Correlates of Early Peer Rejection

When compared to their more socially accepted peers, children who are not accepted are more likely to drop out of school (Ullmann, 1957), become juvenile delinquents (Roff et al., 1972), receive dishonorable discharges from military service (Roff, 1961), and have mental and emotional problems in adulthood (Cowen et al., 1973). In one study, for example, Merrill Roff and colleagues (1976) analyzed the records of men who had been referred, as children, to guidance clinics and who later had adjustment problems in the military service (such as a diagnosis by a military psychiatrist as neurotic or psychotic) or received a dishonorable discharge because of their conduct. The researchers compared records of these men with the records of individuals whose military records were excellent. Specifically, they focused on evidence for early difficulties in peer relationships.

The findings were clear. Half of the neurotic servicemen (versus one eighth of the non-neurotic) and two thirds of the psychotics (versus a quarter of the nonpsychotics) had records indicating poor peer adjustment during childhood. Similarly, 54% of those discharged for bad conduct (versus 24% of the controls) showed indications of poor peer adjustment as children. In short, men whose service records were seriously problematic were two to four times more likely to have had problems with peer relationships during childhood.

However, some of the most interesting work focusing on the importance of childhood peer relationships has come in studies using the "class play" role-nomination technique, in which children are asked to nominate others in their class for a particularly desirable or undesirable role in a class play. Emory Cowen and colleagues (1973) made use of such data that had been generated for a project on early detection and prevention of adjustment problems among third graders. A nationwide psychiatric registry made it possible to follow up with the children to see which ones had received psychiatric treatment 11–13 years later. Those who had received some sort of psychiatric attention were compared with a control group whose names did not appear on the psychiatric register. The results showed that children who later had undergone some type of psychiatric treatment had indeed received a disproportionate number of nominations for undesirable roles in the "class play" study. In other words, those who later developed mental or emotional problems serious enough to require the attention of a psychiatrist had been viewed negatively by their peers as early as the third grade.

In another study of the correlates of rejection and neglect by peers during childhood, Janis Kupersmidt and her colleagues (1990) followed children from the eighth grade to age 18. They found that rejected children were more likely than average to be truant or suspended, to drop out, and to have police records. Over 60% of rejected children had one or more of these problems, but only 35% of the average students did. (The sample was taken from a largely rural, low-income area.) Neglected children, on the other hand, showed no such tendencies.

Taken as a whole, such findings suggest that friendship patterns during childhood offer an important early indicator of long-term psychological adjustment. Those who have behavior disturbances of various kinds later in life, whether in the form of schizophrenia, delinquency, or academic difficulties, tend to show a history of problems with peer acceptance starting early in life. This conclusion is supported by many studies, using quite different methods of data collection, and suggests that indices of peer adjustment during childhood may predict adjustment problems later in life better than the traditional measures, such as intelligence tests, demographics, or socioeconomic standing (Cowen et al., 1973; see also Caspi et al., 1989).

This picture of general support for the "children at risk" hypothesis must be qualified in certain ways, however. First, it's important to note that low peer acceptance and aggressiveness are more closely associated with negative outcomes than are withdrawal and shyness. And although it is true that adults who experience problems often have a history of withdrawal or shyness, withdrawal and shyness in children have not been shown to be predictive of adjustment problems later in adulthood (Parker & Asher, 1987). Accordingly,

Friendship patterns during childhood and adolescence provide insight into long-term psychological adjustment.

Jeffery Parker and Steven Asher caution against being too quick to label children as being at risk. Measures of peer acceptance sometimes have a tendency to err in the direction of too many false alarms, and in the process, labeling itself can cause problems.

Now, for some perspective on the issue, let's turn for a moment to the cross-cultural record. As we see in Box 6-1, the issue of peer rejection would seem to be quite different among the Bangwa. Do they know something we don't?

## Intervention

Several studies have focused on improving the social skills of children who are either rejected or neglected by their peers (Newcomb et al., 1993). These have taken two general forms: experimental programs in schools or laboratory settings involving such things as coaching, modeling, rehearsal, feedback and reinforcement, videotape sessions, play, discussion, verbal instructions and goal setting (Zaragoza et al., 1991), and studies of parenting styles in the home.

*Social Skills Training in School or Laboratory Settings*    Is it possible to identify rejected children early and change their status? The answer seems to be a cautious yes. Sherri Oden and Steven Asher (1977) developed a coaching program that successfully increased the sociometric ratings of children, and a follow-up showed that the gains were maintained 1 year later. The increases in positive social behaviors that one would expect, however, did not seem to occur. And, indeed, no behavioral differences were found in this study between popular and unpopular children prior to the intervention program.

Similarly, when Karen Bierman and Wyndol Furman (1984) compared

*Box 6-1 In a Different Key*
**Arranged Friendships**

In some societies, friendships, like marriages, are "arranged." As strange as this may seem to us, there may be a wisdom to it. People who are lonely, overlooked, and isolated in our own society may well look quite favorably upon the practice in Cameroon where Bangwa children are given a lifelong friend (and a husband or wife) as soon as they are born.

The importance of friendship is emphasized from an early age among the Bangwa. It permeates the folktales, which carry a secondary message of the negative consequences of being without friends. In preadolescence same-sex friends spend long hours together discussing confidences, making plans, sharing aspirations and secrets, and they may be seen in the market together holding hands.

For the Bangwa, friendship is far more important than kinship, where inequities of age, wealth, and status can sometimes strain relationships. The ideal friendship for the Bangwa is one of equality and is characterized by ceremony and the exchange of gifts. Over time, the importance of these friendships continues. When someone is ill among the Bangwa, it is the role of the best friend to seek the advice of the diviner against witchcraft. When a young man decides to marry, his best friend acts as a middle man and negotiates the bride-price; and when the Bangwa are dying, they do not call for their relatives, but their friends. Among the Bangwa, friendship lasts till death (Brain, 1976).

the effectiveness of social skills training, structured (positive) interaction with peers, and a combination of the two, they found that peer interaction alone led to increases in acceptance and increases in the target children's sense of social competence, although a combination of social skills training and peer interaction seemed somewhat more effective. Somewhat surprisingly, researchers have also found that academic skills training tends to increase the peer acceptance of rejected children (Coie & Krehbiel, 1984).

On the other hand, Karen Bierman and colleagues (1987) found that although children receiving some type of treatment showed less in the way of negative behaviors toward their peers, this change in behavior did not seem to translate into improved social status. The reason remains something of a mystery. Perhaps given enough time such changes would occur. Reputations in grade school are hard to live down once they are established.

More recently, Kevin Murphy and Barry Schneider (1994) coached rejected children in various age-appropriate behaviors and noted significant improvements in their interactions with others *as well as* increased liking by others. Zipora Shechtman and colleagues (1994) investigated the effects of therapy/counseling in developing close friendships among preadolescents who were "lacking in social efficacy." Their findings indicated that boys, especially, were helped by such sessions, both as measured by self-report and as indicated by their best friends. Girls undergoing the same treatment showed improvement as well.

Finally, in their review of studies involving social skills training for schoolchildren who showed various disruptive or withdrawn behavior, Nina Zaragoza and her associates (1991) noted that 26 of the 27 studies reported significant gains. However, some problem areas seem to be more resistant to change than others. For example, of the 12 studies assessing sociometric status, only 4 reported significant gains in this measure, and in only 2 of these were the gains maintained at follow-up. Of the studies that focused on specific social skills, on the other hand, significant gains were generally reported during intervention, and upon follow-up these were maintained in all but one of the studies.

The picture on the effectiveness of intervention, then, is somewhat spotty. Programs focusing on training in social skills seem promising in helping rejected children make friends, but we must wait for further research to draw firm conclusions concerning their long-term effectiveness.

***Focus on Parenting Styles***   Because parenting styles are correlated with the social status of children among their peers, some researchers have focused their attention on the home. Parents of popular children tend to be warmer and more responsive to their children's feelings. They talk and play more with their children. They tend to set and enforce consistent boundaries. And, in general, they seem to be more involved in the lives of their children (Berndt, 1992).

Studies have shown that moderate and consistent parental control is correlated with children's popularity. For example, Kevin MacDonald and Rose Parke (1984) found that the parents of popular preschoolers exercised a moderate degree of control over their children, while Martha Putallaz (1987) noted that first graders whose parents were highly controlling, especially in play situations, tended to be lower in social status. And Thomas Dishion (1990a) reported that fourth graders whose parents were inconsistent in their discipline were often rejected by their peers. Why would this be?

It is in the context of the family that children are likely to learn basic social skills. The warmth, control, and modeling of the parents themselves seem to generate social competence in children, and when this social competence is learned at home, it apparently transfers to interactions with peers (Putallaz & Heflin, 1990).

This being the case, programs that focus on modifying parenting practices may be helpful in increasing the social status of children among their peers. However, the relationship between parenting practices and the social status of children tends to be modest. The weight of the evidence suggests that parents may facilitate the entry of their children into the world of peer relationships, but their influence in these matters seems to be limited.

## Conclusion

First we note that children's friendships seem to involve progressively more sophisticated transformations of reciprocity and to serve a variety of functions in the social development of the child. Second, similarity plays a major role in children's friendships. Friends tend to be the same sex and the same race starting in the early elementary grades.

Next we note that although some children's friendships are stable, these tend to be of the classmates or next-door-neighbor variety. Overall, the evidence for stability in children's friendships is not great. It is not unusual for friends to come and go during childhood.

More importantly, research findings indicate a relationship between early problems with peer acceptance and later problems in adjustment, so peer rejection in childhood should be viewed as a serious matter. On the other hand, although there is some evidence for stability in the peer status of children, it is clear that status can change—it is not carved in stone.

Finally, studies are now beginning to identify behaviors of children who do not get along with their peers. And early intervention programs seem to hold some promise in increasing peer acceptance among rejected children, but so far, the long-term effects of such programs are still not clear.

## Suggestions for Further Reading

Asher, S. R., & Coie, J. D. (Eds.). (1990). *Peer rejection in childhood.* New York: Cambridge University Press. An edited volume that features some of the leading authorities reviewing the research on peer rejection in childhood.

Cowen, E. L., Pederson, A., Babijiana, J., Izzo, L. D., & Trost, M. A. (1973). Long-term follow-up of early detected vulnerable children. *Journal of Consulting and Clinical Psychology, 41,* 438–446. A classic study documenting the long-term significance of early peer rejection.

Kupersmidt, J. B., DeRosier, M. E., & Patterson, C. P. (1995). Similarity as the basis for children's friendships: The role of sociometric status and withdrawn behavior, academic achievement and demographic characteristics. *Journal of Social and Personal Relationships, 12,* 439–452. A recent look at the role of similarity in children's friendships.

Maccoby, E. E. (1990). Gender and relationships: A developmental account. *American Psychologist, 45,* 513–520. A highly readable account of gender differences in relationships from a developmental perspective.

Newcomb, A. F., Bukowski, W. M., & Pattee, L. (1993). Children's peer relations: A meta-analysis review of popular, rejected, neglected, controversial and average sociometric status. *Psychological Bulletin, 113,* 99–128. An authoritative overview of research on the significance of sociometric status in children's peer relationships.

Rubin, Z. (1980). *Children's friendships.* Cambridge, MA: Harvard University Press. This prize-winning paperback remains a highly readable look at children's friendships.

# CHAPTER 7

## ❧ *Adolescent Friendships*

*Three boyhood friends—we'll call them Al, Steve, and Mike—grew up in the same neighborhood and were classmates all through grade school. They were like three peas in a pod, you might say. But in middle school Al was held back a grade, and the three began to see less of each other. Because of his size, Mike emerged as the most popular in high school. He made the football team his freshman year. Steve remained close behind, by virtue of his personality, and Al became isolated. A year or two later, however, things changed. Al joined the track team and went on to set the state record in the 100-yard dash. Now the trio began to get together more often, and Al was "number one." Somewhat later, Steve met Beth, fell in love, got a part-time job, and became something of a social dropout. Now there was just Al and Mike. At this point, however, Mike developed a case of acne and became self-conscious around girls, and Al emerged as the more social member of the threesome. It was now Al who dated and danced at the teen dances and Mike who stood on the sidelines talking mostly with the guys. After graduation, Al joined the Army. Mike and Steve went on to college, but Steve remained completely absorbed in his relationship with Beth, and from that time on, the three friends saw each other only infrequently.*

Adolescence is a time of rapid change, physically, socially, and emotionally. These changes take place at an uneven pace, with wide variations between individuals and with significant differences between the sexes. Adolescents often feel adrift as the dependencies of childhood loosen, relationships with family members become less dominant, and progress toward independence begins in earnest. For some semblance of anchorage, they tend to turn to their peers. When they feel isolated and apart, it is from similar others that adolescents gain a sense of shared perspective and the feeling that they are not alone.

## The Significance of Friends in Adolescence

It is in the give and take of relative equals, when neither age nor power differences enter the picture, that adolescents tend to feel the most comfortable. Approximately two out of three adolescents indicate that they can be "more themselves" with their friends and that close friends understand them better than their parents do (Youniss & Smollar, 1985). Friends provide feedback that helps adolescents make realistic appraisals of themselves. And when conflicts arise, each participant is on an equal footing. In the United States adolescents spend more time socializing with friends than anything else, and they seem to be the happiest when they are doing so (Csikszentmihalyi et al., 1977).

Friendships during adolescence tend to be more extensive, more diverse, and more subtle than they are during childhood (Collins & Repinski, 1994). They are likely to be marked by intimate, intense, honest, and open exchanges. With friends, the self-conscious attempts at role playing or putting on airs are muted, and a "warts and all" quality emerges. Friendship goes hand in hand with sharing feelings openly and with assurance of confidentiality. Friends listen, friends share, and friends understand.

In this respect, adolescents' friends are their therapists. When we hear a teenager on the phone saying, "Hi, it's me. Can you talk? I need to talk with somebody," we have a pretty good idea that a friend is on the other end of the line. Some writers have even suggested that peer relationships may be the last chance an adolescent has to repair the inadequacies of a problem childhood (Blos, 1979). Such factors operate to set adolescent friendships apart from those of childhood and adulthood.

## Girls' Friendships in Early, Middle, and Late Adolescence

In their study of adolescent girls, Elizabeth Douvan and Joseph Adelson (1966) noted distinctive patterns of friendships in each of three periods. In early adolescence (11, 12, and 13 years old) friendships tend to be activity centered. Friends at this stage are those who do things together, with little indication of depth. In middle adolescence (14, 15, and 16 years old) the activity-centered relationships begin to give way to relationships of mutuality and interdependence. The personality of the other becomes important. And reciprocal self-disclosure of thoughts and sharing of feelings provide a foundation from which to launch heterosexual relationships, new sex roles, and new identities.

During middle adolescence, we see more emphasis on security. Friends are those who remain loyal, who are trustworthy, and who do not betray. Douvan and Adelson accounted for this emphasis on security by invoking the mechanism of identification—that is, adolescents need someone who is experiencing the same problems at roughly the same time. This concern for security seems to be particularly important at the age when girls start dating.

Sometime around the middle of adolescence, the rules of friendship begin to change. Suddenly, the threat of a girl being abandoned by her friend in

Girls' early adolescent friendships, according to research by Douvan and Adelson, tend to be activity centered; they do things together, but with little indication of depth.

favor of a special boy is very real. The friend who leaves, leaves a young girl to cope with her insecurities on her own. The case of Bev and Jill illustrates this point.

Bev and Jill had been friends for a long time. But when Dan started calling Jill, Bev knew their friendship was going to take a back seat to Jill's relationship with Dan. She never said anything, but she could see it coming. Jill had always been there. Bev couldn't imagine not having her as a best friend.

Friendships during late adolescence (17 years old and beyond) tend to be considerably more relaxed. The suffocating exclusivity of earlier friendships seems to give way to a more equitable sense of *autonomous interdependence* (Selman & Selman, 1979). During this period, an emphasis on emerging heterosexual relationships makes for less dependence upon same-sex friendships. Friends are close but grant each other a measure of freedom. Friendships now emphasize such things as personality, talents, and skills—that is, what friends can bring to the relationship and how interesting, stimulating, and tolerant they are. Sharing confidences is still important, but for the most part, confidences no longer carry with them the earthshaking urgency they did earlier (Conger, 1991). There is also less emphasis on loyalty and security in reference to friendship. In late adolescence, friendship seems to be less needed, and as a consequence there is less concern about being abandoned (Douvan & Adelson, 1966). The case of Bev and Jill provides a continuing example.

Two years later Dan and Jill are still a couple, and Bev still feels like a third wheel, but she no longer feels threatened by their relationship. Dan sometimes fixes Bev up with one of his friends, and they all go out together. Her competitor for Jill's friendship has now been transformed into her "buddy."

## *Adolescent Culture*

Adolescents apparently have a need to create something of an *interim culture* as a staging ground for the great leap forward into adulthood. In striking a balance between the adolescent culture and the adult world that looms before them, peers offer feedback that adults cannot. In order to understand adolescent friendships, it's necessary to look at the wider context in which they take place and the way this changes over time.

### Cliques and Crowds as a Way of Establishing Identity

Building on the earlier work of Dexter Dunphy (1963), B. Bradford Brown (1989) defines **cliques** as small numbers of adolescents who interact, hang out together, and develop more or less close relationships. Cliques vary both in size and significance. There are tight-knit cliques, and there are cliques that have a clear central core with peripheral members who come and go. But, in general, members of a clique tend to be "friends."

In contrast, **crowds** tend to be larger reputation-based groups of similar others, who may or may not spend much time together. For Brown, crowds function more like **reference groups** (others with whom one identifies). In any given high school these are likely to be known by such names as the jocks, the brains, the druggies, the populars, the normals, the loners, the nerds; and the list goes on, varying somewhat from one school to another.

Members of a teenage crowd often hang out together, wear similar clothes, and engage in common activities. Cultural and symbolic labels seem to be more important than actual behavior.

Although the norms of the clique are generated from within the group itself, the reputation of the crowd is not of its own making—it tends to come from outside (Brown, 1989). The most significant thing about a crowd's reputation is that it gives some indication of a crowd member's attitudes and activities and provides something of a commentary on his or her level of social development.

According to Brown, the transition from elementary school to middle or junior-high school is especially significant for the peer relationships of young adolescents (Brown et al., 1994). At this point, their school is likely to be bigger and the student body much larger and more diverse. Adult monitoring of their day-to-day activities becomes looser. And heterosexual relationships loom on the horizon. For some, this new scene presents opportunity. For others, it is threatening. But all young adolescents must negotiate and structure their new social world as best they can.

Using labels to stereotype various crowds is apparently a strategy by which adolescents locate themselves in relation to others and establish where they fit in the social scheme. Categorizing their peers into crowds lends structure to social interactions and facilitates the development of an identity. Crowds may divide along socioeconomic lines (Eckert, 1989), racial/ethnic lines (Matute-Bianchi, 1986), or activity lines. In this sense they tend to reflect the social structure of the larger society.

What is the nature of the process at work in labeling others? How is it that it has such an impact on peer relationships? According to B. Bradford Brown and his colleagues (1994) the process involves caricature, channeling, permeability, and desirability.

***Crowds as Caricatures (Prototypes)***   When we read the descriptions of various adolescent crowds, we are likely to get the impression that they are "real" (for example, see Eckert, 1989). Members of a given crowd often hang out together at a particular place in the hall, lunchroom, or on the street corner. Some crowd members wear the same kinds of jackets, sweaters, or other forms of dress to identify themselves. And sometimes a particular crowd controls certain activities. So there is no question that members of various crowds can be observed and recognized at most high schools.

But a closer look reveals that adolescent crowds are more about cultural and symbolic labels than they are about actual behavior (Lesko, 1988). Crowds represent stereotypical lifestyles, value systems, and activities of adolescent society. Various crowds constitute different **prototypical cases.** Accordingly, adolescents speak of jocks as involved in sports, interested in having a good time, and showing little concern for schoolwork, when they know perfectly well that certain members of the jock crowd do not fit the stereotype (Brown et al., 1994). In addition, some crowds are "invisible." For example, loners are as readily categorized as jocks, nerds, and burnouts, and yet there is no "loner" crowd, even though there is a "loner" prototype (B. B. Brown et al., 1990). So the categories seem to reflect social reality more than anything else.

Adolescents apparently compare notes in an effort to arrive at some sort of shared intelligence about their social world. In the process, the characterizations of the various crowds are based in part on their observations of a given crowd's activities, mode of dress, assumed attitudes, and the like, and also upon the opinions and evaluations of others. The result is a composite picture that combines elements of fact, elements of elaboration, and a fair amount of exaggeration. In other words, **caricatures** of various crowds are constructed, and even though these are distortions, they are still validated socially.

What purpose is served by painting a picture of crowds that clearly embellishes the facts? Caricatures serve to accentuate the central features of each group and so provide readily recognizable social "handles" (Brown et al., 1994). Why is a caricature preferable to reality? The answer seems to lie in the tendency of adolescents to overstate the positives of their own group and the negatives of certain others, and to exaggerate the differences between the two. This exaggeration serves to facilitate consensual validation, affirm group membership, and increase solidarity.

Thus, when researchers asked junior and senior high students to name the major crowds and describe each one in terms of dress, orientation toward achievement, sociability, involvement in extracurricular activities, hangouts, and weekend activities, they found only moderate agreement (B. B. Brown et al., 1990). Why? Because members of each crowd portrayed their own group more positively than did others.

But members of various crowds also tend to differ systematically in their opinions of certain other crowds. For example, in Margaret Mory's (1992) study, the "elites" and "normals" held similar (negative) views of "druggies." Both saw the druggies as hating school. But the druggies and normals held very different views of the elites. Normals tended to view elites much like the elites viewed themselves, while druggies saw the elites as very achievement oriented. Meanwhile, the druggies saw themselves as neutral to moderately positive with respect to school achievement.

In short, out-groups sometimes share a common view of a particular crowd, and sometimes not. And the tendency to view one's own crowd in positive terms is sometimes extended to a crowd to which one aspires (Kinney, 1993).

The advantages of appraising other crowds more or less objectively seem to be offset by the advantages of indulging in self-serving (group-serving) biases. And crowds tend to be described by outsiders in relation to other crowds. Thus, for example, we are likely to hear such comparisons as "The jocks party a lot, but they don't get stoned like the burnouts do" (Brown et al., 1994).

*Channeling*   The importance of crowd caricatures does not end with the caricatures themselves. Crowd caricatures translate into reality in the way they **channel** (or influence) adolescent social behavior. In essence, teenagers tend to gravitate to relationships with certain "eligibles" and away from certain others who are "less eligible," based not on their experience so much as on the reputation of the crowd. For example, a study of popular girls found that they saw befriending certain people as jeopardizing their position in the crowd, and so they became increasingly selective in their friendships, confining them more and more to their own crowd. As a consequence, they became known as snobs (Eder, 1985). Take the case of Jackie and Kay.

Jackie had run around with Kay since they were both in grade school. Both girls were down to earth. Both had a good sense of humor. Their friendship was really solid. Then in their sophomore year, Kay ran for cheerleader and won. And suddenly things changed. Kay was always polite, but she seemed to have less and less time for her old friend. One day, instead of meeting her as she usually did to walk home after school, Kay left a note in her locker saying she had a meeting. Later Jackie learned that Kay rode home with some of the other cheerleaders. Jackie was deeply hurt by this. She had supported Kay and helped her in her campaign for cheerleader, and now she was being abandoned by her old friend.

*Permeability*    Cliques and crowds tend to be somewhat exclusive. Are they all equally so? There seems to be little consensus on the matter. For example, in a study of high school students, Ralph Larkin (1979) found a considerable amount of interaction between members of three different crowds that constituted the social elite, but the same groups were rather unwelcoming of those at the other end of the status hierarchy. It seems, then, that groups not only differ in **permeability** (or how welcoming they are of others) but that a given crowd may be more receptive to overtures from members of one out-group than from members of another. The same process that leads to categorizing in the first place seems to carry with it an element of evaluation.

For example, in his middle school study, David Kinney (1993) found that there were essentially two crowds, the "trendies" and the "dweebs," and there was little interaction between them. With the transition to high school, however, the crowds became more differentiated. Now there were "trendies," "normals," "headbangers," "grits," and "punkers." The headbangers contended with the trendies for high status, while the grits and punkers settled on the bottom of the social hierarchy. But the boundaries between the normals, the trendies, and the headbangers were not strong, and over time the whole hierarchy tended to flatten out as the normals rose to become trendies, and the headbangers and trendies became essentially similar in status. Some students transferred their allegiances from one crowd to another. Indeed, in a study of 7th–12th graders, another team of researchers found that approximately half changed crowds over a 2-year period (Brown et al., 1992). Apparently, these shifts in crowd affiliation come most often because one is befriended by someone from another crowd.

Moving from lower in the social hierarchy to higher is another matter. One study noted that only one of the populars dropped to become rejected or neglected, and not one of the rejected or neglected students changed to a more desirable status over the course of the year (Franzoi et al., 1994). So the potential for mobility seems to depend, in part, on one's initial status.

*Desirability*   What determines the desirability of a crowd? **Desirability** is clearly related to a crowd's status—that is, the higher the crowd's status, the more desirable it tends to be (Eckert, 1989; Eder, 1985). But there seems to be something more to crowd desirability than just status. B. Bradford Brown and colleagues (1994) report data from their study of a midwestern middle school and high school in which students were asked to indicate on a 5-point scale how willing they were to be a member of a given crowd. This allowed the research team to establish the desirability of each crowd. The overall results are summarized in Figure 7-1.

In the figure we see that the "normals" are considered the most desirable, followed closely by the "populars," then the "jocks" and "brains," with the "druggies" considered the least desirable. But the desirability of certain crowds changed dramatically with age and grade level. The "nerds," for example, went from high to low and back to high again in a U-shaped fashion from grades 7 to 12, while the desirability of the populars and the jocks showed essentially the opposite pattern over the same period. Overall, normals were considered the most desirable. So, apparently, there is a distinction between crowd status and crowd desirability. As paradoxical as it sounds, a crowd can have high status and still not be considered particularly desirable.

## Crowds as the Context for Friendship

In adolescent society, crowds are likely to provide the context in which close relationships, such as friendship and romantic relationships, take place. And,

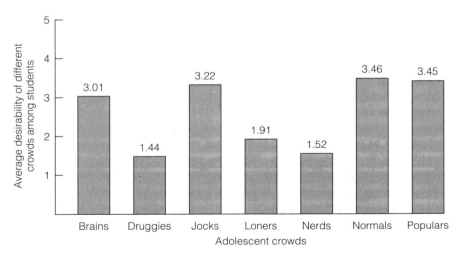

**Figure 7-1**   Adapted from Brown, B. B., Mory, M. S., & Kinney, D. (1994). Casting adolescent crowds in relational perspective: Caricature, channel, and context. In R. Montemayer, G. R. Adams, & T. P. Gullota (Eds.). *Personal Relationships During Adolescence.* Thousand Oaks, CA: Sage. Copyright © 1994 Sage Publications Inc. Used by permission of Sage Publications Inc.

most significantly, for our purposes, the nature and quality of these relationships differ dramatically from one crowd to another. Studies over more than a decade have shown that relationships within high-status groups tend to be superficial and competitive (Brown, et al., 1994). In other words, friendship seems to be used as a way to establish and maintain one's place in the social scheme of things rather than as a way to express emotional support.

For example, Donna Eder (1985) noted that "populars" are somewhat wary of their friendships and continually concerned about image and what a given relationship might do to their standing with the crowd. They even jockey for position within their own ranks, which tends to lead to less than stable friendships (Lesko, 1988). We see this illustrated in the case of Nickie.

Even though Nickie was from a broken home and money was tight, she had always been popular in middle school. She was part of the "in" crowd. In high school, however, things changed. The popular girls in high school "dressed," went out for sports after school, and most of them drove cars. Nickie walked to school and worked every evening at a variety store to bring in a little money. One night Jen, one of the other "counter girls," asked her if she'd like a cup of coffee after work, and Nickie said yes. This was not an easy decision. Jen was older than she was, and she was definitely not part of the "in" crowd. Over time, however, Nickie came to like Jen. She was down to earth, a delight to be around, and in Nickie's terms "would give you the shirt off her back." Over time, Nickie started to ride to work with Jen after school, and soon she was dropped by her old friends, but she had no regrets. Jen was much more "real."

Why are relationships among the "elite" so superficial? One researcher saw it as part of their middle-class upbringing, which makes teens aware of the role of power and status associated with relationships—what some friends can do to help (or hurt) one's place in the social scheme of things (Eckert, 1989).

In contrast, friendships among the "burnouts," "headbangers," and "druggies" tend to be more stable, loyal, deeper, and committed. For example, Nancy Lesko (1988) characterized relationships among burnouts as blunt and undiplomatic, but egalitarian and lasting. They tend not to cultivate a large number of friends, and their friends generally come from their own crowd. Eckert (1989) accounts for these differences by noting that, as children of working-class parents, burnouts are often forced to rely on peers more than family for emotional support, and as a result, there is a sense of solidarity among them. In essence, one's friends become one's family.

We must be careful, however, not to overstate the case. Brown and colleagues (1994) noted in their study of 7th–12th graders that the various crowds tend to be similar in many respects, with differences most marked between the "populars" and the "druggies," on the one hand, and between the "brains" and the "outcasts," on the other. Still, 80–90% of those in each crowd indicated having a best friend, and on average they had known this person for 3 to 3½ years.

There are significant differences from one crowd to another in the amount of time spent with friends. For example, "druggies" spent an average of 13 hours per week with friends, while "brains" spent only about 8 hours, and the others tended to fall somewhere in between. Each crowd seems to have a somewhat different profile in terms of peer relationships, and this tends to be reflected in their friendships (Brown et al., 1994).

### How Important Are Cliques and Crowds?

Wesley Shrum and Neil Cheek (1987) found that the importance of cliques tends to decline from the 6th through the 12th grades, and an increasing number of adolescents become "isolates," and "liaisons." These are marginal members of cliques with ties to outsiders. Similarly, James Coleman (1974) noted that the significance attached to crowd or clique membership reaches a peak in early adolescence and tapers off in the later years of high school.

Eventually, all this leads to what is sometimes called the "senior year dissipation" of crowd boundaries. As adolescents face the uncertainties of the postgraduation world, their jealously guarded turf and peer-group systems seem suddenly a bit beside the point, and those who haven't spoken to each other for years suddenly renew old friendships, write the most endearing notes in each other's yearbooks, and wish each other "all the best" in the future. But, interestingly enough, the most popular and elite groups still show a tendency to remain cliquish and exclusive (Eder, 1985; Larkin, 1979).

## *The Stability of Adolescent Friendships*

Research findings on the stability of adolescent friendships is conflicting and inconclusive. Some researchers have reported an increase in stability of friendships from early to late adolescence (Epstein, 1983a), while others have found that stability in friendship varies little after preadolescence (Berndt, 1982). Looking at the picture as a whole, it's fair to say that there is little evidence for friendship stability during adolescence (Brown, Eicher, & Petrie, 1986).

For example, Joyce Epstein (1983a, 1983b) found that only a third of the participants in her study indicated having *reciprocated* friendships that were stable over a period of 1 year, and other researchers have reported similar findings (for example, Savin-Williams, 1987). As we see in Box 7-1, it is not only in the United States that adolescent friendships can be unstable.

The major factor in determining the stability of friendships seems to be whether or not they are reciprocal (Crockett et al., 1984). Thomas Berndt and colleagues (1986) found that most reciprocal friendships tend to last a year or more. Indeed friendship is typically defined as a close relationship that *is* reciprocal. But, interestingly enough, adolescents sometimes report having more reciprocal friendships than actually are reciprocal (Hartup, 1993).

Factors external to the relationship, such as school transitions, can also affect relationship stability. And both friendships and romantic interests seem to be vulnerable to such external forces. For example, Philip Shaver and his

*Box 7-1  In a Different Key*
**Camaradia**

Rubin Reina (1959) gives an example of friendships among the Chinautleco Indians of Mayan ancestry, who live near Guatemala City. In this culture *camaradia* between adolescent males reaches great intensity. The relationship is institutionalized and recognized publicly. *Camaradia* is treated with great seriousness. Such friends share their dreams, their aspirations, and confidences about their love affairs. One expects complete *confianza* (trust and confidentiality) of his friend. Such relationships are often possessive, fragile, and plagued by jealousy. When friends break up, as they often do, they become enemies, and the *confianza* relationship that they once had comes back to haunt them (Reina, 1959).

Similar relationships have been noted in many parts of the world. Certain Mediterranean cultures place great importance on intense and sentimental relationships between same-sex adolescents, and such relationships are often characterized by public displays of affection (Fine, 1980).

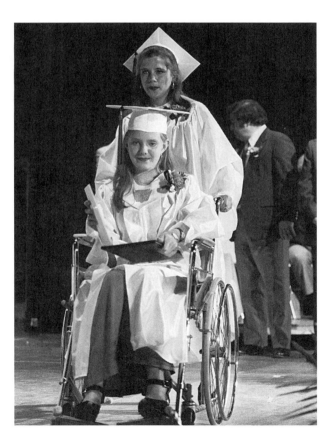

Factors external to a relationship, such as graduation, often affect relationship stability. Both friendships and romantic interests may be vulnerable to major life transitions.

colleagues (1985) found that in the transition from high school to college, high school friendships tended to fall by the wayside.

### Best Friends

As a rule, adolescents have one or two best friends and a number of "good friends," but the numbers reported vary depending on the method of study (Crockett et al., 1984). Joyce Epstein (1986) found that the number of "best friends" reached a peak in early adolescence. John Reisman and Susan Shorr (1978) reported that best friends were mentioned most often in middle adolescence, when individuals sometimes mentioned having four to five best friends. After that the number typically dropped off. Somewhat paradoxically, there is some evidence that "just plain" friendships tend to be more stable than "best" friendships (Epstein, 1983a, 1983b).

### Conflict

Conflict is recognized as an integral part of friendship among adolescents, but at the same time, it is seen as something that can usually be managed (Goodnow & Burns, 1988). Indeed, the way conflicts are resolved is sometimes seen as an indication of the strength of friendships (Selman, 1980).

Conflict between friends usually involves some sort of rule violation signaling a lack of trust, attention, respect, or support (Youniss & Smollar, 1985). And when conflicts are not resolved successfully, friends are likely to reach a parting of the ways (Kandel, 1978a, 1978b; Kandel & Andrews, 1987).

## Correlates of Adolescent Friendships

Among the many factors that play a role in adolescent friendships, those that have received attention in the research literature have been family background, similarity, gender, race, popularity, conformity, and social adjustment. All of these have been shown to influence, or be influenced by, friendship during adolescence.

### Friendship and Family Background

Socioeconomic class is important in the formation of crowds and, as a consequence, influences both the friendships and romantic interests of adolescents. There seems to be surprisingly little cutting across class lines. The "elite," particularly, tend to come from higher socioeconomic backgrounds. The normals, loners, brains, and certain special-interest groups tend to come from more diverse backgrounds (Clasen & Brown, 1985). One of the clearest lines of demarcation, however, is between those who are planning to go on to college and those who are not. Consider the case of Chelsie and Pam.

Chelsie lived in a pleasant neighborhood. Her father was a well-known and very successful lawyer. In high school she was popular and known as a "fashion plate." Over the summer a new girl moved into her neighborhood, and Chelsie was delighted. She and Pam hit it off just like that. Both were on the quiet side. Both were pretty. And it didn't hurt that Pam had an older brother who was a "hunk." When school started that fall, however, the relationship ended as fast as it had begun. The problem was that Chelsie was in the honors program, and Pam wasn't. Pam wasn't even in the regular academic program. She was signed up for "commercial." Consequently, the two girls hung out with very different crowds. All of Chelsie's friends were planning on going to college. Pam wasn't planning on going to college. She hung out with the other girls in the secretarial program and became known as one of the "burnouts."

In addition to socioeconomic and academic factors, studies have reported that a father's absence from the home can seriously affect adolescents and their relationships with their peers (Emery, 1988; Hetherington, 1972). In her study of the social behavior of adolescent girls from father-absent homes, for example, Mavis Hetherington (1972) found a difference in the behavior of girls from homes where the father's absence was due to separation or divorce, and those where the father's absence was due to death. Girls whose fathers were absent due to divorce tended to seek male company and to engage in sex-related behaviors more often. They were seldom seen pursuing typical female activities, preferring to spend their time hanging around the carpentry shop, basketball courts, and the like. Yet, the *interview* data revealed no suggestion of a preference for male company over female company. On the other hand, when the father's absence was due to death, the girls were more likely to be inhibited and lacking in self-confidence and tended to avoid their male peers.

## Friendship and Similarity

During adolescence, friends tend to be similar in age, socioeconomic background, ethnic group, gender, intelligence, academic achievement, and educational aspirations and interests. They also tend to be similar in terms of sociability and in their attitudes toward the use of alcohol, drugs, smoking, church attendance, preferences in music, entertainment, and other activities, and in their attitudes toward the peer culture in general (Ball, 1981; Berndt, 1982; Conger, 1991; Csikszentmihalyi & Larson, 1984; Dishion, 1990b; Epstein, 1983b; Kandel, 1978a, 1978b; Karweit, 1983; Tuma & Hallinan, 1979).

Similarity among friends seems to be achieved in two ways. First, those with similar backgrounds, attitudes, and interests tend to be attracted to each other. This is due in part to the way their social world is structured. Neighborhoods are typically segregated along social class and racial lines. "Tracking" in schools separates the vocational/technical, academic, and honors students. And students with similar interests find themselves together in extracurricular activities, such as band, as well.

Once they find each other, friends tend to become still more similar. This movement toward increased similarity was noted by Denise Kandel (Kandel, 1978a, 1978b, 1985; Kandel & Andrews, 1987), who studied adolescents before they became friends, during their friendships, and following breakups. She found that not only were adolescent friends similar in various ways, but they also became more similar over time in those areas in which they had initially differed. And those who failed to achieve such increased similarity were likely to break up. Other studies have confirmed that friends not only tend to be similar but also tend to become increasingly similar over the course of their friendship (Epstein, 1986, 1989).

The dynamics of similarity "enforcement" can be quite subtle. In observations of a middle-school lunchroom, for example, researchers have documented in some detail the nuances of how group norms were conveyed and conformity enforced (Eder & Sanford, 1986). Specifically, teasing seems to serve as a powerful tool for keeping peers in line. It is used to make the point while allowing the "offender" to save face about such things as weight problems and boyfriends. Gossip about outsiders seems to serve much the same purpose, by making oblique references to "them" as opposed to "us." Such teasing and gossip serves to generate solidarity among in-group members and convey a clear sense of the norms and boundaries that members in good standing dare not violate. This is demonstrated in the case of Donny.

Because of his height, Donny was a valuable member of a neighborhood basketball team. He also had a part-time job at a local gas station. While the team was practicing one day, another group of boys began playing nearby. Later the two teams decided to "shoot around" together, and it soon became clear that they were both very good and very well matched. So they decided to make plans for a real game. Everybody could make it Saturday but Donny. He had to work. Butch spoke for the rest of them: "Well Mr. Moneybags, you gonna play basketball or you gonna pump gas?" But Donny stuck to his guns. He kept his part-time job at the gas station. And with that decision, he lost his status with the rest of the team.

### Friendship and Gender

Friendship patterns of males and females differ significantly during adolescence (Eder & Hallinan, 1978). These differences are consistent with the prevailing stereotypes that suggest females have a stronger interpersonal orientation and put more emphasis upon nurturing and intimacy in their relationships.

Females generally mature earlier than males, and apparently the need to express intimacy comes earlier in females than it does in males. Females typically show more subtlety in their descriptions of others, including their friends, than do males of the same age (Livesley & Bromley, 1973). Females also seem better able to verbalize their feelings (Douvan & Adelson, 1966). In their conversations with friends, females are likely to strike themes that are more personal and intimate, and males are more likely to be activity oriented and interested in making things happen.

Another indication of the sex differences in friendship patterns is that female cliques tend to be more exclusive than male cliques (Eder & Hallinan, 1978). That is, females seem to guard their "social turf" more jealously.

On average, females spend more time with their friends than do males (Wong & Csikszentmihalyi, 1991). And there is some indication that their friendship preferences are also more stable than those of males (Kon & Losenkov, 1978). At the same time, however, females are more likely to express feelings of loneliness and being misunderstood (Kon, 1981), and they are also at greater risk for depression during adolescence than are males (Conger, 1991).

Both males and females acknowledge that female friendships are more intimate (Bukowski & Kramer, 1986), and this seems to be the case across the age range (Furman & Buhrmester, 1985a). It is possible, however, that such differences are more a matter of style than substance. Males may simply convey intimacy through actions rather than words (Buhrmester & Furman, 1987), because, when all is said and done, males and females report having about the same number of friends (Eder & Hallinan, 1978).

### Opposite-Sex Friendships

Friends tend to be the same sex through grade school and high school. Cross-sex friendships (as opposed to romantic interests) seem to be rare among adolescents, but estimates of how common they are vary widely. In a study of 97 adolescent friendship pairs, Steve Duck (1975) found only two opposite-sex choices, both of them unreciprocated. Willard Hartup (1983, 1993) reported that about 5% of middle adolescents indicated having friends of the opposite sex. When Igor Kon and Vladimir Losenkov (1978) asked ninth graders in Leningrad to name their friends, 57% of the boys and 43% of the girls mentioned only same-sex friends. Similar findings have been reported for France, West Germany (Kon, 1981), and the United States (Kandel, 1978a).

In Suzanna Rose's (1985) study of college undergraduates, on the other hand, 100% of the single males and 73% of the single females reported having close friends of the opposite sex, as did 67% of the married males and 53% of the married females. So the picture on opposite-sex friendships seems to change significantly when we move from high school to college.

One of the most intriguing findings in this regard was reported by Stanley Gaines (1994) in a study of 62 male and female college students who had platonic relationships. Among the measures taken were indications of "affection given," "affection denied," "respect given," and "respect denied." The findings indicated that when compared with same-sex friendships, the only thing that differentiated the male-female platonic pairs was their tendency to deny each other respect.

What purpose could this possibly serve? One interpretation is that those in opposite-sex platonic relationships feel a need to leave no doubt, both for themselves and for other interested parties, what their relationship is and what it is not. Left to their imaginations, onlookers might jump to the (wrong) conclusion that the pair is romantically involved. Further, if a disrespectful comment by one went unanswered, it could simply mean that a relationship was asymmetrical, where one was willing (however reluctantly), for the sake of the relationship, to be treated like a doormat. By reciprocating denial of respect for denial of respect, they are apparently able to enjoy the fruits of a male-female relationship and yet remain clearly distanced from the commitment of a romantic one. Denial of respect, then, may serve paradoxically as a relationship maintenance strategy, whereby those involved in opposite-sex platonic relationships seek to achieve some semblance of balance in their tightrope relationship, lest they risk falling into the abyss of romantic involvement.

## Friendship and Race

Race and ethnicity seem to emerge quite early as major defining features of friendship. Even though peer relationships tend to become increasingly diverse in other respects, cross-race friendships tend to decline over the elementary school years and remain low during middle school and high school (Hallinan & Williams, 1983; Shrum et al., 1988; Steinberg, 1985). Although there is some evidence that friendships across racial lines are more common in integrated schools than in more segregated ones (Schofield, 1981), blacks in predominantly white schools show more stability in their (same race) neighborhood friendships than in their school relationships (Clark & Ayers, 1988). Indeed, there is some evidence that blacks tend to avoid associations that would link them with "brainiacs" and shun and deride peers who "act white" (Fordham & Ogbu, 1986).

## Friendship and Popularity

Donna Eder (1985) raised the question of the relationship between popularity and friendship, noting that the pursuit of high status was frequently associated with conflict and tension between females who were popular. Others have suggested that popularity offered a sense of (group) inclusion, while friendship offered loyalty, affection, and intimacy (Furman & Robbins, 1985).

On the other hand, friendship and popularity seem to be similar in that both involve helping, nurturing, companionship, and a sense of self-worth. In general those who are popular are likely to have more opportunities for friendship (Newcomb et al., 1993). The relative importance of popularity and friendship changes from preadolescence to adolescence, however, with the emphasis increasingly on friendship and less on popularity (Berndt, 1986; Bukowski et al., 1987; Furman & Bierman, 1984).

## Friendship and Conformity

One indication of the importance given to the opinions of peers is the heightened level of conformity that we see in the early teens. Negotiating a place in the social scheme of things is not an easy thing to do, and in the face of uncertainty, one of the safest strategies is simply to do what everybody else is doing. There is a measure of security in going along with the crowd.

How much do adolescents let peer pressure affect them? One study showed a modest relationship between peer pressure and self-reported involvement in certain (peer-encouraged) activities, but there were wide individual differences (Brown et al., 1986). Some adolescents reported feeling more vulnerable to peer pressure than others.

How much should we believe the reports of adolescents concerning peer pressure? Apparently not very much. According to another study (Brown, 1982), adolescents are reluctant to admit how much they are influenced by others, so their self-reports are likely to underestimate the amount of peer pressure they actually experience. In a study in which college students were asked to give retrospective accounts, they indicated that peer pressure during their teenage years had been considerably stronger than the responses of the (then current) teenage population suggested.

In general, conformity to peer pressure seems to be at its highest in early to middle adolescence, diminishing significantly in late adolescence. This decline is somewhat less marked for girls, but the sex differences are not great. The major additional factor affecting conformity seems to be one's status within the group. Those who are lower in status tend to be more conforming.

## Friendship and Social Adjustment

Adolescents who have supportive friendships tend to do better in school, have higher scores on standardized tests, be more involved in school activities, and receive more positive behavior ratings from their teachers (Cauce, 1986). However, this general finding must be qualified in certain ways. In a study of gifted students, for example, Judy Dunn and her colleagues (1987) found no relationship between school performance and the support of friends. And in a study of black adolescents, Ana Cauce and colleagues (1982) found an *inverse* relationship between perceived peer support and grades. In this case, however, it might have been that peers did not particularly value school achievement (Cauce, 1986). Stephen Ball (1981) suggests that low-achieving friends may reinforce negative attitudes toward school and schoolwork. And adolescents whose friends have negative attitudes toward school tend to develop negative attitudes themselves.

On the whole, friends during adolescence seem to serve psychological, social, and academic adjustment well, and this is true for both males and females and for various social classes and racial groups (Savin-Williams & Berndt, 1990). In one study, for example, teenagers were asked about various qualities of their friendships, and then this information was correlated with other factors. Those who reported having intimate and supportive friends in the fall tended to become more involved in school over time, while those whose friendships were conflicted became less involved (Berndt & Keefe, 1992). In short, good friendships and school adjustment seem to go hand in hand.

Nevertheless, the long-term consequences of having a stable close friend during adolescence is not clear. Some of the most hurtful, irrevocable injuries in life take place in the company of "friends" during adolescence. People do change, and during adolescence, particularly, maturation can take place at varied rates. It's possible that stability in friendship retards the growth of some and facilitates the growth of others (Bigelow & La Gaipa, 1980). Friends can sometimes interfere with, rather than facilitate, preparation for one's adult role (Csikszentmihalyi & Larson, 1984).

## Conclusion

What can we say about friendships during adolescence? First, adolescence is a time when peer relationships generally, and friendships in particular, take on added significance. We find also that friendships change systematically from early to later adolescence, and there are significant sex differences in the way these changes play out. Friendships during early adolescence tend to be activity centered. During middle adolescence, we see more emphasis on loyalty and security, and during later adolescence, the emphasis tends to be more on autonomous interdependence.

Crowds seem to provide the context for friendship, and within each crowd, we see cliques of varying degrees of exclusivity and stability who interact and hang out together—these we tend to think of as friends.

Friends during adolescence tend to be similar in many ways. They tend to be the same sex and the same race, and socioeconomic status plays a significant role in friendships as well. There is surprisingly little cutting across class lines.

Popularity is not the same as friendship. Popularity is measured unilaterally, while friendships are generally defined as reciprocal relationships. And as teenagers mature, the emphasis on popularity tends to give way to an emphasis on friendship.

Finally, one of the significant issues in adolescent adjustment is peer pressure. Conformity seems to be at a statistical high during middle adolescence. Although friendship during adolescence is generally associated with positive adjustment, it can have its negative side as well.

## Suggestions for Further Reading

Berndt, T. J. (1982). The features and effects of friendship in early adolescence. *Child Development, 53,* 1447–1460. An excellent article on early adolescent friendships.

Csikszentmihalyi, M., & Larson, R. (1984). *Being adolescent: Conflict and growth in the teenage years.* New York: Basic. A classic study of adolescents—authoritative, methodologically inventive, insightful, and well written.

Dunphy, D. C. (1963). The social structure of urban adolescent peer groups. *Sociometry, 26,* 230–246. Despite its age, this classic study of Australian youth is still informative.

Feldman, S. S., & Elliott, G. R. (Eds.). (1990). *At the threshold: The developing adolescent.* Cambridge, MA: Harvard University Press. An edited volume featuring articles by some of the leading authorities in the area of adolescence.

Gaines, S. O. (1994). Exchange and respect denying behaviors among male-female friendships. *Journal of Social and Personal Relationships, 11,* 5–24. Here's how opposite-sex friends remain "just friends."

Hetherington, E. M. (1972). Effects of father absence on personality development in adolescent daughters. *Developmental Psychology, 7,* 313–326. This study of the effects of father absence on teenage girls is a classic.

Laursen, B. (Ed.). (1993). *Close friendships in adolescence.* San Francisco: Jossey-Bass. A brief paperback featuring some excellent articles on adolescent friendship.

Montemayor, R., Adams, G. R., & Gullotta, T. P. (Eds.). (1994). *Personal relationships during adolescence.* Thousand Oaks, CA: Sage. An edited volume featuring articles on relationship continuity and change, relationships with parents and with crowds, romantic relationships, relationship issues among gay adolescents, and relationships between adolescents and adults.

# CHAPTER 8

## ✤ *Adult Friendships*

*They grew up in the same town and went to school together, but they did not get to know each other well until sometime later, when they found themselves attending the same church. Over time they became the closest of friends. They married, raised families, attended the weddings of each other's children, and gave baby showers for each other's grandchildren. They shared their feelings when one or the other's children got divorced. They comforted when one of their sons went off to Vietnam and did not return. When Caroline's husband died and her son became ill, her three friends baby-sat while she took classes, graduated from college, and went on to work in the library to support herself. Later when Myrtle's husband died, the others made sure she was not isolated. She was always included in their get-togethers. And when Edna had eye problems and could no longer drive, the others saw to it that she had transportation. And so they remain to this day. Four women, who had known each other only casually in high school, eventually formed friendships that have now lasted for well over four decades—friends in deed.*

The social circumstances of most adults differ significantly from those of adolescents. Adults tend to have more demands on their time and to devote more time to families and work than do young people. When the social interactions of adults and college students have been compared, for example, adults have been found to interact with more heterogeneous groups of others and spend less time with their friends (Blieszner & Adams, 1992).

## *Issues in Friendship During Adulthood*

In adulthood, friends are expected to share and keep confidences, to refrain from public criticism, to repay debts and favors, and to provide emotional support. They are expected to be loyal, open, and honest, to show warmth and affection, to trust and to be trustworthy, to share time and activities, to treat one another with respect, to value one another's company, to offer aid in time of need, and to work through any disagreements they might have (Argyle & Henderson, 1985; Davis & Todd, 1985; Hays, 1988; Parlee, 1979; Rubin, 1985).

## Defining and Measuring Friendship in Adulthood

One difficulty in the study of friendship in adulthood comes in trying to settle upon a workable definition. We know, for example, that both the young and the old spend more time interacting with friends than do middle-aged adults. We know that singles generally see their friends more often than do marrieds, and neighbors tend to see each other more often than do friends who live slightly farther apart (Reisman, 1979). For example, urban males tend to have more contact with neighbors and coworkers than with their closest friends (Jackson, 1977). Similarly, participants in a *Psychology Today* survey on friendship reported that close friends were often friends from childhood or from college whom they saw only infrequently (Parlee, 1979).

So, although friendship for children and adolescents can be described in terms of behavioral measures such as frequency and length of interactions, such measures are not particularly useful in describing adult friendships. For middle-class adults, especially, friendships can apparently remain intact over long distances and endure long periods of separation. Accordingly, the number and length of contacts seems to be less important in defining friendship for adults than for children or adolescents (Verbrugge, 1983). We see this illustrated in the case of Matt and Steve.

It had been several years since Matt and Steve had seen each other. And even though they both knew they would have dinner, talk a while, and then return to their separate lives, still, it was important to make time. So they walked along the river where they had both learned to swim as boys, where they caught their first fish, read comics, and smoked their first cigarettes. No mention was made of how different their lives had become (Steve was now a doctor, Matt a retired policeman). Now, both in their early 60s, that was set aside. They were back home for the holidays, and for the moment, they were once again two barefoot boys reminiscing and skipping rocks across the surface of the water—still best friends.

## Close Friends and Friendly Relationships

There are different kinds of friends, of course. Close friends convey a sense of caring, support, and ease of communication that makes them special (Hays, 1988). Close friends, especially those who have been friends for some time, enjoy each other's company and make a point of taking time for each other for no reason other than the relationship itself (Wright, 1984).

Friendly relationships, on the other hand, tend to involve interactions that are based not so much on affection or caring for the individual, as on a role

Close relationships, especially those that have lasted a long time, are ones in which the friends make it a point to take time for each other for no other reason than the relationship itself.

relationship, such as relationships between people who work in the same office, or who interact professionally or in business transactions (Kurth, 1970). When someone in such a relationship moves away, for example, a new friendly relationship is likely to develop with the person who takes his or her place.

What exactly leads relationships to become close, as opposed to remaining "friendly relationships," is still something of a mystery. Some relationships remain superficial, even over a long period of time (Babchuck & Bates, 1963). Indeed, there may be advantages in keeping relationships casual. Sometimes one person is interested in pursuing a close friendship and the other is not. The case of Deb and Margaret illustrates this point.

Deb and Margaret were both nurses in their early 40s. Both were divorced and both had grown children. Margaret was the charge nurse on Deb's unit, but the two got along well and shared many interests. One summer they even traveled to Italy together. Over time, however, it became clear that Margaret was interested in having more interaction and a closer relationship than Deb was. Deb liked her independence, and this began to cause a strain in their relationship.

One day, as Deb was checking her mail, she was shocked to find a letter telling her that, after 19 years at the hospital, she was being placed on probation and her performance was "being evaluated." She went to Margaret immediately and asked what was going on. Margaret responded only in vague generalities. But this was no joke, the hospital was in fact cutting staff. The evaluation went forward, Deb came through with flying colors, and her probation was lifted. Later, in airing their differences, it all became clear. It seems Margaret's daughter had been seriously ill, and Deb had not called. Deb never forgot what Margaret made her go through. Margaret had used her position as charge nurse to get back at her for not wanting to be closer friends. A year later Deb left the unit and took a new job.

## Special-Interest Friendships

Although the distinction between friendship and friendly relations is a common one in the literature, Barry McCarthy (1986) has suggested the need for an intermediate category in which friendships are not particularly deep or exclusive, on the one hand, nor merely role-based friendly relationships, on the other. In his study of various recreational groups (a fishing club, a local branch of a conservation organization, and a little theater group), McCarthy noted that although some of these relationships tended to be limited in scope, they were still "successful friendships" in that they were lasting. Of the 52 original friendship pairs in his study, 18 had been friends for over 10 years, and another 20 had been friends for at least 5 years.

The friends in McCarthy's study interacted frequently in what appeared to be well-established routines, and they did so with genuine affection. Yet there was little self-disclosure between them, and, indeed, McCarthy suggests that part of the success of these friendships came from avoiding the weightier matters of the world and the more intimate aspects of their lives. They were close, but not too close.

## Gender Differences in Friendships

There are notable differences in the way men and women relate to their friends. In general, women's friendships tend to involve more nurturing and emotional sharing, and men's friendships tend to involve shared activities (Wright, 1989).

Women view their friendships more positively than do men. They see their friends as dependable companions who are open, affectionate, and helpful. They often exchange favors. They respect each other (Rose, 1985; Wheeler et al., 1983). This approach to friendship seems to be true of women of all ages and many different cultures (Aukett et al., 1988; Wheeler et al., 1989). We see an example of this from the cross-cultural record in Box 8-1.

Women also tend to be more satisfied with their friendships than men. For example, among a group of professionals, ages 21 to 55 and over, older women rated their same-sex friendships highest, and young unmarried males rated theirs the lowest (Sapadin, 1988). Men generally express more satisfaction with their opposite-sex friendships; women are likely to be equally satisfied with their same-sex and opposite-sex friendships (Elkins & Peterson, 1993).

As suggested in the opening paragraph of this chapter, women generally

## Box 8-1 In a Different Key
## Women in Rural Taiwan

When a male is born into a family in rural Taiwan, his place is firmly established. But this is not true for females. One day she will leave her family of origin and become part of her husband's household. There she is likely to be treated with indifference, suspicion, and sometimes hostility by other family members. The relationships that are most meaningful to her psychologically are those she had with her mother and her brothers and sisters. But as she grows up, her brothers marry and the family dynamic begins to change. As her mother plans for the future, it is clear that she means the future of her sons, leaving the daughter with little in the way of family identity, loyalty, or obligation.

The daughter's ties with her family of origin are expressed symbolically when she marries. In the wedding ceremony, as the sedan chair in which she rides crosses the threshold of her father's house, the door is slammed behind her. If she lives nearby, she will likely continue to visit her mother, and when her mother dies, her relationship with her brother(s) remain(s). But, for all intents and purposes, she is now without a family. In her husband's household she is likely to be treated as an outsider. Her mother-in-law may be resentful, her sisters-in-law hostile. Her role is to bear and nurture the next generation of children.

Isolated and lonely, she is likely to turn to other women in the village. The needs, interests, and concerns she shares with other women provide a basis for forging a place in the social scheme of things. Women in rural Taiwan wash clothes together by the river, prepare vegetables together at the community pump, and sew and mend together. They visit each other's kitchens and carry on conversations through open doorways.

In establishing friendships with other women in the community, the new wife gains a certain place and a certain amount of influence. If she is poorly treated in her husband's household, she can now complain to others, and the court of public opinion will pass its judgment. Her story will spread first among the other women and, from them, to their husbands and sons. This discussion will serve to correct the offense.

Mothers are not likely to tell their daughters to form relationships with other women in order to increase their influence at home, but as they see other households settling their differences in order to avoid censure, they too turn to the company of women. For "face" is easily lost in rural Taiwan and once lost is not easily regained. When men behave badly, women talk. In this way they use their social network to influence their circumstances at home (Wolf, 1972).

see their friends as more supportive, especially in the emotional sphere. They also tend to have larger social support networks and receive more help from their friends than do men (Buhrke & Fuqua, 1987; Otten et al., 1988). Men are more likely to name women as important in offering social support than women are to mention men (Buhrke & Fuqua, 1987). And both men and women indicate that their friendships with women are more "therapeutic" (Aukett et al., 1988). These are modal patterns, of course. Exceptions have been reported (Caldwell & Peplau, 1982; Rose, 1985); but, in general, the findings on gender differences in friendship patterns have been consistent (Wright, 1989).

*Number and Types of Friends*   The findings on number of friends and gender, on the other hand, have been somewhat inconsistent. Michael Johnson and Leigh Leslie (1982) reported that college women generally have more friends than college men. Lawrence Weiss and Marjorie Lowenthal (1975) noted the same thing in a study of blue-collar families. However, Alan Booth and Elaine Hess (1974) found that white-collar males reported having more friends than did white-collar females, whereas blue-collar males and females reported having about the same number of friends.

It's possible that these inconsistencies are due to the tendency for men to use the term *friend* somewhat more loosely than women do (Nardi, 1992). Men tend to think of coworkers, neighbors, fellow carpoolers, and bowling buddies as friends, while women seem to use the term somewhat more selectively (Wright, 1982, 1989).

The difference comes through most clearly when studies distinguish between close and casual friends. For example, when Lilian Rubin (1985) asked those in her study about a "best friend," 75% of the single women indicated that they had a best friend, and typically this was another woman. Two thirds of the single men, on the other hand, could not name a best friend, and most of them did not seem to be bothered by the fact. For men who did have a best friend, it was often a woman. Only 10% of the men indicated that they had a close friendship with another male. Most of these men were not married or otherwise involved in a long-term heterosexual relationship. In contrast, Stacy Oliker (1989), in a study of best friends among women, found that such friendships were characterized by visits (a few times a week) and telephone calls (nearly everyday) for most friendship pairs.

One of the most interesting examples of gender differences in friendships came in a study by Roger Little (1990) who observed that, following the Korean conflict, "buddies" who had gone through combat together, who had lost comrades on the battlefield, and who had grieved together tended to look at this period in their lives as an exception—to see the relationships as transitory. They often promised to keep in touch when they returned home, but few did. Generally, when they left the battlefield, these friendships ended.

*Gender and the Social Network*   We also find differences in the way males and females interact with others in their social network. For example, in a study of dual-income families, Leigh Leslie (1989) found that the amount of social support obtained from sources outside the marriage seemed to contribute positively to the well-being of women, even when stress levels from other sources (such as their jobs) were high. But for men, this was not the case. The more embedded men were in their social networks, the more stress they felt. Social networks, then, apparently function somewhat differently for men and women. In times of stress, relationships with friends seem to be therapeutic for women in a way that they are not for men.

### Friendships and the Workplace

Because the work environment figures so prominently in the everyday lives of many adults, it becomes something of a network of "friends." These subcultures tend to develop their own traditions, stories, jokes, and jargon. On the job, similar socioeconomic status, educational levels, and life circumstances (for example, single parent) tend to provide a "level field" on which relationships are played out.

Friendly relations characterize many relationships in the workplace. These tend to have the minimal affective quality necessary for smooth and uncomplicated interactions. Indeed, getting along with coworkers is often necessary for promotion (Fine, 1986). In some cases, jobs are complementary; for example, in a restaurant the server's tips depend very much on the quality of the meals prepared by the chef. Workers often "cover" for each other, sometimes formally, sometimes informally. Production workers, even when their performance is not dependent on each other, tend to adopt a code of ethics against "rate busters"—a practice that generates a measure of solidarity among workers. Those who do not "cooperate" typically find themselves isolated.

So, in the workplace, people tend to interact with each other in a friendly manner, and some of them become close friends. And this presents an important issue for friendships in the workplace. On the one hand, relationships in the workplace have an instrumental quality about them, and, on the other hand, friendships are generally considered voluntary and free of instrumental qualities (Wright, 1984).

It is generally easier to maintain friendships when workers are of equal status. Friends at work tend to be peers (they hold positions at about the same level) rather than supervisors or subordinates (Winstead et al., 1995). Still, friendships with higher-ups can benefit those who are upwardly mobile within the organization. They must decide between associating with their old friends and cultivating relationships with higher-ups, however. And, generally, the choice is clear. When workers are promoted within an organization, they usually drop their old friends (Feld, 1984).

In addition, as men and women find themselves in close proximity in the workplace, and at similar levels of responsibility, it is increasingly likely that they will develop relationships that are more personal. Some of these are defined as "mentor relationships," and the importance of such relationships for career advancement has been well documented (Levinson, 1978). But a senior male acting as a mentor to a younger female can generate a great deal of gossip throughout an organization. Curious onlookers are likely to assume that when a male and female are seen together on a frequent basis there is more to their relationship than appears on the organization charts.

So, although the workplace is a natural environment for friendships to develop and flourish, and although the commonality of purpose legitimizes (if it does not force) close interactions, it is easy for such relationships to involve more than company business. And such extracurricular considerations seem to figure more strongly in some circumstances than in others.

For example, in a study comparing faculty and staff friendships in two university settings, Barbara Winstead and colleagues (1995) found that the quality of best friendships in the workplace was generally predictive of job satisfaction. But, interestingly enough, maintenance difficulty (for example, time and effort necessary in ironing out misunderstandings and disagreements) seemed to operate differently for faculty and staff. It was inversely related to job satisfaction among staff, but not for faculty. Winstead and colleagues suggest that the intrinsically rewarding quality of work for faculty, and greater control over their time and work space, may make interpersonal relationships in the workplace less salient.

Thus, each workplace not only has its own traditions, norms, and values, it also has its own set of problems. And as the context changes, so does the meaning and significance of relationships.

## Adult Friendships Across the Age Range

"To everything there is a season" seems to be especially true in the case of personal relationships. Where people are in the life cycle influences both the types of relationships they are likely to pursue and the types of relationships that are likely to be encouraged by others.

Although age plays a role in adult friendship patterns, just as it does earlier in life, it seems not to be as important as *life transitions*. Marriage, children, children leaving home ("empty nest"), divorce, retirement, widowhood, and health complications are likely to determine friendship patterns in adulthood more than age per se (Litwak, 1989).

Generally, the importance placed on friendships tends to decrease after adolescence (McCandless, 1970). Interest in pursuing friendships tends to wane by about age 30, except for people who have experienced disruptions in their other relationships due to such things as divorce, a change of residence, or the death of a spouse (Reisman, 1981). In such cases, people often make an effort to get back into circulation by pursuing friendships that have been allowed to lapse.

During maturity and middle age, the demands and obligations of marriage, family, and career come first for most adults. Married adults with children indicate having the lowest frequency of interaction with their friends (Fischer & Philips, 1982). In old age the importance of friendship seems to reemerge, especially when retirement and (possibly) bereavement affect other relationships in one's life (Argyle, 1987).

Even after a long separation, friendships often remain intact. The number and length of contacts seems less important in defining the friendship for adults than it does for children and adolescents.

## Friendships Among Young Adults

In our society, young adults (between the ages of about 20 and 30) are confronted with such tasks as finishing their education, launching careers, pursuing romantic relationships, choosing a marriage partner, and beginning a family. This is not a light agenda. Research suggests that, during this time, the amount of interaction with friends is likely to depend very much on the state of one's other relationships (Hause, 1995).

*Single Adults*   Single adults in the United States typically have a lot of freedom. Whether they remain in school or join the workforce, there is very little conflict between what society prescribes and what the demands of friendship require. Coworkers, colleagues, fellow students, and others with whom they routinely come in contact constitute the pool from which single adults are likely to form their friendships (Huston & Levinger, 1978). Both single males and females typically have a large number of friends during young adulthood (Fischer & Oliker, 1983; Reisman, 1981; Verbrugge, 1983).

On the other hand, when love is in bloom, friends are expected to accept the fact that romance takes priority over other relationships. Romantic interests have a preemptive quality about them that forces others to understand, perhaps because they have experienced the same thing, and perhaps because they have no other choice (Rubin, 1985). Similarly, when college beckons, friends leave home (Shaver et al., 1985). When job offers and promotions mean relocating, friendships are likely to be disrupted.

Accordingly, we find that friendships during young adulthood tend to be quite transient. In the *Psychology Today* survey on friendship (Parlee, 1979), for example, the reason most often cited for the end of friendships was "moving." Friends of young adults on the move are likely to come from the neighborhood and the workplace (Newman & Newman, 1975). Newly formed friendships during this period are often considered temporary from the outset. A clear example of this came in a study by Joan Starker and colleagues (1993). They found that after relocating, most "movers" had a functioning network of friends and acquaintances within 3 months, but only about 25% of the friends named at 3 months were named again at 6 and 21 months. In other words there is, among "movers," some evidence for transitional friendships.

Even when romantic relationships and family life are entirely satisfactory, they take place against a backdrop of relationships with relatives, neighbors, work associates, and friends, which seems to constitute something of a social "ecosystem" (La Gaipa, 1981). And the evidence suggests that this broader social network is more important than is sometimes assumed.

***Couples Versus Single Life***    In her interviews with newlyweds, Kimberly Hause (1995) found that they routinely indicated nothing had changed with regard to their premarriage friends, but when they got down to specifics, things had changed considerably. On average, contacts with friends decreased by about 50%. Males, especially, tended to lose their single friends as the new couples turned more and more to their mutual friends, and these tended to be other couples.

Single friends of the newly married sometimes become disgruntled because their long-time buddies can no longer find time to go bowling, go camping, go out for a drink, shop, take in a movie, talk endlessly on the phone, or simply drop everything and go to the shore like they used to. We see this illustrated in the case of Red and Tim.

Red had never given much thought to the idea that once Tim was married his priorities would change. He kept stopping by on the spur of the moment, as he always had, staying until the wee hours of the night, and suggesting things that they might do together. This continued for some time, and finally Tim met him on the porch one evening and said, "Red, you have to understand I'm a married man now. I can't just go running off all the time." Red was completely unprepared for this. He had no idea that his stopping by was a problem.

For a newly married couple, activities with other married couples are likely to be seen as validating their identity as a couple, whereas activities with their single friends tend to be seen as more diversionary. Other couples understand and appreciate the constraints of married life and are less likely than single friends to make demands that are intrusive. As a consequence, young marrieds tend to fashion a social life that is more and more "coupled" (Rubin, 1985).

***Parents With Young Children***    Friendship patterns are likely to change again when children arrive on the scene. Children bring with them certain "nonnegotiables" (for example, baby's feeding schedule) that make it easier (and cheaper) to develop a home-centered social life. Young couples, during the family-building stage, are likely to find themselves pursuing an agenda that essentially shuts out their uncoupled friends by default. Friends are required to accommodate to the family, rather than vice versa, and friendships at this stage tend to be pursued and encouraged, when they are, because of their consolidating effect on marriage and family.

As long as there are children at home, the social agenda is likely to be determined (in large part) by their activities. Parents of young children have to transport them, take in sports events, attend school concerts, go to PTA meetings, and so on. And in all of these activities, they meet other parents with children about the same age, going through the same thing. As children become more independent, however, more time is available to parents to pursue their own interests.

## Friendships During Maturity and Middle Age

Although the coupled life satisfies important needs, it is not necessarily enough (Weiss, 1973). For most couples, married life has both its fulfilling and its stifling sides. Thus, after the children are of an age to stay comfortably by themselves, and life has settled into something of a routine, interest in cultivating friendships reemerges, at least for some adults.

At this point, age does not seem to have the significance that it did earlier in determining friendships. Friendships among adults at maturity (between about 30 and 40) and middle age (between about 40 and 60 or 65) often involve a wider age range than those of younger adults (Rosow, 1968). For those who are content with (or resigned to) their friendship networks, and whose life circumstances are not likely to change dramatically, social life tends to settle into a routine, such as "bridge on Tuesday, bowling on Thursday." Such individuals are not likely to be in the friendship market any more than they are likely to be interested in a new career, a new house, or a new club. On the other hand, those whose life circumstances are disrupted in some way, such as the divorced or the recently transferred, are likely to have a greater interest in forming new friendships.

For some, this is a time of taking stock. Those who tend to be introspective look out at the society around them and shudder at its shallowness. Divorce, death, and the fragmentation of relationships remind them daily that even the best-laid plans can go awry. And one day there comes a watershed moment when they begin to measure time not so much in terms of how long they have lived but in how long they have left. For some, this can be rather disquieting. This sense of having "one last shot" leads some to go off in unlikely directions—to new jobs, new hobbies, new locations, and new spouses. Middle age is also a time when relationships are likely to be reviewed and those found unsuitable, weeded out (Hunt & Hunt, 1975).

Some authors suggest that at this time of life there is less interest in social interactions generally and a preference for fewer close friends (Bischof, 1976).

Others suggest that middle age is second only to adolescence in terms of making friends (Hunt & Hunt, 1975). Something all agree on, however, is that there are gender differences.

*Gender Differences in Mature Adults' Friendships*    Something in the world of the middle-aged male seems to stifle friendship. Possibly in response to career demands and the competitive climate that this often generates, men during this period seem to have fewer friends and have less contact with those friends (Fischer & Oliker, 1983; Levinson, 1978; Reisman, 1981; Verbrugge, 1983).

In his interviews, for example, Daniel Levinson (1978) found that friendship among middle-aged men was largely noticeable for its absence. Men sometimes have friendly relationships with other men and perhaps a few women, casual dating relationships with women, and perhaps complex love affairs, but most do not have the kind of relationship with another male friend that we see for other age groups, nor are they likely to have an intimate nonsexual friendship with a woman.

For women, on the other hand, the tendency to form and maintain friendships seems to persist through the life span (Candy et al., 1981). Women seem to have the ability to mix friendship and other responsibilities—including marriage, family, and work—in a way that men do not (Aries & Johnson, 1983; Hunter et al., 1983; Rubin, 1985).

*Mature Singles*    What is it like to be unattached as an adult? In general, it seems to be neither as good nor as bad as conventional wisdom would have us believe (Cargan & Melko, 1982). Overall, marrieds tend to be happier. Singles, especially the divorced, are more lonely. But there is some indication that the association between marriage and happiness is not as strong today as it once was. For example, in their review of national surveys conducted between 1972 and 1986, Norval Glenn and Charles Weaver (1988) found that the "happiness gap" between marrieds and never marrieds seemed to be narrowing, especially for males between the ages of 25 and 29. In surveys conducted between 1972 and 1976, married men were more than twice as likely as never-married males to indicate that they were "very happy." For surveys taken between 1982 and 1986, the difference was only 5.7 percentage points. Still, although being single is increasingly accepted in our society (Thornton, 1989), the coupled life is still considered the norm for most adults (Ganong et al., 1990).

The pattern of friendships for mature singles is likely to be determined largely by their resources, the presence or absence of dependent children, and the fact that they are "unattached." For both single men and women, friends and an active social life are associated with happiness (Freedman, 1978). In contrast, friends and an active social life are relatively unimportant in predicting happiness among married couples.

Both males and females who are not married are likely to find their social options limited, and as a consequence, they tend to spend more time with relatives. In this respect, the widowed and the divorced share a common social fate. The initial attention of sympathetic friends tends to wane over time.

In some respects, single women seem to have it worse than single men (Rubin, 1985, 1986). They suffer more in the way of cultural stereotypes. Women tend to value and desire marriage more than men do, and single women who want to marry are likely to have fewer opportunities. For example, women 40 and over face a demographic disadvantage. As members of the baby boomers, they are especially likely to be caught in a marriage squeeze (more eligible women than men). Among marrieds, husbands are typically 2–3 years older than their wives, but older men who remarry tend to marry women who are 5–8 years younger. So single men seem to have it easier both in the way they are perceived and in terms of marriage (or remarriage) possibilities.

Among the better educated and financially well-off single women, we often see a small circle of friends who travel, socialize, go to cultural events together, and come to one another's aid in times of crisis, but there seems to be no similar pattern among single men (Rubin, 1985). Unattached males, on the other hand, are likely to have a somewhat wider range of options—they are often sought after socially. But, unlike their female counterparts, they are likely to have more acquaintances than friends.

## Friendships Among Adults 65 and Over

Although the later years offer freedom from many obligations and afford opportunities to form new friendships and rejuvenate old ones, older adults (those 65 and over) also face issues and constraints that do not (ordinarily) affect the young (Adams, 1987; Allan & Adams, 1989; Blieszner, 1989; Chown, 1981). Among these are retirement, widowhood, health problems, living on fixed incomes, relocation, and problems of transportation. Taken together, these factors suggest that friendship patterns among older adults are likely to show considerable diversity. And this is what we find.

For example, in a study of 1,200 adults aged 62 and over, Irving Rosow (1968) found that some had rather few friends, and that's the way they preferred it. Others seemed to have an unquenchable thirst for more friends, even though they already had a relatively large number. The majority of those in the study tended to lead active social lives.

Similarly, a 3-year study of middle-class older women revealed various patterns of friendship networks as well (Adams, 1987). Some women had expanding friendship networks. Others showed a contracting pattern, and still others indicated an increase in the number of friends who remained somewhat distant emotionally.

On the other hand, complete social isolation among older adults seems to be relatively rare. For example, only 4% of Rosow's (1968) sample reported having no friends. These individuals had few contacts with their neighbors and did not wish to have more. And, similarly, in a study of adults 65 and over, Eric Pfeiffer (1977) found that only 9% were socially isolated, and these tended to be individuals who had failed to develop new friendships with the passing of their old ones.

It seems fair to say that the friendship patterns of older adults differ widely, and although some people are socially isolated, many have both the motivation and ability to develop new friendships.

*Gender Differences in Older Adults' Friendships*   For older women, the empty nest typically leads to a decrease in obligations and responsibilities and leaves more time to devote to friendships. Women whose children have left home are freer to follow their social inclinations, which often means spending more time with friends and developing new ones.

But reports on gender differences among older adults, both in terms of the number of friends and frequency of contact with them, have been somewhat conflicting. Some studies have reported that men have more friends and more frequent contacts with those friends (Ferraro et al., 1984). Alan Booth (1972), however, found evidence for a somewhat greater number of friends among older women, and Claude Fischer and Stacy Oliker (1983) reported that the number of friends for men tended to decrease with age, and in the age group 65 and older, women tended to have more friends.

A point on which there is general agreement, however, is that older women have more friends in whom they confide, and their friends tend to be closer and more intimate (Booth, 1972; Powers & Bultena, 1976; Roberto & Scott, 1986). Older men seem to confide almost exclusively in their wives (Keith et al., 1984). Opposite-sex friendships among older adults seem to be rare (Chown, 1981).

*Similarity and Proximity*   Friends among older adults tend to be similar in age, sex, marital status, and socioeconomic circumstances. Those who are retired are particularly likely to have friends drawn from the same age group and socioeconomic status (Chown, 1981). On the other hand, differences in social and economic background tend to be muted in institutional settings such as retirement homes (Retsinas & Garrity, 1985).

Furthermore, although friendships for middle-class young and middle-aged adults are not particularly constrained by proximity, this is not the case for older adults. Physical proximity reemerges as one of the important determinants of whether or not older adults become friends. In one study, for example, the number of friends reported by the elderly was determined largely by the number of people of similar age in the same apartment building and the same block (Rosow, 1976).

A study of older adults in New York City found that, overall, the number of friends tended to depend on the "match" of an individual with those close by (Blau, 1961). A widowed person among a group of marrieds was likely to feel socially isolated, even among age mates. And, somewhat surprisingly, the same was true for marrieds—married couples living in an area where most others were widowed tended to feel socially isolated.

Elderly people report seeing friends who are nearby most frequently, often more frequently than relatives (Lawton, 1977). And friendships across age, race, and gender also tend to be found most often when people live in close proximity (Nahemow & Lawton, 1975), especially among the working class (Rosow, 1967).

*Retirement*    Traditionally, retirement has affected men and women differently. Among those currently reaching retirement age, men have tended to identify more closely with their occupational role than have women. For men, freedom from work and professional responsibilities allows increased time for friends, but at the same time, it often means the loss of relationships associated with the world of work. Given the tendency for men to form activity-centered friendships, retirement raises the issue of whether these lost work relationships will be replaced and, if so, how (Wright, 1989). The loss of work-related contacts seems to be particularly an issue for those in the working class. Working-class males are less likely to have pursued relationships outside the work setting (Allan, 1979).

Women currently reaching retirement age are less likely to have worked outside the home, and, accordingly, the repercussions of retirement for them tend to be less dramatic. Many of their day-to-day activities and interests remain the same. Although loss of employment contacts can decrease relationships for women as well, the identity of older women tends to be less closely tied to employment.

Overall, the evidence suggests that although retirement may cut off certain

Retirement can offer the opportunity to extend both activities and friendships.

avenues of socializing, it does not, by itself, limit sociability or friendship. People both make and lose friends in retirement (Adams, 1987; Jerrome, 1981). For those with the wherewithal, the increased time and flexibility of retirement offer the opportunity to extend both their activities and their friendship networks, especially for those whose earlier life and professional skills made them adept at social relationships.

*Old Friends/New Friends*    Some studies have found that older adults prefer old friends to new ones. For example, older adults with ties to a given neighborhood are reluctant to leave (Langford, 1962). And when older adults relocate, those who are least satisfied with their new circumstances are the ones who have friends in their old location with whom they can no longer keep in touch.

On the other hand, when Laurie Shea and her colleagues (1988) studied the effect of moving to a retirement community on friendship patterns, they found that old friendships tended to remain stable and newly developed ones increased in both affection and exchange of resources. At the same time, however, there were clear differences between the old and new friendships. Information exchanged with new friends tended to focus more on current events, whereas exchanges with old friends tended to involve reminiscing and self-disclosure.

Old friends helped each other in times of need, but such exchanges were less characteristic of relationships with new friends. With new friends, there was much more concern over reciprocity, and although indications of love and affection were generally taken for granted among old friends, these had to be expressed in the case of new friends.

Along these same lines, Rosemary Blieszner (1989) described findings from a study involving new residents in a retirement community. After 5 months, participants in her study rated old friends higher in terms of trust and liking than new friends. And although they saw themselves as likely to provide assistance regardless of how close a friend might be, the reverse was not true. They saw their old friends and newer *close* friends as more likely to offer assistance. Indeed, accounts of actual behavior corresponded to their expectations.

*Widowhood*    Those who are widowed early in life are more likely to be socially isolated simply because most of their age mates are still married. Those who are widowed closer to the average age of widowhood have a larger pool of eligible friends to draw upon. But widowhood need not bring a complete break with one's married friends. Many people whose spouses have died continue to see friends who are still in couples. These relationships now tend to be different, and interactions tend to be less frequent, however (Lopata, 1979). For the widowed, friendships with married couples are most likely to decline if the relationship had revolved primarily around the other spouse.

The psychological well-being of widows seems to be correlated with the support and companionship of friends in complex ways. For example, Elizabeth Bankoff (1990) compared two groups of widows—the recently widowed (18 months or less) and those widowed 2–5 years. These periods she referred to as the "crisis loss phase" and the "transition phase," respectively. For those in the crisis loss phase, well-being was closely tied to the companionship of friends and their friends' *lack of approval* of their new lifestyle. Apparently, although companionship and intimate ties continued to play a role in the well-being of these widows, approval of their new lifestyle was negatively associated with their well-being.

After 2 to 5 years of widowhood, Bankoff found that friends, companionship, intimacy, and the lack of assurance in their friends' dependability was associated with positive well-being. Paradoxically, knowing that their friends could always be counted upon had a negative effect on the widows' long-term well-being. Why would this be?

Although support from friends is important, over the long term, it seems that the widowed can become too dependent on such support, and their long-term adjustment can suffer as a consequence. As in many areas of life, the principle of "no pain, no gain" may apply to the adjustment of widows to their new social circumstances.

## Is There a Downside to Friendship in Adulthood?

Before leaving the topic, we should note that friendships in adulthood can have a negative side. The comfort level that people attain within the cocoon of friendship can inhibit their ability or willingness to grow. A number of investigators have noted that networks of close friends can stifle efforts to change, accept challenge, and cope with the new and unexpected (Hirsch, 1980).

William Rawlins (1983a, 1983b), for example, has looked at friendship in terms of the interplay of forces such as independence and interdependence, expressive tendencies and protective tendencies, interdependence and the contradictory sense of threat and vulnerability, and the need for some balance between too much security and too little. In these respects, casual friendships sometimes provide the advantage of distance, perspective, objectivity, and challenge that close friendships may not (Hays, 1988).

The tension between too much security and too little was illustrated in a study by Jill Suitor (1987), who focused on the changes in interaction patterns of women returning to college in their adult years. Suitor noted that as less time became available for their old friends (who incidentally tended not to be encouraging of their returning to college), these relationships became progressively more difficult to maintain compared to friendships with their new college friends. Part-time returning students, on the other hand, seemed able to maintain friendships with their old friends; for them, it was the relationships with their new friends that suffered.

So, the need to be accepted by one's friends can lead people to act in ways that, however gratifying they may be in the short run, are not particularly wise in the long run. Friendship networks can be insulating, and this insulation can lead to decisions that are more comfortable and less challenging than the individuals might make if they were acting more independently (Hays, 1988).

## Conclusion

What should we conclude concerning friendships during adulthood? First, young adults, mature and middle-aged adults, and older adults pursue friendships in significantly different ways. The state of one's marital and family obligations seems to be a major factor in determining how much time is available for friends.

In addition, there are identifiable differences in the friendship patterns of males and females. However, although such differences have been found often enough that they are by now well established, their significance is another matter. For most purposes, the kinds of experiences and interactions that take place in virtually all friendships are much the same whether those friendships are between two women, two men, or a man and a woman. Gender differences in adult friendship patterns are a matter of degree. They are not polar opposites. Further, as with many statistical differences, there is considerable overlap between men's and women's friendships.

The role that friends play during adulthood seems to depend largely on the state of one's other personal relationships. Marrieds, especially marrieds with children, and singles show quite different friendship patterns. Friends tend to take a back seat to family life during young adulthood and much of maturity and middle age as well. During old age, however, there is some indication that the importance given to friendships increases, at least for some.

Finally, it's important to note that friendships during adulthood can have a stifling effect as well as a supporting one. It's possible to reach a comfort level with a network of friends that inhibits rather than facilitates growth and adapting to change.

## Suggestions for Further Reading

Adams, R. G., & Blieszner, R. (Eds.). (1989). *Older adult friendship*. Newbury Park, CA: Sage. A short edited volume featuring issues-oriented chapters by well-known researchers in the area.

Aries, E. J., & Johnson, F. L. (1983). Close friendships in adulthood: Conversational content between same-sex friends. *Sex Roles, 9,* 1183–1197. What do people talk about with their friends?

Blieszner, R., & Adams, R. G. (1992). *Adult friendship*. Newbury Park, CA: Sage. A brief, highly readable overview of adult friendship.

Lopata, H. Z., & Maines, D. R. (Eds.). (1990). *Friendship in context*. Greenwich, CT: JAI Press. An edited volume featuring chapters by leading researchers in the area. Bankoff's chapter about the effects of friends' support on the psychological well-being of widows and Little's account of friendship in the military are particularly recommended.

McCarthy, B. (1986). Friendship behaviors and perceptions. In R. Gilmour & S. Duck (Eds.), *The emerging field of personal relationships*. Hillsdale, NJ: Erlbaum. A study of three recreational groups and the types of friendships they generate.

Nardi, P. M. (Ed.). (1992). *Men's friendships*. Newbury Park, CA: Sage. The best single source for an overview of the issues in male friendships.

Levinson, D. J. (1978). *The seasons of a man's life*. New York: Knopf. In-depth interviews reveal the dearth of friendships among middle-aged males.

Parlee, M. B. (1979, October). The friendship bond. *Psychology Today, 43–54*, 113. Summary article on a massive questionnaire study on friendship among *Psychology Today* readers.

Reisman, J. M. (1981). Adult friendships. In S. W. Duck & R. Gilmour (Eds.), *Personal relationship, 2: Developing personal relationships*. New York: Academic. Despite its age, this overview of adult friendships provides an excellent introduction to the area.

Rubin, L. B. (1985). *Just friends: The role of friendship in our everyday lives*. New York: Harper & Row. Accessible to the layperson, yet subtle in its analysis, this is one of the best-written books on friendship.

Suitor, J. J. (1987). Friendship networks in transition: Married mothers return to school. *Journal of Social and Personal Relationships, 4*, 445–461. Old friendships experience strain when married women return to school.

# CHAPTER 9

## ❧ *Stigma and Disability*

*Suppose you are the owner of a small real estate business. Things are going well, and you are expanding to a new office and hiring a receptionist. Two candidates come to interview. The first is a pleasant, attractive person with average qualifications who is new to the community. The second is a delightful, friendly woman who has experience, is a longtime resident of the community, and types 90 words a minute. However, she weighs approximately 250 pounds. The thought goes through your mind: Is this the first person I want potential clients to see when they walk in the door? What kind of an impression will this create? Would she turn potential customers off? Could she hurt business just when things seem to be going so well? And so you are faced with a dilemma: Hire the more qualified candidate despite her obesity, or hire the less qualified but slimmer, more attractive applicant. What do you do?*

The word *stigma* comes from the Greek and originally referred to the practice of branding slaves who had been caught trying to escape (Funk, 1950). Since that time its meaning has broadened to apply to anyone who is "marked" in a way that society considers flawed, limited, deviant, undesirable, or spoiled in some way (E. E. Jones et al., 1984). The effects of stigma go beyond the "mark" itself, however, and like all prejudices, stigmatizing carries with it the tendency to treat the other differently, usually less humanely (Crandall & Coleman, 1992; Rodin & Price, 1995).

How does stigma affect personal relationships? What about relationships in the workplace? Are personal relationships different for younger people who are stigmatized than for adults? What about the "spread of stigma" from the one who is stigmatized to other family members? What happens to friendships that center around a particular activity (such as bowling) that becomes impossible due to disability? Are such relationships likely to be abandoned? We don't have the answers to all these questions, and some have more than one answer. Indeed, scholars in the area generally agree that the experiences of the stigmatized are diverse. There is as much variability in the adjustment of the stigmatized and the responses of others as there are people with different types of stigmatizing conditions (Gibbons, 1986).

## Effects of Stigma

Stigma has three kinds of effects. First, there is the direct impact of the condition itself—for example, the economic impact, activity restrictions on work and leisure, and the time and effort associated with caretaking in the case of the disabled. Second, there is the problem of psychological asymmetry in relating to others. The stigmatized, by definition, tend to be looked down upon. And third, there is the subjective feeling associated with being different. In short, the stigmatized are likely to experience **objective consequences, interpersonal consequences,** and **psychological consequences** (French, 1984).

### The "Marked" Versus the "Markable"

Conditions that are potentially stigmatizing are not always obvious to the casual observer. For example, patients who have undergone electroconvulsive shock therapy for depression have no outward signs of their condition. Such people are sometimes described as "markable" rather than "marked." In these cases, Erving Goffman (1963) has distinguished between **known-about-ness** (whether others have been informed of a potentially stigmatizing condition independent of its visibility), **obtrusiveness** (the extent to which a condition interferes with the normal flow of interactions), and the **limitations** that the condition imposes in a particular sphere. Diabetics, for example, can choose not to "go public" with their condition; its known-about-ness can ordinarily be restricted to a few intimate friends and loved ones.

People in wheelchairs, on the other hand, have little choice about whether others know of their condition. Although their mobility is limited, their condition is not obtrusive when they are sitting at a conference table or talking on the telephone. On the other hand, for people with a facial disfigurement, the obtrusiveness of their condition in face-to face interactions is more of a factor than is sitting in a wheelchair.

Known-about-ness, obtrusiveness, and limitation are different aspects of potentially stigmatizing conditions, and they can vary independently of one another. An example of this was given in the opening paragraph of the chapter. What does research have to say on the matter? For some thoughts on this, turn to Box 9-1.

### "Passing"

Face-lifts, nose jobs, breast implants, orthodontics, weight reduction programs, contact lenses, prostheses, acne medications, and a multibillion-dollar

---

### Box 9-1 In a Different Key
### Stigma and Obesity

Obese individuals are stigmatized in U.S. society. This was clearly demonstrated in an experiment by Mary Harris (1990). In this study a female was depicted as being of normal weight, under one condition, or (by wearing extra clothing) as being overweight, in the other. Participants were asked to evaluate such things as her self-esteem and the likelihood of her dating or being married. The results showed that when she was depicted as obese, she was judged to be lower in self-esteem and less likely to be dating or married.

The impact that the evaluations of others can have was further demonstrated in a study by Carol Miller and colleagues (1990). In this study females who were either obese or nonobese en-

gaged in conversations over the telephone. Based on these telephone conversations alone, with no information about their weight, students on the other end of the line rated the obese subjects as less likable, less socially skilled, and less attractive.

The implications of being overweight can be far reaching. For example, college students who are overweight, especially females, tend to receive less financial help from home (Crandall, 1991). This is true regardless of the financial circumstances of the parents or the number of children in the family. And in the business world, research suggests that people are likely to make approximately $1,000 less annually for every pound they are overweight (Kolata, 1992).

---

cosmetic industry all testify to the human tendency to try to fix anything that might detract from one's social desirability. Indeed, entire medical specialties are dedicated to plastic and reconstructive surgery. So we should not be surprised to find that the markable who can, sometimes try to "pass." **Passing** is an effort to hide a stigmatizing condition. For example, people with epilepsy whose seizures can be controlled with medications tend to reveal their condition to very few people (Kleck, 1968). Passing has also been reported among illiterates (Freeman & Kassebaum, 1956) and people who are hard of hearing (Higgins, 1980). For people who pass, initial encounters, at least, can be relatively normal.

The advantages of passing go beyond immediate circumstances. For example, in their study of people with epilepsy, Ernest Rodin and colleagues (1977) found that those whose symptoms were "uncomplicated" by outward signs of neurological impairment led fairly normal lives and were significantly better off socially than were those whose symptoms were more noticeable. Similarly, when Richard Goldberg (1974a) compared the adjustment of children with facial scars to the adjustment of children with congenital heart disease, he found that those with congenital heart disease were better adjusted socially. Visible marks that involve very little in the way of physical limitation can have profound effects interpersonally (Goldberg, 1974a, 1974b). Even facial deformities that have been corrected through plastic surgery often leave their mark long after the deformity is gone (Rodin & Price, 1995).

Sometimes the issue of visibility can be quite subtle. For example, Sister Anne Felice (1977) noted that college students from the lower castes in India were stigmatized by those from the upper castes, even though to the casual observer their "condition" was not evident.

Furthermore, known-about-ness has different consequences in different situations. The mildly retarded who are marked during their school years often simply disappear into the general population as adults (Gottlieb, 1975), when the label no longer serves any purpose. Some of the ramifications of this difference for personal relationships are interesting. For example, mentally retarded people, after being released from the hospital, try to avoid being identified as retarded in an effort to integrate more easily into the community (Edgerton, 1967). One form that such efforts take is to steer clear of others who are retarded, which has significant effects upon these people's immediate social networks.

Passing, then, can sometimes allow people who are markable to function in the mainstream of everyday life. But in so doing they must be careful to avoid associations with anyone similarly "afflicted" (Gibbons, 1986). In addition, they must avoid certain social services associated with the stigmatizing condition and those who frequent them. Thus, by passing, the stigmatized show some of the same ambivalence toward the stigmatized as do the nonstigmatized (Goffman, 1963). We see an example of this in people with AIDS.

The difference between the objective facts of a stigmatizing condition and its psychological and social consequences is vividly illustrated in the case of people diagnosed as HIV positive. HIV (human immunodeficiency virus) is a condition associated with already stigmatized groups such as homosexuals and intravenous drug users. People in the general population who have negative attitudes toward gays tend to view HIV and AIDS as immoral, disgusting, dirty, and the punishment of God for homosexuality (Pryor et al., 1989). Furthermore, these attitudes extend to people with AIDS in the heterosexual population, including children. Approximately half of a representative sample of Americans agreed that most of those with AIDS have no one to blame but themselves for contracting the disease (Gallup poll, 1987). And efforts to change such attitudes seem to be largely ineffective (Pryor et al., 1991).

The impact of dual stigmas like AIDS is especially important when it comes to social support. Because AIDS has significantly increased the health risk of many in the homosexual community, some have responded by keeping their sexual orientation secret and their contacts clandestine. For homosexuals, seeking support in itself can be threatening. Disclosure of an HIV-positive diagnosis sometimes leads to loss of support from family and friends and loss of employment (Altman, 1986). For example, Christian Crandall and Robert Coleman (1992) found in their study of individuals who had been diagnosed HIV positive that 17% indicated having less social support following their diagnosis.

Finally, passing in some cases is easier and less complicated than it is in others. Consider the case of Wendy and Josh.

Wendy and Josh met in college and had been going together since their sophomore year. One evening, out of the clear blue sky, Wendy said, "Josh, we have to talk." "Fine," said Josh, a bit puzzled. "What do you want to talk about?" "Us," said Wendy, looking at him seriously. "I know we've joked around a lot about, you know, getting married and having kids and all that, but there is something you need to know." She paused and took a deep breath. "My dad's been in and out of the hospital with schizophrenia. My grandfather was schizophrenic. I have an uncle who is schizophrenic, a cousin, and a nephew who is probably schizophrenic. You keep talking like you want to get married and have kids, well, married, yes. Kids, no. I could be a carrier, Josh. I'm not going to take the chance of being the mother of a schizophrenic child. No way. So, if you want out, now is the time."

### Deviance Disavowal

Even when visibly afflicted, it is not uncommon for the marked to seek ways of disavowing the limitations of their condition. One such case came to my attention some years ago. A blind student attending our school was absolutely insistent upon negotiating the physical environment completely unaided. He memorized the campus geography, used no cane or guide dog, and continually refused offers of help. During his years in college, he was seen walking full tilt into the side of a parked car, into the railing for the handicapped, not to mention various and sundry chairs; and, most memorable of all, he typed an entire essay with his hands displaced one place to the right on the keyboard.

So it is with us all. We tend to conceal or deny anything that might detract from our desirability. When we do this, we keep the personal limitation from becoming a social issue. Although this concealment might seem like common sense, it does not necessarily make sense in terms of overall adjustment.

Trying to hide a stigmatizing condition comes at a price, and usually the effort is doomed (Wright, 1983). The hard facts of life impose themselves sooner or later; meanwhile the constant tax in defensive measures imposes a second handicap on top of the first.

What, then, can we say to those who suggest that suppressing the problem is one of the most adaptive responses to disability? Some researchers, such as Beatrice Wright (1983), are skeptical, but there is some evidence that the effect of suppression may vary with the condition. In the case of spinal cord injury, for example, denial seems to be associated with a sense of internal control and less psychological distress (Elliott et al., 1991).

### Choice of Friends

Somewhat surprisingly, those who are stigmatized, or potentially stigmatizable, are not always the best friends of others who are similar. People with hearing loss tend to avoid those who are completely deaf (Higgins, 1980). The visually impaired tend to avoid associating with the blind (Criddle, 1953).

People who are slightly disabled tend to avoid the more severely disabled (Wright, 1983). Similarly, people who are somewhat overweight (Richardson, 1983) and those who are mildly retarded (Gibbons, 1981) show a preference for associating with those who are more "normal." In short, those whose conditions are less visible or less serious tend to avoid those who are more seriously affected in an effort to avoid "guilt by association" (Gibbons, 1986).

On the other hand, when a stigmatizing condition is clearly visible, the stigmatized tend to prefer the company of similar others (Wright, 1983). For example, people in wheelchairs indicate that interactions with able-bodied people are sometimes intrusive and make them feel uncomfortable (Braithwaite, 1991; Higgins, 1980). No doubt this is part of the reason why various support groups are as popular as they are. The social significance of the stigmatizing condition itself is greatly diminished when one associates with similar others. Indeed, many of the stigmatized, such as dwarfs (Ablon, 1981) and the deaf (Becker, 1980), who meet at support groups eventually marry. Further, the stigmatizing condition can be something as incidental as an accent. Recent immigrants tend to band together for mutual support.

## The Problem of Norm Ambiguity and Ambivalence

Part of the problem for the stigmatized stems from **norm ambiguity** (not knowing what is expected) and **ambivalence** (mixed feelings) on the part of others about getting involved (Katz, 1981). When interacting with someone who is visibly marked, people tend to monitor their conversation carefully. They also tend to adopt a certain mode of etiquette, an overly polite manner, and a certain formality. As a consequence, their conversations are robbed of spontaneity (Comer & Piliavin, 1972).

Albert Hastorf and his colleagues (1979) have referred to this tendency as the "norm to be kind." Christantina Safilios-Rothschild (1982) referred to it as "fictional acceptance," and others have called it "disabling the normal" (Hilbourne, 1973). By whatever name, the consequence is that the social experience of the stigmatized is likely to be different. Researchers in one study, for example, noted that over half of their sample of cancer patients reported difficulties in communicating with friends and family (Bean et al., 1980). And Robert Kleck and colleagues (1966) reported that social interactions with the physically handicapped were characterized by ending conversations more quickly, avoiding eye contact, and other indications of discomfort.

These kinds of difficulties seem to be especially true for people who have little contact or experience with the stigmatized. This was vividly illustrated in a study by Amerigo Farina and colleagues (1968). They had subjects interact with others who they were led to believe had a history of mental illness. Not all the targets, however, had a history of mental illness (that is, had been in a mental hospital). The results of the study were clear. When the mark was (assumed to be) "known," the subjects behaved in a less competent and more tense manner regardless of the actual history of the target person. So, perception sometimes has a way of creating reality.

In the case of a recently acquired stigmatizing condition, the initial support of friends tends to wane as they anticipate becoming involved in something that they do not feel they can continue. Russell Jones (1970), for example, reported that in the case of the disabled, friends were less likely to help if they thought their continued help might be expected. Edward Jones and colleagues (1984) have dubbed this the "tar baby" effect.

On the other hand, one of the most delightful individuals I have ever met had polio and was paralyzed from the waist down. She was married, had two children, and worked full time in an office. In addition, she was active in the community and her church. One year she headed the March of Dimes drive for a major metropolitan area. Both her coworkers and her family were completely supportive.

In the final analysis, we can read both positive and negative accounts of personal relationships involving the stigmatized. Renee Lyons (1991) reported that 66% of the participants in her study indicated that having an acquired disability had an effect on their friendships, and somewhat surprisingly, the number of advantages reported (99) was greater than the number of disadvantages (85). The advantages included opportunities to meet new people, increased value placed on friendships, reestablishment of old friendships, and more time and occasions available to pursue and maintain friendships. On the negative side were stigma, the social uncertainty that stems from misconceptions, limited physical access to friends, and feelings of low self-esteem. Perhaps most telling was the fact that the disabled reported having to initiate most social interactions themselves.

The way most people handle interactions with the stigmatized is simple indeed. They avoid them when possible. For example, passers-by tend to keep their distance from those who are visibly marked (Rumsey et al., 1982). On average, paraplegics experience a reduction in their social interactions, the number of settings in which they participate socially, and the variety of activities they are involved in (Marinelli & Dell Orto, 1984). Indeed, one review of the literature noted that 40% of disabled adults reported church as their only outside social activity (McCarthy, 1983). Relationships in the workplace tended to be disappointingly impersonal—something for which rehabilitation programs did little to prepare them.

In sum, the social world of the stigmatized is likely to be one in which people are either indifferent or overly solicitous, social interactions are ritualized and rather undiscriminating as to their needs, and behaviors fluctuate unpredictably. The effect on the stigmatized varies from individual to individual along a number of dimensions, as well. Among the most important of these dimensions is age of onset.

## Stigma Across the Age Range

Effects of stigmatizing conditions vary with the age of those affected, the severity of the condition, and its duration. Studies indicate that the young are especially vulnerable to the discrimination associated with stigma.

## Children and Their Peers

Studies of mentally and physically challenged children suggest that they are at a disadvantage socially. Evidence for this comes from sociometric studies, observational studies of interactions, and reports by the children themselves. Sociometric studies of grade-school classrooms, for example, show that the social status of disabled children tends to be significantly lower than that of children who are not disabled and that they are less preferred as friends (Centers & Centers, 1963; Force, 1956).

In "mainstreamed" classrooms, in which disabled children are taught along with other children, the disabled are often isolated or grouped with other disabled children (Sigelman & Singleton, 1986). Furthermore, a negative halo effect or "courtesy stigma" (Birenbaum, 1992) sometimes spreads to those who associate with the stigmatized (Goffman, 1963; Wright, 1983). For example, "normal" siblings of the mentally or physically impaired can experience problems of their own. Not only may they carry the burden of guilt for being "normal" and compensate by becoming oversolicitous, but they also may be resentful that so much of the family's time, attention, and resources are focused on their disabled sibling (Schreiber & Feeley, 1965).

Steven Richardson and his colleagues have painted a somewhat more positive picture. In a series of studies (Richardson, 1971; Richardson et al., 1974), they were able to show that when physically disabled and nondisabled children lived together in a 3-week summer camp setting, the attitudes and behaviors of those with little previous experience with the physically disabled changed significantly toward greater acceptance. How much such findings generalize to the outside world, however, remains an open question. This is exemplified in the case of Tom.

Tom stuttered rather severely. As a boy he was generally accepted by others in his neighborhood, and this acceptance continued in the small neighborhood school he attended. In the sixth grade, however, he moved to a larger, less personal school, and the other kids began to tease him, which only made his stuttering worse. He dreaded being called on in class and often pretended he didn't know the answer when he really did. Those who had been his friends for years began to shun him, and over time, he withdrew more and more. After a year his parents sent him to a private school in the hope that it would be a little more personal.

## Adolescents and Their Peers

During adolescence, problems of friendship and peer relations are joined by other issues. The maturing disabled adolescent faces difficult problems as the demands of vocational planning, relationships, and intimacy come into play. These problems are qualitatively different from those experienced during childhood (Ammerman et al., 1987).

In comparing a sample of physically disabled adolescents with a group of nondisabled ones, Elizabeth Anderson and her colleagues (1982) found that the disabled adolescents were generally more isolated socially, had fewer contacts with peers, had few close friends, made few visits, and had few visitors. Parents and teachers indicated that they were less well adjusted socially than were their nondisabled peers. For example, teachers reported that the disabled adolescents tended to be disliked and isolated, and their few social activities were likely to be organized by adults and involve parents and other disabled adolescents.

Among the adolescents who were orthopedically disabled, 72% showed signs of anxiety and a lack of confidence. They were particularly concerned about interpersonal encounters, worrying about such matters as incontinence, rejection, embarrassment, speech abnormalities, and seizures. The more severely impaired tended to show more anxiety. As a group, they tended to be unhappy, miserable, hopeless, and lonely. They also reported a higher frequency of suicidal thoughts.

Likewise, in interviews with 37 families of adolescents with spina bifida, one researcher found that, on the whole, the adolescents were restricted socially and had little contact with peers and few close friends. Sixty-six percent reportedly had frequent bouts of "misery" (Dorner, 1973; see also McAndrew, 1979). Studies focusing specifically on heterosexual adjustment have noted infrequent contacts with the opposite sex. Boys with mild or moderate disability and greater mobility had more contact than did the more severely afflicted, but as a group they lacked knowledge of heterosexual matters and expressed anxiety over the prospect of sexual performance and marriage (and for some the anxiety was realistic due to damage to the central nervous system) (Dorner, 1977).

Similarly, in remaining "closeted," young gay men and lesbians often face problems in developing relationships that heterosexuals do not ordinarily experience. They are not free to pursue courtship openly. They usually have a smaller pool of eligible partners to draw upon. They cannot depend on heterosexual friends' matchmaking. They cannot anticipate going to the prom. And they are not likely to confide in their parents. As a consequence, the early experiences of romantic involvement, common among heterosexuals, are not available to them. This often leaves secretive encounters during high school and college. Many gay men and lesbians hesitate to join clubs for gay teens. Some even "fall in love" with someone of the opposite sex, marry their heterosexual partner, and only later choose to act on their "true" sexual orientation (Huston & Schwartz, 1995).

On the other hand, Vincent van Hasselt and colleagues (1985) compared 21 visually impaired adolescents with 22 sighted controls on a role-play test and global ratings of overall social skill. Their findings indicated that in spite of more speech disfluencies among the visually impaired group, they showed less hostility and more expressions of appreciation. Overall, in this study, the visually handicapped were rated *more* socially skilled than the sighted controls.

In general, however, limited peer contact, peer rejection, and social withdrawal seem to be common among stigmatized adolescents. And because of the limitations of their social experience, they are sometimes at risk for later maladjustment (Ammerman et al., 1987).

## Personal Relationships and the Stigmatized Adult

Whereas marital and other family relationships have a strong element of obligation about them, friendships are voluntary. It is this voluntary nature that indicates "true" caring. Anybody can be friends during the good times, but when the chips are down, we find out who our true friends are. For this reason, indications of friendship are likely to carry particular significance among those who are stigmatized.

When an adult becomes disabled, for example, not only are changes in activities and interests necessary, but also friendships have to be reassessed. Former activities may no longer be possible or easily accessible, and relationships that were once well balanced are likely to become asymmetrical and strained.

On the other hand, evidence suggests that not only can existing friendships continue and be restructured to adapt to new circumstances, but they can also grow in the process (Fisher & Galler, 1988; Lyons, 1991; Wright, 1983).

*The Role of the Stigmatized*   Although it is sometimes assumed from a therapeutic point of view that anyone experiencing a stigma would find it helpful to talk about it, the evidence suggests that such venting may come at a price—namely, being judged less well adjusted and less attractive (Glick et al., 1974). Other people prefer to interact with stigmatized people who are successful and well adjusted (Kleck et al., 1966). So, we find something of a conflict between what might be wise to encourage in the interest of psychological adjustment (Pennebaker, 1989) and what seems wise in terms of social adjustment.

Insofar as a stigmatizing condition implies dependence, asymmetry, and lack of balance in a relationship, then, it also implies strain. For example, disabled people are not generally perceived as offering help to others and indeed may not perceive themselves as having much to offer (Lyons, 1991). This perceived asymmetry sets in motion a chain of events whereby requests for support by the more savvy disabled people may become muted in an effort not to appear dependent or demanding.

When asked to indicate what type of help they saw themselves able to bring to a relationship, approximately 10% of Renee Lyons's sample indicated they had little or nothing to offer. Most, however, referred to such things as interpersonal skills, such as listening. Beyond this skill, possible contributions tended to be highly individual, for example, baking, knowledge, motorcycle repair, and material possessions. One person in her study even built a swimming pool to provide a place to interact socially (1991).

*Old Friends/New Friends*    One way those with acquired disabilities reenter society is by avoiding their old friends. They are likely to seek contacts initially with individuals somewhat lower in social status and, based on this experience, move into new roles and activities gradually.

Establishing a footing in untried social roles sometimes goes hand in hand with the stepwise progress of physical rehabilitation (French, 1984). Life out from under the shadow of the pretrauma identity may well be more forgiving. New friends seem to offer something of a fresh start. They do not carry with them the baggage of the past. Thus, negotiating an identity with new friends is sometimes preferable to restructuring and retraining old ones, who did not bargain for the role of friend to someone who is newly disabled (Fisher & Nadler, 1974). We see an example of this in the case of Emma.

Emma was a vivacious, popular student at the time of her auto accident in which she was seriously injured. Although her recovery was miraculous, it was never complete. The accident affected her gait and left her speech slightly slurred. Initially, her friends rallied around her. She had many visitors. They went shopping with her. They helped her up the stairs. If anything, she was more the center of attention now than before the accident. But as the months went by, she found herself more and more isolated. Today she spends half of each weekday at a "sheltered workshop" where other physically disabled individuals provide her with friendship and a sense of place. Otherwise, her family and a few neighbors are her only sources of social interaction. Her old friends have all gone their separate ways.

Old friends tend to be aware of the implications of interacting with someone who is now "different." Sometimes they continue the association out of a sense of loyalty while looking for graceful ways of exiting the relationship. At the same time, the stigmatized are aware of the changed circumstances and feel that their friendship now imposes a burden. Their own pride may lead them to seek ways to end the relationship themselves (E. E. Jones et al., 1984).

In her study of adults with acquired physical disabilities, Lyons focused on how they *perceived* that their condition had affected their friendships. Generally, the comments showed that those with acquired disabilities saw themselves as having few bargaining chips. They felt that they had to depend on themselves when the going got tough. Patients with spinal injuries seemed to have more positive experiences, whereas those with degenerative disorders (such as multiple sclerosis) often felt that their friends had deserted them (1991).

Sixty-seven percent of adults with acquired disabilities reported spending less time with friends after becoming disabled. Factors that figured most strongly in reducing social contacts were severity of disability, limitations on mobility, and health restrictions. Sixty-one percent of Lyons's sample indicated that the location of their social interactions changed. Visits typically took place in the disabled person's home. Those in institutional settings indicated that friends seemed to be uncomfortable visiting them there (Lyons, 1986, 1991; Lyons et al., 1995).

## Degree of Impairment and Social Adjustment

Intuitively, we might assume there would be a relationship between the degree of impairment and social adjustment—that is, the greater the impairment, the more difficulty one would have in adjusting. Some researchers have indeed reported such a relationship (Weiss et al., 1971). But others have found no such relationship (Shontz, 1971), and still others have reported an inverse relationship (Macgregor et al., 1953; Wright, 1983; Zahn, 1973).

How are we to account for such diverse findings? One interpretation is that those with minor disabilities or conditions that allow them to pass are more likely to use people in the mainstream as a reference group, and as a consequence, their psychological adjustment is hampered. On the other hand, those with disabilities serious enough to be undeniable have no choice but to accept their condition.

The clearest test of this hypothesis came in a study in which blind children were compared with peers who were visually impaired, and deaf children were compared with peers who were hearing impaired. In 20 of the 28 comparisons, the visually impaired children and the hearing-impaired children, rather than those who were completely blind or deaf, showed the most difficulty in adjusting (Cowen & Bobrove, 1966).

We must keep in mind, however, that research findings have not consistently shown a relationship between degree of disability and adjustment. Disabilities that are less severe generate fewer objective problems by definition, which presumably facilitates adjustment. On the other hand, people with mild afflictions are more likely to use "normals" as a reference group. The net effect seems to be the result of a combination of objective and psychological factors. But objective factors by themselves are not necessarily good predictors of adjustment. Mildly disabled people sometimes wallow in self-pity, while the more severely afflicted sometimes make admirable adjustments (Wright, 1983).

### Adaptation Over Time

Many of the negative effects of disability appear to come during childhood, when the bases for social relationships are being formed. Stigma, stereotypes, and lack of mobility seem to affect children who are visibly handicapped especially severely, as they experience the double jeopardy of coping with disability and dealing with interpersonal relationships.

However, as the disabled grow older and begin to accept their condition, relationships with others who are close to them tend to improve. Those with acquired disabilities often speak of cultivating long-dormant friendships. They can and do learn strategies to set others at ease, such as honest communication and sensitivity as to how others are responding (Fisher & Galler, 1988), which in turn can have a facilitating effect on further social interaction. If, on the other hand, they fail to accept their physical limitations, they are likely to have difficulty in social and personal relationships as well.

## Relationships With Spouse and Family

In a major study of its kind, Margaret Zahn (1973) examined the impact of disability on relationships with spouse and family. She found no indication that severity of physical impairment led to increased disruption in family relationships. Indeed, exactly the opposite seemed to be the case. Overall, the more severely impaired were likely to report better interpersonal relations than the less severely impaired! Moreover, loss of employment skills did not seem to disrupt interpersonal relationships in this study. Those who were not able to work indicated having better relationships with spouse and family members than did those who continued to work.

There are a number of possible explanations for such findings. One is that those who are more seriously disabled simply show a tendency to put a positive face on things. Another is that as ambiguity is removed with increasing impairment, a set of norms applying to the disabled role come clearly into play. In any case, we see that certain characteristics tend to be associated with adaptation and the quality of interpersonal relations. When health is in doubt over the long term, greater problems in interpersonal relations with friends and family alike seem to result. On the other hand, the notion that visibility generates stereotyping, which, in turn, adversely affects adjustment, was not supported in Zahn's study. If anything, clarity in defining the condition seems to facilitate positive interpersonal relations. Within the family, at least, ambiguity seems not to be the friend of the disabled.

## Intimate Relationships

Acquired disability has been shown both to disrupt marriages and to make them stronger—a finding that may be due as much to the pretrauma state of the relationship as to the effect of the disability itself (Croog & Levine, 1977). But the evidence suggests that marriage is possible for many people with physical disabilities. Although some relationship has been shown between severity or visibility of disability and marriage, the degree of impairment does not seem to be a particularly good predictor of satisfaction in marriage (Skipper et al., 1968).

In Zahn's (1973) study, for example, the hypothesis that sexual impairment would lead to impaired personal relationships was not confirmed. Indeed, the sexually impaired had better relationships with their spouses and suffered less disruption with other family members than did the sexually unimpaired! Consistent with this finding, the divorce rate for men with spinal cord injury has been shown to be no greater than that for the general population (El Ghatit & Hanson, 1976).

On the other hand, one of the important factors in any consideration of stigma and intimate relationships seems to be the time of onset of the condition. In marriages in which one partner is disabled and the other is not, it is more common for the disabled partner to be a female if the onset preceded the development of the relationship. Presumably this meshes with traditional sex roles in which the husband is seen as responsible for his wife and family (Goffman, 1963; Wright, 1983).

In a study of 138 paralyzed veterans, Teresa Thompson (1981) found that marriages in which one person was disabled did not, on the whole, appear to be different in sharing and autonomy than those of the nondisabled. On the other hand, when the disability affects sharing of responsibilities in the relationship, couples married *before* the disability occurred appear to be more affected by it than couples married *after* the disability occurred. There seems, in other words, to be some truth to the notion that disability can have negative effects on a marriage unless the couple entered the relationship with a full awareness of the implications.

Finally, we note that some stigmatizing conditions improve over time, others remain stable, and still others get worse. In a study of wives of men hospitalized for mental disorders, for example, Charlotte Schwartz (1957) noted that the wives' outlook and attitude depended very much on whether they believed their husbands' condition would improve.

## Conclusion

What should we conclude with regard to the relationship between stigma, disability, and personal relationships? When a stigmatizing condition is visible, people tend to distance themselves. The stigmatized individuals sometimes respond by passing (if they can) or disavowing their limitations, and one of the implications of this is that they may avoid those who are similarly marked, especially if the condition of the other is more serious.

Norm ambiguity and ambivalence are likely to affect many of the social interactions of stigmatized individuals. Disabilities acquired after a relationship has been established are likely to strain the relationship. The young seem to be particularly vulnerable to discrimination by their peers, and the evidence suggests that the effects can last a lifetime.

On the other hand, we find surprisingly little relationship between severity of a stigmatizing condition and adjustment over time. Particularly within the family, close personal relationships seem to be less affected by stigmatizing conditions than might be assumed.

## Suggestions for Further Reading

Ammerman, R. T., van Hasselt, V. B., & Hersen, M. (1987). The handicapped adolescent. In V. B. van Hasselt & M. Hersen (Eds.), *Handbook of adolescent psychology*. New York: Pergamon. An authoritative account of the psychological problems of disabled adolescents.

Birenbaum, A. (1992). Courtesy stigma revisited. *Mental Retardation, 30,* 265–268. A brief article on the negative halo effect associated with stigma.

Brickman, P., Coates, D., & Janoff-Bulman, R. (1978). Lottery winners and accident victims: Is happiness relative? *Journal of Personality and Social Psychology, 36,* 917–927. The conclusions of this classic study have been challenged, but its general point is still worth making. Those sustaining permanent injuries and those who win the lottery do not differ appreciably in happiness.

Crandall, C. S. (1991). Do heavyweight students have more difficulty paying for college? *Personality and Social Psychology Bulletin, 17,* 606–611. This article provides evidence that our prejudices show up in some of the most unlikely places.

Crandall, C. S., & Coleman, R. (1992). AIDS-related stigmatization and the disruption of social relationships. *Journal of Social and Personal Relationships, 9,* 163–177. A questionnaire study noting the varied effect of AIDS and related illnesses on relationships.

Goffman, E. (1963). *Stigma: Notes on the management of spoiled identity.* Englewood Cliffs, NJ: Prentice-Hall. A noted sociologist looks at stigma.

Jones, E. E., Farina, A., Hastorf, A. H., Markus, H., Miller, D. T., & Scott, R. A. (Eds.). (1984). *Social stigma: The psychology of marked relationships.* New York: W. H. Freeman. A book of independently written chapters on stigma. A good overview of the issues from a psychological perspective.

Lyons, R. F. (1991). Effects of acquired illness and disability on friendships. In W. H. Jones & D. Perlman (Eds.), *Advances in personal relationships: A research annual* (Vol. 3, pp. 233–276). London: Kingsley. A review of the literature and account of her work with patients who have acquired disabilities.

Lyons, R. F., Sullivan, M. J. L., & Ritvo, P. G., with Coyne, J. C. (1995). *Relationships in chronic illness and disability.* Thousand Oaks, CA: Sage. A brief overview of the impact of illness and disability on relationships.

Pryor, J. B., Reeder, G. D., & McManus, J. A. (1991). Fear and loathing in the workplace: Reactions to AIDS-infected co-workers. *Personality and Social Psychology Bulletin, 17,* 133–139. Workers' responses to AIDS-infected coworkers.

Wright, B. (1983). *Physical Disability: A psycho-social approach* (2nd ed.). New York: Harper & Row. Despite its age, this volume remains a landmark in the field.

## CHAPTER 10

### ❧❧ *Liking and Loving*

*Claire looked sadly at what she had written. She couldn't help noticing that it started out "Dear John." She had met John over the summer when they were both counselors at a camp. It was a buddy-buddy relationship all the way. When camp ended, Claire was a bit surprised to get a call from John just to see if she made it home all right. And then, on his way to school that fall, John "just happened to drop by." They stopped by a flea market, went out to dinner, and took in a movie. Still, they were just friends, nothing more. They wrote a time or two, and then John mentioned visiting her over the weekend. Claire agreed. She was ready for a break, and the visit went fine. There wasn't a hint of anything but friendship between them.*

*Then the bombshell came. John wrote a 13-page letter professing his love for her and telling of his plans to transfer to her school so that they could be together. Claire was shocked. She had kissed John once! It was a peck on the cheek. That was all. John had clearly read much more into their relationship than Claire had intended. She hadn't meant to lead John on. How could something like this have happened?*

*That night Claire did some soul searching and decided she had better clarify things before they went any further. She wrote a short note indicating what a good time she had had over the summer and how much she enjoyed the weekend visit, but indicated that she wasn't ready for a serious relationship at this point in her life. She hoped, however, that they could continue to be friends. Her letter closed simply: "I like you, John, but I don't love you, (signed) Claire."*

Ordinarily, we think of liking (sometimes referred to as love in the platonic sense) and loving (in the romantic sense) as two different things. **Love** is typically considered a strong attachment to or affection for someone, or a passionate feeling for someone of the opposite sex; while **liking** is ordinarily seen

175

as a milder form of affection. Like Claire in the chapter opener, it's possible to like someone without loving him or her, but the reverse wouldn't make a lot of sense. We don't ordinarily think it possible to love someone without liking him or her. For most of us, then, liking and loving may be similar, but they are not the same. In this chapter we consider what research has to say about liking and loving and the relationship between the two.

## Rubin's Liking and Love Scales

It was Zick Rubin (1970, 1973, 1974) who first attempted to distinguish between liking and loving in a way that was empirically based, or "scientific." In these early studies, students were asked to respond to a series of items either as they would toward a friend of the opposite sex or as they would toward a romantic partner, such as a boyfriend or girlfriend.

The two different response patterns were then used as the basis for developing scales for measuring liking and loving. Examples of some of the questions appear in Table 10-1.

### Correlates of Liking and Love Scores

When students took the Love Scale with respect to their dating partners, they showed higher scores than when they took it with respect to their friends, while scores on the Liking Scale were essentially the same for dating partners and friends (Rubin, 1970, 1973). In other words, they *liked* their friends and their dating partners about the same but *loved* their dating partners more than their friends. In addition, not only were love scores higher for couples who indicated that they were "in love," but they also tended to be higher for couples who planned to marry (Rubin, 1973). And, further, dating couples who scored higher on the Love Scale tended to gaze at each other for longer periods of time (Rubin, 1970).

Other studies have reported findings consistent with these. For example, couples who are dating casually tend to indicate *liking* their partners, while those who are dating exclusively, engaged, or married tend to indicate more loving (Dion & Dion, 1976). Engaged and married couples have higher love scores than do those who are simply going together, and cohabiting couples tend to have lower love scores than do couples in more committed relationships (Cunningham & Antill, 1981).

Further, when married couples are distinguished on the basis of whether they have lived together before marriage, those who have *not* lived together have higher love scores. As a group, those who have lived with someone other than their present partner, or had sex with someone since their current relationship began, tend to have lower scores on the Love Scale. And, in general, scores on the Love Scale tend to be negatively correlated with the number of sex partners people report (Cunningham & Antill, 1981).

Higher love scores are related to perceived happiness with a relationship, perceived likelihood that a couple will get married, a positive view of the institution of marriage, romanticism, femininity, and self-disclosure. Among

**Table 10-1   Love-Scale and Liking-Scale Items**

Love Scale

1. If _____ were feeling bad, my first duty would be to cheer him (her) up.
2. I feel that I can confide in _____ about virtually everything.
3. I find it easy to ignore _____ 's faults.

Liking Scale

1. When I am with _____, we almost always are in the same mood.
2. I think that _____ is unusually well adjusted.
3. I would highly recommend _____ for a responsible job.

*Source:* Rubin, Z. (1970). Measurement of romantic love. *Journal of Personality and Social Psychology, 16,* 265–273. Used by permission of Z. Rubin.

dating couples, high love scores also tend to be associated with sexual intimacy but in an interesting way. For dating couples who reported having had sex, those who postponed sex beyond the first month of their dating relationship had higher love scores, indicated greater closeness, and were more likely to indicate that they were in love than were those who had sex earlier (Cunningham & Antill, 1981; Critelli & Dupre, 1978; Peplau et al., 1977). Generally, the more conservative someone's views are on such issues as premarital sex, cohabitation, and sex, the higher one's love score tends to be (Cunningham & Antill, 1981).

On the other hand, couples who have lower love scores are more likely to break up (Hill et al., 1976; Peplau et al., 1993; Z. Rubin et al., 1980), especially when the female's love score is low. Feminism among women tends to be associated with lower love scores (Cunningham & Antill, 1981). And a study of couples who were married 0–15 years showed that the longer a couple had been married, the *lower* their scores on the Love Scale tended to be (Cimbalo et al., 1976). Apparently, with time, the "glow" of love tends to fade for most married couples.

Finally, there is some indication that males and females view liking and loving somewhat differently. Females tend to show a pattern of greater liking for their romantic partners (Rubin, 1970) and greater love for their friends (Black & Angelis, 1974; Cunningham & Antill, 1981), although both these findings may simply be due to a greater willingness on the part of females to express their feelings on such matters.

## Different Types of Love

Following the work of Rubin, researchers have taken different approaches to liking and loving. The terms used vary somewhat, but typically they have focused on various dimensions of love both in the platonic sense and the romantic sense. In the following sections we will look at some representative approaches.

## Passionate Versus Companionate Love

Elaine Walster and William Walster (1978) distinguished between passionate (sometimes called romantic) love and companionate (sometimes called pragmatic) love. This distinction has become one of the most widely recognized in the literature.

*Passionate Love*    **Passionate love** is "a state of intense longing for union with another" (Walster & Walster, 1978, p. 9). It tends to be characterized by high levels of arousal, ecstasy, and feelings of fulfillment in being loved by one's "intended" or, in the case of unrequited love, feelings of anxiety, emptiness, and despair (Hatfield, 1988). People experiencing passionate love are likely to be preoccupied with their lovers, to look at them through rose-colored glasses, to feel sexual attraction, to want to be with them, and to feel an emotional need for their love to be returned (Hatfield & Sprecher, 1986a).

Passionate love seems to be quite common across cultures (Hatfield, 1988; Jankowiak & Fischer, 1992). For example, Elaine Hatfield and Richard Rapson (1987) found no differences in passionate love experiences reported by Caucasians, Japanese, and Filipinos living in Hawaii. And in their cross-cultural study, William Jankowiak and Edward Fischer (1992) found evidence for romantic (or passionate) love in about 89% of the cultures in their sample.

Elaine Hatfield and Susan Sprecher (1986a) have developed the Passionate Love Scale (PLS), which appears in Table 10-2. Research using the PLS indicates that both children and young adults report having had passionate love experiences, and males and females do not seem to differ much in this respect.

*Companionate Love*    Walster and Walster (1978) define **companionate love** as "the affection we feel for those with whom our lives are deeply intertwined" (p. 9). Companionate love involves such things as trust, affection, and security. Such love relationships do not just happen; they tend to be accompanied by considerable self-control and are somewhat calculated. They are also likely to be symmetrical in terms of emotional involvement and equitable in terms of their rewards and costs. In many ways, companionate love is similar to liking. The only difference between the two seems to be in the intensity of feeling and the degree to which the lives of those involved are intertwined (Berscheid & Walster, 1978).

The course of passionate and companionate love tends to be quite different. Passionate love can develop very rapidly but typically declines over time, while companionate love tends to develop more slowly and grow deeper with time. Passionate love is characterized by strong, but sometimes mixed, emotions, while in companionate love, the emotional overtones are positive but somewhat muted. Passionate love, then, is the "hot" type, and companionate love the "warm" type (Hatfield, 1988).

What happens when the intensity of passionate love begins to fade? Presumably, its role in the economy of the relationship is taken over by a more enduring companionate love. And when the transition from passionate to companionate love does not take place, the relationship is likely to be at risk.

**Table 10-2   Passionate Love Scale**

　　1. Since I've been involved with _____, my emotions have been on a roller coaster.

　*2. I would feel deep despair if _____ left me.

　　3. Sometimes my body trembles with excitement at the sight of _____.

　　4. I take delight in studying the movements and angles of _____'s body.

　*5. Sometimes I feel I can't control my thoughts; they are obsessively on _____.

　*6. I feel happy when I am doing something to make _____ happy.

　*7. I would rather be with _____ than anyone else.

　*8. I'd get jealous if I thought _____ were falling in love with someone else.

　　9. No one else could love _____ like I do.

　*10. I yearn to know all about _____.

　*11. I want _____ —physically, emotionally, mentally.

　12. I will love _____ forever.

　13. I melt when looking deeply into _____'s eyes.

　*14. I have an endless appetite for affection from _____.

　*15. For me, _____ is the perfect romantic partner.

　16. _____ is the person who can make me feel the happiest.

　*17. I sense my body responding when _____ touches me.

　18. I feel tender toward _____.

　*19. _____ always seems to be on my mind.

　20. If I were separated from _____ for a long time, I would feel intensely lonely.

　21. I sometimes find it difficult to concentrate on work because thoughts of _____ occupy my mind.

　*22. I want _____ to know me—my thoughts, my fears, and my hopes.

　23. Knowing that _____ cares about me makes me feel complete.

　*24. I eagerly look for signs indicating _____'s desire for me.

　25. If _____ were going through a difficult time, I would put away my own concerns to help him/her out.

　26. _____ can make me feel effervescent and bubbly.

　27. In the presence of _____, I yearn to touch and be touched.

　28. An existence without _____ would be dark and dismal.

　*29. I possess a powerful attraction for _____.

　*30. I get extremely depressed when things don't go right in my relationship with _____.

Possible responses to each item range from:

| 1 | 2 | 3 | 4 | 5 | 6 | 7 | 8 | 9 |
|---|---|---|---|---|---|---|---|---|
| Not at all true | | | | Moderately true | | | Definitely true | |

*Indicates items selected for a short version of the PLS.
*Source:* Hatfield, E., & Sprecher, S. (1986a). Measuring passionate love in intimate relationships. *Journal of Adolescence, 9,* 383–410. Used by permission.

Which kind of love is stronger or more lasting—passionate or companionate? For these two couples, is there a difference that matters?

In the broad scheme of things, passionate love seems to set the stage for the warmth, trust, and understanding of companionate love to develop (Kelley, 1983). One way to look at passionate love is as a launchpad from which we blast off in a venture to achieve a more stable, if less exciting, orbit in the haven of companionate love.

Research indicates that many romantic relationships show a practical side as they become more serious. For example, Ellen Berscheid and Jack Fei (1977) noted that those who are in relationships but are not sure whether they are in love or not, tend to be insecure about their partner's feelings toward them. Similarly, in their study of personal accounts of falling in love, Arthur Aron and colleagues (1989) observed that individuals often indicated their feelings were preceded by some signal from the partner that the feeling might be mutual.

## Friendship as a Component of Love

Keith Davis and his associates (Davis & Latty-Mann, 1987; Davis & Roberts, 1985; Davis & Todd, 1982, 1985) have taken a position that is similar in many ways to the distinction between passionate and companionate love, but they refer to these two simply as love and friendship.

Using the Relationship Rating Form (Davis & Latty-Mann, 1987) to assess such things as viability, intimacy, passion, caring, satisfaction, and conflict in relationships, they have made various comparisons between love and friendship. Do the two differ on these dimensions? Indeed they do. As we might expect, romantic love relationships tend to be more passionate, more intimate (sometimes), and more conflicted (sometimes).

The most important finding to come out of Davis's work, however, is that the relationships of spouses and lovers when compared with those of close friends do not differ significantly in terms of a common core of friendship. Friendship underlies both loving and liking (Davis & Roberts, 1985). Friends are supportive and friends reciprocate favor for favor, and, interestingly enough, this is true of same-sex friendships and opposite-sex friendships as well. But friendships do not generate feelings of passion and caring as love relationships do. So, for Davis and his colleagues, love is something added to friendship, rather like frosting on the cake, and is composed, primarily, of two additional ingredients: passion, which includes sexual desire and exclusiveness, and caring, which involves championing the other, being a primary advocate of the other, and giving one's utmost. In short:

$$love = friendship + passion + caring$$

**Preliminary Conclusions**

Now that we have reviewed some of the early work on liking and loving, we must ask, do these address the full range of phenomena that we normally associate with love? Not necessarily. In their analysis of the descriptions of subjective experiences of love, Kenneth and Karen Dion (1973) found evidence for many differences in the way people experience love. For some, love is volatile, for others, it is not. Some approach love with caution, others with abandon. Some take a rational, pragmatic approach, and others are more passionate and impetuous.

Clearly, the word *love* means different things to different people. In the scientific literature, there have been several attempts to capture these differences. And these are the approaches that we turn to next.

## *More Comprehensive Models of Love*

A number of researchers have presented models of love that are more comprehensive than those we have just looked at. As a group, these are efforts to capture a fuller range of phenomena involved in both liking and loving. In the following sections, we will consider some of the better known ones.

**Lee's Typology**

In his book *The Colors of Love* and later writings, John Lee (1973, 1977, 1988) has developed a classification system for various approaches to love that people take, which he calls "love styles." These are represented using the analogy of the color wheel. For Lee, the three primary "colors" of love are *Eros, ludus,* and *storge.*

In the case of **Eros,** the lover considers love to be what life is all about. There is a strong physical component to Eros. Eros is likely to be expressed in terms of touching and verbal expression. Individuals involved are usually attracted to and aroused by each other upon first meeting. Rapport is established quickly, but, still, the relationship is seen to be honest and sincere. There is anticipation of the other and very little mention of anxiety over the relationship. Emotion is intense, and sexual relations are likely to occur early.

In the case of *ludus,* love is considered a game. A ludic type does not seek or make serious commitments and easily transfers his or her affections from one person to another. The ludic type does not become overly excited upon first meeting, and contacts with one person can be considered too frequent. Too little, or too much, involvement spoils the game. Insincerity is a characteristic of ludic love. Several relationships may be pursued simultaneously. Sex is seen as good fun and not as an indication of commitment.

*Storge* (pronounced "STOR-gay") is the type of love one might feel for a brother or sister. It's the sort of love that evolves from friendship. It is more likely to be found in close-knit communities where people have known each other for a long time. It's not particularly exciting or eventful. It has little to do with physical attractiveness, and its development is more likely to be characterized by getting to know someone gradually and making that person more and more a part of one's life. Storgic love is relaxed rather than intense, arousing, and emotional. In storgic relationships, there is more of a tendency to focus on shared interests and activities rather than on the relationship itself. Storgic love may not be exciting, but it is dependable.

When Eros, *ludus,* and *storge* (the three primary colors of love) are combined in various ways, they result in other recognizable love styles, such as mania, pragma, and agape.

**Mania,** according to Lee, is a combination of Eros and *ludus* (love as passion and love as a game). It is similar in many ways to the traditional notion of romantic love. In mania, contradictions abound. On the one hand, there is a yearning for love; on the other hand, this is coupled with the sense that love is likely to be painful. The manic lover is preoccupied with his or her intended and develops imagined scenarios of their future together, coupled with anxiety. Mania is possessive, wishing for more and more control and commitment from one's partner. Life without the other seems as if it is not worth living. For mania there is no happy ending. In this sense, it is the stuff of which soap operas are made.

**Pragma,** as the name suggests, is the type of love that is concerned with compatibility. The pragmatic lover seeks a relationship that works with as few hitches as possible—contentment rather than happiness. Pragmatic partners are not gamblers. They avoid emotional risk taking. They are apt to select from well-known others. Courting is not likely to be forced, and mutuality in relationships is seen not as something that just happens so much as something that can be worked at. Over the long term, compatibility, not excitement, is

## Box 10-1 In a Different Key
## Arranged Marriage

Historically, marriage for the Japanese was a contract made between families, not between individuals. The male's parents typically started the process by investigating a girl's family background to make sure her family was of good social standing and that she had no hereditary diseases that might be transmitted to their grandchildren. Once it was determined that a girl was suitable, they sought the approval of all the close relatives before entering into negotiations with the family of the bride. It was accepted practice for a new bride and groom, who lived as much as 10 miles apart, to meet for the first time at their wedding. One bridegroom in Robert Blood's study even missed his own wedding.

It seems the groom was away at the university studying for civil service exams at the time. Because he was 27, and the eldest son, his parents wanted him to marry, so his uncles made the arrange-

ments. His wife was 17 at the time. She had seen a picture of him, but he had never seen hers. He was too busy studying. At the wedding, he was represented by proxy. After the ceremony, representatives from the two families came to Tokyo, introduced the groom to his new bride and, after some formalities, left the two to live together in wedded bliss. "Love matches" at the time only took place among the lower classes (Blood, 1967).

Although "romantic marriage" is the dominant pattern in Japan today, the criteria for romantic attraction still seem to be much more practical than they are in the United States, with the emphasis on reproduction and financial security rather than psychological well-being. Indeed, single women in Japan today often refer to the "3-highs" in evaluating a prospective husband—height, high education, and high income (Kamo, 1993).

the main concern. And, as we see in Box 10-1, some cultures consider pragmatic concerns to be more important than passion, and in choosing a marriage partner, compatibility is weighted more heavily than romance.

Finally, **agape** (pronounced "A-ga-pay"), which comes from the Christian tradition, is the kind of love that is selfless and giving, focused on the other rather than the self, strong on caring rather than on need. Agape is sometimes associated with sexual abstinence. The body being a temple, sexuality is closely linked to spirituality.

Clyde Hendrick and Susan Hendrick (1986) developed the Love Attitude Scale to measure and validate the various love styles proposed by Lee. In general, their findings have demonstrated the utility of the approach. For example, studies using the scale have shown that males tend to be more ludic than females, while females tend to be more pragmatic and storgic than males. They have also found that when romantic partners both filled out the Love Attitude Scale, their scores on Eros, *storge,* and mania tended to be similar (Hendrick et al., 1988).

Agape is selfless and giving. Both passion and compatibility may be present in agape.

## Sternberg's Triangular Theory

A second comprehensive model of love suggested by Robert Sternberg also features three primary components. Based on an analysis of items from Rubin's Liking and Love scales and a similar scale by George Levinger and his colleagues (1977), Sternberg developed the Triangular Love Scale and proposed a theory in which the major components of love—intimacy, passion, and decision/commitment—are portrayed as the points of a triangle (Sternberg, 1986, 1988a, 1988b; Sternberg & Grajek, 1984). The Triangular Love Scale appears in Table 10-3.

**Intimacy** refers to feelings of closeness, bondedness, and connection. **Passion** is used in much the same way that Walster and Walster (1978) used the term as defined earlier in this chapter. In passionate love, sexual and other related motivational needs predominate. Other feelings, such as self-esteem, need, nurturance, affiliation, dominance, submission, and self-actualization, may also be involved, depending on the person and the type of relationship. Passion is the component most often associated with romantic involvement. Passion itself refers to an arousal state, which may (but does not necessarily) include sexual desire.

For Sternberg, the **decision/commitment** component involves two subsets, the short-term (decision) component indicating that one loves the other, and the long-term (commitment) component, which has more to do with the resolve to maintain the relationship over time. Ordinarily, decision comes first and commitment later. The two often go together, but not always. Commitment varies with the type of relationship. Parents, for example, may be more

**Table 10-3   The Sternberg Triangular Love Scale**

INSTRUCTIONS

The blanks represent the person with whom you are in a relationship. Rate each statement on a 1-to-9 scale, where 1 = "not at all," 5 = "moderately," and 9 = "extremely." Use intermediate points on the scale to indicate intermediate levels of feelings.

1. I am actively supportive of _____'s well-being.
2. I have a warm relationship with _____.
3. I am able to count on _____ in times of need.
4. _____ is able to count on me in times of need.
5. I am willing to share myself and my possessions with _____.
6. I receive considerable emotional support from _____.
7. I give considerable emotional support to _____.
8. I communicate well with _____.
9. I value _____ greatly in my life.
10. I feel close to _____.
11. I have a comfortable relationship with _____.
12. I feel that I really understand _____.
13. I feel that _____ really understands me.
14. I feel that I really can trust _____.
15. I share deeply personal information about myself with _____.
16. Just seeing _____ excites me.
17. I find myself thinking about _____ frequently during the day.
18. My relationship with _____ is very romantic.
19. I find _____ to be very personally attractive.
20. I idealize _____.
21. I cannot imagine another person making me as happy as _____ does.
22. I would rather be with _____ than with anyone else.
23. There is nothing more important to me than my relationship with _____.
24. I especially like physical contact with _____.
25. There is something almost "magical" about my relationship with _____.
26. I adore _____.
27. I cannot imagine life without _____.
28. My relationship with _____ is passionate.
29. When I see romantic movies and read romantic books I think of _____.
30. I fantasize about _____.
31. I know that I care about _____.
32. I am committed to maintaining my relationship with _____.
33. Because of my commitment to _____, I would not let other people come between us.
34. I have confidence in the stability of my relationship with _____.

**Table 10-3   The Sternberg Triangular Love Scale (*continued*)**

35. I could not let anything get in the way of my commitment to _____.

36. I expect my love for _____ to last for the rest of my life.

37. I will always feel a strong responsibility for _____.

38. I view my commitment to _____ as a solid one.

39. I cannot imagine ending my relationship with _____.

40. I am certain of my love for _____.

41. I view my relationship with _____ as permanent.

42. I view my relationship with _____ as a good decision.

43. I feel a sense of responsibility toward _____.

44. I plan to continue in my relationship with _____.

45. Even when _____ is hard to deal with, I remain committed to our relationship.

Items 1 to 15 are for measuring the intimacy component; 16 to 30, for the passion component; and 31 to 45, for the decision/commitment component. In order to obtain your score, add up your ratings for each of the component subscales and divide by 15. This will give you an average rating for each item. (In the scale as it is used outside the context of this book, the scale items appear in a random order, rather than clustered by component, as they are here.)
Source: Sternberg, R. J. (1987). *The triangle of love: Intimacy, Passion, Commitment*, New York: Basic Books. Used by permission of R. J. Sternberg.

committed to their children than to their friends, but are likely to be more intimate with their friends than with their children.

When these three major components are combined in various ways, they generate eight different types of love relationships, all of which have something of an intuitive ring to them. Table 10-4 summarizes the various components.

1. In *nonlove* none of the three elements is present.

2. *Liking* is defined by the presence of the intimacy component only; one feels a sense of closeness but no passion or commitment.

3. *Infatuated love* results from passionate arousal in the absence of either intimacy or commitment. Love at first sight would be an example of this.

4. *Empty love* is characterized by a relationship in which the individuals are committed, but without intimacy or passion. This is the kind of love one sometimes sees in marriages that have stagnated over the years.

5. *Romantic love* is a combination of intimacy and passion.

6. *Companionate love* is a combination of intimacy and decision/commitment. This is a committed friendship, if you like. It may also be seen in marriage relationships after the passion has ebbed.

7. *Fatuous love* is defined as passion and commitment in the absence of intimacy. Fatuous love is the stuff of which old Hollywood movies were

Table 10-4   Taxonomy of Kinds of Love

| Kind of Love | Intimacy | Passion | Decision/Commitment |
|---|---|---|---|
| Nonlove | − | − | − |
| Liking | + | − | − |
| Infatuated love | − | + | − |
| Empty love | − | − | + |
| Romantic love | + | + | − |
| Companionate love | + | − | + |
| Fatuous love | − | + | + |
| Consummate love | + | + | + |

*Note:* + = component present; − = component absent. These kinds of love represent idealized cases based on the triangular theory. Most loving relationships will fit between categories, because the components of love occur in varying degrees, rather than being simply present or absent.
*Source:* Sternberg, R. J. (1986). A triangular theory of love. *Psychological Review, 93,* 119–135. Copyright © 1986 by the American Psychological Association. Adapted with permission.

sometimes made, in which a couple meet, have a whirlwind courtship, and are married shortly after. The passion component can indeed develop very rapidly, but intimacy takes time.

8. *Consummate love* is defined as the presence of intimacy, passion, and commitment. This is what we often hold up as the ideal. It may, however, be an elusive ideal that is apparently easier to achieve in the short term than to maintain over the long term.

***Critique of Sternberg's Theory***   Sternberg's approach has been criticized on several grounds. Any approach that rests on a statistical analysis of response patterns is open to the criticism that what comes out of the operation depends on what goes into it to begin with. For example, if no items characteristic of agape are present in the original scale, obviously the analysis is not going to come up with an agape component. And there are other problems as well.

Clyde Hendrick and Susan Hendrick (1989) have questioned Sternberg's assumption that the three primary components of love are really as independent as his treatment suggests. For example, others have found a significant friendship component to love (Davis & Todd, 1985) and a good deal of commitment as well (Fehr, 1988). The next approach we consider takes this into account.

## Love as a Prototype

Measures of the pencil-and-paper variety, showing correlations between love and other closely related notions, such as liking (Rubin, 1970), commitment (Fehr, 1988), and romanticism (Cunningham & Antill, 1981), suggest that

**Table 10-5    Prototype Analysis of Love and Commitment**

### Mean Centrality Ratings of the Features of Love and Commitment

| Feature | Rating | Feature | Rating |
|---|---|---|---|
| Love | | Love (*continued*) | |
| Trust | 7.500 | Do things for the other | 6.135 |
| Caring | 7.284 | Feel good about self | 6.068 |
| Honesty | 7.176 | Responsibility | 6.041 |
| Friendship | 7.081 | Warm feelings | 6.041 |
| Respect | 7.014 | Patience | 6.000 |
| Concern for the other's well-being | 7.000 | Long-lasting | 6.000 |
| Loyalty | 7.000 | Miss other when apart | 5.986 |
| Commitment | 6.919 | Comfort other | 5.946 |
| Accept other the way s/he is | 6.824 | Attachment | 5.892 |
| Supportiveness | 6.784 | Sex appeal | 5.865 |
| Want to be with the other | 6.784 | Touching | 5.824 |
| Interest in the other | 6.689 | Sexual passion | 5.811 |
| Affection | 6.676 | Need each other | 5.797 |
| Closeness | 6.649 | Mutual | 5.784 |
| Understanding | 6.608 | Contentment | 5.770 |
| Sharing | 6.581 | Put other first | 5.703 |
| Want best for other | 6.581 | Unconditional | 5.689 |
| Forgiveness | 6.554 | Wonderful feelings | 5.622 |
| Intimacy | 6.527 | Physical attraction | 5.581 |
| Other is important | 6.459 | Laughing | 5.473 |
| Openness | 6.392 | Sacrifice | 5.432 |
| Feel relaxed with other | 6.365 | Helping | 5.419 |
| Liking | 6.338 | Empathy | 5.351 |
| Compassion | 6.311 | Admiration | 5.311 |
| Devotion | 6.284 | Positive outlook | 5.284 |
| Giving | 6.230 | Kind | 5.135 |
| Happiness | 6.216 | Protectiveness | 5.108 |
| Feel free to talk about anything | 6.189 | Have a lot in common | 5.108 |

these categories tend to overlap to some extent. In light of such findings, Beverley Fehr (Fehr, 1988, 1993; Fehr & Russell, 1984) has taken the position that our concept of love basically rests on a cognitive model, or prototype, that consists of a number of conceptually overlapping notions. For example, Fehr (1988) found that when college students were asked to list various features of love, they mentioned such feelings as caring, happiness, trust, sharing,

**Table 10-5  Prototype Analysis of Love and Commitment (*continued*)**

### Mean Centrality Ratings of the Features of Love and Commitment

| Feature | Rating | Feature | Rating |
|---|---|---|---|
| **Love** | | **Commitment (*continued*)** | |
| Excitement | 5.027 | Love | 6.053 |
| Security | 4.986 | Respect | 6.039 |
| Think about the other all the time | 4.446 | Caring | 6.013 |
| Energy | 4.284 | A high priority | 5.908 |
| Heart rate increases | 4.257 | Giving | 5.882 |
| Euphoria | 4.122 | A promise | 5.776 |
| Gazing at the other | 4.095 | Obligation | 5.750 |
| See only the other's good qualities | 3.446 | Sacrifice | 5.711 |
| Butterflies in stomach | 3.405 | Sharing | 5.711 |
| Uncertainty | 2.878 | Hard work | 5.658 |
| Dependency | 2.811 | Helping | 5.618 |
| Scary | 2.284 | Working out problems | 5.618 |
| **Commitment** | | Conscious decision | 5.408 |
| Loyalty | 6.724 | Attachment | 5.382 |
| Responsibility | 6.605 | Liking | 5.382 |
| Living up to your word | 6.566 | Giving and taking | 5.355 |
| Faithfulness | 6.553 | Maturity | 5.289 |
| Trust | 6.539 | Long-lasting | 5.250 |
| Being there for the other in good and bad times | 6.526 | Mutual agreement | 5.237 |
| | | Work toward common goals | 5.224 |
| Devotion | 6.421 | Affection | 5.197 |
| Reliable | 6.342 | Put other first | 4.987 |
| Give best effort | 6.276 | Attention focused on other | 4.961 |
| Supportiveness | 6.263 | Contentment | 4.645 |
| Perseverance | 6.118 | Security | 4.592 |
| Concern about the other's well-being | 6.066 | Think about other all the time | 3.829 |
| Honesty | 6.053 | Feel trapped | 2.487 |

*Note:* Ratings made on a scale ranging from 1 *(extremely poor feature of love [commitment])* to 8 *(extremely good feature of love [commitment]).*

*Source:* Fehr, B. (1988). Prototype analysis of the concepts of love and commitment. *Journal of Personality and Social Psychology, 55,* 557–579. Copyright © 1986 by the American Psychological Association. Reprinted with permission.

and understanding. But they also mentioned scary and uncertain—not features we ordinarily think of as being associated with love.

At the same time, Fehr noted other elements, such as laughing, gazing at the other, doing things for the other, and helping. She noted physiological responses (such as butterflies in the stomach, increases in heart rate and sexual passion); cognitive responses (such as thinking about the other); a rational component (such as respect, admiration, and having many things in common); and a more biased component (involving distortion, looking at the other's positive side). Still other elements were lack of inhibitions, feeling relaxed and open, and a component we might call social support, sharing, empathy and altruism, sacrifice and concern for the other. In the case of love, all these seem to come as a package deal—the good and the bad, the exciting and the dull, the rational and the crazy. How, then, are we to analyze this love package without dissecting it to pieces and destroying its essential integrity?

***The Centrality of Features***    Are some features of the love prototype more important than others? Fehr (1988) suggests that they are. She had subjects rate various features on a scale of 1–8 as they related to love, where 1 indicated a less central feature and 8 represented a more central one.

What were the features that college students considered most central to the concept of love? Trust was the most central, followed by caring, honesty, and friendship. Intimacy, affection, and liking were also considered central to the love prototype, while attachment was seen as less central. And, as can be seen in Table 10-5, some items (such as trust, loyalty, supportiveness) were considered central to both love and commitment.

When we compare Fehr's findings to Walster and Walster's (1978) distinction between passionate and companionate love, we note features of both passionate and companionate love in Fehr's love prototype. Items associated with passionate love, such as feelings of sexual arousal, preoccupation with the other, euphoria, and increased arousal, were all considered features of the love prototype, as were such companionate features as trust, caring, respect, friendship, and loyalty. But, interestingly enough, not one feature that is typically associated with passionate love was considered a central feature of love by this group of college students. Indeed, the more passionate aspects were rated among the lowest in centrality.

In addition, about 20% of Fehr's subjects considered love as a feature of commitment, and about 15% considered commitment as a feature of love. Such a finding suggests that the two are not considered completely independent, but neither are they completely overlapping (Fehr, 1988). Further, when we focus on those features that are considered unique to love versus those that are shared with closely related notions (trust, commitment, and liking), it tends to be the *shared* features that are more central and the *unique* attributes that are more peripheral. Trust, commitment, and liking are all seen as central to the notion of love, whereas such things as passion and euphoria are considered as less central.

***Centrality and the Effects of Hedging***    One of the most interesting aspects of Fehr's (1988) study comes in a test of the effects of "hedging" on features that are either central or peripheral to the love prototype. What do we mean

Richard Cline © 1995
from the New Yorker
Collection. All Rights
Reserved.

*"Look, Ellen, haven't I always been fairly honest with you?"*

by hedging? A hedge is a qualifier, such as "sort of," "kind of," or "somewhat," that we use to temper the meaning of a word or phrase. For example, note what hedging does to the statement "Pat trusts Chris": It becomes "Pat *sort of* trusts Chris," or "Pat is faithful to Chris" becomes "Pat is *somewhat* faithful to Chris."

Note, on the other hand, what happens in the case of more peripheral features of the love prototype; for example, when "Pat is dependent upon Chris" is hedged to become "Pat is sort of dependent upon Chris," or when "Pat idolizes Chris" is hedged to become "Pat sort of idolizes Chris."

Fehr hypothesized that such hedges would have much less effect on a hypothetical relationship when applied to features peripheral to the love prototype than when applied to features central to the love prototype. And this is what she found. Subjects judging hypothetical cases viewed the hedges on central features of the love prototype as likely to have more serious consequences for a relationship than hedges of more peripheral features.

***Violation of Central Versus Peripheral Features*** Much the same rationale applies in the case of violations of central versus peripheral features. When subjects were presented with scenarios in which either central or peripheral features of the love prototype were violated, they judged the violations of peripheral features to have fewer repercussions for the relationship than violations of central features. For example, subjects were presented with a description of a romantic relationship such as the following:

Deb and Ed met in their junior year. They were both biology majors, both had an interest in environmental issues, and both loved the outdoors. They found themselves spending more and more time together, taking walks, watching TV, or working on homework assignments. Over time their relationship became more and more intimate. Certain things might happen that would hurt their relationship.

Participants were then given various possible events and asked to rate them for their likely effect on the relationship. What did they consider as likely to have the greatest impact? Loss of caring, loss of trust, loss of feelings of honesty and respect or feeling that friendship was no longer part of the relationship—all violations of features that were central to the love prototype.

On the other hand, violations of peripheral features were seen as relatively inconsequential. For example, whether or not they stopped feeling euphoric, stopped gazing at each other, or stopped seeing only one another's good qualities was not considered likely to have much of an effect on the relationship.

So the picture that emerges from this line of research is that those features of love that correspond to companionate love (such as trust, caring, and friendship) are considered to be more central to love. Violations of these features are seen as more likely to be damaging to a relationship. On the other hand, the passionate aspects of love are considered to be more peripheral to love, and when these are violated, they are not seen as having much of an impact on a relationship.

It would seem, then, that a good case can be made for considering love as a prototype. Such an approach goes well with other things we know about cognitive models, expectations, and emotions generally. But the approach still leaves certain questions unanswered. Most obvious among them are questions concerning the origins of love, why it is such a powerful emotion, why some people respond positively when love beckons and others respond with reserve or anxiety. For some thoughts on that, we turn to a consideration of love as a form of attachment.

## Love as Attachment

As noted in Chapter 1, researchers have pointed out the similarities between mother-infant attachment in humans and other primates. Some have considered this bond the "beginning of love" (Harlow, 1971). There are, indeed, some striking similarities between infant attachment and romantic love in adulthood. For example, both are likely to involve frequent eye contact, smiling, holding, sharing, and other signs of empathy. Both tend to generate a sense of security when the other is present and distress when the other is absent until closeness is restored (Weiss, 1991). Such similarities suggest that a common underlying process is at work (Ainsworth, 1989; Shaver et al., 1988).

Accordingly, researchers focusing on attachment have emphasized the importance of early experience, especially the role of maternal caregiving. Their general findings have been that such things as quality of care, responsiveness, feeding patterns, sensitivity, cooperation, and acceptance are associated with different attachment styles later in life.

Attachment styles, once established, tend to resist change. It is likely each individual in this relationship formed secure and loving attachments early in life.

***Stability in Attachment Patterns***   Attachment theorists assume that, once established in infancy and childhood, early working models of attachment tend to become habitual and resistant to change, and they operate largely outside of awareness. For example, Chante Cox and colleagues (1992) found that the time the mother spent with the infant and the nature of the mother-infant interaction at 3 months predicted an infant's attachment style at age 12 months. Similarly, attachment style at age 12 months predicts attachment style at age 6 years rather well (Main et al., 1985).

Over time, these attachment styles tend to generalize to other situations or persons. If this is indeed the case, we would expect that early attachment experiences would be reflected in the way we relate to others in adulthood. Depending on their early experience, individuals should show attachment styles that are similar to those described for infants—secure, insecure-avoidant, and insecure-anxious/ambivalent (Ainsworth et al., 1978).

When infants' experiences with their primary caregiver are positive, they tend to develop a secure attachment style. And in adulthood they should find it easy to get close to others and feel comfortable in depending on others and having others depend on them. Those who experience inconsistent caregiving early in life should develop an anxious/ambivalent love style as adults. On the one hand, they will tend to seek relationships in which they are totally immersed; on the other hand, they will avoid getting too close to others and worry about whether their partners are really in love with them or might leave.

Those whose early experiences have been negative or who experienced fear of being abandoned should develop avoidant love styles as adults, characterized by discomfort in getting too close to others, distrust of others, and difficulty in being in a position of dependency. They should also be more controlled in their emotional displays and tend not to seek support from others in times of distress (Feeney & Noller, 1996; Hazan & Shaver, 1987; Shaver & Hazan, 1988, 1993; Shaver et al., 1988).

Indeed, in Cindy Hazan and Philip Shaver's (1987) study, adults with a secure attachment style recalled their childhood relationships as warmer. Those with avoidant attachment styles tended to view their mothers as cold and rejecting, and those with an anxious/ambivalent attachment style tended to remember their fathers as unfair.

Having said this, although there can be stability in attachment styles over time, there can also be change (Shaver et al., 1988). For example, when families experience stresses (such as separation or divorce), children tend to show corresponding changes in attachment style. Indeed, Hazan and her associates (cited in Shaver & Hazan, 1993) found that 22% of adults who changed in attachment style over the course of a year were also likely to have experienced relationships that were incongruent with their old style. And although studies have often reported a similar pattern (60% securely attached) when attachment style was measured globally, when individuals have been asked to respond to the same items with respect to specific others (such as mother, father, best friend, and romantic partner), the percentages of "securely attached" varied widely. For example, in one study 98% indicated being secure with their friends (Kojetin, 1993). This suggests that attachment style in adults interacts with other things, such as the nature of specific relationships.

On the other hand, there is some evidence that feelings of attachment can persist even when we would just as soon they did not. For example, when going through a divorce or separation, people often report a sense of attachment to the former spouse (Sarason, 1979). This feeling of attachment does not depend on the relationship being happy, or whether the divorce/separation had been asked for, and it often continues in the absence of respect or liking and despite the fact that alternative relationships are available. Parallels between such feelings of attachment and the bonds that many of us experience with our parents are remarkable.

However, the utility of the attachment-style approach does not rest on attachment patterns being completely stable over time. The approach simply hypothesizes a relationship between early caregiving and attachment.

***Attachment Style and Other Approaches***   When we compare the attachment-style approach to the work of others who have theorized about love, we find some important similarities. For example, in comparing their approach to Lee's love styles, Shaver and Hazan (1988) suggest that a secure love style corresponds to Eros and agape. An avoidant love style corresponds to *ludus,* and an anxious/ambivalent love style corresponds to mania.

What others have called **limerence** (Tennov, 1979), or **desperate love** (Sperling, 1985), attachment theorists see as reflecting an anxious/ambivalent attachment style. The attachment approach suggests that such anxious/

ambivalent love styles can be traced to inconsistent and/or unresponsive care-giving early in life (Feeney & Noller, 1996).

Along these same lines, Marc Levy and Keith Davis (1988) found that intimacy, passion, and commitment as portrayed in Sternberg's triangular theory were all positively correlated with a secure attachment style, and an avoidant attachment style was correlated with lack of commitment.

Consistent with this, Judith Feeney and Patricia Noller (1990) found an association between early family experience and attachment, on the one hand, and "mental models" of relationships, on the other. For example, avoidant types in their study were likely to have experienced long periods of separation from their mother during childhood. Secure subjects tended to be high in self-confidence, low in neurotic love (defined as a preoccupation with and emotional dependence on the partner), and low in avoidance of intimacy. Anxious/ambivalent subjects were high on neurotic love and low on circumspect love (which is similar to friendship).

Similarly, Jeffrey Simpson (1990) found, in a study of dating relationships, that those who were securely attached showed higher levels of trust, commitment, satisfaction, and interdependence. Both avoidant and anxious/ambivalent attachment styles were negatively related to trust, commitment, and satisfaction. Avoidant types were generally less committed to their relationships, and males who were avoidant tended to express less distress upon breaking up. Such findings are generally consistent with Shaver and Hazan's position.

What are the advantages of the attachment approach? First, it offers a developmental perspective. Various orientations to romantic love are seen as having their origins in early attachment experiences. Consistent with Fehr's approach, these early experiences tend to generate models (or prototypes), which eventually result in different approaches to love, or love styles. Second, the approach helps to account for a broad range of findings in close personal relationships. Its application is not limited to romantic love. It also suggests important accounts of loneliness and jealousy (see Chapters 5 and 15).

Finally, the attachment perspective offers an integrative view of romantic love. Attachment style fits well with many of the features of love studied by other researchers, suggesting that there may be certain biases built into our relationships as a result of our early attachment experiences. Accordingly, both healthy and unhealthy relationships can be accounted for by the same general principles.

## Conclusion

Following the early work of Rubin, researchers have taken different approaches to the study of liking and loving. Some have been rather specific, focusing, for example, on companionate and passionate love, or friendship and love. Others have taken a more comprehensive view. Each of these has its strengths and weaknesses.

The application of prototype theory to the area of liking and loving introduces an element of integration into research that seems especially useful in generating testable hypotheses. But the prototypes or working models of a given individual may depend on her or his early experiences. Those whose early childhood experiences are positive tend to develop secure attachment styles, those whose early experiences are inconsistent tend to develop anxious/ambivalent attachment styles, and those whose early experiences caused them to worry about being abandoned tend to develop avoidant attachment styles. Each of these, then, is likely to be reflected in later relationships, especially adult romantic relationships. And so, with the attachment approach, we see that a developmental dimension is added to research on liking and loving, and the area becomes more integrated and more firmly anchored in early experience.

## Suggestions for Further Reading

Jankowiak, W. R., & Fischer, E. F. (1992). A cross-cultural perspective on romantic love. *Ethnology, 31,* 149–155. These researchers find evidence that romantic love is a universal, or nearly universal, phenomenon.

Jeffries, V. (1993). Virtue and attraction: Validation of a measure of love. *Journal of Social and Personal Relationships, 10,* 99–117. An effort to integrate various notions of love using the two broad themes of virtue and attraction.

Kelley, H. H., Berscheid, E., Christensen, A., Harvey, J. H., Huston, T. L., Levinger, G., McClintock, E., Peplau, L. A., & Peterson, D. R. (1983). *Close relationships.* New York: W. H. Freeman. A book of independently written chapters by some of the pioneers in personal relationship research.

Peplau, L. A., Hill, C. T., & Rubin, Z. (1993). Sex role attitudes in dating and marriage: A 15-year follow-up of the Boston couples study. *Journal of Social Issues, 49,* 31–52. Do they all live happily ever after? Not all, but some seem to do better than others.

Shaver, P. R., & Hazan, C. (1993). Adult romantic attachment: Theory and evidence. In D. Perlman & W. H. Jones (Eds.), *Advances in personal relationships* (Vol. 4). London: Kingsley. A recent statement about romantic love from the attachment perspective.

Simpson, J. A., Campbell, B., & Berscheid, E. (1986). The association between romantic love and marriage: Kepart (1967) twice revisited. *Personality and Social Psychology Bulletin, 12,* 363–372. The younger generation is not becoming cynical about romantic love.

Sprecher, S., & Metts, S. (1989). Development of the "Romantic Beliefs Scale" and examination of the effects of gender and gender-role orientation. *Journal of Social and Personal Relationships, 6,* 387–411. A case study in the construction and early attempts at validation of a romantic beliefs scale.

Sternberg, R. J. (1987). Liking versus loving: A comparative evaluation of theories. *Psychological Bulletin, 102,* 331–345. A valuable overview of the liking and loving issue as it stood in 1987.

Sternberg, R. J., & Barnes, M. L. (Eds.). (1988). *The psychology of love.* New Haven, CT: Yale University Press. An edited volume featuring some of the major researchers/theorists in the area of liking and loving.

# CHAPTER 11

## ✂ *Physical Attractiveness*

*During my graduate school days, I often ate in the snack bar, and one weekend I noticed a crowd gathered at the other end of the room. I soon learned what all the excitement was about. One of the fraternities was having a "slave auction," and a number of pledges were lined up on the platform, stripped to their waists, hands tied behind their backs, waiting to be auctioned off to the highest bidder. I had never seen a slave auction before, so I watched as the bidding started. What all the commotion was about, apparently, was that one of the more eligible men on campus was on the auction block. He was a star athlete, movie-star handsome, in other words, a "hunk." The auctioneer checked his teeth and assured potential bidders that none were missing, then noted that he had a strong back, good for heavy lifting, and the bidding started. Higher and higher went the bids. To my amazement, four young women pooled their resources and finally walked off with their "slave" for 3 hours on Saturday night. Price: $135.*

*The next "slave" on the block lived on my floor in the dorm, and I knew him. He weighed about 95 pounds and looked more like someone in middle school than a college student. Again the auctioneer checked his teeth, commented on his good strong back, and so on. This time there was dead silence from the crowd. "Does anybody need their closets cleaned? Clothes washed? Shoes shined?" Still no response. The auctioneer became noticeably anxious. The crowd began to disperse. Finally, one sympathetic coed placed a bid and walked off with her "slave" for 3 hours on Saturday night. Price: 25 cents.*

Physical attractiveness has been defined as "that which best represents one's conception of the ideal in appearance and gives the greatest pleasure to the senses."[1] This isn't something that we ordinarily give much thought to. But

---

[1] From Hatfield, E., & Sprecher, S. (1986). *Mirror, Mirror: The Importance of Looks in Everyday Life.* Albany, NY: State University of New York Press.

research evidence suggests that the influence of physical attractiveness is far more pervasive than most of us realize or care to admit. In this chapter we explore the issue of physical attractiveness and note some of the implications of this for personal relationships.

## Why Physical Attractiveness?

Returning to the evolutionary theme for a moment, we note first that the issue of physical attractiveness does not seem to be unique to the human species. Other animals show various preferences based on physical appearance as well. One or two examples might help us better appreciate what happens over many generations as some characteristics are "selected" (note the term) and some are not. The peacock offers one obvious case. How has such a garish-looking creature managed to survive with hungry predators around? Certainly not by blending in with his surroundings. For all the disadvantages of his brightly colored tail feathers, however, the peacock has one decided advantage. His elaborate plumage is attractive to the peahen. Over many generations, elaborately adorned peacocks apparently attracted mates while their duller looking peers did not. As a consequence, we don't see too many drab peacocks around today (Buss, 1994).

This selection process was dramatically demonstrated in a series of experiments by Nancy Burley (1985), who was studying the mating behavior of

For the female, this peacock's tail enhances his attractiveness. The more attractive the male's appearance, the more likely the female is to accept his advances.

zebra finches. Burley tagged a group of finches with various colored leg bands and then monitored their reproductive activity. Over the next 5 months, it became clear that some of the birds were doing better at the mating game than others. Specifically, 10 of the 14 birds wearing red or pink leg bands were breeding, while 6 of the 9 birds wearing light green were not. When some of the nonbreeding finches were re-banded with red or pink, they were breeding within the next 11 weeks, while those that were still banded green were not.

This finding made it possible to study the effects of "attractiveness" on other aspects of the birds' behavior. By altering the color of their leg bands and keeping other things constant, Burley made some startling discoveries. The zebra finches, it seems, are perfectly capable of establishing their worth in the rating and mating game. And those suddenly made "beautiful" by their colorful leg bands began to take advantage of the fact.

Emboldened by their attractiveness, the red-banded males became "playboys." Some members of this ordinarily monogamous species acquired more than one mate, and their reproductive success soon surpassed that of their less attractive peers. Indeed, over a period of 22 months, the reproductive success of the red-banded males was twice that of orange-banded (neutral) or green-banded (unattractive) males.

Meanwhile, the "more attractive" females also showed higher reproductive success. But they did not become polyandrous. Instead, they became "liberated." They invested less time and effort in the rearing of their offspring, and their plain (unbanded) mates had to compensate (Burley, 1985).

One does not have to be a geneticist to see the genetic advantage in being physically attractive. And as the opening paragraph of the chapter illustrates, the effects of physical attractiveness do not begin and end with peacocks and zebra finches. They also have profound implications for humans.

## Measuring Physical Attractiveness

Despite some variation in what is considered the ideal over time and across cultures, the evidence suggests that overall there is remarkable agreement in our judgments of who is, and who is not, considered physically attractive (Cunningham et al., 1995; Hatfield & Sprecher, 1986b).

In one study, for example, when college students were asked to rate photographs of females from least to most attractive on a 7-point scale, the correlations between male and female raters was very high—.93 (Kopera et al., 1971). In addition, when researchers have varied facial characteristics using computer-generated images, they have found that symmetrical faces are judged to be more physically attractive than asymmetrical faces. Students with symmetrical faces report not only having more friends and romantic interests but also being sexually active earlier than those with less symmetrical faces (Thornhill & Gangestad, 1994).

Such findings suggest that a physical attractiveness bias may be built into our biology. And as we see in Box 11-1, there is some evidence that this is the case. Preferences for certain physical characteristics appear very early in life,

## Box 11-1 In a Different Key
### Is an Appreciation for Beauty Built Into Our Biology?

There is some indication that a physical attractiveness bias may be built into our biology. For example, when infants 2–3 months old are shown pictures of adult faces, they spend more time looking at physically attractive faces than at the less attractive faces (Langlois et al., 1987). It's hard to make the case that 2–3 month old children are showing a cultural bias. And similarly, when young children (2 years, 8 months to 6 years, 1 month) were shown how to push a button to receive 5 seconds exposure time to pictures of attractive and less attractive faces, the children pressed an average of 72 times when the face was physically attractive and an average of 36 times when it was less attractive. The sex of the stimulus person in this case was not significant. Mere exposure to physically attractive faces is more reinforcing than exposure to less attractive faces, even when the subjects have never met the child in question (Dion, 1977).

And when recently arrived Asian and Hispanic students were asked to rate the attractiveness of Asian, Hispanic, black, and white women from photographs of their faces, the correlations between the various groups ranged from .91 to .94 (Cunningham et al., 1995). Apparently, this is not a new finding.

> Mr. Winwood Reade, . . . who has had ample opportunities for observation, not only with the Negroes of the West Coast of Africa, but with those of the interior who have never associated with Europeans, is convinced that their ideas of beauty are on the whole the same as ours. He has repeatedly found that he agreed with Negroes in their estimation of the beauty of native girls; and that their appreciation of the beauty of European women corresponded with ours. (Darwin, 1871, p. 350)

There seems, in other words, to be a universal quality to female facial beauty.

and researchers have noted that there is surprising agreement in what constitutes physical attractiveness cross culturally.

## Physical Attractiveness and Gender

Although both males and females tend to show a preference for those who are physically attractive, they differ significantly in how much importance they place on physical attractiveness. Studies using various methods, such as questionnaire data, studies of personal ads published in lonely hearts columns, and preferences as expressed in video dating services, show that males generally consider physical attractiveness in a partner to be more important than do females (Allgeier & Wiederman, 1991; Bailey et al., 1994; Buss, 1989, 1994; Buss & Barnes, 1986; Cash & Kilcullen, 1985; Feingold, 1990; Garcia et al., 1991; Goodwin, 1990; Green et al., 1984; Harrison & Saeed, 1977; Hatfield & Sprecher, 1986b; Howard et al., 1987; Koestner & Wheeler, 1988; Sprecher

Is there a universal quality to beauty? Charles Darwin suggested as much over a century ago. Since then, researchers have noted that there is surprising agreement in what constitutes physical attractiveness cross culturally.

et al., 1994; Townsend & Levy, 1990a, 1990b; Wiederman & Allgeier, 1992). There are various ways of accounting for this difference. One is to take an evolutionary perspective.

### The Evolutionary Account

In evolutionary terms, the reason males consider physical attractiveness important in a partner is that certain physical characteristics are associated with reproductive success (Buss, 1994; Buss & Schmitt, 1993; Kendrick & Trost, 1989). For example, beauty (and age) are cues to a female's health and reproductive potential (Buss & Schmitt, 1993). So, from an evolutionary perspective, we would expect males to have shown a preference for mates who were young and physically attractive. Males who were selective in this way tended to leave more offspring. Males that didn't have this preference left fewer offspring over time. As a consequence, males today tend to have a preference for young, healthy (physically attractive) females.

By the same token, a female's preference for a mate who showed signs of physical ability, intellect, ambition, and status served to increase the prospects that her offspring would survive, because these characteristics were associated with the ability to generate and control resources. Females who ignored these signs over many generations were less likely to have access to the resources necessary to raise offspring to maturity. So we would expect females today to have a preference for mates who show evidence of having control over resources. And, generally, this is what we find.

For example, studies of ads placed in lonely hearts columns show that males are more likely to emphasize their (own) professional or occupational status and prefer partners who are physically attractive and somewhat younger. Females, on the other hand, tend to emphasize their physical appearance and seek partners who are somewhat older and high in occupational status (Cameron et al., 1977; Harrison & Saeed, 1977; Koestner & Wheeler, 1988).

## The Sociocultural Account

It's important to note that much of the evidence with regard to sex differences in mate preference is consistent with sociocultural explanations as well. The male preference for a physically attractive mate can be accounted for by noting that an attractive female is something of a status symbol, and the female's interest in a partner who is a good provider is consistent with the poorer economic opportunities that women traditionally face, especially when they are encumbered by pregnancy and child care (Feingold, 1990).

In fact, when it comes to romantic partners, the evidence suggests that males and females both prefer physically attractive partners to about the same degree (Feingold, 1990; Sprecher, 1989; Sprecher et al., 1994). For example, in studies of video dating services, the factor that differentiates the most popular (that is, most sought after as dates) from the least popular is physical attractiveness (Green et al., 1984). This is true for males and females alike. It may be that men are more likely to be in a better position to indulge their preference for "trophy mates" in a way that women are not. Women may simply be more likely to compromise their preference for a physically attractive mate out of more practical considerations (Sprecher et al., 1994).

*Radiating Beauty*   The effects of physical attractiveness do not end with the physically attractive themselves. Physically attractive people seem to have a Midas touch. In one study, for example, Harold Sigall and David Landy (1973) investigated the "radiating effects of beauty." Participants were brought into the lab three at a time. One was the actual subject and the other two were accomplices in the experiment. The subject was asked to rate the other two on several different scales. And what were the results? When the male (accomplice) was represented as being with a physically attractive female, the overall impression of him was more positive than when he was with a less attractive female or when the attractive female was merely present but the two were not represented as being together. So the effect of a female's beauty seems to transfer to some extent to the man she is with. And this is true whether the person doing the evaluating is a male or a female. But the radiating effects of physical attractiveness seem to go in only one direction. A handsome male does not seem to do much for a less attractive female (Bar-Tal & Saxe, 1976a; Sigall & Landy, 1973).

Finally, we should note that beauty also seems to rub off on the work of physically attractive people. For example, David Landy and Harold Sigall (1974) had participants judge essays with the "writer's" picture attached, and the photographs varied in attractiveness. The results showed that essays were judged more favorably when participants thought they were written by the more physically attractive authors.

***The Contamination Effect***   If there is a "radiating beauty" effect, is there also a "contamination" effect? What happens, for example, when we associate with someone who is decidedly not physically attractive? The answer seems to be that others tend to judge us by the company we keep in both cases. When we associate with others who are unattractive, physically, we are likely to be perceived as less attractive ourselves (Wedell et al., 1987). And, as we see in the next section, this bias is part of a larger picture.

## Physical Attractiveness and Attributions

We are reluctant to admit to judging others by their appearance, but there is strong evidence that this is exactly what we do (Albright et al., 1988; Eagly et al., 1991). For example, in one study college students were presented with three photographs, one of a less attractive person, one of someone who was average in physical appearance, and one who was highly attractive, and then asked to rate each one on a number of characteristics. The results showed that those who are more physically attractive are seen as warmer, more sexually responsive, more sensitive, kinder, more interesting, stronger, more poised, more sociable, more nurturant, more outgoing, and more exciting on dates than those who are less physically attractive. These findings are true for both male and female judges, and they are true whether the judges are rating the same sex or the opposite sex (Dion et al., 1972).

The physically attractive are also assumed to have more prestigious oc-cupations, to be more competent in the role of husband or wife, to have hap-pier marriages and happier social and professional lives (Dion et al., 1972; Dion & Dion, 1988). Handsome men tend to be seen as more masculine, and beautiful women tend to be seen as more feminine (Gillen, 1981; Lucker et al., 1981). Even adults aged 60 to 93 who are more physically attractive tend to be judged more positively (Johnson & Pittinger, 1984).

Finally, our judgments of physical attractiveness are not based solely on facial features. We attribute more positive personality characteristics to those with athletic builds and more negative ones to those who are either overweight or underweight (Ryckman et al., 1991). In short, there seems to be a physical attractiveness stereotype. What are some of the consequences of this?

## Social Consequences of Physical Attractiveness

Physically attractive individuals tend to get more offers of assistance when they are in need of help (Benson et al., 1976), more cooperation in conflict situations (Kahn et al., 1971), and more in the way of self-disclosure from others in conversations (Brundage et al., 1977). They are also more effective in getting those they approach to agree with (the content of) and to sign a petition. And this is true regardless of the sex of the individual or the sex of those they approach (Chaiken, 1979). And there is more.

## Physical Attractiveness and Occupational Success

It is a fact that physical attractiveness is related to occupational success. Although qualifications are important, physical attractiveness helps as well. In the area of hiring, for example, physically attractive applicants are more likely to get job offers than are their less attractive counterparts with similar qualifications (Dipboye et al., 1975). And once hired, physically attractive employees tend to be seen as more effective (Landy & Sigall, 1974). The case of Lisa recently came to my attention.

When the local state camp for young male offenders recently had an opening for a counselor, the (all-male) staff expected to hire another male. Still, when a female applied, it seemed only fair to grant her an interview and let her see for herself what the situation was like. Imagine their dilemma when Lisa appeared. Her academic record was excellent. She was well qualified. She had experience working with juvenile delinquents, and she interviewed well. There was only one problem. Lisa was a head-turning beauty. This is not necessarily considered an advantage in working at a camp for male juvenile delinquents. Much to their credit, however, the staff did not discriminate against her, and after cautioning her against dressing too provocatively, they offered her the job. A year later, by all reports, the staff (and the "campers") are all very supportive and respectful of their new counselor.

## Physical Attractiveness and "Legal" Settings

There is also some evidence that juries are influenced by physical attractiveness (Efran, 1974). In simulated trials, for example, physically attractive defendants are less likely to be found guilty than are their less attractive counterparts, and they also tend to receive milder sentences for similar crimes.

But there are exceptions to this general rule. For example, when physically attractive defendants are found guilty of swindling, they tend to receive more severe sentences than less attractive defendants, based (presumably) on the assumption that they used their physical appearance to swindle their victims (Sigall & Ostrove, 1975). The seriousness of the crime also seems to make a difference. For less serious crimes, the more physically attractive the defendant (based on police officer judgments), the lower the fine or bail. For more serious crimes, however, fines (or bail) do not seem to be affected by the defendants' physical attractiveness (Downs & Lyons, 1991).

Finally, in cases of rape, physical attractiveness can be a disadvantage for the victim. Physically attractive females are more likely to be seen as responsible for enticing their attackers in cases of rape. Here, however, the physical attractiveness of the judges also enters the picture. Both male and female judges who are less physically attractive themselves are more likely to find that physically attractive rape victims provoked their attacker (Baunach, 1974).

## Physical Attractiveness and Mental Health

In general, physical attractiveness seems to be associated with positive mental health. Physically attractive clients tend to be given more favorable prognoses by counselors (Barocas & Vance, 1974). Physically attractive therapists are viewed as more competent, and there is some evidence that clients show greater improvement when treated by more physically attractive therapists (Shapiro et al., 1976). On the other hand, when physically attractive clients have long-term psychological problems, therapists are less likely to view them as serious. They may assume such individuals tend to have "high-class anxieties" and, at any rate, can depend on a supportive social milieu to see them through (Cash et al., 1977).

## Physical Attractiveness and Personality

In assessing the effects of physical attractiveness on personality, it's necessary to keep in mind the physical attractiveness stereotype. If the physically attractive are assumed to be kinder, more responsive, sexually warmer, happier, and more successful, does believing make it so?

Physically attractive individuals tend to have more social options open to them and can be more selective in choosing both their friends and situations for socializing. They are likely to get more practice in socializing. They tend to enter social situations confident that they will be well received, and as a consequence, they tend to become the very thing others expect them to be.

Evidence consistent with this connection between expectations and behavior came in a study in which unacquainted male and female subjects were given background information on their "partner," but the two remained in separate rooms. Then the males rated females on several characteristics, based on a telephone conversation and a photograph (allegedly) of her (Snyder et al., 1977). In fact, what the experimenters did was vary the appearance of the partners by showing the men pictures of females who were either high or low in physical attractiveness.

What effect did this have? Not only were the physically attractive women rated more positively by the subjects themselves, but independent judges listening to tape recordings of the *male* end of the conversation rated the men as more social, sexually warmer, and more permissive and interesting when they thought they were talking to a highly attractive female. Similarly, judges listening only to the *female* end of the conversation rated the women as more poised, more sociable, sexually warmer, and more outgoing when the males believed they were talking to someone who was physically attractive. Apparently, women who were assumed to be physically attractive talked in a more socially poised and outgoing way. Those who were expected to be beautiful behaved beautifully.

Over time, then, the responses of others seem to become internalized, and as a consequence, physical attractiveness is associated with a more positive self-concept (Adams, 1977). But, again, there is some evidence for sex differences. For example, in a study of adult men and women ages 18–80, Gerald Adams (1979) found very little relationship between physical attractiveness and various personality characteristics among males. Apparently, handsome is as handsome does in our society. However, for females, things are different. Physically attractive women tend to be more self-accepting, and they see themselves as more likable and more in control of their lives. They are also less fearful of negative evaluations, and as a group, they tend to be more assertive and more active socially (Jackson & Huston, 1975).

## Physical Attractiveness Over the Life Span

Evidence suggests that the effects of physical attractiveness start very early in life and continue well into old age. In addition, physical attractiveness is not limited to heterosexual relationships; it affects both same-sex and opposite-sex relationships.

### Physical Attractiveness and Children

Studies of adult-infant interactions show that the physical appearance of a newborn can affect the attitudes and behaviors of adult caregivers. For example, the attractiveness of an infant is a good predictor of the quality of the parent-child attachment (Hildebrandt & Fitzgerald, 1983), and even nurses caring for premature infants see those who are physically attractive as having more positive intellectual prospects (Corter et al., 1978).

Young children also show a preference for peers who are physically attractive. In one experiment, children were shown photographs of other children's faces that varied in physical attractiveness. They were then asked questions about the children pictured. The results indicated that young children prefer other children who are physically attractive and tend to reject those who are less attractive. Similarly, when preschoolers were asked to indicate which children in the photographs might exhibit certain social behaviors, they saw the physically attractive children as being more friendly and more likely to dislike shouting and fighting, and the less attractive children as more likely to be involved in aggression and other negative behaviors. So we see evidence for a physical attractiveness stereotype even in preschool children (Dion, 1973).

Physically attractive children are seen as more socially outgoing, more poised, more confident, kinder, and more likable than their less attractive peers. Teachers view attractive children as less problematic and less mischievous than their less attractive peers (Dion & Berscheid, 1974). When physically attractive children are involved in misbehavior, people generally attribute more positive motives to them and are less inclined to see the misbehavior as truly representative of their personality. Similar behaviors on the part of less attractive children tend to be viewed as representative of an underlying disposition, and the punishment recommended tends to be more severe (Dion, 1974).

In addition, parents of physically attractive children tend to have greater expectations of them in terms of their personal and social success (Adams & LaVoie, 1975). In the classroom, teachers' expectations tend to be higher for physically attractive children than for less attractive children (Adams & Crane, 1980). Not only do teachers expect more, they tend to provide more information to attractive children, give them more opportunities, more support, and more positive evaluations (Adams & LaVoie, 1977). So the effects of physical attractiveness appear quite early in life.

## Physical Attractiveness and Romantic Relationships

The greatest impact of physical attractiveness is likely to come during adolescence and young adulthood when romantic relationships take center stage (Adams, 1980). Let's begin with a look at the effects of physical attractiveness on dating.

*Physical Attractiveness and Dating*   The importance of physical attractiveness in dating was vividly demonstrated in a study based on a dance for freshmen at the University of Minnesota, in which participants were led to believe that their partners had been assigned by computer (Walster et al., 1966). In fact, the dates had been assigned randomly, and participants were later asked to indicate how attracted they were to their dates and how much they would like the relationship to continue. The results indicated that physical attractiveness was the only factor that determined how much the participants liked their dates, how much they wanted to see them again, and (as it turned out later) how much they did pursue the relationship. Every other variable studied turned out to be nonsignificant.

Along these same lines, when college freshmen were asked to keep records of their interactions with others over an 8-month period, the records showed that physically attractive females spent more time at parties and on dates than did their less attractive peers, and physically attractive males spent more time in conversation and socializing with the opposite sex and less time in same-sex activities (Reis et al., 1980). In short, more physically attractive freshmen seem to have a more social first year of college.

In the laboratory, when "couples" meet for the first time, both males and females make an effort to intensify interactions with those of the opposite sex who are physically attractive (Garcia et al., 1991). When women interact with physically attractive men, they tend to adopt a more exclusive conversational tone and try to establish a more intimate and communal relationship, even in the first few minutes of their meeting. When men interact with physically attractive women, they tend to adopt the females' perspective, make repeated efforts to continue the conversation, and rate the interactions more positively even when the responses of the women are not particularly encouraging.

***The Matching Hypothesis***    Briefly stated, the matching hypothesis holds that males and females of approximately equal physical attractiveness tend to end up together. Handsome men tend to pair with beautiful women, homely men with homely women, and the rest fall someplace in between.

*Matching in Naturally Occurring Couples*    Studies show that dating partners do, in fact, tend to be matched in terms of physical attractiveness (Critelli & Waid, 1980; Feingold, 1988; Price & Vandenberg, 1979). In one study, for example, Irwin Silverman (1971) had observers rate naturally occurring heterosexual couples on physical attractiveness. Male observers rated female part-

Could physical attributes be part of a person's self-concept? For couples who look and act in similar ways, it is unlikely that each will demand of the other big changes in the way they look or live their lives together.

ners and female observers rated male partners. When the ratings were analyzed, the results showed a high degree of matching on physical attractiveness.

*What Leads to Matching?*   Suggestions vary as to how and why matching on
physical attractiveness might take place. Some researchers believe that individuals simply prefer partners who are similar in terms of physical attractiveness. Others assume that individuals prefer more attractive partners, but the
hard facts of life lead them eventually to settle for what they can get, and they
tend to get someone of roughly the same level of physical attractiveness as
themselves (Kalick & Hamilton, 1986). In an analysis of 18 studies focusing
on the matching hypothesis, Alan Feingold (1988) found that although there
is evidence for similarity in physical attractiveness among romantic partners,
the correlations tend to be modest. What is going on here? Is there evidence
for matching or isn't there? The answer seems to be yes, but it takes time.

Among dating couples, correlations in physical attractiveness tend to be
weakest for those who are in the early stages of the courtship process. Couples
who are dating seriously, engaged, or married tend to be more closely matched
(White, 1980). What seems to be at work is the availability of other potential
partners. Couples who are mismatched on physical attractiveness are somewhat less stable than well-matched couples because the more attractive of the
pair is likely to be attracted to (or enticed away by) someone else who is more
physically attractive.

Support for the idea that mismatched couples are unstable was found in
the Boston Couples Study. A significant factor in ending a relationship was a
difference in physical attractiveness between the two partners (Hill et al.,
1976). Similarly, a study of dating services found that people who progress
further in the process (for example, dating a second time) tend to be more
closely matched in terms of physical attractiveness than those who stop seeing
each other after the first date (Folkes, 1982).

Have you ever seen a couple that was clearly mismatched on physical
attractiveness? What was your reaction? It turns out that there has been some
research into this. When a couple is clearly mismatched on physical attractiveness, others tend to feel somewhat uneasy about the relationship. For example, when people are asked to evaluate contrived "couples" based on photographs that are either matched or mismatched on physical attractiveness,
couples are judged as more likable and as having a more positive relationship
when they are similar in physical attractiveness (Forgas, 1993). Still, we do
find couples who are mismatched on physical attractiveness. How do we account for these?

## Physical Attractiveness and Social Mobility

Some years ago, researchers noted that middle-class girls were perceived, on
the whole, as being more physically attractive than their working-class counterparts (Elder, 1969). Why would this be? Was there some principle of selection at work?

To test this hypothesis, Glen Elder turned to data from the Oakland Growth Study. As part of this study, fifth- and sixth-grade girls had been rated on physical attractiveness in the 1930s. In his follow-up study, Elder tracked them down to find out how life had treated them. He found that, in general, the more physically attractive the girls had been in the fifth and sixth grades, the "better" they had done in their marriages.

This brings us back to the evolutionary theme touched on earlier. Physically attractive females tended to catch the eye of males and soon found that they could be selective in their choice of a mate. As a consequence, the more physically attractive females tended to marry "up"—that is, the socioeconomic status of their husbands tended to be higher than their own prior to marriage. Twenty years after graduation from high school, a female's physical attractiveness in the fifth and sixth grades tended to be positively correlated with the social status of her spouse. Furthermore, the more the husband's initial social status exceeded that of his wife, the more likely his wife was to be very attractive (Elder, 1969). Such couples are common enough that some researchers have referred to the "symbiotic" relationship between beauty and money, that is, the trade-off we sometimes see in which a wealthy but not particularly attractive male pairs with a physically attractive female (Murstein, 1972).

But the story does not end there. Apparently, as physically attractive working-class females have been selected for upward mobility over many generations, a second trend has been quietly at work as well. Less physically attractive women from the middle class have had to settle for less socially desirable husbands, and as a consequence, they have drifted to the lower socioeconomic levels. This has led, over time, to a difference (on average) in the physical attractiveness of middle- and working-class females (Trivers, 1972).

## Physical Attractiveness and Same-Sex Friendships

The importance of physical attractiveness is not limited to male-female relationships. It is an issue in same-sex relationships as well. For example, Linda Carli and her colleagues (1991) investigated the effect of physical attractiveness on the relationships of college roommates who had been assigned randomly. The students were interviewed individually and asked to give an evaluation of their roommates. The results indicated that the more similar roommates were in terms of physical attractiveness, the more satisfactory their relationship tended to be, and the more likely they were to plan to continue rooming together. When roommates were dissimilar in physical attractiveness, their relationship tended to be less satisfactory.

Where did the dissatisfaction lie? Not with the less attractive roommates. They tended to envy the more attractive ones, wished to be more like them, and generally seemed to be grateful for their help in meeting other people. For the more attractive roommates, the situation was very different. They were likely to see their less attractive roommates as interfering with their social lives and to feel that they were being held back socially. They saw their friends as

These teens' physical characteristics seem to be well matched, one reason they are comfortable in each other's company, if not that of their parents or grandparents. Given time, are they more or less likely to retain their present perceptions of what makes one attractive?

rejecting their less attractive roommates, and they often planned to change roommates. In short, these tended to be very unsatisfactory relationships.

We should not be surprised, then, to find that friends tend to be similar in physical attractiveness, and this general rule holds true for same-sex as well as opposite-sex friends (Cash & Derlega, 1978).

## Physical Attractiveness and Marriage

Physical attractiveness also seems to play a role in marital satisfaction. For example, a survey of *Psychology Today* readers found that marriages were reported to be more stable when partners were matched in terms of physical attractiveness (Berscheid et al., 1973).

Matching on physical attractiveness seems to persist long after initial attraction. This was demonstrated in a study comparing two groups of married couples. One was relatively young (ages 19–31) and recently married, and the other was older (ages 34–64). From what other studies have shown, we would expect the younger couples to be matched on physical attractiveness, but interestingly enough, matching was evident in both of these groups (Price &

Vandenberg, 1979). And a study investigating the role of physical attractiveness among older couples, ages 64–86, found that they also tended to be matched on physical attractiveness, and the physical attractiveness of the spouse was positively correlated with marital satisfaction (Peterson & Miller, 1980).

So while we may see "mismatched" pairs from time to time, in general, the evidence suggests that the physically attractive tend to select each other, and the rest of us are left with a decision either to pursue an impossible dream or return to the real world. Apparently, the real world is what most of us choose, because most of us do find friends and mates. We may aim high initially, but in the end our aspirations are likely to be tempered by a bit of realism (Kalick & Hamilton, 1986).

## Does Physical Attractiveness Have a Downside?

Before leaving the topic of physical attractiveness and its influence on personal relationships, we should note that although physical attractiveness tends to be associated with many positive qualities, it can also bring problems. As a group, the physically attractive tend to be seen as egotistical, snobbish, and vain (Dermer & Thiel, 1975). Among college freshmen, for example, those who are the most physically attractive tend to be rejected by their dorm mates. And although the physically attractive are seen as having greater self-esteem and social competence, they are not viewed as particularly high in integrity or concern for others (Eagly et al., 1991). The less physically attractive (especially females) are considered more honest and moral (Krebs & Adinolfi, 1975).

Still, the physically attractive seem to have greater social acceptance, more opportunities to meet and interact with the opposite sex, greater opportunities in mate selection, and advantages in job interviews and educational situations—all of which suggests that life has stacked the deck in their favor. So, are they happy?

Somewhat surprisingly, there seems to be only a slight (positive) relationship between physical attractiveness and subjective well-being among college students (Diener et al., 1995). How to account for such a finding is a matter of speculation at this point. It may be that those who are physically attractive simply expect more out of life (have a higher CL, if you will), and as a consequence, their subjective well-being is approximately the same as that of others.

When we look at the long term, however, the picture gets a bit more interesting. In one study Ellen Berscheid and her colleagues (1972) interviewed individuals in their 40s and 50s who had been students at the University of Minnesota some 20 years earlier. Next they had judges from the same (student) generation evaluate the interviewees on physical attractiveness based on photographs from old yearbooks. Because of the quality of some of the photos, interjudge reliability was only modest (.39), but it was still acceptable.

What did the researchers find? For men, there was some suggestion that those who had been more physically attractive during their college days turned out to be somewhat better off financially later in life. Otherwise, physical attractiveness seemed to have little long-term effect for males one way or another.

In the case of women, however, the researchers found a marginally significant relationship between their physical attractiveness 20 years earlier and interviewer ratings of their current marital satisfaction and general life adjustment. The physical attractiveness of females during their college years was correlated with happiness later in life, but in the *opposite* direction suggested by the physical attractiveness stereotype. The more physically attractive a female was judged to have been, based on her college photograph, the less happy she reported being later in life, and the less well-adjusted she was judged to be by evaluators. Why would this be?

Apparently, those who spend a good part of their lives operating on the assumption that life will be good to them, based on their physical appearance alone, are less likely to put forth the effort to develop the skills and talents that others might find desirable when their physical appearance is no longer such an asset. So we should not leave the topic of physical attractiveness with the impression that things are all sweetness and light for those who are physically attractive. Apparently they are not.

## Conclusion

From our brief look at physical attractiveness, we can conclude, first, that from an evolutionary point of view, there is a close association between attractiveness and mating. Second, the effects of physical attractiveness are far more pervasive than most people realize. Third, there tends to be considerable agreement among individuals as to who is and who is not physically attractive. This is true of our own culture, and it seems to be true cross culturally as well. And although there is some evidence that physical attractiveness in females is more important to males than vice versa, overall, romantic partners tend to be matched on physical attractiveness to a remarkable degree. The exception to this rule seems to be the "beauty-for-wealth or status" trade-offs that we sometimes see, where men of wealth or reputation who are not particularly attractive pair off with physically attractive women.

Finally, although the cards seem to be stacked in favor of those who are physically attractive, there is some evidence, in the case of females, that this can come back to haunt them later in life when their physical attractiveness is no longer such an asset. Women who were physically attractive earlier in life tend to be less happy and less well adjusted when they are older.

## Suggestions for Further Reading

Carli, L. L., Ganley, R., & Pierce-Otay, A. (1991). Similarity and satisfaction in roommate relationships. *Personality and Social Psychology Bulletin, 17,* 419–426. Roommates who differ greatly in physical attractiveness are not likely to be satisfied as roommates.

Cowley, G. (1996, June 3). The biology of beauty. *Newsweek*, pp. 61–66. An excellent, accessible article on what recent research says about beauty.

Cunningham, M. R., Roberts, A. R., Barbee, A. P., Druen, P. B., & Wu, C. H. (1995). "Their ideas of beauty are, on the whole, the same as ours": Consistency and variability in the cross-cultural perception of female physical attractiveness. *Journal of Personality and Social Psychology, 68,* 261–279. Makes a case for cross-cultural consistency in our ideas of physical attractiveness.

Dion, K. L., Berscheid, E., & Walster, E. (1972). What is beautiful is good. *Journal of Personality and Social Psychology, 24,* 285–290. An early, but still relevant, statement on the "What is beautiful is good" phenomenon.

Downs, A. C., & Lyons, P. M. (1991). Natural observations of the links between attractiveness and initial legal judgments. *Personality and Social Psychology Bulletin, 17,* 541–547. Can the looks of a defendant affect the judicial process? Apparently, but it depends on the nature of the crime.

Feingold, A. (1988). Matching for attractiveness in romantic partners and same-sex friends: A meta-analysis and theoretical critique. *Psychological Bulletin, 104,* 226–235. A comprehensive look at the matching (on physical attractiveness) hypothesis.

Harrison, A. A., & Saeed, L. (1977). Let's make a deal: An analysis of revelations and stipulations in lonely hearts advertisements. *Journal of Personality and Social Psychology, 35,* 257–264. What features do men and women advertise and seek in the personal columns?

Hatfield, E., & Sprecher, S. (1986). *Mirror, mirror . . . The importance of looks in everyday life.* Albany, NY: State University of New York Press. An overview of research on the importance of physical attractiveness.

Patzer, G. L. (1985). *The physical attractiveness phenomena.* New York: Plenum. A comprehensive review of research on physical attractiveness.

Sigall, H., & Landy, D. (1973). Radiating beauty: The effects of having a physically attractive partner on person perception. *Journal of Personality and Social Psychology, 28,* 218–224. The classic study on how having a physically attractive partner makes one look good.

Sprecher, S., Sullivan, Q., & Hatfield, E. (1994). Mate selection preferences: Gender differences examined in a national sample. *Journal of Personality and Social Psychology, 66,* 1074–1080. How males and females differ in what they prefer in a mate.

Walster, E., Aronson, V., Abrahams, D., & Rottmann, L. (1966). Importance of physical attractiveness in dating behavior. *Journal of Personality and Social Psychology, 4,* 508–516. The early "computer dance" study showing the overwhelming importance of physical attractiveness among dating college students.

# CHAPTER 12

## Self and Other

*One of the most interesting "matches" I have ever observed is one that developed in my last year of college. A woman who ate regularly in the cafeteria was generally viewed as being highly social, bubbly, and not especially bright. But the most noticeable thing about Ellen was that she had a complexion problem that was almost shocking. People tried not to notice, but it was impossible. About midyear, an older married student, whom we all knew because he was exceptionally bright, suddenly started eating in the cafeteria. It turned out Sam's wife had died suddenly. It was particularly tragic, in this case, because he was functionally blind. As the year progressed, sure enough, one day Sam and Ellen came in together. She was leading him by the hand. Everybody in the cafeteria smiled at this match made in heaven. She was his eyes, and he was her brains. They were married about a year later.*

The importance of the relationship between the self and other(s) was a central focus of the early writings of sociologists Charles Horton Cooley (1922) and George Herbert Mead (1934). For both of these writers, how we come to think and feel about ourselves is largely due to our relationships with others. These relationships generate what Cooley called the "looking-glass" self—the self the person imagines from the reflected appraisal of others. Mead elaborated upon this theme, focusing particularly on the influence of "significant others" in the life of the child (for example, mother, father, and siblings). As these significant others behave in certain ways, such as treating the child as someone who is helpless or as someone who is capable, the child begins to "take the role of the other," eventually thinking of him- or herself in ways that reflect this treatment.

In this chapter we will review four research programs that extend and sharpen the focus of work in this tradition. These include the work of William Swann and his colleagues on "identity negotiation" (McNulty & Swann,

1994; Swann, 1987, 1996; Swann et al., 1992; Swann et al., 1994); the approach of "interpersonal theory" (Strong et al., 1988; Tracey, 1994); the application of the self-evaluation maintenance (SEM) model to close personal relationships (Campbell, 1980; Pilkington et al., 1991; Tesser, 1988; Tesser & Campbell, 1980; Tesser & Smith, 1980; Yinon et al., 1989); and the work of Daniel Wegner and his associates on "transactive memory" (Wegner, 1986; Wegner et al., 1985; Wegner et al., 1991).

Each of these shows in a somewhat different way how one person in a relationship often facilitates the behavior of the other(s) in ways that contribute to their interaction and mutual effectiveness. We begin with the work on identity negotiation.

## Identity Negotiation

The concept of identity negotiation (Swann, 1987) is based on the assumption that people are motivated to have others see them as they see themselves. The term that Swann and his colleagues use to describe this process is "self-verification."

### The Self-Verification Process

Swann begins by assuming that as humans we are motivated to *know*. The two primary objectives of this knowing are the self and the world around us, and one goal of knowing is to detect patterns and establish relationships between these two objectives. One way of achieving this is to observe our own behavior and the responses of others to it. Broadly speaking, this information provides the basis for our generating and maintaining a self-concept.

Why is the self-concept important? In a world where challenging, awkward, and potentially embarrassing or dangerous possibilities lurk, a stable self-concept helps us to predict future outcomes. Our self-concept functions much like a set of lenses through which we see the world. And because any threat to the self-concept is likely to require significant reorganization of tried-and-true modes of adapting, we tend to be highly invested in our self-concept (Swann, 1987).

This being the case, people should become more and more resistant, over time, to altering their self-concept, possibly because they believe, rightly or wrongly, that they would risk failure if they ventured into unexplored territory (Baumgardner & Brownlee, 1987) or that significant changes in their self-concept would have a negative effect on their relationships with close others (Swann, 1984). And, indeed, the evidence is that the self-concept is highly resistant to change over the long term (e.g., Block, 1981; Caspi et al., 1989; Costa & McCrae, 1980).

An implication of this need for a stable self-concept is that we tend to seek and maintain relationships with others who verify and otherwise support our self-concepts (Swann, 1983, 1984). How do we do this?

Our self-concept functions much like a set of lenses through which we see the world. And because it is so important to how we function in the everyday world, we tend to be highly invested in our self-concept.

*Opportunity Structures*    One strategy we use to verify and maintain our self-concept is to seek or generate **opportunity structures** (McCall & Simmons, 1966). Conceptually, opportunity structures are similar in many ways to the notion of **ecological niche**, a term used in biology to mean the habitat in which a particular species thrives and which is generally supportive of its needs.

According to Swann, we seek social opportunity structures in order to satisfy social needs and desires in much the same way. And one of the ways we do this is through selective interactions with others.

*Selective Interaction*    Several studies have provided evidence that supports the opportunity structure position. For example, Lawrence Pervin and Donald Rubin (1967) found that students were happier in college, and were less likely to drop out, if the college environment was supportive of their view of themselves. William Swann and Brett Pelham (1987) found, in a study of college roommates, that those whose roommate's view of them was incongruent (did not agree) with their own were more likely to plan to switch roommates. Similarly, William Swann and his colleagues (1992) noted that married couples tend to be less committed to their marriage when their partner's view of them does not agree with their own.

In short, people seem to prefer those close to them to see them as they see themselves. And not only do those with a positive view of themselves prefer others who view them positively, but also those who have a negative view of themselves prefer others who view them unfavorably! Furthermore, these preferences are, in fact, the way their friends and associates tend to view them (Pelham & Swann, 1987).

The preference for positive feedback in the case of those with a positive self-concept is not hard to understand. But why would people with a negative self-concept prefer others to view them negatively? The answer according to Swann goes something like this: Although there may be painful moments associated with a negative self-concept, there may also be a measure of security. Better the devil we know than the one we don't.

***Interaction Strategies***    What happens when people get feedback from others that is not in agreement with their self-concept? William Swann and Stephen Read (1981b) had subjects who perceived themselves as either likable or unlikable interact with others. Some of them were led to believe that the others they were about to meet would like them; some were led to believe that the others would dislike them; and some received no indication one way or the other.

The results showed that those who see themselves as more likable tend to behave in ways that *elicit* more positive responses from others, especially when they are under the impression that the others might not like them. Conversely, those who view themselves as unlikable, tend to elicit the least favorable responses from those they are led to believe *would* like them. Both groups behave in ways calculated to elicit feedback that supports their self-concept from those they suspect are going to view them in ways that disagree with their own view.

Along these same lines, William Swann and Craig Hill (1982) had subjects participate in a game with a confederate in which they alternated roles, one playing the dominant (leader) role, the other the assistant (submissive) role, and then switching. Following this, the "subjects" were asked to decide among themselves who would be the leader in the next session. Based on a prearranged plan, the confederate indicated either that the subject seemed dominant and hence should assume the role of leader or that the subject seemed submissive and the confederate would assume the leadership role.

Under these conditions, subjects tended to accept the dominant or submissive role without question when it was consistent with their view of themselves. When the feedback differed from their self-view, however, they tended to react vehemently in an effort to show that they were not what the confederate was making them out to be. Those who saw themselves as dominant and who had been labeled submissive became especially dominant. Those who viewed themselves as submissive and had been labeled dominant became especially submissive.

In real-life interactions, how someone responds to the suggestions of others is likely to vary from one individual to the next. Presumably, those who find a given relationship rewarding respond positively to the role in which they are being cast, while those who are uncomfortable either try to change the role into which they are being cast or leave the relationship. And one important factor in the process is the effort that people make to get others to see them as they see themselves (Swann, 1987). Apparently, it works at least some of the time. In their longitudinal study of college roommates, Shawn McNulty and William Swann (1994) found that a student's view of his or her roommate tended to become more like the roommate's own self-view over time.

## Routine Self-Verification

We need not paint a picture of the person as constantly going through the process of trying to self-verify. On the contrary, most self-verification takes place in a routine way as a by-product of our everyday interactions within an established opportunity structure. For the most part, we live, work, and socialize with others who have agreed to honor the identities that we have negotiated with them and they with us (Swann & Predmore, 1985). We rarely find it necessary to demonstrate that we are dominant or submissive, introverted or extroverted, and so on. All we have to do is remain within familiar social surroundings—that is, interact with our friends and loved ones. But, as we see in the next section, our friends and loved ones are far from being passive in their roles.

## The Role of Friends in Self-Verification

A study by William Swann and Stephen Predmore (1985) has provided perhaps the most interesting evidence of the role of close others in protecting and maintaining one's self-concept in the face of inconsistent feedback. This experiment involved the subjects and either a total stranger or an "intimate" (an individual who had known the subject for approximately 18 months on average). Some of the participants had a positive view of themselves, and some had a more negative view of themselves.

The subjects were first given a personality test (the Thematic Apperception Test) as a pretense for giving them feedback. After this, they returned to a waiting room, either to the company of an intimate or of a total stranger. Shortly afterward, the experimenter appeared with the "results" of the TAT, which consisted (in two of the experimental conditions) of feedback that was contrary to the subject's self-view. Those with a negative view of themselves received positive feedback. Those with a positive view of themselves received negative feedback. The experimenter then left the subjects in the company of their companion for about 5 minutes.

What followed was most interesting. Intimates, especially congruent intimates (those who viewed the subjects as the subjects viewed themselves), tended to "protect" the subjects from discrepant feedback, while the strangers did not. Indeed, intimates even protected those with low esteem from positive feedback! Why would this be?

***A Two-Way Process***   It seems that friends don't let friends make fools of themselves. Friends don't let friends get in over their heads. But, more than that, Swann and Predmore's (1985) findings underscore the mutual investment that intimates have in supporting each other's self-concept.

Identity negotiation is not a one-way process. While we are negotiating an identity with those close to us, they are presumably doing the same thing. Not only do we enlist others as "accomplices" to aid us in our work of self-verification, we in turn are enlisted by them as well. As part of this process, our friends and loved ones tend to look out for us, screening what we should take seriously and what we should ignore in the way of feedback from others. In so doing, those in our opportunity structure—our friends and loved ones—serve to stabilize our self-concept (Swann, 1987).

***What About Those With a Negative Self-Concept?***   People with a positive self-concept show a preference for feedback that verifies their more positive

Most validation of who we are takes place automatically, as a by-product of our everyday interactions and the way we live and work.

characteristics. No surprise there. But what about those who have an unfavorable view of themselves, and who are in an environment that offers them a more positive view of themselves? You guessed it. People with a negative self-concept prefer that their friends and intimates perceive them in a less favorable way. For example, when students with a negative self-concept find themselves rooming with someone who has a favorable view of them, they are likely to plan to change roommates, while those with a negative view of themselves whose roommates also view them less favorably are likely to plan to remain with their roommate (Swann et al., 1989; Swann & Pelham, 1987).

Such findings seem to fly in the face of common sense and contradict research indicating that ordinarily we prefer flattery to honesty in the feedback we get from others (Berscheid & Walster, 1978). But feedback that has few if any long-term consequences (as is often the case in certain laboratory experiments) and relationships in which one is deeply invested are sometimes very different.

## Preliminary Conclusions

What does the work on identity negotiation tell us about the way we interact with others who are close to us? First, we seem to have a vested interest in self-verification, and we prefer to interact with others who are supportive of our self-concept. Second, one way we generate support for our self-concept is to seek opportunity structures, and in order to do this, we often behave in ways that invite certain types of responses from others and discourage certain other types. In the process we tend to attract (and be attracted to) others whose behavior generally complements our own. And when others do not behave in ways that are generally supportive of our self-concept, we tend to drop them from our circle of friends and pursue relationships with those who do. It's likely, however, that this process is mutual and takes place largely outside of awareness. For most of us, our opportunity structures are simply made up of friends and other intimates with whom we are comfortable.

The work of Swann and his colleagues on identity negotiation helps us appreciate some of the dynamics involved in close personal relationships. And, as we see next, identity negotiation is part of a broader and most interesting picture. For example, Swann and colleagues (1994) note that not only do couples in committed relationships share a strong sense of interdependence, but they also come to realize that in order for their relationship to be successful, they must recognize each other's strengths and weaknesses. Presumably this is so that the strengths of one can make up for (or in some way complement) what the other is lacking and vice versa.

Similarly, in their work on the "inclusion of other in self" Elaine Aron and Arthur Aron (1996) found, in comparing students before and after they fall in love, that they not only show increased scores on measures of self-esteem (no surprise there), but they also show increased scores on self-efficacy. People in love generally feel more effective and competent, presumably because they see their partner as complementing their lives in important ways.

Indeed, one of the most important findings in the study of close personal relationships is the tendency of one person in a personal relationship to complement the behavior of the other. In the research literature this is called complementarity, and it is to the work in this area that we turn next.

## Complementarity

We will define **complementarity** as the extent to which the behavior of one person elicits responses from another in a way that facilitates the interaction and/or contributes positively to the relationship (Tracey, 1994). When we look closely, we find many examples of complementarity in personal relationships.

### Early Work on Complementarity

It's fair to say that the notion of complementarity has not fared well over the years. This is partly because of the methodological problems that plagued earlier efforts to demonstrate complementarity (see Campbell, 1980, for a review) and partly because the notions of similarity and complementarity have been seen as incompatible. Either "birds of a feather flocked together" (similarity) or "opposites attracted" (complementarity). Take your pick. Couched in such terms, when similarity was present, complementarity could not be and vice versa. But recent research has led to a reassessment of the relationship between similarity and complementarity.

### Similarity and Complementarity

Similarity and complementarity are not necessarily incompatible notions. This is easily shown by an example. Suppose Joe and Bob are similar in that they are both interested in baseball. If they are also both pitchers, we would predict that as one outperformed the other, competition would heat up, and eventually their relationship would be ripe for conflict. If, on the other hand, one is a pitcher and the other a catcher, their similarity (an interest in baseball) would provide the context in which their different skills and interests would become complementary (see, for example, Tesser, 1988).

On the other hand, say Joe is good at hunting and Bob is good at math; then the two are not necessarily complementary. They're just different. But there is no shared context in which these differences come to complement one another. It is only when there is some common frame of reference that the notion of complementarity has any meaning. And this common frame of reference is often expressed in terms of similarity in a broader domain.

The couple in the opening paragraph of the chapter were similar in many ways. They were both deeply religious. They were both pursuing graduate work. They were both outgoing, and both had a good sense of humor. There was no lack of similarity that could account, in part, for their attraction to each other. But in addition to their similarity, what was striking about the match was the way they also complemented each other.

Similarity and complementarity, rather than being antagonistic notions, are notions that go together quite well. Two people in a personal relationship can be both similar and complementary. The work on interpersonal theory provides us with an example of the way the two sometimes interact.

## Interpersonal Theory

Interpersonal theorists assume that when two people interact, the actions of one person constrain or elicit certain behaviors on the part of the other. The extent to which the behavior of the other reflects these constraints or "invitations" is called complementarity. So considered, complementarity is fundamental to a smooth running relationship (Carson, 1969).

Stanley Strong and his colleagues (1988) provided a convincing demonstration of this. In their study, confederates (those who, unknown to the participants, were part of the experiment) were trained to play various roles portraying, for example, someone who was domineering, self-enhancing, critical, distrustful, docile, cooperative, or caring. Confederates and the actual subjects in the study were then presented with ambiguous pictures and instructed to come to agreement on what the pictures were about.

The question being asked experimentally was this: Would certain types of behavior on the part of the confederates (such as dominance) tend to generate certain complementary responses on the part of the participants? Indeed they did. When the confederate's behavior was "leading," it tended to elicit following (or submissive) behavior on the part of the other person. Critical behavior tended to generate distrustful responses. Cooperative behavior tended to encourage leading. At the same time, however, friendly behavior tended to elicit friendly responses in return, and hostile behavior tended to lead to hostile responses. What's going on here—complementarity or similarity? The answer seems to be both. On emotional dimensions we tend to find similarity (or tit-for-tat reciprocity), that is, friendly responses to friendly behavior, hostile responses to hostile behavior. Complementarity is more likely to be associated with such things as skills and abilities (Tesser, 1984).

When we turn to the study of real people in real relationships, we do not generally find one person responding to others in a passive manner, nor do we find one dominating the other independent of the other's responses over time. Actual relationships tend to have a much more dynamic quality, and researchers are now beginning to capture this process in experimental studies. As they do, the findings are beginning to give us a picture of the role of complementarity that is more complete and compelling than early notions of complementarity suggested.

The work of Tesser and his associates on self-evaluation maintenance provides us with a case in point. And it is to their work that we turn next.

## Self-Evaluation Maintenance

The self-evaluation maintenance (SEM) model (Tesser, 1980, 1988), like the work on identity negotiation described earlier, assumes that others are often enlisted to help in the process of stabilizing (or maintaining) our self-concept.

But the focus, in the case of the SEM model, is on the role that friends and other intimates play in helping us maintain a *positive* view of ourselves. (In practical terms, this assumption does not often contradict the assumptions of identity negotiation because most people do have a positive self-concept.)

According to the SEM model, two important processes in self-evaluation maintenance are **reflection** and **comparison**. In the reflection process, we associate with others who, because of their abilities, reputation, and accomplishments, allow us to "bask in their reflected glory" (Cialdini et al., 1976). Comparison, on the other hand, is a process that leads us to evaluate our accomplishments, abilities, and the like, *relative* to those close to us. The effects of comparison processes and reflection processes are potentially in conflict with one another. For example, the better our friends and associates are at sports, the more we can bask in their reflected glory, but at the same time, the worse we are likely to look in comparison.

These two processes, basking in reflected glory (or BIRGing) and social comparison, present us with a dilemma. How do we bask in the other's reflected glory and at the same time not suffer in terms of comparison? This

The self-evaluation maintenance model assumes that others provide support for the individual, especially at times that are personally relevant, such as important life transitions.

dilemma is resolved, according to the SEM model, by associating with others whose abilities, skills, and talents are in areas that are not particularly important to our own self-concept, while the others (presumably) acknowledge the same in us.

The issues that the SEM model identifies as important in the reflection and comparison processes are (1) how relevant a given skill or activity of the other person is to our own self-evaluation, (2) how the other's performance compares to our own, and (3) how close he or she is to us.

## Relevance

When others are very good at something that is also important to our own self-definition (high relevance) we are likely to compare ourselves with them, and the better they are, the more likely we are to suffer in comparison. On the other hand, if the talents and abilities of others lie in areas that are not particularly important to our own self-definition (low relevance), we tend to bask in their reflected glory rather than to compare ourselves with them.

For example, if Ed is particularly invested in his abilities as a computer scientist, he may quite happily befriend Dan, who is an outstanding pianist, and not feel threatened. Dan, in turn, would presumably be willing to acknowledge Ed's abilities in things having to do with computers. They arrive, in other words, at a tacit agreement: You scratch my back and I'll scratch yours.

## Closeness

Closeness in the SEM model is used in the psychological sense of the term. Closeness increases the likelihood that both reflection and comparison will take place. Accordingly, when someone close is very good at something that is important to our own self-definition, we tend to compare ourselves with her or him, and this is likely to threaten our own self-evaluation. One way we deal with such threats is to distance ourselves from those who make us look bad by comparison. If, on the other hand, someone is good at something that is far removed from our own interests and abilities, we are likely to bask in the reflected glory that the relationship brings with it, and as a consequence, our self-evaluation will be more positive (Campbell, 1980).

## The Dynamics of SEM

According to the SEM model, then, we will be attracted to, and try to remain close to, others whose skills, talents, and abilities complement our own and help maintain our self-evaluation. Specifically, we will seek to maintain relationships with people who do well in areas that are not especially relevant to our own self-evaluation (BIRGing) and whose performance is not threatening (by comparison), while they will (presumably) give us our due in our own areas of accomplishment, expertise, and talents.

Studies across a wide range of relationship types have provided support for the SEM model. Naturally occurring friendship pairs among fifth and sixth graders show a pattern in which one was likely to perform somewhat better on a dimension that was relevant to his or her own self-evaluation and less well on a dimension that was irrelevant. As the performance of a friend becomes more similar on a dimension that is relevant to one's self-definition, the more likely the two are to show complementarity in the *details* of their performance (Tesser et al., 1984). For example, two artists might specialize, one concentrating on landscapes and the other on portraits.

On the other hand, people show a tendency to avoid associations with those whose relevant skills, talents, and accomplishments make them look bad by comparison. For example, when one individual outperforms another on a task that is personally relevant, people tend to distance themselves, perhaps by sitting farther away physically and expressing less willingness to work with the other. In addition, they tend to view the other as less similar to themselves in important ways (Pleban & Tesser, 1981). Siblings who are similar in age report being less close psychologically—that is, they show more discord in their relationships—when one shows superiority in an area that is personally relevant to the other (Tesser, 1980). And, interestingly, college students provide more help to a total stranger than they do to a friend when the task in question is high in personal relevance (Tesser & Smith, 1980).

The effects of closeness and relevance were also vividly demonstrated by Constance Pilkington and her colleagues (1991) in a study of couples who were romantically involved. Following the SEM model, the researchers hypothesized that one partner would remain in the background in certain activities that were of less importance to him or her personally and more relevant to the partner. That is, each partner would allow the other to have his or her chance to shine in those areas that were personally relevant. Their findings indicated that this was indeed the case. When the relevance of art was high for Kate and low for Mike, Mike tended to defer to Kate in matters having to do with art. Moreover, when relevance was similar for both, neither one considered himself or herself to be particularly superior.

In another study, Pilkington and her associates focused on the question of whether romantically involved couples were operating independently in such instances. In other words, were they essentially looking out for themselves first and the other second, or was there evidence of concern for both the interests of the self and the interests of the other? The researchers found that romantic partners consistently took both their own and their partners' self-evaluation needs into account. When something was relevant to Mike (say tennis) and not to Kate, Kate deferred to Mike. As a consequence, Mike benefited in the comparison, while Kate tended to bask in the reflected glory of her partner.

We see in the SEM model, then, an example of the kind of processes that evolve and lead to complementarity in personal relationships. Partners do not just go their own way in close personal relationships. They look out for the needs of each other and, in so doing, tailor their own behavior in ways that tend to complement the needs and abilities of their partner.

## Transactive Memory

The work of Daniel Wegner and his associates (Wegner et al., 1985; Wegner et al., 1991) on transactive memory provides a further example of complementarity in close personal relationships. "Transactive memory" refers to a system whereby one person relies on the other to remember certain kinds of information. The advantage of such a system is that it allows one person to delegate certain areas of memory responsibility to another and still have access to that information. Two people who develop a transactive memory system increase their joint memory capacity.

People in developing relationships do not initially have such a system in place, of course. In the early stages of a relationship, delegation of memory tasks may follow along certain stereotypical lines, based, let us say, on gender. But as relationships mature, so too does the sophistication and subtlety of transactive memory systems, and over time they are likely to move beyond the stereotypical categories in their division of memory tasks, as one person more or less becomes the resident expert in one domain, and the other person becomes an expert in something else.

For example, as a romantic couple gets to know each other's interests, backgrounds, and abilities, a system tends to evolve by which certain memory tasks are delegated automatically to the one in whose bailiwick a particular piece of information happens to fall. In order for this to take place to the best advantage, each must come to appreciate the strengths, weaknesses, interests, and sensitivities of the other. This understanding sometimes leads to formal agreements (for example, who is responsible for the checkbook, the income tax return, who makes sure the car is serviced on time), but it often evolves informally as well, as each one becomes aware of the other's idiosyncrasies.

What happens when a couple is responsible for remembering something? The answer seems to be that they communicate. However, they not only share information, but they also share the basis for that information, who acquires it, and who is responsible for it. In other words, they engage their common transactive memory.

So, when an old Army buddy drops by one weekend, notices the painting in Jack and Mary's den, and asks, "Where did you get that painting?" We hear Jack check with Mary, "Mary, what was the name of that place where you got the painting?" And Mary responds, "It's not a painting, it's a print. We sent off for it. Let me think. It's from a museum. Winter something. Winterhaven, Winter. . . (pause). You know. It's in Delaware. We were there once." And with that Jack says, "Winterthur."

Before such an exchange can take place, however, the two would presumably have to arrive at some way of knowing what kinds of information are likely to be stored in the other's memory. If this is the case, it should be possible to demonstrate experimentally that transactive memory systems exist in naturally occurring couples in a way that they do not for strangers. Indeed, if the couple did not have some agreed-upon method of delegating memory responsibility, the efforts of one partner would be just as likely to disrupt as to complement the efforts of the other.

## Experimental Evidence for Transactive Memory

Evidence for such a transactive memory system in naturally occurring couples came in an experiment by Wegner and colleagues (1991). Participants in this study, working in pairs, were given either an explicit memory task assignment (for example, he would be responsible for remembering things having to do with finance and the garden and she, with vacations and decorating), or they were given no such instructions. The researchers hypothesized that when such category assignments were given to pairs who had not known each other prior to the experiment, it would facilitate their joint memory task performance and help them avoid both duplication of effort and oversights. With naturally occurring couples, on the other hand, it was hypothesized that such assignments, insofar as they were disruptive of well-established transactive memory practices, would prove to be a disadvantage. And the hypothesis was confirmed.

As we see in Figure 12-1, when naturally occurring couples were given categories for which they were to be responsible, it was disruptive. When pairs of strangers were given categories for which each was responsible, it was not disruptive. It actually helped. This difference suggests that the naturally occurring pairs had a system of transactive memory already in place, and the

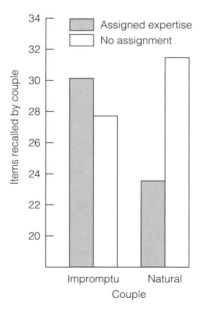

**Figure 12-1**   Couple recall as a function of couple type (natural vs. impromptu) and assignment (assigned expertise vs. no assignment). From Wegner, D. M., Erber, R., & Raymond, P. (1991). Transactive memory in close relationships. *Journal of Personality and Social Psychology, 61*, p. 926. Copyright © 1991 by the American Psychological Association. Reprinted with permission.

imposition of a new system interfered with it. In fact, when naturally occurring couples were left to their own devices, they did better on the memory task than did pairs of strangers (Wegner et al., 1991).

Transactive memory is not unique to romantic couples, of course. The same sort of thing can be found among friends and colleagues in situations where people interact on a routine basis and depend on one another's knowledge and expertise. For example, when one of my colleagues was in the market for a new stereo, the following conversation took place in the hall. Bob: "Why don't you check *Consumer Reports* or whatever?" Dave: "Why? I've got Dale" (resident expert on stereos).

Still, it is in intimate relationships, in which people share a wealth of information and operate somewhat like a single entity, that the notion of transactive memory is most obvious and most advantageous. Ordinarily, when one partner communicates with another, the information is transferred from one memory to the other. And in the case of a couple in a committed relationship, we can conceive of such a transfer of information as taking place within a single transactive memory system. Through such well-established transactive memory systems, couples generate their own storehouse of knowledge and, as a consequence, share a world uniquely tailored to their purposes.

Couples are often involved in self-disclosure in the early stages of their relationship. The information exchanged typically begins with the more general, perhaps mundane, and moves over time to exchanges of more and more intimate information. In the course of these exchanges, one partner gets an idea of the abilities, interests, and resources of the other. This is the general information that is routinely transmitted in self-disclosure. Specific information is exchanged as well, of course, but it is not likely to be remembered as such, but as general information, such as "She likes to travel" or "He enjoys

Michael Maslin © 1992 from the New Yorker Collection. All Rights Reserved.

*"That's right, Phil. A separation will mean—among other things—watching your own cholesterol."*

gourmet cooking." By having this general information, partners can access the specifics at some future time.

Thus, when Suzy meets Doug, the following conversation takes place: "You took Latin? I took French. Went to France my junior year." Two years later, when we find the happy couple honeymooning in Quebec, who is going to depend on whom to order meals, buy tickets to events, and ask for directions to a parking lot?

Such a process increases the efficiency of transactive memory, as the various issues of interest are automatically (and perhaps unconsciously) delegated. Accordingly, the "ignorant" partner in a particular area is not completely ignorant, so long as he or she has information about the other's competencies. The advantage of this is that a pair can be confident of their joint competence in an area and at the same time not duplicate effort and waste memory on all the specific information in their collective transactive memory bank.

## The Generation Effect

Transactive memory involves more than the delegation of memory responsibility, and it has properties that make it qualitatively different from the individual memories that go into making it up. A case in point is the generation effect.

The **generation effect** refers to situations in which partial knowledge on the part of one person combines with partial knowledge on the part of another and leads the pair to arrive at a joint conclusion. For example, in observing a social situation—say a wedding reception—Al may have noticed that the father of the bride seemed a bit miffed about something. Betty, on the other hand, may have noticed that the best man had a bit too much to drink. In recounting the events on their way home later that evening, they may pool their separate bits of information and arrive at the conclusion that the father of the bride was upset because the best man got tipsy.

As you can see, the generation effect may or may not represent a faithful account of the actual events. Still, we tend to remember information that we generate ourselves better than information that we simply receive passively (Slamecka & Graf, 1978). Such memories have a way of becoming validated and supported in close relationships, even though they might not reflect the actual facts.

## Implications of Transactive Memory

Insofar as transactive memory systems are characteristic of close personal relationships, it's easy to see that they would lead to interdependence. And there are some important implications of this when a close relationship of long duration comes to an end. In addition to the emotional fallout, there are likely to be clear cognitive consequences as well. No longer will the partners be able to access their transactive memory in ways that they have taken for granted over the years.

Accordingly, upon separation from Bev, Tom should feel somewhat confused and inefficient. As he loses access to Bev's part of their transactive memory, such as phone numbers, recipes, addresses, and where the candles are stored if the electricity goes off, this loss should make life for him somewhat less efficient and more effortful. Now functioning without the benefit of part of his transactive memory, perhaps it is not too much to say he may feel like something of an invalid.

Not only will the words to "their song" be harder to recall and the special apple pie recipe be lost, but Tom will no longer be able to assume that the bill for the electricity is automatically paid on time, the car inspected, and the Christmas cards sent. Further, with the loss of the priming (or cues) that transactive memory affords, there will be entire areas of experience that fade quietly away totally unnoticed (Wegner et al., 1985).

Because Bev so often provided the "complement," there will also be a personal loss in the ability to retrieve memories. Every memory that was formerly the product of their joint competence is now likely to be more difficult to retrieve in the absence of the old interpersonal context. And what we have said about transactive memory in a long-term relationship could be said to a lesser extent of many other relationships as well.

## Conclusion

Where does this discussion leave us on the matter of self and other in close personal relationships? First, as noted in the work on identity negotiation, we are attracted to others in part because they play a role in supporting our self-concept. Second, it seems clear that the early view of similarity and complementarity as notions that were in some sense incompatible is not appropriate. Today the more global approaches of the past, based on the search for complementary needs or traits, have largely been replaced by a much more dynamic approach. And researchers working from the perspective of interpersonal theory and self-evaluation maintenance are more inclined to look at similarity and complementarity together, with similarity in a wider domain providing the context in which complementarity is likely to operate.

Finally, in close personal relationships of long duration, interdependence, as illustrated in the form of a transactive memory system, allows for a kind of "fit" that is uniquely tailored to a given relationship. As a consequence, those in close relationships can remember more, accomplish more, and do things more efficiently than either partner could by operating independently.

## Suggestions for Further Reading

Campbell, J. (1980). Complementarity and attraction: A reconceptualization in terms of dyadic behavior. *Representative Research in Social Psychology, 11,* 74–92. A review and critique of the work on complementarity and an introduction to the SEM model.

McNulty, S. E., & Swann, W. B., Jr. (1994). Identity negotiation in roommate relationships: The self as architect and consequence of social reality. *Journal of Personality and Social Psychology, 67,* 1012–1023. An application of the identity negotiation theme to relationships among roommates.

Pilkington, C. J., Tesser, A., & Stephens, D. (1991). Complementarity in romantic relationships: A self-evaluation maintenance perspective. *Journal of Social and Personal Relationships, 8,* 481–504. An application of the SEM model to romantic relationships.

Strong, S. R., Hills, J. J., Kilmartin, C. T., DeVries, H., Lanier, K., Nelson, B. N., Strickland, D., & Meyer, C. W., III (1988). The dynamic relations among interpersonal behaviors: A test of complementarity and anti-complementarity. *Journal of Personality and Social Psychology, 54,* 798–810. An experimental demonstration of complementarity under laboratory conditions.

Swann, W. B., Jr. (1987). Identity negotiation: Where two roads meet. *Journal of Personality and Social Psychology, 53,* 1038–1051. An overview of Swann's position on identity negotiation.

Swann, W. B., Jr., De La Ronda, C., & Hixon, J. G. (1994). Authenticity and positivity strivings in marriage and courtship. *Journal of Personality and Social Psychology, 66,* 857–869.

Swann, W. B., Jr., Hixon, J. G., & De La Ronda, C. (1992). Embracing the bitter "truth": Negative self concepts and marital commitment. *Psychological Science, 3,* 118–121. In each of the works by Swann and colleagues, a surprising and important distinction is made between the motivations that characterize our social relationships and those that characterize our more personal ones.

Tesser, A. (1988). Toward a self-evaluation maintenance model of social behavior. In L. Berkowitz (Ed.), *Advances in experimental social psychology* (Vol. 21, 181–227). San Diego, CA: Academic. An overview of work on the SEM model. In this and the next two articles, Tesser and his colleagues apply the model to various types of relationships.

Tesser, A., Campbell, J., & Smith, M. (1984). Friendship choice and performance: Self-evaluation maintenance in children. *Journal of Personality and Social Psychology, 46,* 561–574.

Tesser, A., & Smith, J. (1980). Some effects of friendship and task relevance on helping: You don't always help the one you like. *Journal of Experimental Social Psychology, 16,* 582–590.

Tracey, J. (1994). An examination of complementarity in interpersonal behavior. *Journal of Personality and Social Psychology, 67,* 864–878. An analysis of the notion of complementarity within the context of interpersonal theory. This article is best read in conjunction with the Strong et al. article listed earlier.

Wegner, D. M., Erber, R., & Raymond, P. (1991). Transactive memory in close relationships. *Journal of Personality and Social Psychology, 61,* 923–929.

Wegner, D. M., Giuliano, T., & Hertel, P. (1985). Cognitive interdependence in close relationships. In W. J. Ickes (Ed.), *Compatible and incompatible relationships.* New York: Springer-Verlag. Both Wegner et al. articles explore the implications of the way memory systems evolve as people in close personal relationships come to delegate memory responsibility more or less automatically.

# CHAPTER 13

## ◈ *Commitment*

*Harry and Jill met while they were both in college. They dated casually at first and then more or less steadily. After graduation Harry found a position that involved extensive travel. Jill continued in school, working on her master's degree. They saw each other mostly on weekends. This pattern continued for more than a year, and over time Jill began to feel that the relationship simply wasn't going anywhere.*

*One afternoon Jill was meeting with her advisor, who asked, "What are your plans after graduation?" Jill hesitated. The two were silent for what seemed like a long time, and then Jill's advisor handed her a sheet of paper. It was an announcement of an opening in Jill's area of specialization. Jill read it and noticed that the position was clear across the country. "I think you should look into this," her advisor said, surprisingly firmly. "Opportunities like this don't come along everyday." What should Jill do?*

Why do some relationships last through very difficult times while others seem to fall apart over minor issues? Researchers interested in this question have focused on the role of commitment. Someone who is committed is likely to stick with a task, an activity, or another person in the face of obstacles and setbacks (Becker, 1960). This is expressed in the words of the traditional wedding ceremony, "for richer, for poorer, in sickness and in health." So one of the things that commitment involves is persistence. But there is more to commitment than persistence. Commitment involves such things as decision, investment, and risk. Whether we are speaking of commitment to an employer, commitment to the environment, commitment to a religion, or commitment to a partner, we find a common process at work. And an understanding of this process will help us better appreciate the role of commitment in personal relationships.

233

## Personal and Structural Commitment

It's common to distinguish between two types of commitment. One type is based on internal motivations such as personal dedication, attitudes, feelings, and beliefs. The other focuses on external factors, such as pressures from family, friends, and possibly religious and social institutions. Michael Johnson (1991) refers to these as personal and structural commitment, respectively.

Although these two forms of commitment are conceptually distinct, in practical terms, they are often related. External pressures may serve to generate and support personal commitment (Rosenblatt, 1977), or communication of a personal commitment may lead to expectations in others (external) that in turn bind us more firmly to whatever (internal) commitment we have already made. First we look at the role of external influences on commitment.

External forces can contribute to stability in our activities, associations, and relationships in important ways. For example, pledging a fraternity, announcing an engagement, or taking wedding vows are public indications of intent to become involved in certain relationships with selected others (Kiesler, 1971). Such practices—both formal and informal—call into play an overlapping series of relationship-supporting systems from others (for example, church, kin, social, and friendship circles). These in turn provide context, structure, and stability for our relationships.

At first, such external influences may seem alien to the notion of commitment, which seems to imply an internal motivation—a "state of the person." Someone who acts because he has a gun to his head is surely not acting out of a sense of commitment. But external forces can subtly reinforce internal motives. People often act (or refrain from acting) in order to live up to the expectations of others. For example, the cardinal principle among professional musicians is that "the show must go on," and so, when Ed is asked at the last minute to play bass in a musical, he agrees even though he has been looking forward to the weekend with his family. "Good musicians" among their fellows are those who can be counted on to take a job they may not particularly want. Such "pro-membership" forces are, technically speaking, external to Ed's decision to take the job, and his reputation among his fellow musicians (who, in this case, exert social pressure) becomes the focus of concern (Becker, 1960).

Along these same lines, Larry remains in a dull and unfulfilling job in order to stay close to his aging mother and because the local school system is particularly good and he does not want to move his family. Such examples illustrate the fact that many things in life come in the form of "package deals," and we must take the bad with the good. These forces that are, strictly speaking, external to a commitment and yet supportive of it are sometimes called structural forces, and the commitments that are generated by them are called **structural commitments** (Johnson, 1985, 1991).

On the other hand, for the person who is committed to becoming a concert pianist, committed to being an artist, or committed to mountain climbing, the activity itself seems to be rewarding and in need of no further justification.

Such commitments are sometimes called **personal commitments** (Johnson, 1985). Personal commitments are often pursued in spite of their costs. There are clearly costs to becoming a mountain climber, a concert pianist, or an artist—the effort, training, risk, and sacrifice. Yet some people choose to bear these costs and even bear them joyfully, but costs they are.

So the term *commitment* is used to refer both to actions that we feel we are "required" by the larger society to carry out and to actions we pursue out of our personal preference. In the first case, we feel we *must* do something. In the second case, we feel we *want* to do something. How are we to reconcile these two uses of the term *commitment*? If we examine them closely, we find an underlying compatibility between the two. What is important in commitment is not the distinction between the external and the internal, or between "wanting to" and "having to," but the relationship between the two. Indeed, according to Brickman (1987), the study of commitment is the study of that relationship.

The task before us, then, is to explore how external influence is transformed into internal motivation—how "having to" becomes "wanting to." Commitment, so considered, always involves three things: a positive element (or goal), a negative element (or cost), and a bond between the two (Brickman, 1987). What is the nature of this bond? Where do we find the glue that keeps the negatives and the positives together? For some thoughts on this, we turn to dissonance theory.

## Dissonance Theory and the Commitment Process

In Philip Brickman's (1987) analysis, **cognitive dissonance** provides a model of the basic mechanism underlying the commitment process. According to the theory of cognitive dissonance, when our beliefs are not in harmony with our actions, we experience tension and tend to take steps to bring the two into harmony. This can be done by changing our behavior or by changing our beliefs. The most interesting implication of cognitive dissonance is that, having acted, we feel compelled to bring our beliefs into line with our actions. And one of the ramifications of this is that behavior which takes place in the absence of sufficient justification leads to a tendency to generate a justification.

For example, when we spend time and effort in pursuit of a goal that leads to a disappointing result, it makes us feel uncomfortable. How is this state of dissonance to be resolved? The behavior itself is over and done with. There is not a lot we can do about it. Our beliefs and attitudes, on the other hand, can be changed quite easily. Accordingly, it is tempting to convince ourselves that the outcome wasn't all that bad; in fact, it was really quite positive. How does this tendency play out when it is applied to personal relationships?

### How Costs Increase Perceived Value

In their classic study, Elliot Aronson and Judson Mills (1959) had female volunteers read obscene words in front of a male experimenter as part of an

Even the most committed relationship must weigh the costs as well as the rewards of an unintended or untimely pregnancy.

(alleged) screening for membership in a group that would be discussing sexual material. This exercise was deliberately calculated to make the subjects feel uncomfortable (that is, to increase costs). A comparison group was required only to deal with much less embarrassing material, and a third group underwent no screening at all.

The subjects were then informed that the groups for which they were being screened were already in progress, and they could listen to the discussions but could not participate directly. Then all the subjects heard a rather dull prerecorded discussion. Afterwards, they were asked to evaluate the discussion. Those who had experienced the more severe "initiation" judged the discussion more positively. They seemed to be going on the assumption that "you get what you pay for." Paying a higher cost in terms of initiation meant "their group" was more desirable. Why else would they have been willing to pay such a high price?

Assigning value to something, then, is not a passive process. It is a process whereby we actively transform costs. In order to be transformed, the cost must be seen in relation to at least a tentative goal with which the cost can be linked. The integration of the two not only neutralizes the negative effects (costs), such as time, effort, embarrassment, or sacrifice, but also tends to generate a stronger motivation and more persistent behavior than would have been the case had there not been a cost to overcome. In other words, given a goal, the effort, cost, and sacrifice invested to achieve it tend to increase its (subjective) value (Lawrence & Festinger, 1962) and, as a consequence, serve to generate increased commitment to that goal. Hazing among fraternities, discipline in the Marines, and renunciation of worldly pursuits in religious orders are all ways of increasing commitment.

So, in the cognitive dissonance phenomenon, it seems we have an example of a process whereby we can absorb high costs (overcome obstacles, endure setbacks) and still persist in pursuit of our goals. It is this process that seems calculated in evolutionary wisdom to sustain us during hard times. But how long should we bear such costs? How long should we continue to overcome obstacles and endure setbacks? Let's look at the case of Mr. Jones.

Mr. Jones has worked all his life in a factory. He has always been good at fixing things and has had a little business on the side repairing radios, TVs, and whatnot, in his spare time. Secretly, he has dreamed of opening his own repair shop. He saves over the years, and finally one day he decides to take the plunge. He quits his job, rents a spot downtown, and puts up a shingle—Jones's Electronics Repair. Never has he been so happy. The first month, business is not bad. He doesn't quite break even, but then a new business never does break even in the first month, does it? He advertises in the local newspaper. Business picks up, but the cost of advertising is higher than he anticipated, and he doesn't quite break even the second month. And so it goes. Business stabilizes the next month, and the next, but not quite enough to pay. Winter comes, and the heating bill is more than he expects. After a year, Mr. Jones has invested more than $20,000, and his business is still not profitable. Then one day his old boss from the factory comes in. "Jonesy," he says. "How are things? Hey, we sure do miss you down at the plant. Starting a new product line next month. Sure could use you. Sure you don't want to come back and help get things rolling?" What should Mr. Jones do?

Researchers have studied this issue in different ways, and some of the most intriguing findings have come from a simulation called "the dollar auction game" (Shubik, 1971). In this simulation, players bid for a dollar bill. What makes this interesting is that the rules of the game require that the two top bidders must pay whatever they last bid. So, if the winner bids 80 cents and the loser bids 75 cents, the winner gets the dollar for 80 cents, but the loser is out his entire 75 cents. What happens in playing this game is that the two highest bidders find themselves locked in a battle where it will only cost a little bit more for the second highest bidder to up his bid and possibly avoid losing his entire stake in the game. It's not much more to lose 85 cents than to lose 75 cents, and in the process he just might be the highest bidder. Under these conditions, it is not unusual for someone to pay $5.00 for a dollar bill and the second highest to pay $4.95 and get nothing!

This is much like the dilemma faced by our fictitious Mr. Jones. How long should he risk throwing good money after bad in the hopes of saving his new business? When should he decide to cut his losses and bail out? It is the dilemma faced by medical doctors who must decide how long to use extreme measures at ever increasing costs in an effort to save a patient whose chances of survival are becoming progressively slimmer. It is also the dilemma faced by a military commander in deciding whether or not to escalate a conflict in an effort to win when battle conditions are deteriorating. It's called **entrap-ment.** How long does one continue to invest in the hopes of saving something that looks more and more like it's in trouble?

Now let's return to the case of Jill in the opening of this chapter. Notice that Jill faces a similar dilemma. How long does she continue to invest in a relationship that doesn't seem to be going anywhere? When does she decide to cut her losses and leave?

Faced with such choices, people are likely to weigh the pluses and minuses of the various options available to them and in the process experience a sense of ambivalence.

## Ambivalence and Personal Relationships

For most of us, close personal relationships are high-stakes investments. Over time they involve both significant rewards and significant costs. If the rewards are sufficient, we are likely to experience a degree of satisfaction. If the costs are high, we are likely to experience dissatisfaction. And in between lies a gray area we will call ambivalence.

Perhaps the best model of ambivalence comes from catastrophe theory. The central notion in catastrophe theory is that when two powerful forces are in opposition, no moderate, neutral, or intermediate outcome is likely (Brickman, 1987).

Let's take an example: One of the first lessons to be learned in sailing is how *not* to make a turnabout. It's possible to turn a dinghy downwind, for example, and find yourself in the situation of having the sail begin to fill from both sides, say the top filling from the right and the bottom filling from the left. As the pressure builds, sooner or later one side or the other "wins out." Under such circumstances, the boom can snap around with a vengeance, and many an amateur sailor (the author included) has found him- or herself taking an unexpected swim.

Like the sail filling from both sides, ambivalence describes our feelings when we find ourselves in situations that have reached an unstable state. Under conditions of ambivalence, two opposing forces are powerful, and when change comes, it is likely to be rapid, drastic, and seemingly beyond reason (Brickman, 1987). This seems to characterize the feelings we associate with many of life's most important events—falling in (and out of) love, religious conversion, having a baby, for example. It's hard to feel neutral about any of these.

What are the implications of the concept of ambivalence for close personal relationships? In situations where we feel ambivalent (she loves me, she loves me not), attitudes, feelings, and behavior can shift dramatically as the balance between the positives and the negatives changes (even slightly) one way or the other. Why would this be?

Feelings of ambivalence are not the same as feelings of neutrality or indifference. If close personal relationships were characterized by feelings of neutrality or indifference, as the relationship became more or less satisfying,

When one feels ambivalent in a relationship, emotions may shift back and forth between positive and negative. Honest communication is a crucial part of any close relationship.

people would simply love each other a little bit more on day 1, a little bit less on day 2, with the various episodes perhaps balancing each other out over time. Is this the way we experience close personal relationships? Do marriages decline in satisfaction with the couple returning to the neutral zone and becoming "just friends"? The evidence suggests otherwise. This is why the concept of ambivalence is so important to our understanding of close personal relationships.

The more valuable, important, cherished, and indispensable the other becomes, the more we have to lose if the relationship should end (Berscheid & Walster, 1974). The more we care about someone, the more vulnerable we become. And we must add to this the fact that love places on the other the burden of all of our hopes and dreams. And these are not likely to be realized in the real world (Brickman, 1987). This is the paradox of loving. Love makes us vulnerable, and this is why loving relationships are likely to involve a measure of ambivalence.

We are now in a position to appreciate why close personal relationships generate the strong feelings that they do. The more we invest, the more we stand to lose if the relationship fails. But if we don't invest, there isn't likely to be any relationship at all.

We resolve these feelings of ambivalence by making commitments and accepting the risks that go with those commitments. But, as we noted in the case of Jill, the line between commitment to a good relationship and entrapment in a poor one can be a fine line indeed. This issue—where to draw the line between commitment and entrapment—has been the focus of Caryl Rusbult and her colleagues (Rusbult, 1980; Rusbult et al., 1986b). Her model of commitment has come to be known as the "investment model," and it is to a consideration of her work that we now turn.

## Rusbult's Investment Model

Rusbult's investment model incorporates a number of notions from John Thibaut and Harold Kelley's (1959) exchange theory, such as rewards, costs, comparison level, and outcome (see Chapter 3 for an overview of this theory). Similar notions have been suggested by others, but Rusbult's work stands out both for its clarity of presentation and for the research that it has generated.

For example, it's commonly assumed that when relationships lead to happiness and satisfaction, they tend to last, and when they lead to unhappiness and dissatisfaction, they don't. It's as simple as that. But the problem with using "happiness" or "satisfaction" as an indication of commitment to a personal relationship is that all relationships are likely to go through some difficult times. Accounting for relationships that last during the good times is no particular problem. But why do people stay in relationships when the relationships are not satisfying? People remain in relationships that they are not happy with because they are in some sense committed (Rusbult & Buunk, 1993).

Commitment to a relationship depends on more than just happiness or satisfaction. Among the other factors that enter the picture are such things as concern for the other, the length of the relationship, and the availability of alternative relationships (Rusbult & Buunk, 1993).

### Satisfaction Versus Commitment

According to the investment model, individuals should be satisfied with a relationship as long as outcomes are favorable, that is, as long as rewards are high and costs are low. Such satisfaction is likely to be determined, in part, by comparison level (CL)—in other words, what the individual has come to expect from his or her relationships. And insofar as individuals are satisfied with their relationships, they should become increasingly committed to them. No surprise there. What other factors enter into the picture?

In investigating the importance of various other factors in the prediction

Satisfaction        Investment    **Figure 13-1**   Rusbult's
                                  commitment model
        Commitment

(minus) Availability of attractive alternatives

of relationship outcomes, Rusbult (1980a) collected data on the subjective ratings of probable and desired duration of relationships among romantic partners, asking participants specifically how attractive an alternative relationship would have to be before they would terminate their present relationship, and what the probability was of ending the present relationship in the near future. She found that *attraction* to the current relationship is a matter of rewardingness—period. *Commitment,* on the other hand, is a matter of rewards, plus investment, plus the presence or absence of other desirable alternatives.

As individuals become more invested in a relationship, they are likely to become more committed to it. Such investments come in a number of forms. There are direct investments, such as time, effort, energy, resources, access to shared deep emotional experiences and emotional bonds. And there are indirect investments, such as shared social networks, shared memories, activities, and possessions.

In addition, there are likely to be such things as the development of nontransferable skills, opportunities forgone, and options foreclosed. These kinds of investments also tend to contribute to relationship stability because they are irretrievable (Kelley, 1983; Rusbult, 1980a). Insofar as such investments, direct and indirect, tangible and intangible, are cumulative and nonrecoverable, they serve to generate commitment by increasing the costs of disengagement.

Rusbult's model also predicts that individuals are likely to be more committed to relationships when they perceive their other options to be limited or unattractive. Or, to put it another way, the availability of an attractive alternative, such as one or more other potential partners, tends to pull the individual away from commitment when the primary relationship is unsatisfactory. For example, when there are more eligible females than males in a given social environment, males are less likely to commit themselves to one partner (Buunk, 1987; Drigotas & Rusbult, 1992). The more that other possibilities are available and attractive, then, the less committed individuals tend to be.

These findings suggest not only that satisfaction with and commitment to a relationship are not the same thing but also that they are not necessarily highly correlated. While satisfaction offers an indication of how rewarding or unrewarding a relationship might be, commitment is clearly influenced by other things. People remain in unsatisfactory relationships because they perceive (rightly or wrongly) that ending the relationship would mean the loss of certain irretrievable investments associated with the relationship or that their alternatives are even less attractive. (An old saying goes, "If it weren't for bad luck, I'd have no luck at all.")

Support for the investment model has been demonstrated in various kinds of relationships, including friendships, dating relationships, marriage, relationships between homosexuals, and employee commitment in the workplace (Duffy & Rusbult, 1986; Rusbult, 1980b; Rusbult et al., 1986b; Rusbult & Farrell, 1983). In general, such studies have shown (1) that commitment and investment are positively correlated; (2) that they are related to satisfaction in relationships (Duffy & Rusbult, 1986; Rusbult, 1980a; Rusbult et al., 1986a, 1986b); and (3) that they are negatively correlated with perceived attractiveness of alternatives (Duffy & Rusbult, 1986; Felmlee et al., 1990; Johnson & Rusbult, 1989; Parks & Eggert, 1991; Simpson et al., 1990).

For example, in the case of friendships, Rusbult (1980b) found that commitment was positively correlated with investment ($r = .58$) and satisfaction ($r = .43$) and negatively correlated with the perceived availability of alternatives ($r = -.40$). However, when all three variables were considered together, the multiple correlation was even more significant ($R = .65$), and when any one of these was removed from the equation, the ability to predict commitment declined significantly.

Similarly, in a study of dating relationships, Rusbult (1983) found that those who stayed in relationships showed different trends than did those who eventually left. Over time, those whose relationships lasted indicated increasing investment and satisfaction in the relationship and decreasing interest in alternative relationships.

In a study comparing homosexual and heterosexual relationships, Sally Duffy and Caryl Rusbult (1986) found that lesbians, gay men, and heterosexuals described their relationships in much the same ways. All indicated having high satisfaction with their relationships, relatively high investment, and few desirable alternatives. Still, because lesbian and gay couples experience fewer barriers to separation, we would expect that this would affect relationship commitment.

This possibility has been explored by Lawrence Kurdek and Patrick Schmitt (1986) in a study comparing attraction (satisfaction), barriers to dissolution, and the availability of alternative relationships among gay, lesbian, cohabiting, and married couples. In this study, all four groups indicated similar levels of attraction and satisfaction, but married couples reported significantly more barriers to relationship dissolution than did gays, lesbians, or cohabiting couples. Cohabiting and gay couples indicated having higher availability of alternative relationships (but see Duffy & Rusbult, 1986, for different findings). Still, for all groups, love was related to barriers to leaving, fewer alternatives, and relationship satisfaction. The issue of commitment among lesbians and gay males is explored further in Box 13-1.

Studies relating commitment to why people choose to leave or stay in less satisfactory relationships have also been supportive of the investment model. For example, Caryl Rusbult and John Martz (1995) interviewed women at a shelter for abused spouses. Included in the interviews were questions dealing with other options the women had available to them. The significant findings in this study were that (1) those who indicated feelings of commitment tended to return to their partners; and (2) the investment level (as indicated by such things as length of the relationship and marital status) and (3) the availability of alternatives (as indicated by such things as education level and amount of money on hand), were key to their decision to stay in the marriage or leave it. However, feelings of satisfaction or lack of satisfaction with the relationship did not differentiate between those who returned and those who left. The

## Box 13-1 In a Different Key
## Commitment Among Lesbians and Gay Males

Commitment seems to operate somewhat differently in homosexual and heterosexual relationships. In the case of heterosexual relationships, for example, commitment is affected not only by positive attraction but by barriers to separation—a married couple has many barriers to dissolution of their relationship, such as the cost of divorce, property settlement, and responsibility for children.

Accordingly, when we think about successful marriages, we usually think in terms of longevity. Lesbian and gay couples, however, are not likely to face the same types of costs. Their relationships do not ordinarily have the legal status of marriage, and they are less likely to have responsibility for children. Accordingly, homosexuals tend to think in terms of equity, satisfaction, and fulfillment. This difference has significant effects on the way they evaluate their relationships and conduct themselves.

There is some evidence that gay and lesbian relationships are not as long lasting as heterosexual marriages (Blumstein & Schwartz, 1983), but we must be careful of the way we interpret these findings. Much of the early research on gay males tended to focus on bath houses, bars, and tea rooms. Traditionally, these have offered a meeting place for gay men interested in casual sex. Sometimes these relationships developed into long-term committed relationships, but this seems to be the exception (Silverstein, 1981).

The AIDS epidemic has led gay males to reassess casual contacts, however, and stable relationships seem to be increasingly common (Davidson, 1991). Estimates are that 40% to 60% of gay men are involved in steady relationships, and this may actually be a low estimate because older gay males are more likely to have long-term relationships and at the same time are less likely to "go public" (Peplau, 1991). Approximately 75% of lesbians are in stable relationships. And among older lesbians and gays, it is common to see relationships that last 20 years or more (McWhirter & Mattison, 1984).

In their study, Philip Blumstein and Pepper Schwartz (1983) found a 22% breakup rate among lesbian couples, 16% for gay male couples, 17% for cohabiting heterosexual couples, and 4% for married couples over a period of 18 months. But contrary to what has sometimes been suggested, they found no evidence that lesbian relationships were more stable than the relationships of gay males. On the other hand, casual sex is of less interest to lesbians; they are more likely not to make their homosexuality known (Huston & Schwartz, 1995). And lesbians involved in committed relationships are more likely to view sex outside the relationship as betrayal (Peplau et al., 1982).

women who returned to what most certainly were unsatisfactory relationships were primarily women whose other options were limited.

So, the decision to remain in an unsatisfactory relationship (including an abusive one) is not as irrational as it might appear on the surface. Such decisions are not usually motivated by masochism or learned helplessness, as is sometimes suggested, but rather by the lack of options. The (perceived) lack of desirable alternatives can turn *dependency* into commitment. The implication of this finding for intervention programs is that they are most likely to be effective if they focus on increasing options by providing such things as housing, driving lessons, and job training (Rusbult & Buunk, 1993).

### Commitment and Relationship Maintenance Strategies

Being in a loving, satisfying, and committed relationship does not mean that attractive alternatives disappear. But people make choices that increase or decrease the likelihood of their being in the path of attractive alternatives and often choose to restrict their activities so as to keep themselves out of harm's way, for the sake of the primary relationship.

What are some of the strategies that people use to steer a steady course in personal relationships in spite of feelings of ambivalence from within and distractions from without? In the early stages of a developing romantic relationship, it is common for partners to display signs of their affection, such as class rings and fraternity pins, and to be seen together, as well as to proclaim that they are "going with" each other. This identifies them as a couple and, as a consequence, off-limits to would-be contenders.

In addition, when attractive alternatives appear on the scene, people in committed relationships often use prorelationship biases in responding to

It is common for partners to display signs of affection—a public acknowledgement of their commitment to one another.

them. One of the most interesting examples is the strategy of **derogation of attractive alternatives**. For example, Jeffry Simpson and his colleagues (1990) found that people involved in dating relationships evaluated photographs of opposite-sex others less favorably than did those who were not involved in dating relationships. But perhaps the most compelling demonstration of a pro-relationship bias came in a study by Dennis Johnson and Caryl Rusbult (1989). They found that those who were highly committed to a relationship not only showed a tendency to downgrade the qualities of potential alternative partners, but the more attractive the potential alternative partner, the more they tended to downgrade his or her qualities.

In addition, people in happy marriages are likely to think less in terms of themselves and their own outcomes, and more in terms of their partner—seeing, feeling, and experiencing their partner's ups and downs as if these were their own. The positives and the negatives of the partner are experienced as "yoked"—both carry their weight—and the costs and rewards are shared. A good indication of this comes in the finding that couples who pool their financial resources tend to have more stable marriages (Kurdek, 1993).

### Sacrifice and Attribution

One further indication of commitment to a relationship is the willingness to sacrifice in order to support and preserve it. When partners are willing to make mutual sacrifices for the sake of the relationship, the relationship is more likely to run smoothly (Cox et al., 1995). For example, Paul van Lange and his colleagues (1992, 1997) asked dating couples to name four things, other than their (dating) relationship, that were important to them—such as career, education, family, travel, recreation, and religion—and to indicate how willing they would be to give each one up if it proved detrimental to their relationship. Relationships in which the partners were more willing to sacrifice were more likely to lead to satisfaction, more likely to lead to further investment, and more likely to last.

Brickman (1987) referred to the notion of attribution to account for such findings. His rationale was as follows: When we try to analyze feelings such as love, caring, and commitment, we don't feel very comfortable about it. "Does John love Joan because of sex, money, power, physical attractiveness?" None of these or any number of other explanations are likely to provide a very satisfactory account of one's commitment to a close personal relationship. Indeed, Clive Seligman and colleagues (1978) found that making the extrinsic reasons for a relationship more obvious tends to *decrease* our perceptions of love. Love, once dissected, seems to lose much of its magic. It is only when one goes beyond the tangibles—for example, when one acts "above and beyond the call of duty"—that attributions of caring, commitment, and love are likely to be made (Brickman, 1987).

Let's look at this curiosity for a moment. In most other areas of life, we would be quite happy to take advantage of a bargain. We wouldn't hesitate, for example, to say we got a pair of shoes on sale or that we got a good deal on a new car. But we wouldn't say the same thing about our husband or wife, boyfriend or girlfriend—that we went for him or her "because he or she came cheap." We would, on the other hand, be quite happy to note the costs and to say that whatever the costs, he or she was (is) worth it. Why is it that the same cost-benefit analysis, which is so common in other areas of life, is totally inappropriate when it comes to close personal relationships?

When the reasons for an action (or feeling) are obvious from extrinsic factors alone, we need not make an attribution of caring, thoughtfulness, respect, or love. It is only when the reasons for our beliefs, actions, and feelings are not clear from the externals that such personal attributions are made. Thus, to return to the case of Jill in the opening of this chapter, when one partner takes a less preferred position to remain in the same locale where the other is employed, such a sacrifice is one indication of how committed he or she is to the relationship. When two people save together rather than spending their money on their individual wants and desires, an attribution of caring is likely to be made.

This leads us, then, to a fundamental paradox when we apply exchange theory and its several variations to commitment in personal relationships. What attributions are we likely to make when fairness and equity prevail in a relationship? Fairness and equity are not bad notions, but they do not have much to say about the dynamics of commitment in close personal relationships. For example, precisely the same act, sexual intercourse, is taken as an indication of love under one set of circumstances and, under other circumstances, is called prostitution. Why?

The idea of loving for what we can get does not describe how we experience committed love. It is only when the externals cannot account for our feelings and actions that deeply felt personal motives are implicated. So, it would seem that it is in the departures from tit-for-tat exchange that we find grist for the mill of making personal attributions, such as love, caring, and commitment—that is, when the usual explanations fail us. And so we should not be troubled by our inability to account for why we love someone. The mystery of love does not raise questions so much as it provides an answer. To love means to go beyond the tangible qualities (Brickman, 1987).

Turning the argument around for a moment, whenever problems, emotional stresses, and strains can be attributed to externals, such as pressure at work, a dip in the stock market, or the fact that the car broke down again, they do not fall into the default category of a negative personal attribution (such as negligence or laziness). Making external attributions for negative aspects of one's partner's behavior is, in fact, characteristic of stable adult relationships. And we see this most especially in the accommodations that partners in healthy relationships make for each other in times of distress.

Studies comparing distressed and nondistressed couples show that relationship stability is best served when partners do not respond in tit-for-tat fashion to negative behaviors during conflict (for example, Jacobson et al., 1982; Schaap et al., 1988). In the heat of the moment, when one partner snaps at the other, the other is better off responding in terms that suggest external attributions, such as asking if he or she had a bad day or ignoring the incident altogether.

In accommodative behavior, negativity is transformed into a concern for the other's well-being rather than taken as a personal attack (Rusbult et al., 1996). For example, among satisfied couples, when problems come up, the actual behaviors enacted tend to be far more restrained and benign than some of the behaviors the partners considered (Rusbult et al., 1991). In practical terms, this may be one of the most important findings to come out of the study of commitment in close personal relationships. Of course, our grandmothers already knew this technique for maintaining relationship stability: "A soft voice turneth away wrath."

The tendency to accommodate is closely related to an individual's relationship with his or her partner. When people are satisfied, are highly invested in a relationship, and have few or poor alternatives, they tend to be more accommodating. Even in cases involving extramarital affairs, "offended" partners who are generally more satisfied with their relationship tend to be more accommodating and make more constructive efforts at conflict resolution than do those whose relationships were less satisfying before their partner had an affair (Schaap et al., 1988).

### Commitment Testing

Because certain types of sacrifice, effort, and accommodation are signs of a healthy, mature relationship, sometimes people are curious to know how their partner would respond if "such and such" happened. Paul Rosenblatt (1977) calls this "commitment testing" and notes that it takes place particularly when young married couples face crises. Sometimes this testing involves direct questioning and asking for reassurances. But just as often it is more subtle. For example, a pregnant wife may send her husband chasing all over town in the wee hours for some special food she is craving. This request can be interpreted as a test to see if the husband will come through at a time when the expectant mother is feeling especially vulnerable and in need of reassurance (Rosenblatt, 1977).

## Individual Differences in Commitment

Individual differences also play a role in commitment. For example, personality characteristics such as a need for independence are associated with lower levels of commitment to personal relationships (Eidelson, 1983). Similarly, individuals with high self-esteem are more likely to leave an unsatisfactory relationship (Rusbult et al., 1987). And, among dating couples, high need for power in males does not seem to bode well for a long-term relationship. Not only is it associated with dissatisfaction in relationships, it also predicts future problems. For example, over a period of 2 years, 50% of the couples in which the male had scored high in need for power had broken up, while 9% had

---

### Box 13-2 *In a Different Key*
### Till Death Do Us Part

Cross culturally, commitment is expressed in ways undreamed of in the West. In Thailand, same-sex friends make a public declaration of their relationship in terms we would reserve for marriage. In such cases blood is exchanged between two men who form a "friendship to the death." And failure to live up to the commitment of such a friendship is thought to lead to dire consequences for oneself and one's family. Such friendships are formal, and yet personal and passionate, and offer something of a break from the dangers and isolation of a repressive society (Foster, 1976).

In another example, in the state of Orissa in India, it is considered inappropriate for a widow to eat fish, because eating fish is associated with sexual appetite, and it is thought that a widow who eats fish might be tempted to have sex with another man. But she is still considered to be married to her husband. In Orissa marriage does not end, not even in death (Shweder et al., 1990).

---

married. For couples in which the male was low in need for power, 15% broke up and 52% married (Stewart & Rubin, 1976).

Conversely, although males in our society are not encouraged to be dependent, those who were dependent as children are more likely to have successful marriages. Males who have a history of dependency during childhood seem to be transformed (caterpillar-to-butterfly style) into adult men who are calm, generous, warm, understanding, perceptive, and poised. Apparently, dependency in childhood turns into a surprisingly positive quality in adulthood, and this is especially apparent in their personal relationships. As a group, they are more likely to remain married (to their first wife), and their wives are more likely to be satisfied with their marriage than are wives of other males (Caspi et al., 1989).

Finally, as we see in Box 13-2, commitment operates differently for different types of relationships in other cultures.

## Conclusion

What are we to conclude from our look at the concept of commitment as it applies to personal relationships? First, we have seen that the notion of commitment includes elements of dependence, interdependence, and felt obligation—personal, social, and moral. It is likely to involve investment, feelings of satisfaction in relationships, and potential costs of leaving. Much of the time, the positive and negative forces operate in concert, and people are likely to be both happy in a relationship and pay little attention to the alternatives that might be available.

At other times, people may not be particularly happy in their relationships but may see no attractive alternatives. The same forces that lead to satisfaction and stability in relationships, such as investing exclusively in a relationship, operate in less satisfying relationships as well. Putting all of our eggs in one basket and limiting our options is a way of investing in a satisfactory relationship, but it is also a recipe for entrapment in an unsatisfactory one.

In addition, people in committed relationships tend to use certain strategies and show certain biases in order to maintain them. And, finally, certain personality characteristics seem to be associated both with a willingness to commit oneself to a personal relationship and a tendency to follow through on that commitment.

## Suggestions for Further Reading

Aronson, E., & Mills, J. (1959). The effect of severity of initiation on liking for a group. *Journal of Abnormal and Social Psychology, 59*, 179–181. The classic study on the effect of costs of initiation increasing attraction to a group.

Brickman, P. (1987). *Commitment, conflict and caring.* Englewood Cliffs, NJ: Prentice-Hall. This volume is a series of independent chapters compiled by Brickman's students and friends following his death. What it lacks in organization it makes up for in brilliance and subtlety of analysis.

Johnson, M. P. (1991). Commitment to personal relationships. In W. H. Jones & D. Perlman (Eds.), *Advances in personal relationships* (Vol. 3). London: Kingsley. A chapter emphasizing the distinction between personal and structural commitment, by one of the major proponents of the structural position.

Rusbult, C. E., & Buunk, B. P. (1993). Commitment processes in close relationships: An interdependence analysis. *Journal of Social and Personal Relationships, 10*, 175–204. Excellent overview of Rusbult's investment model.

Rusbult, C. E., & Martz, J. (1995). Remaining in an abusive relationship: An investment model of non-voluntary dependence. *Personality and Social Psychology Bulletin, 6*, 558–571. A compelling application of the investment model to a population of women at a shelter for abused spouses.

Shubik, M. (1971). The dollar auction game: A paradox in non-cooperative behavior and escalation. *Journal of Conflict Resolution, 15*, 109–111. The single best example of "entrapment" research in the literature. Makes an ideal classroom demonstration.

# CHAPTER 14

 *Power*

*Cindy and Ed had been married for some years. Their marriage had always been a traditional one, with Ed the wage earner and Cindy the full-time mother. This suited them both until the children became old enough to be more or less independent. At this point Cindy started a small photography business. It grew steadily, and even Cindy was surprised at how well things went. She was a natural at working with people, and she was especially good with children. Over the years she had to hire some additional help.*

*Then the company where Ed worked started cutting back, and Ed found himself out of a job. Now Cindy's business was their only source of income, and eventually Ed accepted the once unthinkable—he started working in Cindy's photography business. With this came a change in their relationship. Cindy never made a point of it, but it showed in subtle ways. Sometimes she made decisions that affected the household without checking with Ed first. With his loss of an independent income, Ed lost much of his power in their marriage.*

The term *power* is used in many different ways in the area of personal relationships. Sometimes it refers to influence in general; sometimes it is used as a synonym for dominance, meaning one individual is clearly in charge; and sometimes it's used more specifically to indicate control.

Influence is the broadest of these terms. By **influence** we mean simply that one person has an effect on another. For example, it's possible to speak of the influence of one artist on the work of another, without implying any personal relationship at all. However, influence is basic to personal relationships. The notion of a personal relationship loses all meaning unless those involved influence one another.

The extent and direction of influence varies from one relationship to another. Sometimes influence is limited to specific areas, such as the functioning of the household, shopping, choice of furniture, and planning vacations. Influence in a limited area does not imply dominance. Only when the influence of one person extends over a wide range of issues can we speak meaningfully of **dominance** (Huston, 1983). If Dick makes all the financial decisions, controls the conversations, chooses the furniture, and decides how the children are to be disciplined, and his wife Sandy simply accepts this, it's fair to say Dick is dominant in his relationship with his wife and children. This does not mean, however, that he is dominant in all relationships. He may be quite submissive in his interactions with his employer, for example.

Where influence leaves off and control begins is often difficult to say. Indeed, Judith Howard and her colleagues (1986) see **control** as power in which the power holder has the potential to influence and alter another's behavior.

When we speak of power in personal relationships, then, we are speaking of the ability to influence another toward some desired outcome. Sometimes this involves dominance or obvious control, but not always (Huston, 1983). There are times when the use of power is quite subtle.

## The Dynamics of Power

The kinds of things that one person might do to influence another are virtually infinite. For example, the power tactics that romantic partners use to influence each other include such things as asking, bargaining, discussing, whining, hinting, reasoning, suggesting, demanding, threatening, persisting, charming, shaming, withdrawing, and using physical violence (Buss et al., 1987; Falbo & Peplau, 1980; Frieze & McHugh, 1992).

How we get our way, if indeed we do, is likely to be determined by the resources at our disposal, the culture in which we live, the circumstances of those we hope to influence, and the type of relationship we have. For example, one study found that couples whose marriages are more traditional tend to be open in their communication and to use the relationship itself as a basis for achieving agreement, acceptance, or compliance; whereas couples who do more outside the relationship are likely to have a communication style that is more adversarial and to gain compliance by emphasizing the negative consequences of noncompliance (Witteman & Fitzpatrick, 1986). This brings us to one of the most important issues in the use of power in personal relationships: its short-term versus long-term effects.

### Power as a Double-Edged Sword

By definition, people in close personal relationships have a good deal of influence over one another, both to reward and to impose costs. The closeness that is characteristic of personal relationships creates vulnerability. This ability to influence the other may or may not be translated into action, however. Power in the theoretical sense differs from power in the practical sense. The immediate effects of the use of power can be quite different from the long-term consequences. Much like a military general allocating resources in an armed conflict, care must be taken not to win the battle and lose the war.

Anyone exercising power through her or his ability to offer rewards or impose costs generates some ambivalence in the other person (Homans, 1961). Too much influence, or too arbitrary a use of power, can cause the less powerful person to turn to alternative relationships where better outcomes are available. As a consequence, the more powerful person loses whatever power she or he had in the relationship in the first place. An example of this was reported by Charles Hill and his colleagues (1976) in their study of relationship breakups among college couples. When one partner was clearly more involved in the relationship than the other, it was often the less powerful partner that initiated the breakup. In personal relationships, the wise person uses power sparingly.

## Liking as a Source of Power

A number of theorists have noted that liking (or interpersonal attraction) is a source of power (French & Raven, 1959). This was demonstrated in an experiment by Kelly Shaver (1970) in which similarity (versus dissimilarity) was used to generate liking. In this study, subjects were presented with the description of a moral dilemma in which a driver leaves his car parked on a hill with the emergency brake securely set. It rolls down the hill, resulting in injury to two people, because, as is later discovered, the brake was faulty. When participants in the study were led to believe that the driver was very similar to themselves, their attribution of blame and assessment of penalties was significantly more forgiving than it was if they believed the driver was dissimilar.

When we like someone, we tend to give them the benefit of the doubt, to go out of our way more, forgive more, risk more, cooperate more, and put ourselves out more on their behalf. And the greater the liking, the more we tend to be willing to do such favors, make such sacrifices, and provide such benefits. Indeed, liking that does not translate into some sort of preferential treatment would be hollow indeed.

So, people like to be liked, in part because those who are liked receive benefits and have influence that the disliked and the less liked do not. In other words, being liked is a potential source of power. It is no accident that one of the most successful books in publishing history is Dale Carnegie's (1937) *How to Win Friends and Influence People.*

The small talk that characterizes much of our everyday interactions may not seem on the surface as if it is motivated by self-interest; but chitchat, gossip, reminiscences, self-disclosure, joking, and everyday courtesies communicate a great deal in terms of trust, similarity, common interests, common values, and shared symbolic culture (Duck, 1994). In this way, everyday conversation serves to generate and maintain liking and the power and influence that go with it (Bell & Daly, 1984).

The disliked, or less liked, on the other hand, are those who give us reason to suspect their intentions, their good will, and their attempts at influence. Accordingly, we are likely to keep them at a distance when possible.

## Power and Friendship

We tend to be tolerant of temporary imbalances in exchange with our friends. As a consequence, friends may be entirely unaware of each other's power in the relationship until one makes a misguided attempt to influence the other in ways that the other feels she or he must resist (Roiger, 1993). Here is a case in point: When Ron's car slid on the ice and sideswiped Bob's pickup, Ron asked Bob not to report it so that it would not go on his insurance record. "I'll take care of it. There's nothing to worry about," he pleaded. After all, they were friends. But Bob said he couldn't take the chance, and he reported it to the insurance company. Their friendship went only so far.

In addition to such clear-cut cases, we sometimes see subtle hints of imbalances in power, even among friends. For example, the use of subtle strategies tends to decrease as one's power in a relationship increases (Miller, 1982), and the one who is more powerful in a relationship tends to be less polite (Baxter, 1984). In other words, those in a position of power seem to be less concerned about being diplomatic in exerting their influence.

This was demonstrated in a study by James Roiger (1993), who presented students with scenes depicting people in various power relationships. For example, the scene depicting someone in a condition of favorable power was something like this: "Suppose you and Joe have been friends for some time. You are going to see your mother, who is ill, and you need a ride to the airport. The airport is not far away, and Joe has no particular plans at the time." Other examples varied the urgency of the request, the imposition it caused, and the debt one person owed the other from previous favors. Following each scene, some strategies were listed, such as asking politely or insisting more aggressively, and participants in the study were asked to indicate the likelihood of someone in that situation using each of these.

As predicted, Roiger found that those in a position of power were considered more likely to use aggressive power strategies than were those in situations where both parties were equal, but, somewhat surprisingly, so were those in a less powerful position. When we are in a less favorable power position, we are likely to use blatant influence strategies, presumably because we feel our friend has an obligation to help us in time of need. ("Look, pea brain, I'm in a bind. If I don't get to the airport by three, I'll miss my plane—OK?") This curvilinear relationship is shown in Figure 14-1.

However, as we saw in the case of Ron and Bob, using aggressive tactics doesn't always work. And, further, power tactics that are effective over the short term may not be the most effective over the long term. We see the reason for this in the next section.

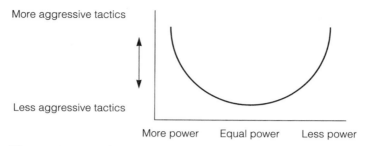

**Figure 14-1**    People in positions of more power and less power are more likely to use aggressive tactics to get their way.

## The Principle of Least Interest

Researchers have noted that power in personal relationships rests with the one who is less involved (or less "interested") in maintaining the relationship(s). This notion has been expressed in a number of ways over the years. It has been called the "law of personal exploitation"—that is, the one who cares the least is in a position to exploit the one who cares the most (Ross, 1921). But it's more commonly known as the "principle of least interest" (Waller, 1938). Put simply, the principle of least interest says that one who has the most power in a relationship is the one who cares the least.

The principle of least interest has been shown to apply across a wide range of relationships, including friendships, heterosexual dating relationships, marriage, and relationships between lesbians (Caldwell & Peplau, 1984). Not surprisingly, then, to "be in love" is sometimes characterized as "being in another's power."

This relationship between power and "least interest" was demonstrated by Christantina Safilios-Rothschild (1976) in her study of 100 Athenian couples. Based on self-reports, participants in the study were classified as (1) couples who were not in love (these tended to be arranged marriages), (2) couples in which the husband was more in love, (3) couples in which the wife was more in love, and (4) couples in which both partners were equally in love. Her findings indicated that when the wives perceived their husbands to be more in love, they (the wives) tended to have more say in the important decisions dealing with family life. When both spouses were equally in love, decision making was more likely to be shared equally.

Consistent with this finding, researchers have noted that women who are more career oriented and, as a consequence, less dependent on a dating partner, report having more power in their romantic relationships (Caldwell & Peplau, 1984). But perhaps the clearest example comes in cases where people have alternative relationships available.

## Power and the Availability of Alternative Relationships

According to John Thibaut and Harold Kelley's (1959) concept of CLalt (see Chapter 3), one factor that determines who is the most and who is the least

Richard Cline © 1995
from The New Yorker
Collection. All Rights
Reserved.

*"Your clock may be telling you to get married, but
mine's telling me to have lunch."*

"interested" in a relationship is the perceived availability (or lack of availability) of alternative relationships. Those without desirable alternatives are dependent on their present relationship(s), while those with access to desirable alternative relationships are less so. As a consequence, the relative power of one person in a dyad (or group) tends to be a matter of the number and quality of options available to the other(s). This is vividly illustrated in the case of Harriet and Sue.

Harriet and Sue were girlhood chums. They lived in the same neighborhood and went to the same school. But Harriet was a year older than Sue and clearly the dominant one in the relationship. She had a tendency to be overbearing, dictating what they would do and when they would do it. Sue tended to be rather shy. For the most part, Sue accepted this, until a new girl, Kathy, moved into the neighborhood. Kathy was the same age as Sue, and as it turned out, she too was on the quiet side. At first the girls formed a threesome, but it soon became evident that Kathy and Harriet did not get along at all.

Summer came, and with it came the acid test. Kathy had a swimming pool, and more often than not, Harriet was not included in their swim times. Soon,

Sue began spending more and more time with her new friend Kathy, and slowly but surely, Harriet's power over her began to fade. The next fall, Sue and Kathy walked to school together, and Harriet rode with her father on his way to work.

***The Interpersonal Arena***    Many of the trials and tribulations of the young in their initial ventures into peer relationships, both same sex and opposite sex, stem from trying to establish their "value" (and power) in the interpersonal arena. In the case of heterosexual relationships, for example, conventional wisdom has it that the value of a female's affections in the eyes of males depends on her popularity with the other males. The more popular she is, the less likely she is to make a commitment to one individual.

The female who indicates her interest in a particular male quite early in their dating relationship gives tacit evidence of her lack of other desirable options and, as a consequence, runs the risk of depreciating her value in the interpersonal arena. On the other hand, the one who waits before making a commitment gives an indication that "there are other fish in the sea" and that weighing the many possibilities available to her will simply take time. A female who plays hard to get increases the value of her affections when and where she chooses to offer them. According to conventional wisdom, then, when a woman's affections are too easily available, men will tend to keep looking. In other words, the value of "easy women" tends to fall in the rating and dating game. A wise woman plays hard to get. True or false?

***Playing Hard to Get***    There has been a fair amount of research on the issue of playing hard to get. In one study, participants were presented with descriptions of members of the opposite sex as being "very selective," "moderately selective," or "not particularly selective" in who they dated and then asked to indicate the desirability of each. The results showed that, in general, the more selective ones were considered more desirable. At the same time, however, it was possible for someone to come across as being too choosy. Those who were portrayed as extremely selective tended to be viewed as conceited. And females were more likely than males to respond negatively to members of the opposite sex who were portrayed as being extremely selective. Apparently, in our society, it's considered more acceptable for a female to be selective in who she dates. But, generally, participants in this study showed a preference for those who were moderately selective (Wright & Contrada, 1986).

Such findings, of course, are part of a much larger picture dealing with the relationship between power and gender, and it is to this topic that we turn next.

## Power and Gender

Researchers have noted differences in the interaction styles of males and females. In general, females tend to be more sensitive and more expressive of their feelings, and males tend to be more instrumental and "agentic" (interested in making things happen). And such differences do not seem to be limited to U.S. culture (Block, 1973; Buss, 1994; Gilmore, 1990).

There is also some indication that men and women express power differently in personal relationships. Women are more likely to use affection, sexuality, and various forms of manipulation that are sometimes quite subtle, such as helplessness; men tend to prefer more direct expressions of power, such as shows of authority, competence, knowledge, and skills (Johnson, 1976).

### Power Tactics

In their study of power in heterosexual relationships, Judith Howard and her colleagues (1986) found that males reported being the recipients of more "indirect" efforts to influence them. But women in this study did not report being the recipients of more direct tactics.

In a study of sex differences in manipulation tactics, David Buss and colleagues (1987) found some indication that females used more "whining," and males were more likely to allow themselves to be debased (or shamed) to get their way. However, neither of these findings stood up when the study was repeated, and the researchers concluded that (for their sample, at least) there were no sex differences in the tactics used by males and females.

A questionnaire study of professional couples by Janice Steil and Karen Weltman (1992) resulted in much the same findings. In this study, women reported using subtle tactics such as smiling and making suggestions more often, but overall, males and females were more similar than different in their influence strategies.

So, when we look closely at the issue of power and personal relationships, the styles of influence do not seem to be as gender loaded as conventional wisdom has sometimes led us to believe. What are the implications of this for the balance of power in heterosexual relationships? For some insights on that, we turn to the Boston Couples Study.

### The Boston Couples Study

The Boston Couples Study (Hill et al., 1979; Peplau et al., 1977; Peplau et al., 1993) was a research project in which 231 couples were recruited from colleges and universities in the Boston area. In order to be included in the study, students had to be going with someone, and both partners had to agree to participate. Most of those involved were white, from middle-class backgrounds, and on average, they had been going together for about 8 months when the study began.

For the most part, the study showed that dating partners considered their relationships reasonably well balanced or "egalitarian." Ninety-five percent of the females and 87% of the males indicated that each partner *should* have equal say in their relationship.

Still, there were differences in the expectations that males and females had of each other. For example, when they were asked which one would prevail if the male preferred to spend the weekend with his friends and the female preferred to spend the weekend with hers, females generally felt that the males were more likely to get their way and that they (the females) were more likely to give in (Peplau, 1979). At the same time, however, males indicated that they expected to get their way much less often than the females thought they would. So we see that males and females in this study saw things somewhat differently when it came to who held the power in their relationships. What have other researchers found?

### Other Research Findings on Power and Gender

Other studies suggest that power may in fact operate somewhat differently for males and females. For example, in a study of dating couples, females who indicated being more involved also indicated having less power in the relationship—an example of the principle of least interest. But this was not true for males, at least not based on self-reports. Males seemed to have about the same amount of power in a relationship whether they were highly involved or only moderately involved (Sprecher, 1985).

On the other hand, in a study of 413 dating couples, Diane Felmlee (1994) found that less than half of those participating viewed their relationship as equal in terms of power. And in a study of the balance of power, decision making, and control in dating couples, Susan Sprecher and Diane Felmlee (1995) noted that although most couples considered their relationships egalitarian overall, very few indicated that they were equal in terms of all three of the measures taken (power, decision making, and control). Further, both males and females in this study generally agreed on who had more power in the relationship, who made more of the decisions, and who had more control.

Somewhat surprisingly, in the Sprecher and Felmlee study, the perceived level of benefits received and resources contributed seemed to have very little effect on perceived power. Desirability of and access to alternative relationships were found to be associated with increased power in the case of males but not females.

Finally, in a 4-year follow-up of 41 couples who had remained together, relative power, decision making, and control seemed to remain quite stable over time. And although a majority of the couples perceived the power and decision making in their relationships to be unequal in some respects, the differences were not large. When there were differences, it tended to be the male who was seen as having more power. Perception of "control over the relationship," on the other hand, was seen as essentially equal by both males and females. Overall, these were not lopsided relationships.

So, during courtship, males and females may express power somewhat differently and in somewhat different areas. But as relationships progress, imbalances seem to decrease. For most couples, the issue of who gets their way fades over time, and shared goals and the relationship itself become the primary focus.

*Power in Lesbian and Gay Male Relationships*   Another way of approaching the question of the relationship between gender and power is to compare same-sex and opposite-sex couples. In the case of lesbian and gay male couples, both partners typically work, both tend to be economically independent, and the division of labor is likely to be determined on the basis of individual interests and skills rather than traditional husband/wife roles (Peplau, 1991). What are the implications of this for power?

In their study comparing the influence tactics of lesbians, gay men, and heterosexual couples, Toni Falbo and Letitia Peplau (1980) concluded that gender affected power tactics for heterosexual couples only. Peter Kollock and colleagues (1985) found that among lesbians and gay men, those who saw themselves as more powerful in a relationship tended to use bargaining and persuasion (masculine tactics). Those who saw themselves as lower in power tended to withdraw and use emotion (feminine tactics). Similarly, in their comparison of power tactics by homosexual and heterosexual couples, Judith Howard and her colleagues (1986) noted that the most dependent partner generally used "weak tactics" (for example, manipulation), and the more powerful partner tended to use "strong tactics" (for example, being autocratic).

On the other hand, when we compare lesbians with gay males, we find some significant differences in the way they express power. Lesbians tend to be relationship oriented; they are sensitive to differences in power; they communicate in ways that maintain emotional intimacy; and they tend not to interrupt or challenge each other (Kollock et al., 1985). Gay men, on the other hand, tend to be more career oriented and less relationship oriented than lesbians, and they are more likely to challenge each other as a normal part of relating (Tannen, 1990). Consistent with this, in the case of gay male couples, the one who earns the most money is likely to have more power in the relationship. But there is no similar association between money and power for lesbians (Blumstein & Schwartz, 1983).

So, although the relationships of lesbians and gay males shed some light on the gender-power issue, it is not safe to say that issues of power do not enter into their relationships. Power may operate somewhat differently in such relationships, but it is still apparent.

*"In" and "Out" of Role Behaviors*   When we turn to the question of how various styles of influence or power tactics are received, does it matter what type of influence style one uses? And does this in any way interact with gender? Here the answer seems to be a cautious yes. Falbo and colleagues (1982) found that either sex might pay a price for using tactics that are "out of role." That is, males seem to pay a price for acting helpless or dependent, and females seem to pay a price for acting assertive and expert. Such out-of-role behaviors are likely to be less well received, and the individuals who use them tend to be less well liked than those who behave in a more gender-appropriate manner.

Linda Carli (1990), however, has suggested that the costs of acting out of role may be greater for females than for males. In this study, subjects listened to either a male or a female who, in turn, spoke in either an assertive or a more tentative manner. When the speaker was a male, the style of his presentation (assertive or tentative) did not seem to affect his perceived competence, knowledge, or persuasiveness. In the case of a female speaker, however, the effects depended both on the style of presentation (assertive or tentative) and the sex of the listener.

Females who spoke more tentatively were considered more influential by male listeners but less influential by female listeners. Male listeners liked the tentative female speakers more, but female listeners responded more favorably to assertive female speakers. And, consistent with this, Doré Butler and Florence Geis (1990) found that female leaders in mixed-sex groups were the recipients of more negative responses than male leaders.

One message that seems to come through loud and clear is that female dominance is less acceptable to both males and females than is male dominance. Although both males and females may enjoy taking charge, they are likely to be more comfortable when the balance of power is tipped in favor of the male than they are when it is tipped in favor of the female.

One of the most telling demonstrations of male dominance came in a study in which researchers surreptitiously recorded the spontaneous conversations of college students in public places (later obtaining permission to use the data for research purposes). What they found was one set of rules for same-sex pairs in conversation and a quite different set of rules for opposite-sex pairs. In conversations between opposite-sex pairs, males interrupted their female partners more often than females interrupted males—a behavior typically associated with greater power (Kollock et al., 1985). Females were more often listeners in the conversation, and the responses of males to the females tended to be superficial (Zimmerman & West, 1975).

Along these same lines, Valerian Derlega and associates (1985) found that males were more self-disclosing in initial encounters with the opposite sex. This seemed to meet with the expectation of their female partners. Indeed, it tends to be the more active, dominant, and forceful males that women find most attractive (Sadalla et al., 1987).

In the case of heterosexual pairs, males are more likely to set the conversational agenda and exert more control over the conversation. The apparent exception to this is when the topic of conversation is clearly feminine (for example, cooking, shopping). In these cases, females tend to dominate (G. W. Brown et al., 1990).

What are some of the practical implications of these findings? Erik Filsinger and Stephen Thomas (1988) studied the verbal interactions of dating couples in the laboratory. The indicator of dominance in the relationships was whether the female had interrupted the male during the verbal interaction. Twenty-one of the original 31 couples were followed over a 5-year period. And what did the researchers find? When the female had interrupted the male, 80% of the couples had broken up. Among those still together, the more often the female had interrupted the male 5 years earlier, the less happy the relationship tended to be for both males and females.

The preference for male dominance is not limited to either brief encounters or dating relationships. Studies of marital satisfaction have shown repeatedly that both males and females are more satisfied in relationships that are either male dominant or egalitarian than in female-dominated relationships (Felmlee, 1994; Gray-Little & Burks, 1983). And in situations of distress, both males and females tend to be more comfortable when a male is in the role of mastery and a female is the one experiencing the distress rather than vice versa (Zillmann et al., 1986).

In short, we see a delicate balancing act for females who wish to wield power in close personal relationships. A personal style that commands respect and influence among other women seems to decrease liking and influence among men and vice versa. There appears to be a rather clear taboo against female dominance in our society, and personal relationships characterized by it are likely to experience dissatisfaction and strain. One of the clearest indications of this comes in the asymmetry we typically see in marriage.

*Marriage Asymmetry*   Charles Hill and his colleagues (1976) noted that dating couples in the college population they studied were matched to a significant degree on such characteristics as physical attractiveness, educational goals, and SAT scores. Gerald Leslie (1976) reported that dating partners and marrieds tend to be similar on many social characteristics. And Brant Burleson and Wayne Denton (1992) found that married couples tend to be similar in terms of social skills as well. In other words, naturally occurring couples seem to be similar in many ways.

Within this general rule, however, there is a systematic difference among heterosexual partners that results in what has come to be known as the "marriage asymmetry" phenomenon. Husbands tend to be somewhat older, taller, more educated, and higher on the occupational or professional ladder than their wives (Shepard & Strathman, 1989). And this arrangement seems to be preferred by both sexes. There is a tendency, in other words, for males to marry "down" and females to marry "up."

Such findings fit well with evolutionary theory. In our evolutionary past it has been the more powerful (bigger), more skillful, and more intelligent males who have controlled resources, and as a consequence, these qualities were associated with survival. Females who paired with less powerful males were less likely to rear offspring to maturity.

This tendency for females to marry "up" is still with us, and it is not an inconsequential matter, as William Philliber and Dana Vannoy-Hiller (1990) have noted. One of the implications of this is that a husband's accomplishments (occupationally and professionally) are likely to generate a **ceiling effect** so that a wife's accomplishments tend not to exceed those of her husband's.

For those interested in marrying, the impact of marriage asymmetry, demographically, is to reduce the pool of eligible partners for the less successful, lower status males. No surprise there. But the pool is also likely to be smaller for more educated and occupationally successful females. The average male

> **Box 14-1  In A Different Key**
> **Whom Does a Princess Marry?**
>
> Among the Bangwa, princesses marry men of lower rank, by way of preserving their own autonomy and independence. One princess, Mafwa, had her own wife! She could then become the "father" of her children and pocket the bride-price when her daughters married. This practice allowed a wealthy and titled female to establish her own line of descent as a "husband," have her own compound, and have a wife to cook for her. Such a practice is by no means extraordinary (Brain, 1976).

increases his options when he increases his socioeconomic status; the average female decreases hers. How so? For the answer to that, let's turn to the case of Dorothy, Helen, and Barbara.

Three single professional women, Dorothy, a lawyer, and Helen and Barbara, both professors, were having lunch one day and lamenting the lack of men in town. What was interesting about their conversation was the setting. Even as they spoke, the women were being served by an unmarried male waiter, their food had just been cooked by an unmarried male cook, not more than 20 feet away, and the floor around them was being swept by an unmarried male janitor. Yet, for all intents and purposes, these men were invisible. Successful females in U.S. society are reluctant to marry beneath their station (Doundna & McBride, 1981). And the problem doesn't end there.

When we combine the number of single, separated, divorced, and widowed individuals in the United States, we find, overall, that about 45% of those over the age of 15 are unattached (Bureau of Census, 1992). For blacks, however, the figures are very different. In our society, about 65% of black adults are single, divorced, widowed, or not living with a spouse. College-educated black women, especially, are less likely than their white counterparts to find a partner who is similar in status. Middle-class black men, on the other hand, are likely to make a favorable marriage. Their pool of eligible partners is approximately 10 times larger than it is for middle-class black females (Staples & Johnson, 1993).

As we see in Box 14-1, however, other cultures approach both marriage and the marriage asymmetry issue quite differently.

### Gender, Careers, and Personal Relationships

What effect is the trend toward more and more women working outside the home likely to have on personal relationships and vice versa? Here, interestingly enough, there seem to be important differences, not only in the way men and women approach relationships but also in the way they approach *preparation* for the world of work.

For example, in a study of college students who were involved in exclusive dating relationships, Anisa Zvonkovic and associates (1994) focused on the relationship between romantic involvement and level of achievement in academic pursuits. In the case of women, they found clear evidence for a trade-off. Women whose relationships came to an end tended to be more involved in their education and had achieved more in the way of academic recognition than had those whose relationships remained intact. For women, conflict in their relationships tended to increase as their workload increased. In other words, involvement in schoolwork and involvement in a romantic relationship seem to represent opposing commitments for females (Holland & Eisenhart, 1990).

For college men, on the other hand, increased workload was associated with *decreased* conflict in their romantic relationships. Women, then, seem more likely to "think with their hearts" and invest in romantic relationships rather than career preparation (Holland & Eisenhart, 1990). And insofar as women during their college years put romantic considerations first, they trade their academic record for love (Zvonkovic et al., 1994).

Consistent with this picture, Latitia Peplau (1979) reported that 70% of the students in her study planned on going on to graduate school. Out of this number, however, 50% of the women planned to go on for a master's degree only (versus 32% for men). Men were much more likely to plan on going for a Ph.D. or comparable degree (38% versus 19% for women).

So there seems to be a residue of traditional gender roles in the attitudes of many young people, and balancing investments in education and career preparation with investments in personal relationships still tends to be handled somewhat differently by males and females. And, as we shall see, this difference does not end with college.

*Division of Labor*    John Robinson (1977) found that the average husband spent about 11.2 hours per week in "family work," whether his wife was working outside the home or not. Wives who were full-time homemakers averaged 53.2 hours per week in family work, while wives who were employed full time averaged 28.1 hours. Given a working wife, a husband, and a preschool child, approximately 339 minutes per day could be called "free time" for the husband, while 221 minutes per day of free time was available to the wife (Robinson et al., 1977). Still, in the case of dual-income couples, more than two thirds of the wives were satisfied with the division of labor (see, for example, Bryson et al., 1976; Robinson et al., 1977).

There is some indication that this picture has changed somewhat over the years. Lucia Gilbert (1985) noted that in the 1970s, the amount of family work women did decreased, and the amount that males did increased, signaling something of a convergence in their relative contributions. More recently, John Robinson and Geoffrey Godbey (1997) found that the amount of free time for men (41.6 hours per week) and women (39.3 hours per week) was about the same. They also estimate that men spend approximately 17.4 hours a week in family-related work (such as child care, cooking, shopping, and cleaning), while women spend approximately 35.1 hours. So, in this respect, the traditional division of labor still seems to be characteristic of the typical marriage in the United States (Gilbert, 1993). The tacit assumption remains that a wife's primary responsibility is to be a homemaker, and the husband's responsibility is to put bread on the table (Peplau & Gordon, 1985).

## Power and Individual Differences

People differ in how motivated they are to pursue power, what kinds of costs they are willing to pay in the process, and the style they are likely to use in expressing it.

### Need for Power

David Winter and his colleagues saw the need for power as reflecting an interest in having an impact, making things happen, and being preoccupied with such matters as reputation and position (Winter, 1988; Winter & Barenbaum, 1985; Winter et al., 1977). What are the ramifications for personal relationships of such a need?

In the Boston Couples Study, Abegale Stewart and Zick Rubin (1976) found that a high need for power in males was associated with decreased satisfaction in relationships for both males and females, lower levels of love, and an increased number of anticipated problems. Males who were high in need for power reported having a longer list of former relationships and were more likely to indicate an interest in someone else at the time. For women, on the other hand, a high need for power was correlated only with increased anticipated problems.

In a 2-year follow-up, couples in which the male had a high need for power were, in fact, more likely to have broken up and less likely to have married if they were still going together. For females there was no similar link between need for power and relationship outcome.

What happens when males high in need for power do marry? David Winter and colleagues (1977) explored this question. In this study, need for power was assessed from data gathered while participants were students. In a follow-up 14 years later, the students were contacted and asked about their marriage (for those who were married) and their wife's career. And what were the findings? Males who were high in need for power as college students were less likely to have wives who were pursuing full-time careers. In another study, Avonne Mason and Virginia Blankenship (1987) found some indication that males high in need for power were also more likely to be involved in physical abuse both in dating relationships and in marriage.

Although high need for power clearly affects the type of personal relationships males pursue and the way they pursue them, this does not seem to be the case for women. For example, drinking, drug use, aggression, and gambling are associated with high need for power in men but not in women. And although displaying symbols of wealth and power tends to be similar for males and females, for females, the need for power is likely to be associated with such things as holding office and pursuing a career that gives them power.

Such differences may stem in part from differences in socialization. Females in our society tend to get more training in terms of social responsibility, which may lead them to channel their power needs in more socially responsible ways (Winter, 1988; Winter & Barenbaum, 1985).

## Power and Aversion to Conflict

One's willingness to engage in conflict also plays a significant role in the way power is expressed. Such concerns are affected by social norms, of course, but they are not just a matter of norms. There are wide differences in what people are willing to risk in terms of confrontation and the interpersonal costs they are willing to pay in order to win the day. Some people prefer to avoid conflict of any sort and see the direct expression of anger as a breach of a relationship. As a consequence, they develop an "early warning system" that leads them not to push the other too far or too hard. Others don't seem to care so much. How do such differences affect personal relationships? One way is in the tactics partners use to influence one another.

## Strong Versus Weak Tactics

Judith Howard and colleagues (1986) reasoned that when people were bargaining from a position of strength, they would tend to show increased use of what they called "strong tactics" (such as direct request, bilateral negotiation), and those who were dealing from a position of weakness would show an increased use of "weak tactics" (such as hinting, manipulation). And, indeed, in an analysis of data from 320 couples, their findings included the expected association between being relatively less masculine and more feminine, and being more dependent on one's partner. These characteristics, in turn, were correlated with the use of strong or weak power tactics, but interestingly enough, they were not correlated with the sex of the actor. Relatively less masculine males tended to use weak tactics, while more masculine females tended to use strong tactics (see Sagrestano, 1992, for related findings). And, similarly, once power differences are controlled for, gender differences in communication style tend to disappear (Kollock et al., 1985).

On the other hand, the sex of the *target person* was important. The power associated with being male appears to be expressed in behaviors that elicit weak strategies from one's partner. Thus, males tended to elicit manipulation and supplication from both male and female partners. But, somewhat surprisingly, married women who were unemployed (hence assumed to be operating from a position of "structural weakness") tended to use more strong tactics, such as bullying and autocratic tactics, than did women who worked outside the home. So, it seems we have come full circle. Consistent with the findings of James Roiger (1993), we again see evidence for less diplomacy when people have their backs to the wall. Need on the part of one partner translates into obligation on the part of the other.

## Conclusion

To conclude our brief look at power and personal relationships, first, it's important to note that whenever there are close personal relationships, questions of power are likely to arise. It's fair to say that in our society, and many others as well, males have historically assumed a dominant role in heterosexual relationships. Such differences in "structural power" are not completely a thing of the past, but today there are clear indications of a preference for more egalitarian relationships among younger couples—especially among the college educated.

Still, there are important differences in the way males and females express and respond to issues of power. Males tend to be more agentic in their dealings with others, females more sensitive and diplomatic.

In addition, people differ widely in the need to express power and the way they express it. One of the most important aspects of this comes in the case of males who have a high need for power. High need for power in males is associated with less positive relationship outcomes.

Finally, when we look closely at the issue of power in personal relationships, we find that means and ends are easily confused. Coercive power tactics can be quick and effective in the short term but often come at some cost to personal relationships in the longer term. If there is a lesson to come out of our look at the issue of power, it is probably this: When it comes to personal relationships, she or he uses power best who uses it least. But, as we look around us, we are likely to conclude that this is not an easy lesson to learn. We find this illustrated in our next two chapters on jealousy and conflict. Most of the issues in jealousy and conflict in personal relationships are about power.

## Suggestions for Further Reading

Blau, P. M. (1964). *Exchange and power in social life.* New York: Wiley. A consideration of power from an exchange perspective. Despite its age, this book remains one of the most insightful accounts of power in personal and social relationships.

Carli, L. L. (1990). Gender, language, and influence. *Journal of Personality and Social Psychology, 59,* 941–951. There may be a price to pay for acting out of (gender) role, especially for women.

Doundna, D., & McBride, F. (1981). Where are the men for the women at the top? In P. J. Stein (Ed.), *Single life: Unmarried adults in social context.* New York: St. Martin's Press. Where does a female chief executive find an eligible man? Women in U.S. society are reluctant to marry beneath their station. Oh, the problems of life at the top!

Filsinger, E. E., & Thomas, S. J. (1988). Behavioral antecedents of relationship stability and adjustment: A five-year longitudinal study. *Journal of Marriage and the Family, 50,* 785–795. Want a quick way to predict whether or not a romantic relationship will last? Count how many times the female interrupts the male.

Howard, J. A., Blumstein, P., & Schwartz, P. (1986). Sex, power, and influence tactics in intimate relationships. *Journal of Personality and Social Psychology, 51,* 102–109. One of the standard references in the area of power and personal relationships.

Mongeau, P. A., Hale, J. L., Johnson, K. L., & Hills, J. D. (1993). Who's wooing whom? An investigation of female initiated dating. In P. J. Kalbfleisch (Ed.), *Interpersonal communication: Evolving interpersonal relationships.* Hillsdale, NJ: Erlbaum. Contrary to what conventional wisdom suggests, female initiated dating seems to be alive and well.

Peplau, L. A. (1979). Power in dating relationships. In J. Freeman (Ed.), *Women: A feminist perspective* (2nd ed., pp. 107–121). Palo Alto, CA: Mayfield. Females tend to see males as more powerful, but males see themselves as much less likely to prevail than females think.

Philliber, W. W., & Vannoy-Hiller, D. (1990). The effect of husband's occupational attainment on wife's achievement. *Journal of Marriage and the Family, 52,* 323–329. Does the "glass ceiling" on women's achievement begin at home?

Roiger, J. F. (1993). Power in friendship and use of influence strategies. In P. J. Kalbfleisch (Ed.), *Interpersonal communication: Evolving interpersonal relationships.* Hillsdale, NJ: Erlbaum. A simulation study that presents some surprising findings about the dynamics of power.

Winter, D. G. (1988). The power motive in women—and men. *Journal of Personality and Social Psychology, 54,* 510–519. The need for power seems to be expressed quite differently in males and females.

# CHAPTER 15

## 🌀 *Jealousy*

*All of his friends assumed that Navy Lieutenant (JG) Alton Lee Grizzard was destined to become an admiral. No one expected him to die the way he did—not in combat, but as the result of a love triangle. Ensign Kerryn O'Neill was curled up nearby; she too had been shot in the head. Kerryn had been an honor student and a track star at Annapolis. Ensign George P. Smith, like Alton and Kerryn, was due to report for duty aboard the nuclear attack submarine USS Salt Lake City. He apparently shot himself in the head with the same gun he used to kill Alton and Kerryn.*

*George and Kerryn, it seems, had been engaged at Annapolis. However, two days before the murder, Kerryn had broken off the engagement. George sent her a letter pleading with her to reconsider. They had argued that evening. She left in tears. Later, George came to Kerryn's apartment and found Alton visiting her. Seconds later, all three were dead.*

*Alton had passed for 12 touchdowns his senior year at Annapolis. Kerryn had earned 12 varsity letters. George had been selected "best all-around" by his high school class. They say the heart has its reasons. What could possibly be the reason for this? (Time, December 13, 1993)*

Jealousy has been defined as a "negative emotion resulting from the actual or threatened loss of love to a rival" (Mathes, 1992, p. 6). Such a definition is useful, however, only if we recognize that jealousy is usually accompanied by several other emotions. The jealous person is also likely to be angry, hurt, and depressed. This raises a fundamental question. Is jealousy a single emotion, or are there different types of jealousy?

## Types of Jealousy

Gerrod Parrott (1991) distinguished between three different types of jealousy. One type follows from a clear indication that a relationship is over. Parrott calls this **fait accompli jealousy**. A second type of jealousy, **suspicious jealousy,** is generated by interactions with a third party that are ambiguous and yet can be interpreted as jealousy provoking.

In the case of suspicious jealousy, someone believes that a partner is transferring his or her interest to a rival. Such an experience is likely to involve a measure of anxiety and insecurity. In the case of fait accompli jealousy, however, anxiety about the relationship seems not to be an issue. The relationship, after all, is over. Now the focus of attention becomes important. When the focus is on the loss of the loved one, jealousy is likely to be accompanied by sadness. When it is on betrayal, the feeling is likely to be one of anger or hurt. When the focus is on adjusting to one's new status, the feeling is likely to be one of apprehension, and when it is on the rival, the feeling is likely to be one of envy (Parrott, 1991).

In addition to suspicious jealousy and fait accompli jealousy, Parrott suggests a third type. This is the kind of jealousy that sometimes occurs when someone, entertaining the possibility of a relationship that has not materialized, finds the intended partner in the company of someone else. In such cases, jealousy seems to be accompanied by wishfulness, longing, embarrassment, and sometimes even guilt (Parrott, 1991).

At least three sets of circumstances, then, seem to be capable of provoking jealousy—relationships that are over, relationships that are perceived to be threatened, and relationships that are only hoped for. And each of these seems to be accompanied by somewhat different feelings.

Jealousy also sometimes occurs in contexts that have nothing to do with romantic relationships. For example, it's possible to generate jealousy in small children simply by having the mother pay extensive attention to another child of similar age (Masciuch & Kienapple, 1993). Jealousy also seems to be common between siblings during childhood and adolescence (Newman, 1994) and among young adults and their siblings as well (Stocker et al., 1997). Nonetheless, when we think of jealousy, we typically think in terms of romantic couples, and that will be our primary focus in this chapter.

## What Provokes Jealousy?

Although any number of situations may be jealousy provoking, the one interpretation that leads most people to feel jealous is the anticipated loss of a relationship to a rival. The behavior of the partner, a rival, or both may give good reason for jealousy, but the behavior never stands alone. It is always subject to an evaluation process in which we assess the situation, the rival (and her or his presumed motives), and experience emotions, such as jealousy, anger, sadness, or fear, as a result (DeSteno & Salovey, 1996; White, 1981a).

Two issues seem to be particularly important in causing someone to perceive that his or her partner is attracted to a third party: the feeling that he or she is not adequate to meet the expectations of the partner and the sense of being more involved in the relationship than the partner (White, 1981b). For example, imagine yourself in the following study: you are asked how upset you would feel if your partner and someone else of the opposite sex were involved in various activities, ranging from dancing and having fun together to having an extended affair. How do you respond? When researchers have asked people such questions, the results indicate that situations involving some sort of erotic or sexual element (flirting, petting, or sexual intercourse) with a third party are more likely to provoke jealousy than are other forms of intimacy. For the most part, if someone's partner and a third party are engaged in such things as self-disclosure or talking about intimate matters, this does not seem to be jealousy provoking.

Although intimacy that does not involve a sexual component is not ordinarily considered jealousy provoking, sexual relationships are, even when they do not involve "emotional intimacy" (Bringle & Buunk, 1986). In our society (and most Western cultures) it seems to be the violation of sexual exclusivity that provokes jealousy in heterosexual couples (Buunk, 1980).

On the other hand, the loss, or threat of loss, of a relationship is not sufficient to generate feelings of jealousy. The presence or perception of a rival is necessary. A relationship that simply ends may lead us to feel sad or angry, but not jealous (DeSteno & Salovey, 1996). Indeed, in a study involving individuals whose partner had been involved in an extramarital affair at some time in the previous two years, researchers asked what it was that the respondents didn't like about their partner being involved with a third party. Most often mentioned were such things as getting less attention, the sense that the partner enjoyed certain activities more with someone else, feeling excluded, uncertainty, and loss of exclusivity. But the fear of losing the partner was not considered much of an issue. So, apparently, jealousy can occur in situations where losing one's partner is not considered likely (Bringle & Buunk, 1986).

If certain specific circumstances tend to lead to jealousy—some interactions with third parties are more likely to provoke jealousy and others less so—then it may be possible to measure these and determine what is considered more central and what is considered less central in provoking jealousy. This is the assumption made by researchers who view jealousy from the standpoint of prototype theory.

## Jealousy as a Prototype

The prototype approach assumes that we construct cognitive representations (or prototypes) of typical jealousy-provoking situations out of repeated exposures to portrayals of jealousy in the mass media, such as television, newspapers, and popular literature, as well as our own personal experience. As a consequence, when we are faced with situations that are similar to these prototypical cases, we tend to experience jealousy.

In addition, the prototype approach assumes that some responses to jealousy-provoking situations are more representative or central than others (just as we found in the case of the love prototype noted in Chapter 10).

*Centrality*    When people are asked to indicate how characteristic a particular feature is to their idea of jealousy, they can do so and do so reliably (Sharp-

**Table 15-1   Prototypic Jealousy Features in Order of Centrality**

### Central Features

| Feature | Frequency (percent) | Centrality |
|---|---|---|
| Hurt | 28 | 6.4 |
| Bad thoughts toward "other man/woman" | 9 | 6.2 |
| Threatened | 9 | 6.1 |
| Broken hearted | 3 | 6.1 |
| Upset | 3 | 6.1 |
| Insecure | 31 | 6.0 |
| Think someone has invaded what is yours | 3 | 6.0 |
| Always thinking about the situation | 2 | 5.9 |
| Think the relationship is under stress | 6 | 5.8 |
| Betrayed | 11 | 5.8 |
| Rejected | 5 | 5.7 |
| Anger at the "other man or woman" | 3 | 5.7 |
| Possessive | 8 | 5.6 |
| Sad | 9 | 5.6 |
| Ask yourself "Why did this happen?" | 4 | 5.6 |
| Constantly ask for affirmations of love | 2 | 5.6 |
| Envious | 10 | 5.5 |
| Unhappy | 5 | 5.5 |
| Confused | 5 | 5.5 |
| See someone you like with someone else | 7 | 5.5 |
| Frustrated | 8 | 5.5 |
| Cheated | 6 | 5.5 |
| Think partner pays too much attention to the opposite sex | 25 | 5.4 |
| Lonely | 17 | 5.4 |
| Feel depressed | 8 | 5.4 |
| Disappointed | 4 | 5.4 |
| Untrusting | 22 | 5.3 |
| Feel angry | 58 | 5.3 |
| Argue with partner | 12 | 5.3 |
| Don't like partner looking at members of the opposite sex | 6 | 5.3 |
| Tend to jump to conclusions | 4 | 5.3 |
| Empty inside | 2 | 5.3 |
| Act depressed | 5 | 5.2 |
| Unwanted | 5 | 5.2 |

*(continued)*

**Table 15-1   Prototypic Jealousy Features in Order of Centrality** (*continued*)

### Central Features

| Feature | Frequency (percent) | Centrality |
|---|---|---|
| Talk to others about the situation | 3 | 5.2 |
| Resentful | 10 | 5.2 |
| Keep track of partner's whereabouts | 5 | 5.2 |
| Scared | 7 | 5.1 |
| Want to make partner jealous | 10 | 5.0 |
| Act defensive | 2 | 5.0 |
| The situation is beyond control | 4 | 4.9 |
| Feel under pressure to do better | 3 | 4.8 |
| Paranoid | 6 | 4.8 |

### Peripheral Features

| Feature | Frequency (percent) | Centrality |
|---|---|---|
| Feel inferior | 11 | 4.8 |
| Jealousy occurs in relationships | 3 | 4.8 |
| Low self-esteem | 20 | 4.8 |
| Don't want partner to go anywhere without you | 4 | 4.8 |
| Don't think before reacting | 3 | 4.8 |
| Worry about what is going to happen next | 4 | 4.8 |
| Ruins the relationship | 2 | 4.8 |
| Someone gives attention to partner | 2 | 4.8 |
| Feel less important | 3 | 4.7 |
| Interrogate partner | 5 | 4.7 |
| Blame yourself for what has happened | 4 | 4.6 |
| Try to make partner feel guilty | 5 | 4.6 |
| Cry | 4 | 4.6 |
| Shocked | 2 | 4.5 |
| Behave irrationally | 3 | 4.5 |
| Think your behavior shows you care | 2 | 4.5 |
| Want revenge | 9 | 4.4 |
| Hate | 6 | 4.4 |
| Act sarcastically | 2 | 4.3 |

steen, 1993). As Table 15-1 shows, feeling hurt is generally considered a more central feature of jealousy than is feeling betrayed, and feeling threatened is considered more central than feeling resentful. In other words, people do think of certain responses as particularly characteristic of jealousy and others less so.

Table 15-1   Prototypic Jealousy Features in Order of Centrality (*continued*)

### Peripheral Features

| Feature | Frequency (percent) | Centrality |
|---|---|---|
| Rationalize feelings | 2 | 4.3 |
| Act grouchy | 3 | 4.2 |
| Feel hopeless | 2 | 4.2 |
| Feel sick to your stomach | 4 | 4.1 |
| Don't want to be alone | 2 | 4.1 |
| Think the future doesn't look bright | 3 | 4.1 |
| Find fault with others to build self up | 3 | 4.1 |
| Deny the feelings | 2 | 4.0 |
| Pretend you don't care | 2 | 4.0 |
| Overwhelmed | 2 | 3.9 |
| Look at the world differently | 2 | 3.8 |
| Frown | 6 | 3.8 |
| Feel like no one else cares | 2 | 3.7 |
| Defeated | 2 | 3.7 |
| Keep your feelings to yourself | 2 | 3.6 |
| Fight with the "other man/woman" | 11 | 3.6 |
| Brings partners closer together | 3 | 3.5 |
| Act mean | 2 | 3.4 |
| Want to hurt someone | 7 | 3.4 |
| Ultimately gives feeling of reassurance | 2 | 2.9 |
| More interested in self than in others | 5 | 2.9 |
| Become violent | 2 | 2.9 |
| Lack energy | 6 | 2.8 |
| Hate everyone of the opposite sex | 2 | 2.2 |

Frequencies represent the percentage of 100 subjects listing that feature. Centrality ratings were made on a scale ranging from 1 (extremely poor feature of romantic jealousy) to 8 (extremely good feature of romantic jealousy).
*Source:* Sharpsteen, D. J. (1993). Romantic jealousy as an emotion concept: A prototype analysis. *Journal of Social and Personal Relationships, 10,* 74–75. Copyright © 1993 Sage Publications Ltd. Reprinted by permission of Sage Publications Ltd.

***Components of Jealousy Responses***   In addition, theorists have distinguished between the cognitive, affective, and behavioral components of jealousy. In one study, for example, subjects were asked to imagine jealousy-provoking scenes (**cognitive component**) and then to indicate their feelings on a check list (**affective component**). The results indicated that feelings of possessiveness,

## Box 15-1 In a Different Key
### What Provokes Jealousy Cross Culturally?

Among the Pawnee Indians in the 19th century, a husband "bewitched" any man who dared so much as to ask his wife for a cup of water (Weltfish, 1965). A Samoan husband in the 1800s was completely supported by the society in cutting out the eyes or biting off the nose and ears of his wife's lover (Turner, 1884). And at the turn of the century the king of the plateau of northern Rhodesia (now Zimbabwe), upon discovering adultery in his harem, had the male lovers summarily executed and the wife subjected to mutilation (Gouldsbury & Sheane, 1911).

In contrast, a peasant in 19th-century Italy was concerned primarily about his unfaithful wife besmirching the family honor (Hupka, 1981). And among the Waran Indians of Guiana, indications that a male was about to lose or had lost his beloved to a rival was met with such controlled emotion that he seemed by all accounts to be apathetic. It was only when he was drunk that he was free to vent his emotion (Brett, 1868). Among the Ammassalik Eskimos, on

the other hand, a good host offers his wife to a guest and indicates his approval of their having sex by the culturally sanctioned ritual of putting out the lamp (Hupka, 1981). And, similarly, when Chuchchee men (of Siberia) visit in a distant community, they are offered sexual privileges with their host's wife and are expected to reciprocate in kind when the visit is returned (Ford & Beach, 1951).

Finally, we note Margaret Mead's (1931/1977) reference to the attitude of women toward secondary wives in cultures where polygamy was the norm. She cites the case of a woman who took her husband to court, charging that he had not yet taken a second wife. In response to her complaint the court passed down its judgment, ordering the irresponsible husband to get a second wife within six months. In this case, it seems, a second wife added to the prestige of the first, enabling her to assume the role of "chief wife." Additionally, a second wife provided help with the work and bearing children.

shame, anger, disgust, and contempt increased following these imagined scenes, and feelings of joy decreased (Bush et al., 1988).

**Behavioral responses** to jealousy-provoking situations also fit well with this approach. Many of the responses to jealousy-provoking situations are similar to those we associate with anger, sadness, and fear (Shaver et al., 1987). For example, verbal attacks and threats are typical anger responses, and these are also likely to be associated with jealousy-provoking episodes that are considered undeserved and unfair. Responses such as blaming oneself and trying to improve are associated with sadness, and pretending to feel indifferent is a common response to anxiety and fear (Shaver et al., 1987).

So the "blended" nature of jealousy seems to be due, in part, to the fact that some of the feelings we associate with jealousy are also characteristic of other related emotions. Depending on the circumstances, feelings of jealousy are likely to be combined with other emotions such as anger, sadness, envy, anxiety, and apprehension.

Having said all of this, it's important to note that situations thought of as jealousy provoking in U.S. culture are not necessarily considered jealousy provoking in others. However prototypical certain jealousy-provoking situations may be to us, jealousy is clearly influenced by culture. In Box 15-1 we see examples of the variety of responses to jealousy-provoking situations from other times and places.

## *Jealousy and Individual Differences*

Besides the differences among cultures and eras, individuals differ in how easily they are provoked to jealousy. Some people become jealous at the slightest hint of their partner's interest in someone else. Others are relatively unconcerned when their partner becomes involved with a third party. In the research literature, such individual differences in the tendency of people to feel jealous is referred to as **dispositional jealousy** (Bringle, 1991; Bringle et al., 1983).

### Measuring Jealousy

A number of instruments have been developed to measure jealousy as an individual difference variable (for example, Bringle, 1982; Bringle et al., 1979; Pfeiffer & Wong, 1989). One example, the Multidimensional Jealousy Scale, by Susan Pfeiffer and Paul Wong (1989), appears in Table 15-2.

In this particular scale, subjects are asked to respond to each of the items on a 7-point scale, with 1 indicating "never" and 7 indicating "all the time" for the cognitive and behavioral subscales, and 1 indicating "very pleased" and 7 indicating "very upset" for the emotion subscale. Each subscale is treated separately, yielding three different scores, with higher scores indicating greater jealousy in each case.

We must keep in mind, however, that the scales used to measure jealousy are really measuring an individual's ability and willingness to acknowledge jealousy. Jealousy is not always an easy thing to admit, and some people are more open in these matters than others. So when we find that college students who are jealous are also dissatisfied with their lives in general (Bringle, 1981), we cannot interpret this as indicating that students who are jealous are (in fact) more dissatisfied with their lives. We can only conclude that students who are willing to admit feeling jealous are also willing to admit that they are dissatisfied with their lives (Clanton & Kosins, 1991).

With this caution in mind, we note that certain personality characteristics have been associated with a disposition to be jealous. Those that have received the most attention in the research literature have dealt with such things as negative self-concept, low self-esteem, anxiety, dogmatism, arousability, dependency, femininity, and the perception of oneself as inadequate. These

**Table 15-2    Multidimensional Jealousy Scale**

*Cognitive:*

How often do you have the following thoughts about X?

1. I suspect that X is secretly seeing someone of the opposite sex.
2. I am worried that some member of the opposite sex may be chasing after X.
3. I suspect that X may be attracted to someone else.
4. I suspect that X may be physically intimate with another member of the opposite sex behind my back.
5. I think that some members of the opposite sex may be romantically interested in X.
6. I am worried that someone of the opposite sex is trying to seduce X.
7. I think that X is secretly developing an intimate relationship with someone of the opposite sex.
8. I suspect that X is crazy about members of the opposite sex.

*Emotional:*

How would you emotionally react to the following situations?

1. X comments to you on how great looking a particular member of the opposite sex is.
2. X shows a great deal of interest or excitement in talking to someone of the opposite sex.
3. X smiles in a very friendly manner to someone of the opposite sex.
4. A member of the opposite sex is trying to get close to X all the time.
5. X is flirting with someone of the opposite sex.
6. Someone of the opposite sex is dating X.
7. X hugs and kisses someone of the opposite sex.
8. X works very closely with a member of the opposite sex (in school or office).

*Behavioral:*

How often do you engage in the following behaviors?

1. I look through X's drawers, handbag, or pockets.
2. I call X unexpectedly, just to see if he or she is there.
3. I question X about previous or present romantic relationships.
4. I say something nasty about someone of the opposite sex if X shows an interest in that person.
5. I question X about his or her telephone calls.
6. I question X about his or her whereabouts.
7. I join in whenever I see X talking to a member of the opposite sex.
8. I pay X a surprise visit just to see who is with him or her.

*Source:* Pfeiffer, S. M., & Wong, P. T. (1989). Multidimensional jealousy. *Journal of Social and Personal Relationships, 6,* 181–196. Copyright © 1989 Sage Publications Ltd. Reprinted by permission of Sage Publications Ltd.

tendencies in an individual seem to provide the most fertile soil for the seeds of jealousy to take root and grow (Bringle & Buunk, 1986; White & Mullen, 1989), and there is even some evidence that such tendencies run in families (Bringle & Williams, 1979).

Looking at this list of characteristics for a moment, we see that they all have a common denominator: They all involve the self. This suggests that the reason why a threat to a romantic relationship is the prototypical cause of jealousy (in our society) may be due to the significance romantic relationships have in defining and maintaining the self-concept in the wider culture (Parrott, 1991).

## Jealousy and Self-Concept

If we assume that the self is nurtured and sustained, in part, by personal relationships—that is, that certain aspects of the self-concept are intrinsically interpersonal—then a number of puzzling issues in the research on jealousy begin to fall into place. The significance of the loss, or threatened loss, of a close personal relationship is always twofold: There is the threat to the relationship itself and the threat to those aspects of the self-concept that the relationship supports.

After all, when we think of ourselves in certain ways, such as being social, being fun to be with, being sexually attractive, and being agreeable, none of these makes any sense in isolation. No one can be social by him- or herself. One cannot be fun to be with unless others are involved, nor can one be sexually attractive in a social vacuum. We should not be surprised, then, that the loss of a close personal relationship, or the threat of such a loss, would typically have a negative effect upon the self-concept (Parrott, 1991; DeSteno & Salovey, 1996).

## Jealousy and Self-Esteem

Along these same lines, several writers have taken the position that jealousy is really little more than wounded pride. For example, Margaret Mead (1931/1977) contended that the more shaky our sense of self-esteem, the more susceptible we are to feeling jealous. When we experience jealousy, then, it is not a measure of the depth of our love. It's merely an indication of our sense of insecurity and inferiority in our relationships.

Indeed, research has implicated low self-esteem both as a cause and an effect of jealousy. In one study, for example, participants were presented with vignettes featuring loss of a partner caused by various reasons, for example, (1) fate (such as accidental death), (2) destiny (such as moving away for professional reasons), (3) rejection with no rival involved, and (4) loss to a rival. Participants were then asked to indicate how they would feel in response to each of these.

The results indicated that all four conditions would lead to a sense of loss, but self-esteem would suffer most when the loss was due to a rival or rejection and least when the loss was due to destiny or fate (Mathes et al., 1985). Consistent with this, college students who score high on measures of jealousy also tend to score low on measures of self-esteem (Bringle, 1981).

### Jealousy and Attachment Style

As we noted in Chapters 1 and 10, attachment apparently evolved initially as a mechanism to help ensure the care and safety of young offspring. Recently, however, researchers have extended the attachment theme to other relationships as well. The assumption here is that we continue to form attachments throughout life, but the objects of these attachments change. In adulthood, our attachment figures are likely to be romantic partners.

Consistent with the prototype approach, attachment theory assumes that we form "working models," or expectations of the world early in life, and for good or ill, these result in a particular attachment style—secure, anxious/ambivalent, or avoidant. Once these attachment styles are established early in life, do they continue to affect the way we relate to others in adulthood? There is some evidence that they do, or at least that they can. This is the assumption behind research focusing on the relationship between attachment style and jealousy.

When we look closely, we find many parallels between attachment and romantic jealousy. Both are triggered by separation, perceived threat to a relationship, or loss of a close other (caregiver or romantic partner). Both play a role in maintaining close relationships. And both tend to be accompanied by other emotions, such as fear, anger, and sadness (Sharpsteen & Kirkpatrick, 1997).

Accordingly, a secure, anxious/ambivalent, or avoidant attachment style may lead us to experience and express jealousy in different ways. For example, when Don Sharpsteen and Lee Kirkpatrick (1997) presented subjects with scenes depicting various jealousy-provoking situations, securely attached subjects indicated that they would feel more intense anger and would be more likely to express it toward their partner. Those with an anxious/ambivalent attachment style also reported that they would feel anger but indicated that they would be more likely to express it in the form of irritability rather than directly. And those with an avoidant attachment style indicated that they would simply feel sad.

In addition, attachment style apparently affects the way people cope with threats to relationships. Those with anxious/ambivalent attachment styles indicate that they would be more likely to blame themselves, and those with avoidant attachment styles indicate that they would be less likely to seek social support from others. It seems, then, that attachment styles act somewhat like perceptual filters through which we appraise events, interpret circumstances, and select ways of coping when faced with jealousy-provoking events (Radecki-Bush et al., 1993).

**Jealousy and Self-Evaluation Maintenance**

According to David DeSteno and Peter Salovey (1996), jealousy is basically a special case of self-evaluation maintenance. When we feel that a relationship is threatened by a rival who is outstanding in an area that is relevant to our own self-definition, we tend to be more jealous. This, you will note, is just as the SEM model would predict (see Chapter 12).

The position of DeSteno and Salovey is interesting because it provides us with something of a conceptual bridge between the various approaches to the study of jealousy. By considering jealousy as self-maintenance, the evolutionary approach (Buss et al., 1992), attachment theory (Sharpsteen & Kirkpatrick, 1997), prototype theory (Sharpsteen, 1993), and the personality trait (or individual difference) approach (Bringle, 1981) can be reconciled with the view that jealousy is a social or cultural construction (Bryson, 1981; Hupka, 1981; Mead, 1931/1977).

For example, researchers studying jealousy from the perspective of evolutionary theory note that males are likely to be especially jealous in cases involving sexual infidelity, but as we noted earlier, in some cultures this is not the case. DeSteno and Salovey account for this difference by noting that when sexual fidelity is considered important in a particular culture, it is also linked to self-evaluation. In cultures where monogamy is not the norm—not expected or practiced—an individual's self-evaluation is not likely to be affected by the sexual liaisons of his or her partner(s), and as a consequence, these are not likely to lead to jealousy (Mead, 1931/1977). So, in viewing jealousy as a special case of self-evaluation maintenance, we can have our cake and eat it too. Jealousy may be influenced by our evolutionary past, attachment history, or personality traits, but it is still likely to be experienced and expressed in terms of the culture in which we live.

## *Gender Differences in Jealousy*

Freud assumed that females were the more jealous sex. Mead (1931/1977) held that women have been the most jealous, historically, because they have been the most insecure. Others have suggested that males are more likely to be more jealous as an outgrowth of sexual competition (Buss et al., 1992; Buss, 1994; Westermark, 1922). However, there is little evidence in the research literature to suggest that one sex is more jealous than the other. Some studies have found gender differences in self-reported jealousy, but there has been little consistency in the findings (Aune & Comstock, 1991; Bringle & Buunk, 1986; Hupka & Eshett, 1988; White, 1981a, 1981b, 1981c).

For example, Laura Guerrero and her colleagues (1993) recently compared jealousy among dating and married couples. Overall, they found that females were more likely than males to experience jealousy. But such findings are hard to interpret. There is always the question of whether the term *jealousy* means the same thing for males and females. There is some indication that

## Box 15-2 In a Different Key
## Polyandry

Attitudes often have to do with what a culture deems necessary for survival. For example, the hard biological fact that females bear children means that it is important that they not be involved in certain dangerous activities during pregnancy. As a consequence, in cultures where fishing in rough seas, or hunting in the wild, is necessary for survival, such activities tend to be glorified as a way of making them desirable for males so that the job gets done. Thus a status difference that was initially generated for ecological reasons can generate differences along gender lines as well. This link between ecology, economic necessity, and the status of women is clearly demonstrated in the case of fraternal polyandry, in which two or more brothers marry a single wife. This is often practiced in Tibet and Nepal where the land is barren, and families must work the fields, tend herds, and trade out of economic necessity. Since fewer children will be produced with only one wife, polyandry is a means of population con-

trol. Both monogamy and polyandry are accepted in Nepal, but polyandry is often preferred so that the land will not have to be divided.

How do Tibetan males handle jealousy? From early childhood, boys are raised to value loyalty and cooperation among brothers. Accordingly, marriages of two or more brothers to one wife are not only likely to be more successful economically, but they are also considered more prestigious. For her own part, the wife makes an effort to be equitable in sharing her favors so as to promote harmony within the household.

Nancy Levine (1988) has noted that when problems arise, they tend to occur in households involving three or more brothers. Considerable effort is made to avoid such "failed marriages," but when this happens, a second marriage sometimes takes place, and typically the second wife is a sister of the first (Levine, 1988; Strong & DeVault, 1995; Triandis, 1994).

men are more likely to deny feelings of jealousy, and women are more likely to acknowledge them (Clanton & Smith, 1977/1986; Francis, 1977).

Although the evidence for sex differences in quantitative measures of jealousy is somewhat unclear, there is some evidence for qualitative differences in the way males and females experience and express jealousy. For example, researchers taking an evolutionary approach suggest that jealousy evolved as a mechanism to protect parental investments and provide for child care. Males and females face very different issues in this regard. A female always knows who the mother of her child is. A male is not always sure who the father is. Accordingly, researchers predict that males and females should experience jealousy in different ways. And research suggests that this is indeed the case.

Males tend to be especially jealous when faced with sexual infidelity in their partner (Buss, 1994; Buss et al., 1992; Buss et al., 1996); they are concerned with issues of status and competition implicit in jealousy-provoking situations (DeSteno & Salovey, 1996; Francis, 1977; White, 1981a); and they tend to be jealous of rivals who have some ability that they envy. The rival that is most likely to make a male jealous not only attracts his partner but also performs well on some dimension that is important to his self-definition (DeSteno & Salovey, 1996).

Females, on the other hand, are more likely to see loss of shared time and attention as threatening (Francis, 1977; Teismann & Mosher, 1978); they focus on the consequences of their partner's behavior on the relationship (White, 1981a); they tend to be concerned about living up to their partner's expectations (DeSteno & Salovey, 1996); and they acknowledge their feelings, blame themselves, and attempt to salvage the relationship (Clanton & Smith, 1977).

Again, culture clearly influences the way males respond to sexual infidelity in a partner (Mullen, 1996). For example, as we see in Box 15-2, in Tibet and Nepal, marital practices (and presumably jealousy among males) are closely tied to the economy. So when conditions require it, whatever tendency males may have to feel jealous seems to take a back seat to the hard facts of economic life.

## *Jealousy and Violence*

Violence is common in cases involving romantic jealousy. In one study, for example, over 15% of a sample of men and women reported having relationships that involved some sort of physical violence due to their partner's jealousy (Mullen, 1996; Mullen & Martin, 1994). Estimates of violence due to jealousy among battered women have varied from about half of those sampled (Dobash & Dobash, 1980) to about two-thirds (Gayford, 1975, 1979). Interviews with battering men indicate that the alleged infidelity of their partner is the reason most often given for their violence (Brisson, 1983). And jealousy is the most common reason for murder in cases of domestic disputes (Daly & Wilson, 1988; Daly et al., 1982). In short, there is evidence that males, especially, tend to respond to jealousy-provoking situations with violence (Bringle & Buunk, 1985; Buss et al., 1992; Clanton & Smith, 1977/1986).

However, we have to be careful how we interpret such findings. Although it's true that most serious injury resulting from domestic violence is the result of male aggression against females, it is not clear that males are more likely to be aggressive in such situations. For example, Paul Mullen and Judy Martin (1994) found that men and women reported being the recipients of about the *same amount* of aggression. What this suggests is that male aggression is more serious, but it is not necessarily more common.

The problem with assuming a simple relationship between jealousy and violence is that jealousy-provoking situations tend to involve many issues, including a sense of betrayal and broken trust. At the same time that John accuses Mary of infidelity, he also makes a judgment that she is no longer easily influenced. She is "out of control," and this is likely to leave John with a sense of helplessness and resentment. One possible response to this is to try and reassert his power by intimidating her.

Many males who are jealous are not violent, however. And males who are violent are not necessarily jealous. In their interview study on marital violence, for example, Ola Barnett and her associates (1995) found that violent men were no more jealous on average than were nonviolent men. On the other hand, the men who used violence against their wives tended to be more dependent on their partners and had both observed and received more physical abuse in childhood than did their nonviolent counterparts.

Returning to the chapter's opening example, we can only speculate on what might have been the outcome had Ensign Smith been raised as a Quaker and had learned to value nonviolence. We can only guess what might have happened had he been in a situation, unlike a military setting, in which guns and aggression were not an essential part of his immediate environment. And we can only suppose what might have happened had he found Kerryn visiting with the paper boy instead of Lieutenant Grizzard. But such speculations help remind us that many things influence whether or not jealousy will result in violence.

## Jealousy and the Nature of the Relationship

Feelings of jealousy have been found to be related to such things as relationship satisfaction, dependence on the partner, the way people conceive of their relationship, and relative involvement in the relationship. For example, couples who are generally satisfied with their marriage make more of an effort to reconcile conflicts, even when one of the partners becomes involved in an extramarital affair (Schaap et al., 1988). So events that lead to jealousy in some relationships do not in others. And part of the reason for the difference seems to lie in the (perceived) nature of the relationship.

### Relationship Status

Research findings on the association between relationship status, or length of relationship, and jealousy have been somewhat conflicting. Some studies have reported that jealousy increases at the point where a developing relationship becomes serious or exclusive (Braiker-Stambul, 1975). Others have found that dating couples tend to experience and express jealousy more than do married couples (Guerrero et al., 1993). Still others have reported that jealousy is especially a problem among couples who are cohabiting (Macklin, 1972). On the other hand, Eugene Mathes (1986) found that higher jealousy scores were correlated with the *continuation* of relationships over a 7-year period. And others have found no relationship between relationship status, or length, and jealousy (Bush et al., 1988; White, 1981c).

Such mixed findings make it difficult to know what to conclude about the effect of relationship status, or length, and feelings of jealousy. But perhaps this in itself leads us to the conclusion that there seems to be no point in a romantic relationship when the partners can say of jealousy, "Well, we're glad that's behind us."

### Attribution and Jealousy

An individual's response to jealousy-provoking situations seems due, in large part, to the causes attributed to the partner's behavior (Kelley, 1979). If one partner becomes involved with a third party, the other is likely to ask why. In general, there are two types of answers: One places responsibility on the partner, and the other places responsibility on the situation.

According to attribution theory, as jealousy-provoking behavior deviates more and more from the norm (what is accepted or expected), the offended partner is increasingly likely to make a personal attribution (Kelley, 1979). And when someone makes a personal attribution, she or he should feel more jealous. There is some evidence that this is indeed the case.

For example, in a study of individuals whose spouses had been involved in an extramarital affair, Bram Buunk (1991) found that when the affair was attributed to aggression, marital deprivation, or need for variety, the offended partner indicated being more jealous than when the affair was attributed to external circumstances, such as pressure from a third party.

So the circumstances surrounding jealousy-provoking behavior can influence the interpretations made by those affected. And, as we see in the next

William Hamilton © 1993 from The New Yorker Collection. All Rights Reserved.

*"Oh, you were on automatic pilot? And what about her? Was she on automatic pilot, too?"*

section, this need to consider the circumstances is well illustrated by some of the predictions derived from equity theory.

### Equity Theory and Jealousy

A basic assumption of equity theory is that people in inequitable relationships will seek to restore equity, and the way this plays out in the case of jealousy is particularly interesting. Equity theory would predict that individuals should *not* feel jealous if their partners behave the same way they do, so long as some sort of dance-for-dance, flirt-for-flirt, affair-for-affair balance is maintained. On the other hand, when one partner is not involved with a third party, this should lead to an expectation that his or her partner would not be either. If Ed becomes involved with a third party, Sally should be more or less jealous to the extent that she is not (or has not been) involved in a similar relationship.

This hypothesis was tested by Buunk (1980). Participants in the study were offended parties whose partner had been involved in an extramarital affair. They were asked to indicate whether they were also involved with a third party or had been in the past. The results were generally supportive of equity theory. Those who were most jealous were those who were not involved, had never been involved, or were less involved extramaritally.

In a similar study (Buunk, 1991), participants were simply asked to anticipate their feelings of jealousy under certain circumstances, such as their partner's flirting, being involved in light petting, sexual involvement, and a long-term affair. They then filled out the Extramarital Behavioral Intention Scale (Buunk, 1986), a measure of their intention or desire to be involved in an extramarital affair. Again, the results were generally supportive of equity theory; that is, the less anticipation participants had of ever becoming involved in an extramarital affair themselves, the more jealous they indicated they would be if their partner were to have an extramarital affair.

Along these same lines, Karin Prins and her colleagues (1993) explored the relationship between equity and marital satisfaction, as these were related to someone entertaining the notion of, or actually becoming involved in, an extramarital relationship. Specifically, the researchers focused on whether inequity in marriage increased the likelihood that the underbenefited partner would seek to restore equity by becoming involved in an extramarital affair. For example, if Betty is unsatisfied with her marriage and considers her husband to be inequitable in his treament of her, is she likely to take this out on him by becoming involved in an extramarital affair? What did Prins and her associates find?

First of all, there were some interesting gender differences. In general, males indicated a stronger *desire* to become involved in extramarital affairs, but there was no difference in actual (reported) behavior between males and females. In fact, inequity in marriage was related to extramarital inclinations and behavior only for women. Women who felt either overbenefited or underbenefited indicated that they were more likely to have an extramarital affair.

But this was true independent of marital satisfaction or dissatisfaction (Prins et al., 1993).

## Jealousy, Attitudes, and Alternate Lifestyles

Several studies have reported correlations between certain attitudes and practices and feelings of jealousy. Specifically, attitudes of permissiveness and such alternative lifestyles as open marriage and group marriage tend to be associated with less jealousy.

*Permissiveness*   Permissive attitudes about such matters as sexual exclusivity tend to be negatively correlated with jealousy (Buunk, 1980). People who indicate that they would indulge in extramarital activities themselves, should the opportunity present itself, report being less jealous. Moreover, jealousy tends to be low among individuals who themselves either had, or are having, an extra-dyadic relationship. So, apparently, the less exclusive people are in their attitudes and behaviors about relationships in general, the less jealous they tend to be with respect to their partners' behavior (Buunk, 1982a; White, 1981c).

*Open Marriage*   Couples involved in open marriages (so-called swingers) tend to rate themselves as less jealous than those in traditional marriages (Jenks, 1985). Those involved in such relationships, however, routinely report taking certain measures in an effort to prevent jealousy. These include such ground rules as having casual contacts only, putting one's marriage first, being completely open, having only brief encounters with others, having no contacts outside of organized parties, and swinging only with other married couples (Buunk, 1991; Denfeld, 1974; Varni, 1974).

But these rules do not seem to guarantee that jealousy will not occur. Bram Buunk (1981) found that about 80% of those involved in open marriages reported being jealous at one time or another. And Brian Gilmartin (1977) noted that participants in his study often distinguished between "body-centered" and "emotion-centered" sex. Body-centered sex was limited to a physical relationship, while emotion-centered sex included a psychological relationship, and when one partner was thought to have crossed the line from body-centered sex to an emotion-centered relationship, the other partner was likely to feel jealous.

Marriage counselors report a great deal of jealousy among swingers (Denfeld, 1974). Indeed, estimates are that about one third of swingers "drop out" because of jealousy (White & Mullen, 1989). On the other hand, when couples report having a stable swinging lifestyle, they also tend to indicate satisfaction with their marriage (Gilmartin, 1977).

*Group Marriage*   Group marriage is the other alternative lifestyle that has attracted the attention of researchers studying jealousy. Unlike open marriage, group marriage typically involves a commitment to the group, which includes provisions for child rearing, income sharing, and shared involvement in other activities as well. In their investigation of 30 group marriages, Larry Constantine and Joan Constantine (1973) reported that jealousy was a problem in 80% of them. One possible exception has been reported by Ayala Pines and Elliot Aronson (1981) in their study of the Kerista commune, which advocated "polyfidelity," in which individuals married a small group of others but remained faithful within the group. The commune itself was reportedly quite free of jealousy. Elaborate measures were taken to induct individuals into the ethos of the community before sexual relationships took place, and a standard sleeping routine was established. Sex outside the group, meanwhile, was met with strong negative reactions.

Nonetheless, in a later study Pines and Aronson (1983) found it was necessary to note that because of the self-selection involved among those embracing such a lifestyle, it is hard to know what to make of the findings. Such arrangements presumably attract a certain type of individual, and elaborate efforts are typically made to reduce jealousy. All of this raises a number of questions. When something is new and different, and a little bit daring, attention getting, and naughty, presumably it can be its own reward.

## Conclusion

We see from this brief review that individuals experience and express jealousy in different ways. Depending on the circumstances, jealousy is often accompanied by a mix of other emotions, such as anxiety, anger, hurt, and sadness.

The loss, or threatened loss, of a romantic partner to a rival is most likely to provoke feelings of jealousy in U.S. culture, but in other cultures this is not always the case. Clearly, the way jealousy is experienced and expressed depends on differences in attitudes, personality, and culture.

In trying to capture the underlying processes, researchers have approached the topic of jealousy from the perspective of evolutionary theory, cognitive (prototype) theory, attachment theory, personality traits, and cross-cultural comparisons, to name a few. Each approach has its advantages and disadvantages. There is no clear winner, but researchers are increasingly viewing jealousy as a prototype. Interest in the relationship between attachment style and jealousy is increasing, and jealousy viewed from the standpoint of self-evaluation maintenance promises to provide an important integrative theme for some of the research.

Although evidence that one sex experiences or expresses more jealousy than the other has been conflicting and inconclusive, there is some evidence for qualitative differences in the way males and females experience and express jealousy. Males are more likely to be jealous in cases involving sexual infidelity. Females seem to be more concerned about emotional estrangement and are more likely to try and save a relationship.

The relationship between jealousy and violence remains a matter of debate. The association between jealousy and violence depends on a number of things, such as dependency upon the partner and exposure to (and experience of) violence as a child.

Somewhat surprisingly, research findings on the relationship between jealousy and relationship status (for example. whether partners are engaged, married, cohabiting) has been equivocal, but the importance of relationship satisfaction, attribution, and equity have all been clearly demonstrated. In general, when people are more satisfied with their relationships, attribute jealousy-provoking behaviors to external pressures, or see their relationships as equitable, they tend to be less jealous.

Finally, permissive attitudes toward sex and certain lifestyles, such as open marriage and group marriage, are associated with lower levels of (reported) jealousy.

## *Suggestions for Further Reading*

Bringle, R. G., & Buunk, B. (1986). Examining the causes and consequences of jealousy: Some recent findings and issues. In S. W. Duck & R. Gilmour (Eds.), *The emerging field of personal relationships*. Hillsdale, NJ: Erlbaum. A review of the jealousy literature by two major researchers in the area.

Clanton, G., & Smith, L. G. (Eds.). (1977). *Jealousy*. Lanham, MD: University Press of America. A collection of some of the classic works on jealousy up to 1977.

Guerrero, L. K., Eloy, S. V., Jogensen, P. F., & Anderson, P. A. (1993). Hers or his? Sex differences in the experience and communication of jealousy in close relationships. In P. J. Kalbfleisch (Ed.), *Interpersonal communication: Evolving interpersonal relationships*. Hillsdale, NJ: Erlbaum. A certain amount of jealousy seems to be normal in marriage. There is evidence for reciprocity in the way jealousy is expressed in a marital dyad. Wives are somewhat more likely to express it than husbands.

Mathes, E. W. (1992). *Jealousy: The psychological data*. Lanham, MD: University Press of America. Overview of the research on jealousy by one of the leaders in the area.

Pines, A., & Aronson, E. (1983). Antecedents, correlates and consequences of sexual jealousy. *Journal of Personality, 51*, 108–136. A look at jealousy and group marriages.

Salovey, P. (Ed.). (1991). *The psychology of jealousy and envy*. New York: Guilford. An edited volume featuring chapters by the major researchers/theorists in the area.

Sharpsteen, D. J. (1993). Romantic jealousy as an emotion concept: A prototype analysis. *Journal of Social and Personal Relationships, 10*, 69–82. How prototype analysis can profitably be applied to the concept of jealousy.

White, G. L., & Mullen, P. E. (1989). *Jealousy: Theory, research and clinical strategies*. New York: Guilford. A major work in the area of jealousy.

# CHAPTER 16

## ᏬᎤ *Conflict*

*They were both new to the neighborhood, both stay-at-home moms. They jogged together. They baby-sat for each other. They became really close over time. Then Marie began to notice hints that things were not all that well with Grace. For one thing, her husband was a heavy drinker. He and Grace never had people over to their house. Still, Grace was a strong person. She always seemed to be in control. Then one night Marie woke to a pounding on her door. It was 2 o'clock in the morning and here was Grace on her doorstep, suitcase in hand, with her kids still in their pajamas. "I hate to bother you like this, but I just left my husband. Any chance we can stay the night?"*

In this chapter we will look at the role of conflict in personal relationships. Following the work of Jeffrey Rubin and his colleagues (1994), we will consider conflict as stemming from the perception that one person's goals, plans, or aspirations are incompatible with another's. So considered, the potential for conflict may be found in nearly any personal relationship. Interdependence implies that people touch each other's lives in various ways, and their effect on one another is valued. Indeed, the importance of a relationship is reflected in whatever conflict the parties may have. People who do not have an interest in maintaining their relationship are not likely to be in conflict (Braiker & Kelley, 1979).

## Conflict Between Friends

Conflict between friends has received relatively little attention in the research literature (Canary et al., 1995; Hays, 1988; Healey & Bell, 1990). We do know, however, that friends engage in conflict more often than do nonfriends, and negativity is more likely to be expressed during conflicts between friends than between nonfriends. Further, when friends become involved in conflicts, these are resolved to the satisfaction of both parties only about 30% of the time (Davis & Todd, 1985; see also Legge & Rawlins, 1992).

In their interviews with undergraduates, Leslie Baxter and colleagues (1993) were able to identify 12 different types of conflict, but they found that, for the most part, conflict was expressed in terms of "civil discussion." Others have found that roommates are likely to blame each other for difficulties, and this tends to escalate the level of conflict (Canary & Cupach, 1988; Sillars, 1980; Waln, 1982). But it's hard to know what to make of these findings.

It's important to keep in mind that studies of conflicts between friends have often involved college students, especially roommates, and how much we can generalize from these to the general population is an open question. For example, in a comparison of student and community populations, researchers found that students interacted more often and had more "grievances" than did members of the community in general (Stern, 1995). Campus life, the forced closeness of dorm living, the brashness of youth, and the competitive atmosphere may indeed make conflict more likely.

Robert Hays (1988) has suggested that friendships, especially close friendships, are subject to much the same kinds of emotional strains as are heterosexual relationships. But whether the two play out in the same way has yet to be established. Friendships and romantic relationships involve quite different sets of expectations, and these may well generate different types of conflicts (Davis & Todd, 1985). For example, the expectation of exclusivity can lead to conflict among romantic pairs in a way that is less likely to occur in other types of relationships, and the implied loss of independence in exclusive relationships can strain romantic relationships in ways that are less likely to occur in friendships. It's probable, then, that there are systematic differences both in the kinds of issues that generate conflicts in romantic relationships and friendships and in the way these conflicts are expressed.

Faced with unresolved conflicts, apparently friends tend to part, quietly or otherwise (Duck & Allison, 1978). But (at least in the West) there seems to be little in the way of long-term fallout from conflicts between friends. Former friends are not likely to end up in court, for example.

## Conflict and Romantic Relationships

Conflict in romantic relationships seems to be a bit more complicated than conflict between friends. Indeed, the lion's share of research on conflict in personal relationships has focused on heterosexual relationships.

### Areas of Conflict

In interviews with young couples, Harold Kelley and his associates (1973) found that conflicts occurred in just about every imaginable area of their relationships. How they spent their time, how they spent money, how they expressed affection, sex, division of labor, personal habits, politics, religion, jealousies, and interactions with relatives all provided grist for the mill of conflict.

In all, the researchers found evidence for 65 different categories in which couples mentioned having conflicts. And others have reported similar findings (for example, Lloyd, 1987, 1990). Clearly, heterosexual relationships offer plenty of opportunity for conflict.

### Precipitating Events

Open conflict is typically ignited by some precipitating event. For example, when Donald Peterson (1979) asked couples to give detailed accounts of significant interactions in everyday life, he found that many of these dealt with conflict. And when the events immediately prior to the conflict were studied, the problem areas involved such things as criticism, inconsiderate demands, rebuffs, and cumulative annoyance.

Apparently, as one partner criticized the other, the implication was that the other was not holding up her or his end of an implicit bargain. Similarly, when demands exceeded what one partner thought were appropriate, the bounds of legitimacy and the definition of the relationship were strained. Rebuffs were seen in a similar light. When one person did not receive the response she or he anticipated, her or his expectation for the relationship was not confirmed.

The fourth type of problem, cumulative annoyance, seemed to operate somewhat differently. Norm violations tended to be less at issue here, and abrasive behaviors (perhaps unwittingly) seemed to accumulate gradually in a "straw-that-broke-the-camel's-back" fashion.

## Conflict and Relationship Development

Both successful couples and "unsuccessful" couples experience conflicts. But research shows that there are significant differences between the two.

### Conflict and Successful Relationships

Harriet Braiker and Harold Kelley (1979) asked 20 married couples to give accounts of the course of their relationship, as they progressed from casual dating to serious dating, engagement, and marriage, by indicating levels of conflict, love, maintenance, and ambivalence.

The results were then analyzed, coded, and categorized as (among other things) indications of love, conflict/negativity, ambivalence, and relationship maintenance. The **conflict/negativity category** included such things as arguments or problems. The **ambivalence category** referred to such things as confusion about one's feelings and anxiety about increased levels of commitment, and **relationship maintenance** included such things as self-disclosure.

As shown in Figure 16-1, each of these categories changed significantly as couples progressed from casual dating to serious dating, engagement, and marriage. In general, indications of love increased gradually, as did indications of relationship maintenance (such as self-disclosure). But most significantly, for

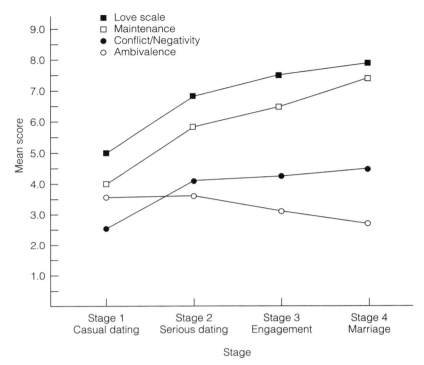

**Figure 16-1**   Mean scores on the four scales as a function of stage (sex and order factors collapsed). From Braiker, H. B., & Kelley, H. H. (1979). Conflict in the development of close relationships. In R. L. Burgess & T. L. Huston (Eds.). *Social Exchange in Developing Relationships.* New York: Academic Press. Used by permission of publisher and authors Harriet B. Braiker, Clinical Psychologist and H. H. Kelley.

our purposes, the overall level of conflict increased as relationships progressed from casual dating to serious dating and greater interdependence. After that, it stabilized, showing no further significant increase. But, interestingly enough, there was no relationship between indications of love and indications of conflict at any stage.

There is a logic of sorts to the finding that conflict increases as close personal relationships become more serious. At the casual dating stage, individuals are likely to put their best foot forward; be less invested; and, of course, major conflicts at an early stage are likely to end less serious relationships. As relationships move from the more casual and tentative toward greater commitment, partners are likely to pursue common activities on a more frequent basis. As a consequence, there are more things to disagree about. Serious dating, engagement, and marriage are much more "for keeps," which both generates and *supports* more conflict.

Consistent with this, Braiker and Kelley (1979) found that feelings of ambivalence (mixed feelings) increased during the transition from the casual to the serious dating stage and then tended to decline as couples moved toward engagement and marriage. In the early stages of relationship development, ambivalence and conflict increase together, suggesting that early in dating relationships, conflict may give rise to ambivalence and vice versa. On the other hand, ambivalence *decreases* as the relationship progresses from dating to engagement and marriage, but conflict does not.

The serious dating stage, then, seems to be something of a turning point. As interdependence increases, so does conflict and ambivalence. Sparks can fly as partners try to hammer out the form that their relationship is to take.

Braiker and Kelley (1979) found no relationship between the levels of love and interdependence, on the one hand, and levels of conflict, on the other. These seemed to rise and fall independent of each other. As strange as it may seem, the presence of conflict, for these couples, did not indicate an absence of either feelings of love or interdependence.

So much for the role of conflict in "successful" relationships. What about relationships that are not successful?

## Conflict and Unsuccessful Relationships

Sally Lloyd and Rodney Cate (1985) took an approach that was similar to that of Braiker and Kelley (1979). Their study involved 49 males and 48 females who had been in serious romantic relationships (the average length of the relationship was 15.7 months) but who had broken up in the last 12 months. Measures of conflict, love, relationship maintenance behaviors (such as self-disclosure), and feelings of ambivalence were similar to those reported by Braiker and Kelley. And, as noted in Table 16-1, Lloyd and Cate also found evidence for an increase in conflict over the course of the relationship for both males and females.

When we compare the findings of Lloyd and Cate with those of Braiker and Kelley, we see that for those whose relationships led to marriage, conflict tended to increase initially and then level off. But for those who later broke up, the pattern was quite different. First, consistent with the findings of Braiker and Kelley, Lloyd and Cate found no correlation between love and conflict in the early stages of relating. As relationships moved to higher levels of involve-

**Table 16-1   Means of Conflict by Gender at Five Involvement Levels**

|  | Casual | Couple | Committed | Uncertain | Certain |
|---|---|---|---|---|---|
| | | | **Involvement Level** | | |
| Male | 10.51 | 14.71 | 16.57 | 23.90 | 24.14 |
| Female | 10.17 | 14.63 | 18.90 | 27.35 | 27.00 |
| Total | 10.34 | 14.67 | 17.72 | 25.61 | 25.56 |

*Source:* Lloyd, S. A., & Cate, R. M. (1985). The developmental course of conflict in premarital relationship dissolution. *Journal of Social and Personal Relationships, 2,* 179–194. Copyright © 1985 Sage Publications Ltd. Reprinted by permission of Sage Publications Ltd.

ment, however, this changed. Relationships entered a stage of "uncertainty," soon to be followed by "certainty" (that the relationship was over). At that point, as conflict increased, indications of love decreased.

These relationships (that eventually ended) also showed a correlation between conflict and efforts at maintenance initially. This suggests that in the early stages of relationship development, both conflict and maintenance efforts seemed to be focused on keeping the relationship intact. Later, however, conflict and maintenance functions for this group of couples were no longer related, suggesting that the relationships had reached a point where efforts to resolve conflicts no longer served any useful purpose.

## Confronting Versus Avoiding Conflict

Some theorists have taken the position that confronting differences tends to aggravate conflict (Rands et al., 1981). Others hold that conflict avoidance is likely to leave problems unresolved and lead over time to increased anger and resentment (Roloff & Cloven, 1990). Patricia Noller and Angela White (1990), for example, found that couples whose marriages were distressed tended to report avoiding critical issues and as a consequence reported less conflict. What's going on here? Is a certain amount of conflict good for a relationship?

*Evidence for a Paradoxical Effect of Conflict*   John Gottman and Lowell Krokoff (1989) reported that although conflict was correlated with marital dissatisfaction in the short term, it actually predicted marital satisfaction 3 years later. Accordingly, they suggested that marriages in which couples never disagreed were at risk (see also Gottman, 1994a, 1994b).

Other researchers have questioned the Gottman and Krokoff interpretation. Erik Woody and Philip Costanzo (1990) argued that the proposed relationship between "early agony and later ecstasy" may simply have been due to the way the data were analyzed. On the other hand, Paul Haefner and colleagues (1991) videotaped "problem-solving sessions" between husbands and wives. These were then coded for indications of facilitating problem solving (each partner cooperated in arriving at a solution rather than inhibiting problem solving) and emotional validation (partners expressed empathy and understanding of the other's feelings rather than lack of validation).

Haefner and colleagues found that husbands were most satisfied when their wives showed high rates of *facilitative* behavior in problem solving and emotional validation. Wives, on the other hand, were most satisfied when their husbands showed fewer problem-solving *inhibiting* behaviors. It is this sensitivity to negative inputs from the husband that Haefner and colleagues suggest may be responsible for the "paradoxical effect" noted by Gottman and Krokoff. Wives may sometimes use conflict to encourage change, and as a consequence, couples may indeed pay a price in the short term but gain in the long term (Haefner et al., 1991). For example, when Al comments on Nancy's weight, Nancy may take the opportunity to note that they could both use a little more exercise, with the result that they agree (however reluctantly) to work out 3 nights a week.

***Stability in Level of Conflict***    Not everyone has found evidence for a paradoxical effect of conflict. For example, Carol Kelly and colleagues (1985) studied 21 couples over a period of 2 years. Their findings (based on retrospective accounts) indicated that the level of premarital conflict tended to predict the level of conflict later in marriage. And a number of other researchers have found the same thing. Couples who show a certain level of premarital conflict generally continue to show the same pattern later in marriage. Much the same thing can be said for certain deceptive practices and manipulation. But although there is general consensus in the research literature as to the negative effects of coercion and manipulation, there is less agreement on the relative merits of confronting versus avoiding conflict in the long term (Sillars & Weisberg, 1987).

For example, Ted Huston and Anita Vangelisti (1991) reported that early relationship satisfaction tends to predict later social-emotional behavior, suggesting that the initial mode of interacting may establish a climate in which positive or negative patterns stabilize. And Patricia Noller and colleagues (1994), in a 2-year study, found essentially no change in conflict patterns from 4–6 weeks prior to marriage to about 21 months into marriage. Those who were lower in relationship satisfaction (none of these couples were considered "distressed") reported more negativity in their relationships, such as threats and verbal and physical aggression. They also reported more demand-and-withdrawal patterns in response to conflict, fewer positive behaviors, and more avoidance. And although there was some indication of an increase in positive behaviors and a decrease in negative behaviors in the first year, this pattern did not last. The only notable trend in this study came later. Wives who were lower in satisfaction reported showing very little support after 2 years, suggesting that efforts to be more constructive had not been particularly successful.

In the study by Noller and her colleagues (1994), patterns of premarital conflict predicted wives' marital satisfaction after a year of marriage. Negativity, disengagement, and destructive processes predicted it later. Coercion and threatening behavior seemed to be especially aversive for women and led to long-term negative effects on marital satisfaction. Such findings are clearly at odds with the position of Gottman and Krokoff (1989). There was no evidence that conflict early in the relationship led to satisfaction later, in the Noller study.

***The Issue of Congruence***    Taking a somewhat different approach, Linda Acitelli and her associates (1993) asked 219 married couples to recount a disagreement and give their perception of themselves and their spouse during that time by indicating their agreement or disagreement about the incident (such as calmly discussing the matter or yelling and screaming at each other). In this way, the researchers were able to arrive at measures of *perceived* similarity (the degree to which Tom and Mary saw each other responding similarly) and *actual* similarity (the degree to which Tom's account and Mary's account were, in fact, similar).

Assuming that conflict itself might be one of the ways in which a couple generate a shared reality, Acitelli and colleagues hypothesized that there would be a positive relationship between perceived similarity in the way conflicts were expressed and the state of the marriage. And, indeed, this is what they found when they compared the accounts of the conflicts with other measures of marital well-being. The more congruent a couple thought they were with regard to conflict, the more positive they felt about their relationship. Apparently it's important for couples to believe that they are on the same wavelength, even when the issue is one of how they perceive their conflicts.

## The Role of Attribution in Conflict

Interactions are often open to various interpretations, especially in situations that generate conflict. For example, when Harold Kelley and associates (1973) asked couples about problems encountered in their relationships, not only did the researchers find that couples mentioned a striking variety of problems, but they also found that problems were described in different ways. At times couples stated the problems in concrete and specific terms, and at other times they couched them in general terms, dealing, for example, with norms and values of the relationship or highly generalized attributes of their partner's personality, disposition, or attitudes.

### Levels of Interdependence

Findings such as those by Kelley and colleagues (1973) led Braiker and Kelley (1979) to suggest that personal relationships, and the interdependence that they generate, operate at different levels, with *specific behaviors* (such as cleaning the house, doing the dishes, taking out the garbage) at one level, *normative interdependence* (such as social roles) on a second level, and *personality characteristics* (such as caring, selfishness, unreliability) at yet a third level.

What is the significance of these different levels for a consideration of conflict? When two people see their relationship as involving different levels of interdependence, they must be experiencing rewards and costs on different levels as well. Rewards and costs at the level of specific behaviors have been well documented, and we simply take these for granted. But rewards and costs at the higher levels of social roles and personality characteristics tend to be more subtle. They suggest that we take satisfaction in applying and conforming to certain norms and in being known and treated as a certain kind of person. And when either the normative "rules" or our self-concept are not supported, we tend to feel ill at ease.

In other words, we enter into personal relationships with certain expectations in mind and tend to evaluate relationships in light of these expectations. Implicit in our expectations for our relationships are notions of the ideal boyfriend or girlfriend, husband or wife, the way they should interact, attitudes that should characterize the relationship, and so on. And we feel rewarded or disappointed as our partners measure up or fail to measure up to these ideals (Braiker & Kelley, 1979).

In looking at conflict and personal relationships, then, we are dealing not only with specific actions but also with the way these actions, however well intended, are interpreted and received. Two people in a close personal relationship are interdependent not only at the level of behavior but also at the level of perceived attitudes and dispositions.

One form of conflict, **normative conflict,** seems to revolve around felt obligations and rights. Resolution of conflicts at the normative level can (in principle) eliminate, or at least decrease, various conflicts at a more specific level. For example, the policy (at the normative level) of taking turns choosing summer vacation spots (John's to the mountains, Joan's to the shore) might replace repeated conflicts at a lower level about where to spend summer vacation.

In a similar vein, the attribution of personal characteristics or attitudes (such as selfishness or thoughtlessness) may be seen as summary statements for the number of times one person has insisted on getting her or his way or pressing her or his interests at the expense of the other ("You're just selfish, John. You always want to go to the mountains, and there's nothing for me to do there"). Labels applied at the level of attitudes or personal characteristics, then, can implicate a number of more specific issues at lower levels and vice versa.

So, although conflicts may be triggered by specific events, they do not necessarily stay there. Conflicts tend to move to higher levels of generality. Even when researchers take great pains to emphasize the importance of defining problems in terms of specific behaviors, they are repeatedly faced with attributions about the other's attitudes or personal characteristics—attributes that are more general (Braiker & Kelley, 1979).

It seems, then, that the distinction between behavior and the attributions generated by those behaviors is easily blurred. Such terms as *affection, caring, support,* and *love* are used to refer to both specific behaviors (such as an act of caring) and to attitudes and dispositions (such as a caring person). And we easily slide back and forth between these without realizing it. Kelley (1979) illustrates the type of problem that can arise by noting the case of a husband who was instructed by the marriage counselor to express more affection, and in response he went out and washed his wife's car!

## Attributions Among Distressed Versus Nondistressed Couples

When we turn to studies that compare couples who are experiencing problems with those who are not, we find that distressed couples differ from nondistressed couples in several ways. For example, in their study comparing clinic (distressed) and nonclinic (nondistressed) couples, Valentin Escudero and his colleagues (1997) noted that for clinic couples, domineering behavior tends to be associated with negative emotion, while for nonclinic couples, this is not the case. In the face of domineering behavior, nonclinic couples tend to show more neutralizing responses rather than eye-for-an-eye reciprocity. Accordingly, potential conflicts among nonclinic couples tend not to escalate.

Taking a different example, we see that although distressed couples show higher levels of negative behavior than do nondistressed couples (Weiss & Dehle, 1994), the number of negative events seems to be only weakly related to marital satisfaction for happily married couples (Fincham, Beach, & Nelson, 1987). Margaret Madden and Ronnie Janoff-Bulman (1981) found that wives who were most satisfied with their marriages were more likely to blame themselves than their husbands in cases of marital conflict, and they were also more likely to see themselves as more able to resolve conflicts. To some extent, then, what is at the root of marital satisfaction or dissatisfaction seems to be in the eye of the beholder. And among the differences that seem to play a role are the attributions that distressed and nondistressed couples make about their partner's behavior.

Research has consistently shown that couples in distressed relationships make more attributions that cast their partner in a negative light. Further, these negative attributions tend to involve stable features of the partner (that is, their actions are seen as intentional, blameworthy, and selfishly motivated). At the same time their positive behaviors tend to be seen as situation specific, unstable, and largely unintentional (Fincham, Beach, & Baucom, 1987; Holtzworth-Munroe & Jacobson, 1985, 1988; Jacobson et al., 1985; Weiss & Dehle, 1994).

In addition, researchers have found it important to distinguish between **causal attributions** and **responsibility attributions.** For example, Donald Baucom and colleagues (1989) found that distressed couples not only tend to attribute negative behaviors of their partners to dispositional, stable, and global characteristics, but they also tend to make attributions of blame or

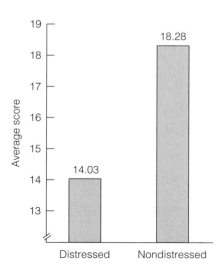

**Figure 16-2** Responsibility attributions to partners for positive behaviors in distressed and nondistressed couples. From Finchham, F. D., Beach, S. R., & Baucom, D. H. (1987). Attribution processes in distressed and nondistressed couples: 4. Self-partner attribution differences. *Journal of Personality and Social Psychology, 53,* 739–748. Copyright © 1986 by the American Psychological Association. Adapted with permission.

responsibility. Such an attributional style seems to be "distress maintaining" (Holtzworth-Munroe & Jacobson, 1985). An example of the difference for distressed versus nondistressed couples in the motivation attributed to partners for positive behavior is illustrated in Figure 16-2 (Fincham, Beach, & Baucom, 1987).

## Other Issues in the Study of Conflict

Attributions are not the only things that distinguish distressed from nondistressed couples. Distressed couples also show patterns of interaction that we tend not to see in more satisfied couples. Certain issues that touch on core values, beliefs, and goals can generate "irreconcilable differences." The longer a couple is married, the less satisfying their marriage tends to be, on the whole. And patterns of conflict established early in a relationship seem to persist.

### The Demand-Withdraw Pattern

Andrew Christensen and Christopher Heavey (1990) have noted a common pattern of "demand-withdraw," in which one partner (usually the wife) prefers more closeness, while the other (usually the husband) prefers distance. This demand-withdraw pattern seems to be especially characteristic of distressed couples. Linda Roberts and Lowell Krokoff (1990), for example, found that withdrawal on the part of the husband tends to lead to increased hostility on the part of the wife among distressed couples, while no similar pattern is evident among satisfied couples.

### Conflict Over Values, Beliefs, and Goals

Many times, the actual content of disputes is significant. We have all heard accounts of breakups in which those involved referred to certain litmus tests, such as "What it came down to was I wanted children and Joan didn't" or "Greg wanted a stay-at-home wife, so when I got into law school, that was pretty much it." In certain cases, it may be important to distinguish between conflicts growing out of problems in interpersonal processes and conflicts due to irreconcilable differences. Why?

Flexibility in addressing conflicts tends to decline when differences are closely tied to fundamental values, beliefs, or goals, and one's position is especially likely to be characterized by rigidity when issues are seen as important and dichotomous. For example, abortion, extramarital sex, and marriage (as opposed to cohabiting) represent dichotomous issues for many people. The conflicts that these generate tend to be closely tied to fundamental values, and their resolution is likely to be couched in terms of a zero-sum game—when one person (group or cause) wins, the other loses automatically. In such cases, there is no middle ground and no room for compromise. One does not *sort of* have an abortion. One does not *sort of* get married or *sort of* have an extramarital fling. And, as suggested in the opening paragraph of the chapter, physical abuse is likely to fall into this category as well.

Of course, not all conflicts are of this type, and not all of those that appear to be of this type actually are. Conflicts arising over the role of wife and mother, involvement of the father in parenting, spending habits, and leisure activities need not be couched in terms of a zero-sum game. There is often the possibility for compromise or "integrative agreements"—solutions that, although they may not be ideal, are acceptable to both parties (Pruitt & Carnevale, 1982; Pruitt & Lewis, 1977).

## Marital Conflict and Duration of Marriage

In general, researchers have noted that marital satisfaction declines over time. The longer the marriage, the less satisfying it tends to be (Huston et al., 1986). The longer relationships last, the more the partners are likely to blame each other for negative events (Christensen et al., 1983).

What are the implications for conflict of this general decline in marital satisfaction? John Gottman and Lowell Krokoff (1989) found that the effects of frequency, style, and outcome of conflict were all significantly related to marital disruption over the course of their study. This led them to suggest that underlying the various types of marital disagreement is a common core of negativity. But the effects of this seemed to interact in subtle ways with how long couples had been married. For example, in the case of couples married less than 8 years, when all the measures were taken together, only the general negativity factor was significant. For those married 8 or more years, on the other hand, the frequency of disagreements was most significant (Gottman & Krokoff, 1989).

More recently, Katherine McGonagle and her colleagues (1993), in a longitudinal study of 691 couples, focused on frequency, negativity, conflict style, outcome of disagreements, and their effects on marital disruption. Specifically, the researchers were interested in the question of whether the effects of disagreements were cumulative and incremental, like a festering sore, or more explosive, like a volcano.

Like Gottman and Krokoff, McGonagle and colleagues found evidence for the changing effects of conflict over time. Negativity predicted disruption among the newly married, whereas frequency of conflict predicted disruption for couples who had been married longer. Couples who had been married 9 or more years experienced fewer conflicts, but their conflicts were more serious and less likely to be resolved satisfactorily than were the conflicts of couples married 8 years or less (McGonagle et al., 1993).

How do we interpret such findings? Do couples become adapted and more tolerant of negativity over time, or do they simply feel stuck? Lynn White and Alan Booth (1991) suggest that barriers to marital dissolution, such as the presence of children, home ownership, and fewer attractive alternatives, combine over the years to increase tolerance for dissatisfaction in marriage. There is, however, a more positive interpretation of the same findings; that is, over time, marriage partners may simply feel that their relationship is strong enough to withstand more in the way of insults, and as a consequence, they don't bother much with diplomacy (Notarious & Vanzetti, 1983). It's only reasonable, after all, to acknowledge that marriages of long duration are "survivors" of sorts, by definition. They must have something going for them.

### What About Couples Who Never Fight?

As noted earlier, one school of thought has it that a certain level of conflict is to be expected and may actually be healthy for the development of stable relationships (Gottman & Krokoff, 1989; Lloyd & Cate, 1985; Peterson, 1983). According to this line of reasoning, couples who do not air their differences are destined to have relationships full of time bombs ticking away, waiting to go off at some point in the future.

Are the marriages of couples who never fight more at risk than those of couples who do? McGonagle and colleagues (1993) found no evidence that they were. In their study, the relationship between disagreement and marital disruption was essentially linear—the more disagreement, the more disruption. But most significantly, they also noted that couples who had the most disagreements were also the most likely to avoid addressing their problems. These were the marriages that were most at risk. Couples who neither disagreed nor avoided problem issues were least at risk.

In view of the popular literature suggesting ways for couples to "fight fair," it is also useful to note that McGonagle and her associates found no evidence that the effects of disagreement were modified by the style or outcome of conflict. In their study, disagreement frequency was a powerful factor regardless of whether couples discussed issues calmly and were satisfied with the outcome, or engaged in conflicts characterized by anger and acrimony.

## Conflict Resolution

Once conflict begins, it seems to take one of two general courses: negotiation (and possibly resolution) or escalation (Peterson, 1983). Two main themes suggested by researchers studying conflict resolution are conciliation and integrative agreements. But, as we see in Box 16-1, efforts at conflict resolution take many forms.

### Negotiation

Most conflicts involving personal relationships are settled through negotiation. People look for ways to accommodate and problem solve, both on their own part and from the perspective of the other, and eventually the issue is resolved (Baxter et al., 1993).

In addition, however, the way one partner responds to dissatisfaction on the part of the other is important in conflict management and conflict reso-

---

*Box 16-1 In a Different Key*
**Conflict Resolution Among the Nzema**

Different cultures resolve conflicts between husbands and wives in various ways. Sometimes the extended family becomes involved. Sometimes officials intervene. Sometimes the husband and wife are left to resolve their problems on their own. But among the Nzema of southern Ghana, marital disputes are handled in a unique way. Here, institutionalized friendships are recognized between men and women. For all intents and purposes, opposite-sex friends become like brother and sister. Indeed, they may even sleep together, but they are not lovers, and they do not have sex. And no one in the community thinks it strange. Any indications of sexual desire are fought, and the families would never give permission for them to marry once the two were bound in friendship. The male may even play a role in the female's choice of a husband, because the friendship continues after her marriage. One role played by such male friends is to act as a go-between in the case of a marital conflict and serve to protect the female against any possible brutality on the part of her husband (Brain, 1976).

---

lution. When one partner engages in negative behavior, the relationship is best served if the other inhibits his or her impulse to respond in a destructive way and makes an effort to be accommodative. For example, if Bev comes home after an exhausting day and makes a rude remark, it's better for Mike to resist the temptation to snap back and, instead, accommodate her, either by asking if she had a rough day or by ignoring the incident entirely (Rusbult et al. 1991).

### Escalation

When conflicts are not resolved through negotiation, they may simmer quietly, or they may escalate. Gerald Patterson and his associates (for example, Patterson, 1982; Patterson & Reid, 1970) have offered insights into why this would be. According to their analysis, as one person introduces negativism (such as criticism or threat) to get his or her way, and the partner responds with noncompliance, this often leads the first to increase the negativism in magnitude and/or frequency. Eventually, one partner or the other gives in, but in so doing, she or he reinforces the use of negativism at a higher level. Suppose, for example, that early in their courtship, Mike sulks, and Bev ignores it. Later, however, Mike blows his stack, and Bev gives in to his demands. Because it is effective, it is reinforcing for Mike to blow his stack, and consequently, "stack blowing" is likely to increase over time. Once set in motion, such a pattern is difficult to reverse, because the immediate effects of getting his way are so rewarding, even though the long-term consequences may be disastrous.

## Conciliation

After a conflict has escalated to high levels, it's difficult to restore things to a problem-solving mode. An intermediate step seems necessary before meaningful progress can be made. This step requires a **conciliatory gesture** in which negative affect is reduced and a willingness to pursue mutually acceptable outcomes is expressed.

Donald Peterson (1979) saw two issues as important in conciliation. First, the conflict should be placed in perspective such that maintaining the relationship is seen as primary. Second, the individual making the conciliatory gesture should assume some of the responsibility for the conflict. Ideally, conciliatory moves on the part of one partner are followed by conciliatory moves on the part of the other. When this happens, the level of emotional arousal declines, and both partners are more likely to move in the direction of resolving their differences.

The form that this takes is not well established. Peterson (1979), for example, found that many conflicts end with one or the other partner withdrawing in anger. In such cases, no obvious resolution of the conflict is in sight. Sometimes a trial separation provides the chance to cool off and look at the relationship in a new light, but it is just as likely that withdrawal will have a negative effect, with both partners becoming more obstinate than before. Withdrawal is common among couples seeking professional help in dealing with marital conflicts. There is no evidence that withdrawal per se facilitates conflict resolution.

Compromise is the first thing that comes to mind when two parties are trying to resolve a conflict. In compromise, one or both parties sacrifice their interests to a greater or lesser extent. But compromise is not the same as flexibility in conflict resolution, and there may be other, more desirable possibilities.

## Integrative Agreements

It is unusual for both parties in a conflict to come away completely satisfied. If conflict resolution were easy, there would be no conflict to begin with. **Integrative agreements** are solutions that satisfy the goals and aspirations of both partners. Dean Pruitt and his colleagues (Pruitt & Carnevale, 1982; Pruitt & Lewis, 1977; Rubin et al., 1994) suggest a number of ways that integrative agreements can come about. Sometimes the answer lies in finding ways to cut costs to one partner or the other, finding ways to compensate one or the other for losses, or perhaps pursuing a third option that is satisfactory to both parties.

For example, Dean Pruitt and Peter Carnevale (1982) noted that goals and aspirations tend to come as a package. If selective concessions are to be made, components must be analyzed and a determination made as to how central or peripheral each component might be. Central concerns are not good candidates for concessions. On the other hand, peripheral issues are good candidates, but such concessions are not likely to make much of a difference. So this leaves components of an intermediate level of concern, and it is here that we are most likely to find realistic possibilities for concessions and the most willingness to give significant ground. Should this middle ground be found, an outcome may be reached that is satisfactory, if not ideal, to both parties.

Pruitt and his colleagues use the term "flexible rigidity" to indicate that it is possible for both parties to be firm about their core concerns and flexible about the means used to attain them. Compromising one's major concern is unlikely to resolve conflicts in personal relationships for long. On the other hand, insisting upon one's major goals while showing a readiness to consider various ways of meeting those goals leaves intact the ends that (presumably) were the reason for the conflict in the first place but also communicates an interest in finding a mutually acceptable solution (Peterson, 1983).

Meanwhile, a new process of openness is generated, in which problems are no longer allowed to fester and trivial issues are placed in perspective. Partners who have weathered the storm of conflict in a personal relationship may now be better equipped to understand and support the other in fashioning a new relationship, with new priorities, new focus, and a new level of maturity (Peterson, 1983).

## Conclusion

What are we to conclude from our consideration of conflict in personal relationships? First, whenever two or more people are in a close personal relationship, conflict is possible and even likely. But conflict between friends and conflict between romantic partners seem to operate somewhat differently. In our society, when friends experience serious conflict, they tend to part. Consequently, we find that the lion's share of research on conflict in personal relationships has focused on romantic relationships.

The research tells us that once patterns of conflict are established in personal relationships, they tend to remain relatively stable. And although conflict seems to be a normal part of relating, couples whose relationships are distressed seem to "do conflict" differently than those whose relationships run more smoothly. Especially important is the role played by attribution in generating and maintaining conflict. Indeed, the most important insight in the literature on conflict in personal relationships may be how easily we move from acts to dispositions in attributing responsibility and blame for the negative events in personal relationships. If there is a key to unlocking the mysteries of conflict in personal relationships, it would seem to lie in understanding the nature of this process.

A third theme that we see in the literature focuses on the nature of the issue in dispute. When conflicts touch on core values, beliefs, and goals, they tend to be couched in terms of a zero-sum game—one person's gain is the other's loss. Putting issues in such terms tends to decrease flexibility on the part of those involved.

Finally, researchers have suggested that conflict resolution is best served by distinguishing between concerns of central, intermediate, and peripheral importance in an effort to reach integrative agreements. Matters of central importance are not good candidates for compromise. Concerns of peripheral importance are, but they are not likely to make much difference. Therefore, concerns of intermediate importance seem to offer the most hope for achieving resolution of the conflict. Such integrative agreements, in which each partner gives something and gets something without sacrificing his or her central concern, seem to offer a practical approach to conflict resolution. But how these are achieved and how effective they are in the long term has yet to be established.

## Suggestions for Further Reading

Baxter, L. A., Wilmot, W. W., Simmons, C. A., & Swartz, A. (1993). Ways of doing conflict: A folk taxonomy of conflict events in personal relationships. In P. J. Kalbfleisch (Ed.), *Interpersonal communication: Evolving interpersonal relationships*. Hillsdale, NJ: Erlbaum. A descriptive look at conflicts in personal relationships. Most conflicts are handled in terms of civil discussion.

Braiker, H. B., & Kelley, H. H. (1979). Conflict in the development of close relationships. In R. L. Burgess & T. L. Huston (Eds.), *Social exchange in developing relationships*. New York: Academic. Report on a major study of conflict among young couples, complete with a perceptive analysis of the dynamics involved.

Cahn, D. D. (1992). *Conflict in personal relationships*. Hillsdale, NJ: Erlbaum.

Cahn, D. D. (Ed.). (1990). *Intimates in conflict: A communication perspective*. Hillsdale, NJ: Erlbaum. Both of the Cahn volumes are short paperbacks, which students will find accessible.

Canary, D. J., Cupach, W. R., & Messman, S. J. (1995). *Relationship conflict*. Thousand Oaks, CA: Sage. A brief overview of relationship conflict.

Gottman, J. M. (1994). *Why marriages succeed or fail*. New York: Simon & Schuster. A work written for the popular audience by one of the major researchers in marital conflict and intervention.

Hocker, J. L., & Wilmot, W. W. (1991). *Interpersonal conflict* (3rd ed.). Dubuque, IA: Wm. C. Brown. This brief paperback gives an overview of the area of interpersonal conflict from the communication perspective.

Lloyd, S. A., & Cate, R. M. (1985). The developmental course of conflict in premarital relationship dissolution. *Journal of Social and Personal Relationships, 2,* 179–194. An insightful study of relationships that do not succeed.

Markman, H. J., Floyd, F. J., Stanley, S. M., & Storasli, R. D. (1988). Prevention of marital distress: A longitudinal investigation. *Journal of Personality and Social Psychology, 56,* 210–217. Research on how an ounce of prevention may indeed be worth a pound of cure.

Rubin, J. Z., Pruitt, D. G., & Kim, S. H. (1994). *Social conflict: Escalation, stalemate and settlement* (2nd ed.). New York: McGraw-Hill. A well-written, accessible general overview of conflict by some of the leading researchers in the area.

# Bibliography

Ableson, R. (1981). Psychological status of the script concept. *American Psychologist, 36,* 715–729.

Ablon, J. (1981). Dwarfism and social identity: Self-help group participation. *Social Forces and Medicine, 15,* 25–30.

Acitelli, L. K., Douvan, E., & Veroff, J. (1993). Perceptions of conflict in the first year of marriage: How important are similarity and understanding? *Journal of Social and Personal Relationships, 10,* 5–19.

Adams, G. R. (1977). Physical attractiveness: Toward a developmental social psychology of beauty. *Human Development, 20,* 217–239.

Adams, G. R. (1979). *Beautiful is good: A test of the "kernel of truth" hypothesis.* Unpublished manuscript, as cited in Adams, G. R. (1980).

Adams, G. R. (1980). The effects of physical attractiveness on the socialization process. In Lucker, G. W., Ribbens, K. A., & McNamara, J. A. (Eds.), *Psychological aspects of facial form.* Ann Arbor, MI: University of Michigan, Center for Human Growth and Development. Monograph #11, Craniofacial Growth Series.

Adams, G. R., & Crane, P. (1980). An assessment of parents' and teachers' expectations of preschool children's social preference for attractive and unattractive children and adults. *Child Development, 51,* 224–231.

Adams, G. R., & LaVoie, J. C. (1975). Parental expectations of educational and personal-social performance and child rearing patterns as a function of attractiveness, sex and conduct of the child. *Child Study Journal, 5,* 125–142.

Adams, G. R., & LaVoie, J. C. (1977). Teacher expectations: A review of student characteristics used in expectancy formation. *Journal of Instructional Psychology, Monograph 4,* 1–28.

Adams, R. G. (1987). Patterns of network change: A longitudinal study of friendships of elderly women. *The Gerontologist, 27,* 222–227.

Agras, S. W., Leitenberg, H., Barlow, D. H., & Thomson, L. E. (1969). Instructions and reinforcement in the modification of neurotic behavior. *American Journal of Psychiatry, 125,* 1435–1439.

Ainsworth, M. D. S. (1973). The development of infant-mother attachment. In B. Caldwell & H. Ricculti (Eds.), *Review of child development research* (Vol. 3). Chicago: University of Chicago Press.

Ainsworth, M. D. S. (1989). Attachments beyond infancy. *American Psychologist, 44,* 709–716.

Ainsworth, M. D. S., & Bell, S. M. (1970). Attachment, exploration and separation: Illustrated by the behavior of one-year olds in a strange situation. *Child Development, 41,* 49–67.

Ainsworth, M. D. S., Blehar, M. C., Waters, E., & Wall, S. (1978). *Patterns of attachment: A study of the strange situation.* Hillsdale, NJ: Erlbaum.

Albright, L., Kenny, D. A., & Malloy, T. E. (1988). Consensus in personality judgments at zero

305

acquaintance. *Journal of Personality and Social Psychology, 55,* 387–395.

Alexander, R. D. (1979a). *Darwinism and human affairs.* Seattle, WA: University of Washington Press.

Alexander, R. D. (1979b). Natural selection and social exchange. In R. L. Burgess & T. L. Huston (Eds.), *Social exchange in developing relationships.* New York: Academic.

Allan, G. A. (1977). Class variations in friendship patterns. *British Journal of Sociology, 28,* 389–393.

Allan, G. A. (1979). *A sociology of friendship and kinship.* London: George Allen & Unwin.

Allan, G. A. (1985). *Family life: Domestic roles and social organization.* Oxford: Basil Blackwell.

Allan, G. A., & Adams, R. G. (1989). Aging and the structure of friendship. In R. G. Adams & R. Blieszner (Eds.), *Older adult friendship* (pp. 45–64). Newbury Park, CA: Sage.

Allgeier, E. R., & Wiederman, M. W. (1991). Love and mate selection in the 1990s. *Free Inquiry, 11,* 25–27.

Altman, D. (1986). *AIDS in the mind of America.* New York: Anchor Press/Doubleday.

Altman, I. (1974). The communication of interpersonal attitudes: An ecological approach. In T. Huston (Ed.), *Foundations of interpersonal attraction.* New York: Academic.

Altman, I., & Haythorn, W. W. (1965). Interpersonal exchange in isolation. *Sociometry, 23,* 411–425.

Altman, I., & Taylor, D. A. (1973). *Social penetration: The development of interpersonal relationships.* New York: Holt, Rinehart & Winston.

Altman, I., Vinsel, A., & Brown, B. A. (1981). Dialectic conceptions in social psychology: An application to social penetration and privacy regulation. In L. Berkowitz (Ed.), *Advances in experimental social psychology* (Vol. 14). New York: Academic.

Alvares, V., & Adelman, H. S. (1986). Overestimates of self-evaluation by students with psychoeducational problems. *Journal of Learning Disorders, 19,* 567–571.

Ammerman, R. T., van Hasselt, V. B., & Hersen, M. (1987). The handicapped adolescent. In V. B. van Hasselt & M. Hersen (Eds.), *Hand-book of adolescent psychology.* New York: Pergamon.

Anderson, C. A., Horowitz, L. M., & French, L. M. (1983). Attributional style of lonely and depressed people. *Journal of Personality and Social Psychology, 45,* 127–136.

Anderson, E. M., Clarke, L., & Spain, B. (1982). *Disability in adolescence.* London: Methuen.

Argyle, M. (1987). *The psychology of happiness.* London: Methuen.

Argyle, M., & Henderson, M. (1984). The rules of friendship. *Journal of Social and Personal Relationships, 1,* 211–237.

Argyle, M., & Henderson, M. (1985). The rules of relationships. In S. Duck & D. Perlman (Eds.), *Understanding personal relationships: An interdisciplinary approach.* London: Sage.

Aries, E. J., & Johnson, F. L. (1983). Close friendships in adulthood: Conversational content between same-sex friends. *Sex Roles, 9,* 1183–1197.

Armstrong, J. C. (1969). Perceived intimate friendship as a quasi-therapeutic agent. *Journal of Counseling Psychology, 16,* 137–141.

Aron, A., & Aron, E. N. (1996). Self and self-expansion in relationships. In G. J. O. Fletcher & J. Fitness (Eds.), *Knowledge structures in close relationships: A social psychological approach.* Mahwah, NJ: Erlbaum.

Aron, A., Dutton, D. G., Aron, E. N., & Iverson, A. (1989). Experiences of falling in love. *Journal of Social and Personal Relationships, 6,* 243–257.

Aronson, E., & Mills, J. (1959). The effect of severity of initiation on liking for a group. *Journal of Abnormal and Social Psychology, 59,* 179–181.

Asher, S. R., Hymel, S., & Renshaw, P. D. (1984). Loneliness in children. *Child Development, 55,* 1456–1464.

Asher, S. R., Oden, S. L., & Gottman, J. M. (1977). Children's friendships in school settings. In L. G. Katz (Ed.), *Current topics in early childhood education* (Vol. 1). Norwood, NJ: Ablex.

Atkins, C. J., Kaplan, R. M., & Toshima, M. T. (1991). Close relationships in the epidemiology of cardiovascular disease. In W. H. Jones & D. Perlman (Eds.), *Advances in personal relationships* (Vol. 3, pp. 207–231). London: Kingsley.

Atkinson, R. L., Atkinson, R. G., Smith, E., Bem, D. J., & Nolen-Hoeksema, S. (1996). *Hilgard's introduction to psychology* (12th ed.). New York: Harcourt Brace.

Aukett, R., Richie, J., & Mill, K. (1988). Gender differences in friendship patterns. *Sex Roles, 19,* 57–66.

Aune, K. S., & Comstock, J. (1991). Experience and expression of jealousy: Comparison between friends and romantics. *Psychological Reports, 69,* 315–319.

Axelrod, R., & Hamilton, W. (1981). The evolution of cooperation. *Science, 211,* 1390–1396.

Babchuck, N., & Bates, A. P. (1963). The primary relations of middle-class couples: A study in male dominance. *American Sociological Review, 28,* 377–384.

Bailey, J. M., Gaulin, S., Agyei, Y., & Gladue, B. A. (1994). Effects of gender and sexual orientation on evolutionarily relevant aspects of human mating. *Journal of Personality and Social Psychology, 66,* 1081–1093.

Bakan, D. (1966). *The duality of human existence: Isolation and communion in Western man.* Boston: Beacon Press.

Ball, S. J. (1981). *Beachside comprehensive.* Cambridge, UK: Cambridge University Press.

Bandura, A. (1986). *The social foundations of thought and action: A social cognitive theory.* Englewood Cliffs, NJ: Prentice-Hall.

Bankoff, E. A. (1990). Effects of friendship support on the psychological well-being of widows. In H. Z. Lopata & D. R. Maines (Eds.), *Friendship in context.* Greenwich, CT: JAI Press.

Barash, D. P. (1979). *The whisperings within: Evolution and the origins of human nature.* New York: Harper & Row.

Barnett, O. W., Martinez, T. E., & Bluestein, B. W. (1995). Jealousy and romantic attachment in maritally violent and nonviolent men. *Journal of Interpersonal Violence, 10,* 473–486.

Barocus, R., & Vance, F. L. (1974). Referral rate and physical attractiveness in third-grade children. *Perceptual and Motor Skills, 39,* 731–734.

Barretta, D., Dantzler, D., & Kayson, W. (1995). Factors related to loneliness. *Psychological Reports, 76,* 827–830.

Barrett-Lennard, G. T. (1986). The relationship inventory now: Issues and advances in theory, method, and use. In L. S. Greenberg & W. M. Pinsof (Eds.), *The psychotherapeutic process: A research handbook.* (pp. 325–366). New York: Guilford.

Bar-Tal, D., & Saxe, L. (1976). Perception of similarly and dissimilarly attractive couples and individuals. *Journal of Personality and Social Psychology, 33,* 772–781.

Bartrop, R. W., Luckhurst, E., Lazarus, L., Kiloh, L. G., & Penny, R. (1977). Depressed lymphocyte function after bereavement. *Lancet, 97,* 834–836.

Bass, T. A. (1993). *Reinventing the future.* Reading, MA: Addison-Wesley.

Baucom, D. H., Sayers, S. L., & Duhe, A. (1989). Attributional style and attributional patterns among married couples. *Journal of Personality and Social Psychology, 56,* 596–607.

Baumeister, R. F., & Leary, M. R. (1995). The need to belong: Desire for interpersonal attachments as a fundamental human motivation. *Psychological Bulletin, 117,* 497–529.

Baumgardner, A. H., & Brownlee, E. A. (1987). Strategic failure in social interaction: Evidence for expectancy disconfirmation processes. *Journal of Personality and Social Psychology, 52,* 525–535.

Baunach, P. J. (1974). Physical attractiveness and attribution of victim responsibility for attractiveness-related and attractiveness unrelated crimes. Who blames beauty and when? Unpublished doctoral dissertation, University of Minnesota, as cited in Adams, G. R. (1980).

Baxter, L. (1984). An investigation of compliance-gaining as politeness. *Human Communication Research, 10,* 427–456.

Baxter, L. A., & Bullis, C. (1986). Turning points in developing relationships. *Human Communication Research, 12,* 469–493.

Baxter, L. A., & Dindia, K. (1990). Marital partners' perceptions of marital maintenance strategies. *Journal of Social and Personal Relationships, 7,* 187–208.

Baxter, L. A., & Wilmot, W. W. (1984). Secret tests: Social strategies for acquiring information about the state of the relationship. *Human Communication Research, 11,* 171–201.

Baxter, L. A., Wilmot, W. W., Simmons, C. A., &

Swartz, A. (1993). Ways of doing conflict: A folk taxonomy of conflict events in personal relationships. In P. J. Kalbfleisch (Ed.). *Interpersonal communication: Evolving interpersonal relationships.* Hillsdale, NJ: Erlbaum.

Bean, G., Cooper, S., Alpert, R., & Kipnis, D. (1980). Coping mechanisms of cancer patients. A study of 33 patients receiving chemotherapy. *CA-A, Cancer Journal for Clinicians, 30,* 256–259.

Becker, G. (1980). *Growing in silence.* Berkeley, CA: University of California Press.

Becker, H. S. (1960). Notes on the concept of commitment. *American Journal of Sociology, 66,* 32–40.

Bell, R. A. (1985). Conversational involvement and loneliness. *Communication Monographs, 52,* 218–235.

Bell, R. A., & Daly, J. A. (1984). The affinity-seeking function of communication. *Communication Monographs, 51,* 91–115.

Belloc, N. B., & Breslow, L. (1972). Relationship of physical health status and health practices. *Preventive Medicine, 1,* 409–421.

Bendtschneider, L., & Duck, S. (1993). What's yours is mine and what's mine is yours: Couple friends. In P. J. Kalbfleisch (Ed.), *Interpersonal communication: Evolving interpersonal relationships.* Hillsdale, NJ: Erlbaum.

Benson, P. L., Karabenick, S. A., & Lerner, R. M. (1976). Pretty please: The effects of physical attractiveness, race and sex on receiving help. *Journal of Experimental Social Psychology, 12,* 409–415.

Berg, J. H. (1983). *Attraction in relationships: As it begins so it goes.* Paper presented at the annual meeting of the American Psychological Association, Anaheim, California, as cited in Berg, J. H., & Clark, M. S. (1986).

Berg, J. H. (1984). The development of friendship between roommates. *Journal of Personality and Social Psychology, 46,* 346–356.

Berg, J. H., & Archer, R. L. (1980). Disclosure or concern: A second look at liking for the norm-breaker. *Journal of Personality, 48,* 245–257.

Berg, J. H., & Archer, R. L. (1982). Response to self-disclosure and interaction goals. *Journal of Experimental Social Psychology, 18,* 501–512.

Berg, J. H., & Clark, M. S. (1986). Differences in

social exchange between intimate and other relationships: Gradually evolving or quickly apparent? In V. J. Derlega & B. A. Winstead (Eds.), *Friendship and social interaction* (pp. 101–128). New York: Springer-Verlag.

Berg, J. H., & McQuinn, R. D. (1986). Attraction and exchange in continuing and noncontinuing dating relationships. *Journal of Personality and Social Psychology, 50,* 942–952.

Berg, J. H., & Peplau, L. A. (1982). Loneliness: The relationship of self-disclosure and androgyny. *Personality and Social Psychology Bulletin, 8,* 624–630.

Berg, J. H., & Piner, K. (1990). Social relationships and the lack of social relationships. In S. W. Duck (Ed.), *Personal relationships and social support.* London: Sage.

Berger, C. R. (1975). Proactive and retroactive attribution processes in interpersonal communication. *Human Communication Research, 2,* 33–50.

Berger, C. R. (1987). Communicating under uncertainty. In M. E. Roloff & G. R. Miller (Eds.), *Interpersonal processes: New directions in communication.* Newbury Park, CA: Sage.

Berger, C. R. (1988). Uncertainty and information exchange in developing relationships. In S. Duck (Ed.), *Handbook of personal relationships: Theory, research and interventions.* New York: Wiley.

Berger, C. R., & Calabrese, R. J. (1975). Some explorations in initial interaction and beyond: Toward a developmental theory of interpersonal communication. *Human Communication Research, 1,* 99–112.

Berkman, L. G. (1985). The relationships of social networks and social support to morbidity and mortality. In S. Cohen & S. Syme (Eds.), *Social support and health* (pp. 141–160). New York: Academic.

Berkman, L. G. (1986). Social network, support and health: Taking the next step forward. *American Journal of Epidemiology, 109,* 186–204.

Berkman, L. F., & Syme, S. L. (1979). Social networks, host resistance and mortality: A nine year follow-up of Alameda County residents. *American Journal of Epidemiology, 109,* 186–204.

Berman, J. S., & Norton, N. C. (1985). Does professional training make a therapist more effective? *Psychological Bulletin, 98,* 401–406.

Berndt, T. J. (1979). Developmental changes in conformity to peers and parents. *Developmental Psychology, 15,* 608–616.

Berndt, T. J. (1981). The effects on friendship of prosocial intentions and behavior. *Child Development, 52,* 636–643.

Berndt, T. J. (1982). The features and effects of friendship in early adolescence. *Child Development, 53,* 1447–1460.

Berndt, T. J. (1986). Children's comments about their friends. In M. Permutter (Ed.), *Minnesota symposium on child psychology* (Vol 18). Hillsdale, NJ: Erlbaum.

Berndt, T. J. (1992). *Child development.* New York: Harcourt Brace Jovanovich.

Berndt, T. J., & Keefe, K. (1992). Friends' influence on adolescents' perception of themselves at school. In D. H. Shunk & J. L. Meece (Eds.), *Student perceptions in the classroom.* Hillsdale, NJ: Erlbaum.

Berndt, T. J., & Perry, T. B. (1986). Children's perceptions of friendships as supportive relationships. *Developmental Psychology, 22,* 640–648.

Berndt, T. J., Hawkins, J. A., & Hoyle, S. G. (1986). Changes in friendship during a school year: Effects on children's and adolescents' impressions of friendship and sharing with friends. *Child Development, 57,* 1284–1297.

Bernikow, L. (1982, August 15). Alone: Yearning for companionship in America. *New York Times Magazine,* pp. 25–34.

Berry, D. S. (1991). Attractive faces are not all created equal: Joint effects of facial babyishness and attractiveness on social perception. *Personality and Social Psychology Bulletin, 17,* 523–531.

Berscheid, E. (1994). Interpersonal relationships. In L. W. Porter & M. R. Rosenzweig (Eds.), *Annual review of psychology* (Vol. 45). Palo Alto, CA: Annual Reviews Inc.

Berscheid, E., & Fei, J. (1977). Romantic love and sexual jealousy. In G. Clanton & L. G. Smith (Eds.), *Jealousy.* Lanham, MD: University Press of America.

Berscheid, E., & Peplau, L. A. (1983). The emerging science of relationships. In H. H. Kelley, E. Berscheid, A. Christensen, J. J. Harvey, T. L.

Huston, G. Levinger, E. McClintock, L. A. Peplau, & D. R. Peterson, *Close relationships.* New York: W. H. Freeman.

Berscheid, E., & Walster, E. (1974). Physical attractiveness. In L. Berkowitz (Ed.), *Advances in experimental social psychology* (Vol. 7, pp. 157–215). New York: Academic.

Berscheid, E., & Walster, E. (1978). *Interpersonal attraction* (2nd ed.). Reading, MA: Addison-Wesley.

Berscheid, E., Walster, E., & Bohrnstedt, G. (1973). The happy American body: A survey report. *Psychology Today, 7,* 119–131.

Berscheid, E., Walster, E., & Campbell, R. (1972). Grow old along with me. Unpublished manuscript, as cited in Berscheid, E., & Walster, E. (1974).

Bierman, K. L., & Furman, W. (1984). The effects of social skills training and peer involvement on the social adjustment of preadolescents. *Child Development, 55,* 151–162.

Bierman, K. L., Miller, C. L., & Stabb, S. D. (1987). Improving the social behavior and peer acceptance of rejected boys: Effects of social skill training with instructions and prohibitions. *Journal of Consulting and Clinical Psychology, 55,* 194–200.

Bigelow, B. J., & La Gaipa, J. J. (1975). Children's written descriptions of friendship: A multidimensional analysis. *Developmental Psychology, 11,* 857–858.

Bigelow, B. J., & La Gaipa, J. J. (1980). The development of friendship values and choice. In H. C. Foot, A. J. Chapman, & J. R. Smith (Eds.), *Friendship and social relations in children.* New York: Wiley.

Birenbaum, A. (1992). Courtesy stigma revisited. *Mental Retardation, 30,* 265–268.

Bischof, L. J. (1976). *Adult psychology* (2nd ed.). New York: Harper & Row.

Black, H., & Angelis, V. B. (1974). Interpersonal attraction: An empirical investigation of platonic and romantic love. *Psychological Reports, 34,* 1243–1246.

Blasband, D., & Peplau, L. A. (1985). Sexual exclusivity versus openness in gay male couples. *Archives of Sexual Behavior, 14,* 395–412.

Blau, P. M. (1964). *Exchange and power in social life.* New York: Wiley.

Blau, Z. S. (1961). Structural constraints on friendships in old age. *American Sociological Review, 26,* 429–439.

Blaxter, M. (1976). *The meaning of disability.* London: Heineman Educational Books.

Blieszner, R. (1989). Developmental processes of friendship. In R. G. Adams & R. Blieszner (Eds.), *Older adult friendship* (pp. 108–126). Newbury Park, CA: Sage.

Blieszner, R., & Adams, R. G. (1992). *Adult friendship.* Newbury Park, CA: Sage.

Block, J. (1981). Some enduring and consequential structures of personality. In A. I. Rabin et al. (Eds.), *Further explorations in personality.* New York: Wiley.

Block, J. H. (1973). Conceptions of sex roles: Some cross-cultural and longitudinal perspectives. *American Psychologist, 28,* 512–526.

Blood, R. O. (1967). *Love match and arranged marriage: A Tokyo-Detroit comparison.* New York: Free Press.

Blood, R. O., & Wolfe, D. M. (1960). *Husbands and wives: The dynamics of married living.* New York: Free Press.

Bloom, B. L., White, S. W., & Asher, S. J. (1979). Marital disruption as a stressful event. In G. Levinger & O. C. Moles (Eds.), *Divorce and separation: Context, causes and consequences* (pp. 184–200). New York: Basic.

Blos, P. (1979). *The adolescent passage: Developmental issues.* New York: International Universities Press.

Blumstein, P., & Schwartz, P. (1983). *American couples: Money, work, sex.* New York: Morrow.

Boissevain, J. (1974). *Friends of friends.* New York: Basic.

Boivin, M., & Begin, G. (1989). Peer status and self-perception among early elementary school children: The case of the rejected child. *Child Development, 60,* 591–596.

Booth, A. (1972). Sex and social participation. *American Sociological Review, 37,* 183–193.

Booth, A., & Hess, E. (1974). Cross-sex friendship. *Journal of Marriage and the Family, 36,* 38–47.

Borys, S., & Perlman, D. (1985). Gender differences in loneliness. *Personality and Social Psychology Bulletin, 11,* 63–74.

Bowlby, J. (1969). *Attachment and loss: Vol. 1. Attachment.* New York: Basic.

Bowlby, J. (1973). *Attachment and loss: Vol. 2.*

*Separation, anxiety and anger.* New York: Basic.

Brage, D., Meredith, W., & Woodword, J. (1993). Correlates of loneliness among Midwestern adolescents. *Adolescence, 28,* 685–693.

Braiker, H. B., & Kelley, H. H. (1979). Conflict in the development of close relationships. In R. L. Burgess & T. L. Huston (Eds.), *Social exchange in developing relationships* (pp. 135–168). New York: Academic.

Braiker-Stambul, H. B. (1975). *Stages of courtship: The development of premarital relationships.* Unpublished doctoral dissertation, University of California at Los Angeles, as cited in White, G. L., & Mullen, P. E. (1989).

Brain, R. (1976). *Friends and lovers.* New York: Basic.

Braithwaite, D. O. (1991), "Just how much did that wheelchair cost?": Management of privacy boundaries by persons with disabilities. *Western Journal of Speech Communication, 55,* 254–274.

Brehm, S. S. (1992). *Intimate relationships* (2nd ed.). New York: McGraw-Hill.

Brennan, T., & Auslander, N. (1979). *Adolescent loneliness: An exploratory study of social and psychological dispositions and theory* (Vol. 1). Bethesda, MD: National Institutes of Health, Juvenile Problems Division.

Brennon, T. (1982). Loneliness in adolescence. In L. A. Peplau & D. Perlman (Eds.), *Loneliness: A sourcebook of theory, research and therapy* (pp. 269–290). New York: Wiley.

Brett, W. H. (1868). *Indian tribes in Guiana: Their condition and habits.* London: Bell & Daldy.

Brickman, P. (1987). *Commitment, conflict and caring.* Englewood Cliffs, NJ: Prentice-Hall.

Brickman, P., Coates, D., & Janoff-Bulman, R. (1978). Lottery winners and accident victims: Is happiness relative? *Journal of Personality and Social Psychology, 36,* 917–927.

Bringle, R. G. (1981). Conceptualizing jealousy as a disposition. *Alternative Lifestyles, 4,* 274–290.

Bringle, R. G. (1982). Preliminary report on the Revised Self-Report Jealousy Scale. Unpublished manuscript, as cited in Bringle, R. G. (1991).

Bringle, R. G. (1991). Psychosocial aspects of jealousy: A transactional model. In P. Salovey (Ed.), *The psychology of jealousy and envy.* New York: Guilford.

Bringle, R. G., & Buunk, B. (1985). Jealousy and social behavior. *Review of Personality and Social Psychology, 6,* 241–264.

Bringle, R. G., & Buunk, B. (1986). Examining the causes and consequences of jealousy: Some recent findings and issues. In S. W. Duck & R. Gilmour (Eds.), *The emerging field of personal relationships.* Hillsdale, NJ: Erlbaum.

Bringle, R. G., Renner, P., Terry R. I., & Davis, S. (1983). An analysis of situation and person components of jealousy. *Journal of Research in Personality, 17,* 354–368.

Bringle, R. G., Roach, S., Andler, C., & Evenbeck, S. (1979). Measuring the intensity of jealous reactions. *Catalog of Selected Documents in Psychology, 9,* 23–24.

Bringle, R. G., & Williams, L. J. (1979). Parental-offspring similarity on jealousy and related personality dimensions. *Motivation and Emotion, 3,* 265–286.

Brinkerhoff, M., & Lupri, E. (1978). Theoretical and methodological issues in the use of decision-making as an indicator of conjugal power: Some Canadian observations. *Canadian Journal of Sociology, 3,* 1–20.

Brisson, N. J. (1983). Battering husbands: a survey of abusive men. *Victimology: An International Journal, 1,* 338–344.

Brody, G. H., Stoneman, Z., & McCoy, J. K. (1994). Forecasting sibling relationships in early adolescence from child temperaments and family processes in middle childhood. *Child Development, 65,* 771–784.

Brown, B. B. (1982). The extent and effects of peer pressure among high school students: A retrospective analysis. *Journal of Youth and Adolescence, 11,* 121–133.

Brown, B. B. (1989). The role of peer groups in adolescents' adjustment to secondary school. In T. J. Berndt & G. W. Ladd (Eds.), *Peer relationships in child development* (pp. 188–216). New York: Wiley.

Brown, B. B., Clasen, D. R., & Eicher, S. A. (1986). Perceptions of peer pressure, peer conformity dispositions, and self-reported behavior among adolescents. *Developmental Psychology, 22,* 521–530.

Brown, B. B., Eicher, S. A., & Petrie, S. (1986). The importance of peer group ("crowd") affiliation in adolescence. *Journal of Adolescence, 9,* 73–96.

Brown, B. B., Freeman, H., Huang, B. H., & Mounts, N. S. (1992). *"Crowd hopping": Incidents, correlates, and consequences of change in crowd affiliation during adolescence.* Paper presented at the biennial meeting of the Society for Research in Adolescence, Washington, DC.

Brown, B. B., Lohr, M. J., & Trujillo, C. M. (1990). Multiple crowds and multiple lifestyles: Adolescents' perceptions of peer group characteristics. In R. E. Muss (Ed.), *Adolescent behavior and society: A book of readings.* New York: Random House.

Brown, B. B., Mory, M. S., & Kinney, D. (1994). Casting adolescent crowds in relational perspective: Caricature, channel, and context. In R. Montemayor, G. R. Adams, & T. P. Gullotta (Eds.), *Personal relationships during adolescence.* Thousand Oaks, CA: Sage.

Brown, G. W., Bhrolchain, M. N., & Harris, T. (1975). Social class and psychiatric disturbance among women in an urban population. *Sociology, 9,* 225–254.

Brown, G. W., Dovidido, J. F., & Ellyson, S. L. (1990). Reducing sex differences in visual displays of dominance: Knowledge is power. *Personality and Social Psychology Bulletin, 16,* 358–368.

Brown, G. W., & Harris, T. (1978). *Social origins of depression: A study of psychiatric disorder in women.* New York: Free Press.

Bruhn, J. G., & Wolf, S. (1978). *The Roseto Story: An Anatomy of Health.* Norman, OK: University of Oklahoma Press.

Brundage, L. E., Derlega, V. J., & Cash, T. F. (1977). The effects of physical attractiveness and need for approval on self-disclosure. *Personality and Social Psychology Bulletin, 3,* 63–66.

Bruner, J. (1972). Nature and uses of immaturity. *American Psychologist, 27,* 687–708.

Bryson, J. B. (1991). Modes of responses to jealousy-evoking situations. In P. Salovey (Ed.), *The psychology of jealousy and envy.* New York: Guilford.

Bryson, R. B., Bryson, J. B., Licht, M. H., & Licht, B. G. (1976). The professional pair: Husband and wife psychologists. *American Psychologist, 31,* 10–16.

Buhrke, R., & Fuqua, D. (1987). Sex differences in same- and cross-sex supportive relationships. *Sex Roles, 17,* 339–352.

Buhrmester, D., & Furman, W. (1984). *The need fulfilling role of friendship in children's social networks*. Paper presented at the Second International Conference on Personal Relationships, Madison, Wisconsin, as cited in Buhrmester, D., & Furman, W. (1986).

Buhrmester, D., & Furman, W. (1986). The changing functions of friends in childhood. In V. Derlega and B. Winstead (Eds.), *Friendship and social interaction*. New York: Springer-Verlag.

Buhrmester, D., & Furman, W. (1987). The development of companionship and intimacy. *Child Development, 50,* 1101–1115.

Bukowski, W. M., & Hoza, B. (1989). Popularity and friendship: Issues in theory, measurement and outcome. In T. J. Berndt & G. W. Ladd (Eds.), *Peer relationships in child development*. New York: Wiley.

Bukowski, W. M., & Kramer, T. L. (1986). Judgments of the features of friendship among early adolescent boys and girls. *Journal of Early Adolescence, 6,* 331–336.

Bukowski, W. M., & Newcomb, A. F. (1984). Stability and determinants of sociometric status and friendship choice: A longitudinal perspective. *Developmental Psychology, 20,* 941–952.

Bukowski, W. M., Newcomb, A. F., & Hoza, B. (1987). Friendship conceptions among early adolescents: A longitudinal study of stability and change. *Journal of Early Adolescence, 7,* 143–152.

Bullis, C., Clark, C., & Sline, R. (1993). From passion to commitment: Turning points in romantic relationships. In P. J. Kalbfleisch (Ed.), *Interpersonal communication: Evolving interpersonal relationships*. Hillsdale, NJ: Erlbaum.

Bureau of Census. (1992). *Marital status and living arrangements: March 1991*. Washington, DC: U.S. Government Printing Office.

Burggraf, D. S., & Sillars, A. L. (1987). A critical examination of sex differences in marital communication. *Communication Monographs, 54,* 276–294.

Burgoon, J. K., & Koper, R. J. (1984). Nonverbal and relational communication associated with reticence. *Human Communication Research, 10,* 601–626.

Burke, R., & Weir, T. (1977). Marital helping relationships: Moderators between stress and well-being. *Journal of Psychology, 95,* 121–130.

Burleson, B. R. (1995). Personal relationships as a skilled accomplishment. *Journal of Social and Personal Relationships, 12,* 575–581.

Burleson, B. R., & Denton, W. H. (1992). A new look at similarity and attraction in marriage: Similarities in social-cognitive and communication skills as predictors of attraction and satisfaction. *Communication Monographs, 59,* 268–287.

Burley, N. (1985). Unpublished data, as cited in Trivers, R. (1985).

Burman, B., & Margolin, G. (1992). Analysis of the association between marital relationships and health problems: An interactional perspective. *Psychological Bulletin, 112,* 39–63.

Bush, C. R., Bush, J. P., & Jennings, J. (1988). Effects of jealousy threats on relationship perception and emotions. *Journal of Social and Personal Relationships, 5,* 285–303.

Buss, D. M. (1989). Sex differences in human mate preferences: Evolutionary hypothesis tested in 37 cultures. *Behavioral and Brain Sciences, 12,* 1–14.

Buss, D. M. (1994). *The evolution of desire: Strategies of human mating*. New York: Basic.

Buss, D. M., & Barnes, M. (1986). Preferences in human mate selection. *Journal of Personality and Social Psychology, 50,* 559–570.

Buss, D. M., Gomes, M., Higgins, D. S., & Lauterback, K. (1987). Tactics of manipulation. *Journal of Personality and Social Psychology, 52,* 1219–1229.

Buss, D. M., Larsen, R. J., & Westen, D. (1996). Sex differences in jealousy: Not gone, not forgotten, and not explained by alternative hypotheses. *Psychological Science, 7,* 373–375.

Buss, D. M., Larsen, R. J., Westen, D., & Semmelroth, J. (1992). Sex differences in jealousy: Evolution, physiology and psychology. *Psychological Science, 3,* 251–255.

Buss, D. M., & Schmitt, D. P. (1993). Sexual strategies theory: An evolutionary perspective on human mating. *Psychological Review, 100,* 204–232.

Butler, D., & Geis, F. L. (1990). Nonverbal affect responses to male and female leaders: Implications for leadership evaluations. *Journal of Personality and Social Psychology, 58,* 48–59.

Buunk, B. P. (1980). Sexually open marriages: Ground rules for countering potential threats to marriage. *Alternative Lifestyles, 3,* 312–328.

Buunk, B. P. (1981). Jealousy in sexually open marriages. *Alternative Lifestyles, 4,* 357–372.

Buunk, B. P. (1982). Anticipated sexual jealousy: Its relationship to self-esteem, dependency and reciprocity. *Personality and Social Psychology Bulletin, 8,* 310–316.

Buunk, B. P. (1984). Jealousy as related to attributions for the partner's behavior. *Social Psychology Quarterly, 47,* 107–112.

Buunk, B. P. (1986). Husband's jealousy. In R. A. Lewis & R. E. Salt (Eds.), *Men in families.* Beverly Hills, CA: Sage.

Buunk, B. P. (1987). Conditions that promote breakups as a consequence of extradyadic involvements. *Journal of Social and Clinical Psychology, 5,* 271–284.

Buunk, B. P. (1991). Jealousy in close relationships: an exchange-theoretical perspective. In P. Salovey (Ed.), *The psychology of jealousy and envy.* New York: Guilford.

Buunk, B., & Hupka, R. B. (1986). Autonomy in close relationships: A cross-cultural study. *Family Perspective, 20,* 209–221.

Buunk, B., & Hupka, R. B. (1987). Cross-cultural differences in the elicitation of sexual jealousy. *Journal of Sex Research, 23,* 12–22.

Buunk, B. P., & Van Yperen, N. W. (1991). Referential comparisons, relational comparisons and exchange orientation: Their relation to marital satisfaction. *Personality and Social Psychology Bulletin, 17,* 709–717.

Buunk, B. P., Van Yperen, N. W., Taylor, S. E., & Collins, R. L. (1991). Social comparison and the drive upward revisited: Affiliation as a response to marital stress. *European Journal of Social Psychology, 21,* 529–546.

Byrne, D. (1992). The transition from controlled laboratory settings to less controlled settings: Surprise! Additional variables are operative. *Communication Monographs, 59,* 190–198.

Cahn, D. D. (1990). Perceived understanding and interpersonal relationships. *Journal of Social and Personal Relationships, 7,* 231–244.

Cairns, R. B., Cairns, B. D., Neckerman, H. J., Gest, S., & Garieppy, J. L. (1988). Peer networks and aggressive behavior: Peer support or peer rejections? *Developmental Psychology, 24,* 815–823.

Caldwell, M. A., & Peplau, L. A. (1982). Sex differences in same-sex friendships. *Sex Roles, 8,* 721–732.

Caldwell, M. A., & Peplau, L. A. (1984). The balance of power in lesbian relationships. *Sex Roles, 10,* 587–599.

Cameron, C., Oskamp, S., & Sparkes, W. (1977). Courtship American style: Newspaper ads. *Family Coordinator, 26,* 27–30.

Cammeron, P., Titus, D. G., Dostin, J., & Kostin, M. (1973). The life satisfaction of the non-normal persons. *Journal of Consulting and Clinical Psychology, 41,* 207–214.

Campbell, D. T. (1975). On the conflicts between biological and social evolution and between psychology and the moral tradition. *American Psychologist, 30,* 1103–1126.

Campbell, J. (1980). Complementarity and attraction: A reconceptualization in terms of dyadic behavior. *Representative Research in Social Psychology, 11,* 74–95.

Canary, D. J., & Cupach, W. R. (1988). Relational and episodic characteristics associated with conflict statistics. *Journal of Social and Personal Relationships, 5,* 305–325.

Canary, D. J., Cupach, W. R., & Messman, S. J. (1995). *Relationship conflict.* Thousand Oaks, CA: Sage.

Canary, D. J., & Stafford, L. (1992). Relational maintenance strategies and equity in marriage. *Communication Monographs, 59,* 243–267.

Canary, D. J., & Stafford, L. (1993). Preservation of relational characteristics: Maintenance strategies, equity and locus of control. In P. J. Kalbfleisch (Ed.), *Interpersonal communication: Evolving interpersonal relationships.* Hillsdale, NJ: Erlbaum.

Canary, D. J., Weger, H., Jr., & Stafford, L. (1991). Couple's argument sequences and their associations with relational characteristics. *Western Journal of Speech Communication, 55,* 159–179.

Candy, S. G., Troll, L. E., & Levy, S. G. (1981). A developmental exploration of friendship functions in women. *Psychology of Women Quarterly, 5,* 456–472.

Cappella, J. N., & Palmer, M. T. (1992). The effect of partner's conversation on the association between attitude similarity and attraction. *Communication Monographs, 59,* 180–189.

Cargan, L., & Melko, M. (1982). *Singles: Myths and realities.* Beverly Hills, CA: Sage.

Carli, L. L. (1990). Gender, language, and influence. *Journal of Personality and Social Psychology, 59,* 941–951.

Carli, L. L., Ganley, R., & Pierce-Otay, A. (1991). Similarity and satisfaction in roommate relationships. *Personality and Social Psychology Bulletin, 17,* 419–426.

Carnegie, D. (1937). *How to win friends and influence people.* New York: Simon & Schuster.

Carson, R. C. (1969). *Interaction concepts in personality.* Chicago: Aldine.

Cash, T. F., & Derlega, V. J. (1978). The matching hypothesis: Physical attractiveness among same-sex friends. *Personality and Social Psychology Bulletin, 4,* 240–243.

Cash, T. F., Kehr, J., Polyson, J., & Freeman, V. (1977). Role of physical attractiveness in peer attribution of psychological disturbance. *Journal of Consulting and Clinical Psychology, 45,* 987–993.

Cash, T. F., & Kilcullen, R. N. (1985). The aye of the beholder: Susceptibility to sexism and beautyism in the evaluation of managerial applicants. *Journal of Applied Social Psychology, 15,* 591–605.

Caspi, A., Bem, D. J., & Elder, G. H. (1989). Continuities and consequences of interactional styles across the life course. *Journal of Personality, 56,* 375–406.

Caspi, A., & Herbener, E. S. (1990). Continuity and change: Assortive marriage and the consistency of personality in adulthood. *Journal of Personality and Social Psychology, 58,* 250–258.

Cate, R. M., Huston, T. L., & Nesselrode, J. R. (1985). Premarital relationships: Toward the identification of alternative pathways to marriage. *Journal of Social and Clinical Psychology, 4,* 3–22.

Cate, R. M., & Lloyd, S. A. (1992). *Courtship.* Newbury Park, CA: Sage.

Cate, R. M., Lloyd, S. A., & Henton, J. M. (1985). The effect of equity, equality, and reward level on the stability of students' premarital relationships. *Journal of Social Psychology, 125,* 715–721.

Cate, R. M., Lloyd, S. A., & Long, E. (1988). The role of rewards and fairness in developing premarital relationships. *Journal of Marriage and the Family, 50,* 443–452.

Cauce, A. M. (1986). Social network and social competence: Exploring the effects of early adolescent friendships. *American Journal of Community Psychology, 14,* 607–628.

Cauce, A. M., Feiner, R. D., & Primavera, J. (1982). Social support in high risk adolescents: Structural components and adaptive impact. *American Journal of Community Psychology, 10,* 417–428.

Causian, F. M. (1987). *Love in America: Gender and self development.* New York: Cambridge University Press.

Cavior, N. (1970). *Physical attractiveness, perceived attitude similarity and interpersonal attraction among fifth and eleventh grade boys and girls.* Unpublished dissertation, University of Huston, as cited in Hatfield, E., & Sprecher, S. (1986).

Center for Disease Control. (1996). *Suicide in the United States, 1980–1992.* CDC Suicide Surveillance, 4770 Buford Highway, N.E., Mailstop K-60, Atlanta, GA 30341–3724.

Centers, L., & Centers, R. (1963). Peer group attitudes toward the amputee child. *Journal of Social Psychology, 61,* 127–132.

Chaiken, S. (1979). Communicator physical attractiveness and persuasion. *Journal of Personality and Social Psychology, 37,* 1387–1397.

Chambliss, W. J. (1965). The selection of friends. *Social Forces, 43,* 370–380.

Chapdelaine, A., Kenny, D. A., & LaFontana, K. M. (1994). Matchmaker, matchmaker, can you make me a match? Predicting liking between two unacquainted persons. *Journal of Personality and Social Psychology, 67,* 83–91.

Charlesworth, W. R. (1988). Resources and resource acquisition during ontogeny. In K. B. MacDonald (Ed.), *Sociobiological perspectives on human development.* New York: Springer-Verlag.

Check, J. V. P., Perlman, D., & Malamuth, N. M. (1985). Loneliness and aggressive behaviour. *Journal of Social and Personal Relationships, 2,* 243–252.

Cheek, J. M., & Bush, C. M. (1981). The influence

of shyness on loneliness in a new situation. *Personality and Social Psychology Bulletin, 7,* 572–577.

Chown, S. M. (1981). Friendship in old age. In S. W. Duck & R. Gilmour (Eds.), *Personal relationships, 2: Developing personal relationships.* New York: Academic.

Christensen, A., & Heavey, C. L. (1990). Gender and social structure in the demand/withdraw pattern of marital conflict. *Journal of Personality and Social Psychology, 59,* 73–81.

Christensen, A., & Jacobson, N. S. (1994). Who (or what) can do psychotherapy: The status and challenge of nonprofessional therapies. *Psychological Science, 5,* 8–14.

Christensen, A., Sullaway, M., & King, C. (1983). Systematic error in behavioral reports of dyadic interaction: Egocentric bias and content analysis. *Behavioral Therapy, 5,* 129–140.

Cialdini, R. B., Borden, R. J., Thorne, A., Walker, M. R., Freeman, S., & Sloan, L. R. (1976). Basking in reflected glory: Three (football) field studies. *Journal of Personality and Social Psychology, 34,* 366–375.

Cimbalo, R. S., Faling, V., & Mousaw, P. (1976). The course of love: A cross-sectional design. *Psychological Reports, 38,* 1292–1294.

Clanton, G., & Kosins, D. J. (1991). Developmental correlates of jealousy. In P. Salovey (Ed.), *The psychology of jealousy and envy.* New York: Guilford.

Clanton, G., & Smith, L. G. (1977/1986). Preface. In G. Clanton & L. G. Smith (Eds.), *Jealousy.* Lanham, MD: University Press of America.

Clark, M. L., & Ayers, M. (1988). The role of reciprocity and proximity in junior high school friendships. *Journal of Youth and Adolescence, 17,* 403–411.

Clark, M. L., & Drewry, D. L. (1985). Similarity and reciprocity in friendships in elementary school children. *Child Study Journal, 15,* 251–263.

Clark, M. S., & Mills, J. (1979). Interpersonal attraction in exchange and communal relationships. *Journal of Personality and Social Psychology, 37,* 12–24.

Clark, R. D., & Hatfield, E. (1989). Gender differences in receptivity to sexual offers. *Journal of Psychology and Human Sexuality, 2,* 39–55.

Clasen, D. R., & Brown, B. B. (1985). The multidimensionality of peer pressure in adolescence. *Journal of Youth and Adolescence, 14,* 451–468.

Clayton, P. J. (1979). The sequelae and nonsequelae of conjugal bereavement. *American Journal of General Psychiatry, 136,* 530–534.

Cochran, S. D., & Peplau, L. A. (1985). Value orientations in heterosexual relationships. *Psychology of Women Quarterly, 9,* 477–488.

Cohen, S. (1988). Psychosocial models of the role of social support in the etiology of physical disease. *Health Psychology, 7,* 269–297.

Cohen, S. (1989). Social supports and physical health: Symptoms, health behaviors and infectious disease. In M. Cummings, A. L. Greene, & K. H. Karraker (Eds.), *Life-span developmental psychology: Perspectives on stress and coping.* Hillsdale, NJ: Erlbaum.

Cohen, S., & Syme, S. L. (1985). Issues in the study and application of social support. In S. Cohen & S. L. Syme (Eds.), *Social support and health* (pp. 3–22). New York: Academic.

Coie, J. D., & Dodge, K. A. (1983). Continuities and changes in children's social status: A five-year longitudinal study. *Merrill-Palmer Quarterly, 29,* 261–282.

Coie, J. D., Dodge, K. A., & Coppotelli, H. (1982). Dimensions and types of social status: A cross-age perspective. *Developmental Psychology, 18,* 557–570.

Coie, J. D., & Krehbiel, G. (1984). Effects of academic tutoring on social status of low-achieving, socially rejected children. *Child Development, 55,* 1465–1478.

Coleman, J. C. (1974). *Relationships in adolescence.* Boston: Routledge and Kegan Paul.

Collins, N. L., Dunkel-Schetter, C., Lobel, M., & Scrimshaw, S. C. (1993). Social support in pregnancy: Psychosocial correlates of birth outcomes and post partum depression. *Journal of Personality and Social Psychology, 65,* 1243–1258.

Collins, W. A., & Repinski, D. J. (1994). Relationships during adolescence: Continuity and change in interpersonal perspective. In R. Montemayor, G. R. Adams, & T. P. Gullotta (Eds.), *Personal relationships during adolescence.* Thousand Oaks, CA: Sage.

Comer, R. J., & Piliavin, J. A. (1972). The effects of physical deviance upon face-to-face interaction: The other side. *Journal of Personality and Social Psychology, 23,* 33–39.

Comstock, G. W. (1971). Fatal arteriosclerotic heart disease, water hardness at home, and socio-economic characteristics. *American Journal of Epidemiology, 94,* 1–10.

Comstock, G. W., & Partridge, K. B. (1972). Church attendance and health. *Journal of Chronic Diseases, 25,* 665–672.

Conger, J. J. (1991). *Adolescence and youth: Psychological development in a changing world* (4th ed.). New York: Harper & Row.

Constantine, L., & Constantine, J. M. (1973). *Group marriage: A study of contemporary multilateral marriage.* New York: Macmillan.

Cook-Gumperz, J., & Corsaro, W. A. (1977). Social-ecological constraints on children's communicative strategies. *Sociology, 11,* 411–434.

Cooley, C. H. (1922). *Human nature and the social order.* New York: Scribner.

Coppinger, R. M., & Rosenblatt, P. C. (1968). Romantic love and subsistence dependence of spouses. *Southwestern Journal of Anthropology, 24,* 310–319.

Corter, C., Trehub, S., Boukydis, C., Ford, L., Celhoffer, L., & Minde, K. (1978). Nurses' judgments of the attractiveness of premature infants. *Infant Behavior and Development, 1,* 373–380.

Costa, P. T., & McCrae, R. R. (1980). Still stable after all these years: Personality as a key to some issues in adulthood and old age. In P. B. Baltes & O. G. Brim (Eds.), *Life span development and behavior* (Vol. 3). New York: Academic.

Cottington, E. M., Matthews, K. A., Talbott, E., & Kuller, L. H. (1980). Environmental events preceding sudden death in women. *Psychosomatic Medicine, 42,* 567–574.

Courtright, J. A., Miller, F. E., & Rogers-Miller, L. E. (1979). Domineeringness and dominance: Replication and extension. *Communication Monographs, 46,* 179–192.

Cowen, E. L., & Bobrove, P. H. (1966). Marginality of disability and adjustment. *Perceptual and Motor Skills, 23,* 869–870.

Cowen, E. L., Pederson, A., Babigian, H., Izzo, L. D., & Trost, M. A. (1973). Long-term follow-up of early detected vulnerable children. *Journal of Consulting and Clinical Psychology, 41,* 438–446.

Cox, C. L., Boland, B., & Rusbult, C. E. (1995). *Willingness to sacrifice in marital relationships.* Paper presented at the conference of the International Network on Personal Relationships, College of William & Mary, Williamsburg, Virginia.

Cox, M. J., Owen, M. T., Henderson, V. K., & Margand, N. A. (1992). Prediction of infant-father and infant-mother attachment. *Developmental Psychology, 28,* 474–483.

Crago, M. A. (1972). Psychopathology in married couples. *Psychological Bulletin, 77,* 114–128.

Crandall, C. S. (1991). Do heavy weight students have more difficulty paying for college? *Personality and Social Psychology Bulletin, 17,* 606–611.

Crandall, C. S., & Coleman, R. (1992). AIDS-related stigmatization and the disruption of social relationships. *Journal of Social and Personal Relationships, 9,* 163–177.

Criddle, R. (1953). *Love is not blind.* New York: Norton.

Critelli, J. W., & Dupre, K. M. (1978). Self-disclosure and romantic attraction. *Journal of Social Psychology, 106,* 127–128.

Critelli, J. W., & Waid, L. R. (1980). Physical attractiveness, romantic love and equity restoration in dating relationships. *Journal of Personality Assessment, 44,* 624–629.

Crocker, J., & Major, B. (1989). Social stigma and self-esteem: The self-protective properties of stigma. *Psychological Review, 96,* 608–630.

Crockett, L., Losoff, M., & Peterson, A. C. (1984). Perception of the peer group and friendship in early adolescence. *Journal of Early Adolescence, 4,* 155–181.

Croog, S. H., & Levine, S. (1977). *The heart patient recovers: Social and psychological factors.* New York: Human Science Press.

Csikszentmihalyi, M., & Larson, R. (1984). *Being adolescent: Conflict and growth in the teenage years.* New York: Basic.

Csikszentmihalyi, M., Larson, R., & Prescott, S. (1977). The ecology of adolescent activity and experience. *Journal of Youth and Adolescence, 6,* 281–294.

Cunningham, J. D., & Antill, J. K. (1981). Love in developing romantic relationships. In S. W.

Duck & R. Gilmour (Eds.), *Personal relationships, 2: Developing personal relationships* (pp. 27–51). New York: Academic.

Cunningham, M. R., Roberts, A. R., Barbee, A. P., Druen, P. B., & Wu, C. H. (1995). "Their ideas of beauty are, on the whole, the same as ours": Consistency and variability in the cross-cultural perception of female physical attractiveness. *Journal of Personality and Social Psychology, 68,* 261–279.

Cutrona, C. E. (1982). Transition to college: Loneliness and the process of social adjustment. In L. A. Peplau & D. Perlman (Eds.), *Loneliness: A sourcebook of theory, research and therapy* (pp. 291–309). New York: Wiley.

Cutrona, C. E., Suhr, J. A., & MacFarline, R. (1990). Interpersonal transactions and the psychological sense of support. In S. Duck (Ed.), *Personal relationships and social support.* Newbury Park, CA: Sage.

Daly, M., & Wilson, M. (1988). *Homicide.* New York: Aldine de Gruyter.

Daly, M., Wilson, M., & Weghorst, S. J. (1982). Male sexual jealousy. *Ethology and Sociobiology, 3,* 11–27.

Darwin, C. (1859). *The origin of species by means of natural selection or the preservation of favoured races in the struggle for life.* London: John Murray.

Darwin, C. (1871/1981). *The descent of man, and selection in relation to sex* (Vol 2). Princeton, NJ: Princeton University Press.

Davidson, A. G. (1991). Looking for love in the age of AIDS: The language of gay personals, 1978–1988. *Journal of Sex Research, 28,* 125–137.

Davidson, S., & Packard, T. (1981). The therapeutic value of friendship between women. *Psychology of Women Quarterly, 5,* 495–510.

Davis, J. M., & Franzoi, S. L. (1986). Adolescent loneliness, self-disclosure and private self-consciousness: A longitudinal investigation. *Journal of Personality and Social Psychology, 51,* 595–608.

Davis, K. E., & Latty-Mann, H. (1987). Love styles and relationship quality: A contribution to validation. *Journal of Social and Personal Relationships, 4,* 409–428.

Davis, K. E., & Roberts, M. K. (1985). Relationships in the real world: The descriptive approach to personal relationships. In K. J. Gergen & K. E. Davis (Eds.), *The social construction of the person.* New York: Springer-Verlag.

Davis, K. E., & Todd, M. J. (1982). Friendship and love relationships. In K. E. Davis (Ed.), *Advances in descriptive psychology, 2,* 79–122. Greenwich, CT: JAI Press.

Davis, K. E., & Todd, M. J. (1985). Assessing friendship: Prototypes, paradigm cases and relationship description. In S. W. Duck & D. Perlman (Eds.), *Understanding personal relationships: An interdisciplinary approach* (pp. 17–38). London: Sage.

De Jong-Gierveld, J. (1986a). Loneliness and the degree of intimacy in personal relationships. In R. Gilmour & S. W. Duck (Eds.), *The emerging field of personal relationships* (pp. 241–249). Hillsdale, NJ: Erlbaum.

De Jong-Gierveld, J. (1986b). Men and loneliness. In R. Lewis & R. E. Salt (Eds.), *Men in families.* Newbury Park, CA: Sage.

De Jong-Gierveld, J., & Raadschelders, I. (1982). Types of loneliness. In L. A. Peplau & D. Perlman (Eds.), *Loneliness: A sourcebook of theory, research and therapy.* New York: Wiley.

Denfeld, D. (1974). Dropouts from swinging: The marriage counselor or informant. In J. P. Smith & L. G. Smith (Eds.), *Beyond monogamy* (pp. 260–267). Baltimore: Johns Hopkins University Press.

Derlega, V. J., Hendrick, S. S., Winstead, B. A., & Berg, J. H. (1991). *Psychotherapy as a personal relationship.* New York: Guilford.

Derlega, V. J., & Margulis, S. T. (1982). Why loneliness occurs: The interrelationship of social-psychological and privacy concepts. In L. A. Peplau & D. Perlman (Eds.), *Loneliness: A sourcebook of theory, research, and therapy.* New York: Wiley.

Derlega, V. J., Margulis, S. T., & Winstead, B. A. (1987). A social-psychological analysis of self-disclosure in psychotherapy. *Journal of Social and Clinical Psychology, 5,* 205–215.

Derlega, V. J., Wilson, M., & Chaikin, A. L. (1976). Friendship and disclosure reciprocity. *Journal of Personality and Social Psychology, 34,* 578–582.

Derlega, V. J., Winstead, B. A., Wong, P. T. P., & Hunter, S. (1985). Gender effects in an initial encounter: A case where men exceed women in disclosure. *Journal of Social and Personal Relationships, 2,* 25–44.

Dermer, M., & Pyszczynski, T. A. (1978). Effects of erotica upon men's loving and liking responses to women they love. *Journal of Personality and Social Psychology, 36,* 1302–1309.

Dermer, M., & Thiel, D. L. (1975). When beauty may fail. *Journal of Personality and Social Psychology, 31,* 1168–1176.

DeSteno, D. A., & Salovey, P. (1996). Jealousy and the characteristics of one's rival: A self-evaluation maintenance perspective. *Personality and Social Psychology Bulletin, 22,* 920–932.

de Waal, F. B. M. (1982). *Chimpanzee politics: Power and sex among apes.* New York: Harper & Row.

de Waal, F. B. M. (1989). *Peacemaking among primates.* Cambridge, MA: Harvard University Press.

de Waal, F. B. M. (1993). Reconciliation among primates: A review of empirical evidence and unresolved issues. In W. A. Mason & S. P. Mendoza (Eds.), *Primate social conflict.* Albany, NY: State University of New York Press.

de Waal, F. B. M., & van Roosmalen, A. (1979). Reconciliation and consolation among chimpanzees. *Behavioral Ecology and Sociobiology, 5,* 55–66.

Diener, E., Wolsic, B., & Fujita, F. (1995). Physical attractiveness and subjective well-being. *Journal of Personality and Social Psychology, 69,* 120–129.

Dion, K. K. (1972). Physical attractiveness and evaluations of children's transgressions. *Journal of Personality and Social Psychology, 24,* 207–213.

Dion, K. K. (1973). Young children's stereotyping of facial attractiveness. *Developmental Psychology, 9,* 183–188.

Dion, K. K. (1974). Children's physical attractiveness and sex as determinants of adult punitiveness. *Developmental Psychology 10,* 772–778.

Dion, K. K. (1977). The incentive value of physical attractiveness for children. *Personality and Social Psychology Bulletin, 3,* 67–70.

Dion K. K., & Berscheid, E. (1974). Physical attractiveness and peer perception among children. *Sociometry, 37,* 1–12.

Dion, K. K., Berscheid, E., & Walster, E. (1972). What is beautiful is good. *Journal of Personality and Social Psychology, 24,* 285–290.

Dion, K. L., & Dion, K. K. (1973). Correlates of romantic love. *Journal of Consulting and Clinical Psychology, 41,* 51–56.

Dion, K. L., & Dion, K. K. (1976). Love, liking and trust in heterosexual relationships. *Personality and Social Psychology Bulletin, 2,* 187–190.

Dion, K. L., & Dion, K. K. (1988). Romantic love: Individual and cultural perspectives. In R. J. Sternberg & M. L. Barnes (Eds.), *The psychology of love.* New Haven, CT: Yale University Press.

Dipboye, R. L., Fromkin, H. L., & Wiback, K. (1975). Relative importance of applicant sex, attractiveness and scholastic standing in evaluation of job applicant resumes. *Journal of Applied Psychology, 60,* 39–43.

Dishion, T. J. (1990a). The family ecology of boys' peer relations in middle childhood. *Child Development, 61,* 874–892.

Dishion, T. J. (1990b). The peer context of troublesome child and adolescent behavior. In P. Leone (Ed.), *Understanding troubled and troublesome youth.* Newbury Park, CA: Sage.

DiTommaso, E., & Spinner, B. (1993). The development and initial validation of the Social and Emotional Loneliness Scale for Adults (SELSA). *Personality and Individual Differences, 14,* 127–134.

DiTommaso, E., & Spinner, B. (1997). Social and emotional loneliness: A re-examination of Weiss' typology of loneliness. *Personality and Individual Differences, 22,* 417–427.

Dobash, R. E., & Dobash, R. P. (1980). *Violence against wives: A case against the patriarchy.* London: Open Books.

Dorner, S. (1973). Psychological and social problems of families of adolescent spina bifida patients: A preliminary report. *Developmental Medicine and Child Neurology, 15 (suppl. 29),* 24–26.

Dorner, S. (1977). Sexual interests and activity in adolescents with spina bifida. *Journal of Child Psychology and Psychiatry, 18,* 229–237.

Douglas, J. W. B. (1975). Early hospitalization and later disturbances of behavior. *Developmental Medicine and Child Neurology, 17,* 456–480.

Douglas, W. (1987). Affinity testing in initial interaction. *Journal of Social and Personal Relationships, 4,* 3–15.

Doundna, D., & McBride, F. (1981). Where are the men for the women at the top? In P. J. Stein (Ed.), *Single life: Unmarried adults in social context.* New York: St. Martin's.

Douvan, E., & Adelson, J. (1966). *The adolescent experience.* New York: Wiley.

Downs, A. C., & Lyons, P. M. (1991). Natural observations of the links between attractiveness and initial legal judgments. *Personality and Social Psychology Bulletin, 17,* 541–547.

Drigotas, S. M., & Rusbult, C. E. (1992). Should I stay or should I go? *Journal of Personality and Social Psychology, 62,* 62–87.

Dubbert, P. M., & Wilson, G. T. (1984). Goal-setting and spouse involvement in the treatment of obesity. *Behavior Research and Therapy, 22,* 227–242.

Duck, S. W. (1975). Personality similarity and friendship choices by adolescents. *European Journal of Social Psychology, 5,* 351–365.

Duck, S. W. (1977). *The study of acquaintance.* Farnsborough, UK: Gower Press.

Duck, S. W. (1991). *Understanding relationships.* New York: Guilford.

Duck, S. W. (1994). *Meaningful relationships.* Thousand Oaks, CA: Sage.

Duck, S. W., & Allison, D. (1978), I liked you but I can't live with you: A study of lapsed friendships. *Social Behavior and Personality, 6,* 43–47.

Duck, S. W., & Barnes, M. K. (1992). Disagreeing about agreement: Reconciling differences about similarity. *Communication Monographs, 59,* 199–208.

Duck, S. W., Pond, K., & Leatham, G. (1994). Loneliness and the evaluation of relational events. *Journal of Social and Personal Relationships, 11,* 253–276.

Duck, S. W., & Sants, H. (1983). On the origins of the specious: Are personal relationships really interpersonal states? *Journal of Social and Clinical Psychology, 1,* 27–41.

Duffy, S., & Rusbult, C. E. (1986). Satisfaction and commitment in homosexual and heterosexual relationships. *Journal of Homosexuality, 12,* 1–23.

Dunn, J. (1983). Sibling relationships in early childhood. *Child Development, 54,* 787–811.

Dunn, J. (1984). Sibling studies and the developmental impact of critical incidents. In P. B. Baltes & O. G. Brim (Eds.), *Life-span development and behavior* (Vol. 6). New York: Academic.

Dunn, J. (1993). *Young children's close relationships, Beyond attachment.* Newbury Park, CA: Sage.

Dunn, J., & Kendrick, C. (1982). *Siblings: Love envy and understanding.* Cambridge, MA: Harvard University Press.

Dunn, S. E., Putallaz, M., Sheppard, B. H., & Lindstrom, R. (1987). Social support and adjustment in gifted adolescents. *Journal of Educational Psychology, 79,* 467–473.

Dunphy, D. C. (1963). The social structure of urban adolescent peer groups. *Sociometry, 26,* 230–246.

Dush, D. M., Hirt, M. L., & Schroeder, H. E. (1989). Self statement modification in the treatment of child behavior disorders: A meta-analysis. *Psychological Bulletin, 106,* 97–106.

Eagly, A. H., Ashmore, R. D., Makhijani, M. G., & Longo, L. C. (1991). What is beautiful is good, but . . . : A meta-analytic review of research on the physical attractiveness stereotype. *Psychological Bulletin, 110,* 109–128.

Eaton, J. W., & Weil, R. J. (1953). The mental health of the Hutterites. *Scientific American, 189,* 31–37.

Eaton, J. W., & Weil, R. J. (1955). *Culture and mental disorders.* Glencoe, IL: Free Press.

Eckert, P. (1989). *Jocks and burnouts: Social categories and identity in high school.* New York: Teachers College Press.

Eder, D. (1985). The cycle of popularity: Interpersonal relations among female adolescents. *Sociology of Education, 58,* 154–165.

Eder, D., & Hallinan, M. T. (1978). Sex differences in children's friendships. *American Sociological Review 43,* 237–250.

Eder, D., & Sanford, S. (1986). The development and maintenance of interactional norms among early adolescents. In P. Adler, (Ed.), *Sociological studies of child development* (Vol. 1, pp. 283–300). Greenwich, CT: JAI Press.

Edgerton, R. G. (1967). The cloak of competence: Stigma in the lives of the mentally retarded. Berkeley, CA: University of California Press.

Efran, M. G. (1974). The effect of physical appearance on the judgment of guilt, interpersonal attraction and severity of recommended punishment in a simulated jury test. *Journal of Research in Personality, 8,* 45–54.

Eggert, L. L., & Parks, M. R. (1987). Communication network involvement in adolescents' friendships and romantic relationships. In M. L. McLaughlin (Ed.), *Communication yearbook, 10.* Beverly Hills, CA: Sage.

Eibl-Eibesfeldt, I. (1979). *The biology of peace and war.* New York: Viking.

Eidelson, R. J. (1983). Affiliation and independence issues in marriage. *Journal of Marriage and the Family, 45,* 683–688.

Ekman, P. (1992). An argument for basic emotions. *Cognition and Emotion, 6,* 169–200.

Elder, G. H. (1969). Appearance and education in marriage mobility. *American Sociological Review, 34,* 519–533.

Elder, G. H., & Clipp, E. C. (1988). Wartime losses and social bonding: Influences across 40 years in men's lives. *Psychiatry, 51,* 177–198.

El Ghatit, A., & Hanson, R. (1976). Marriage and divorce after spinal cord injury. *Archives of Physical and Medical Rehabilitation, 57,* 470–472.

Elkins, L. E., & Peterson, C. (1993). Gender differences in best friendships. *Sex Roles, 29,* 497–508.

Elliott, T. R., Witty, T. E., Herrick, S., & Hoffman, J. T. (1991). Negotiating reality after physical loss: Hope, depression, and disability. *Journal of Personality and Social Psychology, 61,* 608–613.

Ellsworth, P. C. (1991). Some implications of cognitive appraisal theories of emotion. In K. T. Strongman (Ed.), *International review of studies on emotion* (Vol. 1). New York: Wiley.

Emery, R. E. (1988). *Marriage, divorce, and children's adjustment.* Newbury Park, CA: Sage.

Epstein, J. L. (1983a). Examining theories of adolescent friendship. In J. L. Epstein & N. L. Karweit (Eds.), *Friends in school: Patterns of selection and influence in secondary schools* (pp. 39–61). New York: Academic.

Epstein, J. L. (1983b). Selection of friends in differently organized schools and classrooms. In J. L. Epstein & N. L. Karweit (Eds.), *Friends in school: Patterns of selection and influence in secondary schools* (pp. 73–92). New York: Academic.

Epstein, J. L. (1986). Friendship selection: Developmental and environmental influences. In R. C. Mueller & C. R. Cooper (Eds.), *Process and outcome in peer relationships* (pp. 129–160). New York: Academic.

Epstein, J. L. (1989). The selection of friends: Changes across the grades and in different school environments. In T. J. Berndt & G. W. Ladd (Eds.), *Peer relationships in childhood* (pp. 158–187). New York: Wiley.

Escudero, V., Rogers, L. E., & Gutierrez, E. (1997). Patterns of relational control and nonverbal affect in clinic and nonclinic couples. *Journal of Social and Personal Relationships, 14,* 5–29.

Etkin, W. (1967). *Social behavior from fish to man.* Chicago: University of Chicago Press.

Eysenck, H. J. (1952). The effects of psychotherapy: An evaluation. *Journal of Consulting Psychology, 16,* 319–324.

Falbo, T., Hazen, M. D., & Linimon, D. (1982). The costs of selecting power bases associated with the opposite sex. *Sex Roles, 8,* 147–158.

Falbo, T., & Peplau, L. A. (1980). Power strategies in intimate relationships. *Journal of Personality and Social Psychology, 38,* 618–628.

Farberow, N. L. (1974). *Suicide.* Morristown, NJ: General Learning Press.

Farina, A., Allen, J. G., & Saul, B. B. B. (1968). The role of the stigmatized person in affecting social relationships. *The Journal of Personality, 36,* 169–182.

Farr, W. (1858/1975). Influence of marriage on the mortality of the French people. In N. Humphreys, *Vital statistics: A memorial volume of selections from reports and writings of William Farr.* New York: Methuen.

Feeney, J., & Noller, P. (1990). Attachment style as a predictor of adult romantic relationships. *Journal of Personality and Social Psychology, 58,* 281–291.

Feeney, J., & Noller, P. (1996). *Adult attachment.* Thousand Oaks, CA: Sage.

Fehr, B. (1988). Prototype analysis of the concepts of love and commitment. *Journal of Personality and Social Psychology, 55,* 557–579.

Fehr, B. (1993). How do I love thee? Let me consult my prototype. In S. Duck (Ed.), *Individuals in relationships.* Newbury Park, CA: Sage.

Fehr, B. (1996). *Friendship processes.* Thousand Oaks, CA: Sage.

Fehr, B., & Russell, J. A. (1984). Concept of emotion viewed from a prototype perspective. *Journal of Experimental Psychology: General, 113,* 464–486.

Feingold, A. (1988). Matching for attractiveness in romantic partners and same-sex friends: A meta-analysis and theoretical critique. *Psychological Bulletin, 104,* 226–235.

Feingold, A. (1990). Gender differences in the effects of physical attractiveness on romantic attraction: A comparison across five research paradigms. *Journal of Personality and Social Psychology, 59,* 981–993.

Feld, S. L. (1984). The structured use of personal associates. *Social Forces, 62,* 640–652.

Felice, A. (1977). Status of Harijan students in colleges. *Indian Journal of Social Work, 38,* 15–25.

Felmlee, D. (1994). Who's on top? Power in romantic relationships. *Sex Roles, 31,* 275–295.

Felmlee, D., Sprecher, S., & Bassin, E. (1990). The dissolution of intimate relationships: A hazards model. *Social Psychology Quarterly, 53,* 13–30.

Ferraro, K. F., Mutran, E., & Barresi, C. M. (1984). Widowhood, health and friendship support in later life. *Journal of Health and Social Behavior, 25,* 246–259.

Festinger, L. (1954). A theory of social comparison processes. *Human Relations, 7,* 117–140.

Festinger, L. (1957). *A theory of cognitive dissonance.* Stanford, CA: Stanford University Press.

Festinger, L., Schachter, S., & Back, K. (1950). *Social pressures in informal groups: A study of human factors in housing.* New York: Harper.

Filsinger, E. E., & Thomas, S. J. (1988). Behavioral antecedents of relationship stability and adjustment: A five-year longitudinal study. *Journal of Marriage and the Family, 50,* 785–795.

Fincham, F. D., Beach, S., & Baucom, D. (1987). Attribution processes in distressed and nondistressed couples: IV. Self-partner attribution differences. *Journal of Personality and Social Psychology, 52,* 739–748.

Fincham, F. D., Beach, S., & Nelson, G. (1987). Attribution processes in distressed and nondistressed couples: III. Causal and responsibility attributions for spouse behavior. *Cognitive Therapy and Research, 11,* 71–86.

Fine, G. A. (1980). The natural history of preadolescent male friendship groups. In H. C. Foot,

A. J. Chapman, & J. R. Smith (Eds.), *Friendship and social relations in children.* New York: Wiley.

Fine, G. A. (1986). Friendship in the workplace. In V. J. Derlega & B. A. Winstead (Eds.), *Friendship and social interaction.* New York: Springer-Verlag.

Fischer, C. S., & Oliker, S. J. (1983). A research note on friendship, gender and the life cycle. *Social Forces, 62,* 124–133.

Fischer, C. S., & Philips, S. L. (1982). Who is alone? Social characteristics of people with small networks. In L. A. Peplau & D. Perlman (Eds.), *Loneliness: A sourcebook of current theory, research and therapy.* New York: Wiley.

Fisher, B., & Galler, R. (1988). Friendship and fairness: How disability affects friendships. In M. Fine & A. Asch (Eds.). *Women with disabilities: Essays in psychology, culture and politics* (pp. 172–194). Philadelphia: Temple University Press.

Fisher, J. D., & Nadler, A. (1974). The effect of similarity between donor and recipient on reactions to aid. *Journal of Applied Social Psychology, 4,* 230–243.

Folkes, V. S. (1982). Forming relationships and the matching hypothesis. *Personality and Social Psychology Bulletin, 8,* 631–636.

Folkes, V. S., & Sears, D. O. (1977). Does everybody like a liker? *Journal of Experimental Social Psychology, 13,* 505–519.

Foot, H. C., Chapman, A. J., & Smith, J. R. (1977). Friendship and social responsiveness in boys and girls. *Journal of Personality and Social Psychology, 35,* 401–411.

Force, D. G. (1956). Social status of physically handicapped children. *Exceptional Children, 23,* 104–107.

Ford, C. S., & Beach, F. A. (1951). *Patterns of sexual behavior.* New York: Harper & Row.

Fordham, S., & Ogbu, J. U. (1986). Black students' school success: Coping with the burden of "acting white." *Urban Review, 18,* 176–206.

Forgas, J. P. (1993). On making sense of odd couples: Mood effects on the perception of mismatched relationships. *Personality and Social Psychology Bulletin, 19,* 59–70.

Foster, B. T. (1976). Friendship in rural Thailand. *Ethnology, 15,* 251–267.

Francis, J. L. (1977). Toward the management of heterosexual jealousy. *Journal of Marriage and Family Counseling, 10,* 61–69.

Franzoi, S. I., & Davis, M. H. (1985). Adolescent self-disclosure and loneliness: Private self-consciousness and parental influence. *Journal of Personality and Social Psychology, 48,* 768–780.

Franzoi, S. I., Davis, M. H., & Vasques-Suson, K. A. (1994). Two social worlds: Social correlates and stability of adolescent status groups. *Journal of Personality and Social Psychology, 67,* 462–473.

Freedman, J. (1978). *Happy people: What happiness is, who has it, and why.* New York: Harcourt Brace Jovanovich.

Freeman, H. E. (1961). Attitudes toward mental illness among relatives of former patients. *American Sociological Review, 26,* 59–66.

Freeman, H. E., & Kassebaum, G. G. (1956). The illiterate in American society: Some general hypotheses. *Social Forces, 34,* 371–375.

French, J. R. P., Jr., & Raven, B. H. (1959). The bases of social power. In D. Cartwright (Ed.), *Studies in social power* (pp. 150–167). Ann Arbor, MI: University of Michigan Press.

French, R. D. (1984). The long-term relationships of marked people. In E. E. Jones, A. Farina, A. H. Hastorf, H. Markus, D. T. Miller, & R. A. Scott (Eds.), *Social stigma: The psychology of marked relationships.* New York: W. H. Freeman.

Frieze, I. H., & McHugh, M. C. (1992). Power and influence strategies in violent and nonviolent marriages. *Psychology of Women Quarterly, 16,* 449–465.

Frieze, I. H., Parson, J. E., Johnson, P. B., Ruble, D. N., & Zellman, G. L. (1978). *Women and sex roles.* New York: Norton.

Fromm, E. (1956). *The art of loving.* New York: Harper.

Fromm-Reichman, F. (1959). Loneliness. *Psychiatry, 22,* 1–15.

Fuchs, V. R. (1974). *Who shall live? Health, economics and social choice.* New York: Basic.

Funk, C. E. (1950). *Thereby hangs a tale.* New York: Harper & Row.

Furman, W., & Bierman, K. L. (1983). Developmental changes in young children's conception of friendship. *Child Development, 54,* 549–556.

Furman, W., & Bierman, K. L. (1984). Children's conceptions of friendship: A multi-method study of developmental changes. *Developmental Psychology, 20,* 925–931.

Furman, W., & Buhrmester, D. (1985a). Children's perceptions of personal relationships in their social networks. *Developmental Psychology 21,* 1016–1024.

Furman, W., & Buhrmester, D. (1985b). Children's perceptions of the qualities of sibling relationships. *Child Development, 56,* 448–461.

Furman, W., & Buhrmester, D. (1992). Age and sex differences in perceptions of networks of personal relationships. *Child Development, 63,* 103–115.

Furman, W., & Robbins, P. (1985). What's the point? Issues in the selection of treatment objectives. In B. H. Schneider, K. Rubin, & J. E. Ledingham (Eds.), *Children's peer relations: Issues in assessment and intervention* (pp. 141–154). New York: Springer-Verlag.

Gaines, S. O. (1994). Exchange and respect denying behaviors among male-female friendships. *Journal of Social and Personal Relationships, 11,* 5–24.

Gallup poll. (1987, October 23). As cited in Hereck, G. H., & Glunt, E. K. (1988). An epidemic of stigma: Public reactions to AIDS. *American Psychologist, 43,* 886–891.

Ganong, L. H., Coleman, M., & Mapes, D. (1990). A meta-analytic review of family structure stereotypes. *Journal of Marriage and the Family, 52,* 287–297.

Garcia, S., Stinson, L., Ickes, W., Bissonette, V., & Briggs, S. R. (1991). Shyness and physical attractiveness in mixed-sex dyads. *Journal of Personality and Social Psychology, 61,* 35–49.

Gayford, J. J. (1975). Wife battering: a preliminary survey of 100 cases. *British Medical Journal, 1,* 194–197.

Gayford, J. J. (1979). Battered wives. *British Journal of Hospital Medicine, 22,* 496–503.

Gelso, C. J., & Carter, J. A. (1985). The relationship in counseling and psychotherapy: Components, consequences, and theoretical antecedents. *The Counseling Psychologist, 13,* 155–243.

Gerson, A. C. (1978, August). Loneliness and the social influence process. In D. Perlman (Chair), *Toward a psychology of loneliness.* Symposium presented at the annual meeting of the American Psychological Association, Toronto, Canada, as cited in Jones, W. H., Loneliness and social behavior (1982).

Gerson, A. C., & Perlman, D. (1979). Loneliness and expressive communication. *Journal of Abnormal Psychology, 88,* 258–266.

Gibbons, F. X. (1981). The social psychology of mental retardation: What's in a label? In S. S. Brehm, S. M. Kassin, & F. X. Gibbons, (Eds.), *Developmental social psychology: Theory and research* (pp. 249–270). New York: Oxford University Press.

Gibbons, F. X. (1986). Stigma and interpersonal relationships. In S. C. Ainlay, G. Becker, & L. M. Coleman (Eds.), *The dilemma of difference* (pp. 123–256). New York: Plenum.

Gilbert, L. A. (1985). *Men in dual-career families: Current realities and future prospects.* Hillsdale, NJ: Erlbaum.

Gilbert, L. A. (1993). *Two careers/one family: The promise of gender equality.* Beverly Hills, CA: Sage.

Gillen, B. (1981). Physical attractiveness: A determinant of two types of goodness. *Personality and Social Psychology Bulletin, 7,* 277–281.

Gilmartin, B. G. (1977). Jealousy among the swingers. In G. Clanton & L. G. Smith (Eds.), *Jealousy* (pp. 152–158). Lanham, MD: University Press of America.

Gilmore, D. D. (1975). Friendship in Fuenmayer. *Ethnology, 14,* 311–324.

Gilmore, D. D. (1990). *Manhood in the making: Cultural concepts of masculinity.* New Haven, CT: Yale University Press.

Gilmore, D. D. (1991). Commodity, comity, community: Male exchange in rural Andalusia. *Ethnology, 30,* 17–30.

Ginsberg, D., & Gottman, J. M. (1986). Conversations of college roommates: Similarities and differences in male and female friendships. In J. M. Gottman & J. Parker (Eds.), *Conversations of friends: Speculations on affective development.* New York: Cambridge University Press.

Gleitman, H. (1991). *Psychology* (3rd Ed.). New York: Norton.

Glenn, N. D., & Weaver, C. N. (1988). The changing relationship of marital status to reported happiness. *Journal of Marriage and the Family, 50,* 317–324.

Glick, I. O., Weiss, R. S., & Parkes, C. M. (1974). *The first year of bereavement.* New York: Wiley.

Glover, E. (1955). *The technique of psychoanalysis.* New York: International Universities Press.

Goffman, E. (1959). *The presentation of self in everyday life.* Garden City, NY: Doubleday.

Goffman, E. (1963). *Stigma: Notes on the management of spoiled identity.* Englewood Cliffs, NJ: Prentice-Hall.

Goldberg, R. T. (1974a). Adjustment of children with invisible and visible handicaps: Congenital heart disease and facial burns. *Journal of Counseling Psychology, 21,* 428–432.

Goldberg, R. T. (1974b). Rehabilitation of the burn patient. *Rehabilitation Literature, 35,* 73–78.

Goldfarb, W. (1947). Variations in adolescent adjustment of institutionally reared children. *American Journal of Orthopsychiatry, 17,* 449–457.

Goldstein, L. D., & Russell, S. W. (1977). Self-disclosure: A comparative study of reports by self and others. *Journal of Counseling Psychology, 24,* 365–369.

Gomes-Schwartz, B. (1978). Effective ingredients in psychotherapy: Prediction of outcome from process variables. *Journal of Consulting and Clinical Psychology, 46,* 1023–1035.

Gomes-Schwartz, B., & Schwartz, J. M. (1978). Psychotherapy process variables distinguishing the "inherently helpful" person from the professional psychotherapist. *Journal of Consulting and Clinical Psychology, 46,* 196–197.

Goodall, J. (1986a). *The chimpanzees of Gombe: Patterns of behavior.* Cambridge, MA: Belknap Press.

Goodall, J. (1986b). Social rejection, exclusion and shunning among the Gombe chimpanzees. *Ethology and Sociobiology, 7,* 227–236.

Goodall, J. (1990). *Through a window: My thirty years with the chimpanzees of Gombe.* Boston: Houghton Mifflin.

Goode, W. J. (1959). The theoretical importance of love. *American Sociological Review, 24,* 38–47.

Goodnow, J. J., & Burns, A. (1988). *Home and school: A child's eye view.* Sydney, Australia: Allen & Unwin.

Goodwin, R. (1990). Sex differences among partner preferences: Are the sexes really very similar? *Sex Roles, 23,* 501–513.

Gordon, S. (1976). *Lonely in America.* New York: Simon & Schuster.

Gorer, G. D. (1965). *Death, grief and mourning.* New York: Doubleday.

Gottlieb, J. (1975). Attitudes toward retarded children: Effects of labeling and behavioral aggressiveness. *Journal of Educational Psychology, 67,* 581–585.

Gottman, J. M. (1979). *Marital interaction: Experimental investigations.* New York: Academic.

Gottman, J. M. (1983). How children become friends. *Monographs of the Society for Research in Child Development, 48* (3, Serial No. 201).

Gottman, J. M. (1994a). *What predicts divorce? The relationship between marital processes and marital outcomes.* Hillsdale, NJ: Erlbaum.

Gottman, J. M. (1994b). *Why marriages succeed or fail.* New York: Simon & Schuster.

Gottman, J. M., & Krokoff, L. J. (1989). Marital interaction and satisfaction: A longitudinal view. *Journal of Consulting and Clinical Psychology, 57,* 47–52.

Gouldner, A. W. (1960). The norm of reciprocity: A preliminary statement. *American Sociological Review, 25,* 161–178.

Gouldner, H., & Strong, M. S. (1987). *Speaking of friendship: Middle-class women and their friends.* New York: Greenwood.

Gouldsbury, C., & Sheane, H. (1911). *The great plateau of northern Rhodesia.* London: Edward Arnold.

Gove, W. R. (1972). The relationship between sex roles, marital roles and mental illness. *Social Forces, 51,* 34–44.

Gray-Little, B., & Burks, N. (1983). Power and satisfaction in marriage: A review and critique. *Psychological Bulletin, 93,* 513–538.

Green, R. G., & Sporakowski, M. J. (1983). The dynamics of divorce: Marital quality, alternative attraction, and external pressure. *Journal of Divorce, 7,* 77–88.

Green, S. K., Buchanan, D. R., & Heuer, S. K. (1984). Winners, losers and choosers: A field investigation of dating initiation. *Personality and Social Psychology Bulletin, 10,* 502–511.

Greenson, R. R. (1967). *The technique and practice of psychoanalysis* (Vol. 1). New York: International Universities Press.

Greer, D. S., Mor, V., & Sherwood, S., et al. (1983). National Hospice Study analysis plan. *Journal of Chronic Diseases, 36,* 737–780.

Grove, W. R., & Geerken, M. R. (1977). The effect of children and employment on the mental health of married men and women. *Social Forces, 56,* 66–76.

Gubrium, J. F. (1974). Marital desolation and the evaluation of everyday life in old age. *Journal of Marriage and the Family, 36,* 107–113.

Guerrero, L. K., & Eloy, S. V. (1992). Relational satisfaction and jealousy across marital types. *Communication Reports, 5,* 23–41.

Guerrero, L. K., Eloy, S. V., Jogensen, P. F., & Anderson, P. A. (1993). Hers or his? Sex differences in the experience and communication of jealousy in close relationships. In P. J. Kalbfleisch (Ed.), *Interpersonal communication: Evolving interpersonal relationships.* Hillsdale, NJ: Erlbaum.

Gupta, U., & Singh, P. (1982). Exploratory studies in love and liking and types of marriages. *Indian Journal of Applied Psychology, 19,* 92–97.

Haefner, P. T., Notarius, C. I., & Pellegrini, D. S. (1991). Determinants of satisfaction with marital discussions: An exploration of husband-wife differences. *Behavioral Assessment, 13,* 67–82.

Hallinan, M. T., & Kubitschek, W. N. (1990). Sex and race effects of the response to interactive sentiment relations. *Social Psychology Quarterly, 53,* 252–263.

Hallinan, M. T., & Williams, R. A. (1983). Interracial friendship choices in secondary schools. *American Sociological Review, 54,* 67–78.

Hamilton, W. D. (1964). The evolution of social behavior. *Journal of Theoretical Biology, 7,* 1–52.

Hamilton, W. D. (1971). Geometry for the selfish herd. *Journal of Theoretical Biology, 31,* 295–311.

Hanley-Dunn, P., Maxwell, S. E., & Santos, J. F.

(1985). Interpretation of interpersonal interactions: The influence of loneliness. *Personality and Social Psychology Bulletin, 11,* 445–456.

Hansen, G. L. (1983). Marital satisfaction and jealousy among men. *Psychological Reports, 52,* 363–366.

Harlow, H. F. (1959). Love in infant monkeys. *Scientific American, 200,* 68–74.

Harlow, H. F. (1971). *Learning to love.* San Francisco: Albion.

Harlow, H. F., & Harlow, M. K. (1969). Effects of various mother-infant relationships on rhesus monkey behaviors. In B. M. Foss (Ed.), *Determinants of infant behavior* (Vol. 4). London: Methuen.

Harlow, H. F., Harlow, M. K., & Hansen, E. W. (1963). The maternal affectional system of rhesus monkeys. In H. L. Rheingold (Ed.), *Maternal behavior in mammals.* New York: Wiley.

Harris, M. B. (1990). Is love seen as different for the obese? *Journal of Applied Social Psychology, 20,* 1209–1224.

Harrison, A. A., & Saeed, L. (1977). Let's make a deal: An analysis of revelations and stipulations in lonely hearts advertisements. *Journal of Personality and Social Psychology, 35,* 257–264.

Hartup, W. W. (1983). Peer relations. In E. M. Hetherington (Ed.), & P. H. Mussen (Series Ed.), *Handbook of child psychology* (4th ed., Vol. 4). New York: Wiley.

Hartup, W. W. (1993). Adolescents and their friends. In B. Laursen (Ed.), *Close friendships in adolescence.* San Francisco: Jossey-Bass.

Harvey, J. H., Flanary, R., & Morgan, M. (1986). Vivid memories of vivid loves gone by. *Journal of Social and Personal Relationships, 3,* 359–373.

Harvey, J. H., & Omarzu, J. (1997). Minding the close relationship. *Personality and Social Psychology Review, 1,* 224–240.

Hastorf, A. H., Northcraft, G., & Picciotto, S. (1979). Helping the handicapped: How realistic is the performance feedback received by the physically handicapped? *Personality and Social Psychology Bulletin, 5,* 373–376.

Hatfield, E. (1988). Passionate and companionate love. In R. J. Sternberg & M. L. Barnes (Eds.), *The psychology of love.* New Haven, CT: Yale University Press.

Hatfield, E., & Rapson, R. L. (1987). Passionate love: New directions in research. In W. H. Jones & D. Perlman (Eds.), *Advances in personal relationships* (Vol. 1, pp. 109–139). Greenwich, CT: JAI Press.

Hatfield, E., & Sprecher, S. (1986a). Measuring passionate love in intimate relationships. *Journal of Adolescence, 9,* 383–410.

Hatfield, E., & Sprecher, S. (1986b). *Mirror, mirror . . . The importance of looks in everyday life.* Albany, NY: State University of New York Press.

Hatfield, E., Traupmann, J., Sprecher, S., Utne, M., & Hay, J. (1985). Equity and intimate relations: Recent research. In W. Ickes (Ed.), *Compatible and incompatible relationships* (pp. 91–118). New York: Springer-Verlag.

Hatfield, E., Traupmann, J., & Walster, G. W. (1979). Equity and extramarital sex. In M. Cook & G. Wilson (Eds.), *Love and attraction.* New York: Pergamon.

Hattie, J. A., Sharley, C. F., & Rogers, H. F. (1984). Comparative effectiveness of professional and paraprofessional helpers. *Psychological Bulletin, 95,* 534–541.

Hause, K. S. (1995). *Friendship after marriage: Can it ever be the same?* Paper presented at the conference of the International Network on Personal Relationships, College of William & Mary, Williamsburg, Virginia.

Hays, R. B. (1984). The development and maintenance of friendship. *Journal of Social and Personal Relationships, 1,* 75–98.

Hays, R. B. (1985). A longitudinal study of friendship development. *Journal of Personality and Social Psychology, 48,* 909–924.

Hays, R. B. (1988). Friendship. In S. Duck (Ed.), *Handbook of personal relationships: Theory, research and interventions* (pp. 391–408). New York: Wiley.

Hazan, C., & Shaver, P. (1987). Romantic love conceptualized as an attachment process. *Journal of Personality and Social Psychology, 52,* 511–524.

Healey, J. G., & Bell, R. A. (1990). Assessing alternative responses to conflicts in friendships. In D. D. Cahn (Ed.), *Intimates in conflict: A communication perspective* (pp. 25–48). Hillsdale, NJ: Erlbaum.

Helsing, K. J., & Szklo, M. (1981). Mortality after bereavement. *American Journal of Epidemiology, 114,* 41–52.

Helsing, K. J., Szklo, M., & Comstock, G. W. (1981). Factors associated with mortality after widowhood. *American Journal of Public Health, 71,* 802–809.

Henderson, S., & Bostock, T. (1975). Coping behaviour: Correlates of survival on a raft. *Australian and New Zealand Journal of Psychiatry, 9,* 221–223.

Hendrick, C., & Hendrick, S. S. (1986). A theory and method of love. *Journal of Personality and Social Psychology, 50,* 392–402.

Hendrick, C., & Hendrick, S. S. (1989). Research on love: Does it measure up? *Journal of Personality and Social Psychology, 56,* 784–794.

Hendrick, S. S., & Hendrick, C. (1992). *Liking, loving & relating* (2nd ed.). Pacific Grove, CA: Brooks/Cole.

Hendrick, S. S., Hendrick, C., & Adler, N. L. (1988). Romantic relationships: Love, satisfaction, and staying together. *Journal of Personality and Social Psychology, 54,* 980–988.

Herman, C. P., Zanna, M. P., & Higgins, E. T. (Eds.). (1986). *Physical appearance, stigma, and social behavior: The Ontario symposium* (Vol. 3). Hillsdale, NJ: Erlbaum.

Hetherington, E. M. (1972). Effects of father absence on personality development in adolescent daughters. *Developmental Psychology, 7,* 313–326.

Hibbard, J. H., & Pope, C. R. (1993). The quality of social roles as predictors of morbidity and mortality. *Social Science and Medicine, 36,* 217–225.

Higgins, P. C. (1980). *Outsiders in a hearing world: A sociology of deafness.* Beverly Hills, CA: Sage.

Hilbourne, J. (1973). On disabling the normal. *British Journal of Social Work, 2,* 497–507.

Hildebrandt, K. A., & Fitzgerald, H. E. (1983). The infant's physical attractiveness: Its effect on bonding and attachment. *Infants Mental Health Journal, 4,* 3–12.

Hill, C. T., Rubin, Z., & Peplau, L. A. (1976). Breakups before marriage. The end of 103 affairs. *Journal of Social Issues, 32,* 147–168.

Hill, C. T., Rubin, Z., Peplau, L. A., & Willard, S. G. (1979). The volunteer couple: Sex differences, couple commitment, and participation in research on interpersonal relationships. *Social Psychology Quarterly, 4,* 415–420.

Hinterkopf, E., & Brunswick, L. K. (1975). Teaching therapeutic skills to mental patients. *Psychotherapy, Research and Practice, 12,* 8–12.

Hirsch, B. J. (1980). Natural support systems and coping with major life changes. *American Journal of Community Psychology, 8,* 159–172.

Hlasny, R. G., & McCarrey, M. W. (1980). Similarity of values and warmth effects on client's trust and perceived therapist's effectiveness. *Psychological Reports, 46,* 1111–1118.

Holland, D. C., & Eisenhart, M. A. (1990). *Educated in romance: Women, achievement, and college culture.* Chicago: University of Chicago Press.

Holmes, J. G., & Rempel, J. K. (1989). Trust in close relationships. In M. Clark (Ed.), *Close relationships: Review of personality and social psychology.* (Vol. 10). Newbury Park, CA: Sage.

Holtzworth-Munroe, A., & Jacobson, N. S. (1985). Causal attributions of marital couples: When do they search for causes? What do they conclude when they do? *Journal of Personality and Social Psychology, 48,* 1398–1412.

Holtzworth-Munroe, A., & Jacobson, N. S. (1988). Toward a methodology for coding spontaneous causal attributions: Preliminary results with married couples. *Journal of Social and Clinical Psychology, 7,* 101–112.

Homans, G. C. (1961). *Social behavior: Its elementary forms.* New York: Harcourt Brace & World.

Homans, G. C. (1974). *Social behavior: Its elementary forms* (Rev. ed.). New York: Harcourt Brace Jovanovich.

Horne, R. L., & Pickard, R. S. (1979). Psychosocial risk factors for lung cancer. *Psychosomatic Medicine, 41,* 503–514.

Horowitz, L. M., & French, R. S. (1979). Interpersonal problems of people who describe themselves as lonely. *Journal of Consulting and Clinical Psychology, 47,* 762–764.

Horowitz, L. M., French, R. S., & Anderson, C. A. (1982). The prototype of a lonely person. In L. A. Peplau & D. Perlman (Eds.), *Loneliness: A sourcebook of current theory, research and therapy* (pp. 183–205). New York: Wiley.

Hostetler, J. A. (1993). *Amish society.* Baltimore: The Johns Hopkins University Press.

House, J. S., Robbins, C., & Metzner, H. L. (1982). The association of social relationships and activities with mortality: Prospective evidence from the Tecumseh Community Health Study. *American Journal of Epidemiology, 116,* 123–140.

House, J. S., Umberson, D., & Landis, K. R. (1988). Structures and processes of social support. In W. R. Scott & J. Blake (Eds.), *Annual review of sociology* (Vol. 14, pp. 293–318). Palo Alto, CA: Annual Reviews Inc.

Howard, J. A., Blumstein, P., & Schwartz, P. (1986). Sex, power, and influence tactics in intimate relationships. *Journal of Personality and Social Psychology, 51,* 102–109.

Howard, J. A., Blumstein, P., & Schwartz, P. (1987). Social or evolutionary theories? Some observations on preferences in human mate selection. *Journal of Personality and Social Psychology, 53,* 194–200.

Howes, C. (1988). Peer interactions of young children. *Monographs of the Society for Research in Child Development, 53* (1, Serial no. 217).

Hrdy, S. (1981). *The woman that never evolved.* Cambridge, MA: Harvard University Press.

Hunt, B., & Hunt, M. (1975). *Prime time.* New York: Stein & Day.

Hunter, M. S., Saleebey, D., & Shannon, C. (1983). Female friendships: Joint defense against power inequity. *Psychology: A Quarterly Journal of Human Behavior, 20,* 14–20.

Hupka, R. B. (1981). Cultural determinants of jealousy. *Alternative Life Styles, 4,* 310–356.

Hupka, R. B., & Eshett, C. (1988). Cognitive organization of emotions: Differences between labels and descriptions of emotion in jealousy situations. *Perceptual and Motor Skills, 66,* 935–949.

Hupka, R. B., Jung, J., & Silverthorn, K. (1987). Perceived acceptability of apologies, excuses and justifications in jealousy predicaments. *Journal of Social Behaviour and Personality, 2,* 303–313.

Huston, M., & Schwartz, P. (1995). The relationships of lesbians and gay men. In J. T. Wood & S. Duck (Eds.), *Understudied relationships: Off the beaten track.* Thousand Oaks, CA: Sage.

Huston, T. L. (1983). Power. In H. H. Kelley et al., *Close relationships* (pp. 169–219). New York: W. H. Freeman.

Huston, T. L., & Ashmore, R. D. (1986). Women and men in personal relationships. In R. D. Ashmore & F. K. Del Boca (Eds.), *The social psychology of female-male relations* (pp. 167–210). New York: Academic.

Huston, T. L., & Levinger, G. (1978). Interpersonal attraction and relationships. In M. R. Rosenzweig & L. W. Porter (Eds.), *Annual review of psychology, 29,* 115–156. Palo Alto, CA: Annual Reviews Inc.

Huston, T. L., McHale, S. M., & Crouter, A. C. (1986). When the honeymoon's over: Changes in the marriage relationship over the first year. In R. Gilmour & S. Duck (Eds.), *The emerging field of personal relationships* (pp. 109–132). Hillsdale, NJ: Erlbaum.

Huston, T. L., Surra, C. A., Fitzgerald, N. M., & Cate, R. M. (1981). From courtship to marriage: Mate selection as an interpersonal process. In S. Duck & R. Gilmour (Eds.), *Personal relationships, 2: Developing personal relationships* (pp. 53–88). London: Academic.

Huston, T. L., & Vangelisti, A. L. (1991). Socioemotional behavior and satisfaction in marital relationships: A longitudinal study. *Journal of Personality and Social Psychology, 61,* 721–733.

Hymel, S., Wagner, E., & Butler, L. J. (1990). Reputational bias: View from the peer group. In S. R. Asher & J. D. Coie (Eds.), *Peer rejection in childhood.* New York: Cambridge University Press.

Jablensky, A., Sartorius, N., Ernberg, G., Anker, M., Korten, A., Cooper, J. E., Day, R., & Bertelsen, A. (1992). Schizophrenia: Manifestations, incidence, and course in different cultures. A World Health Organization ten-country study. *Psychological Medicine* (Monograph Supplement 20): 1–97.

Jackson, D. J., & Huston, T. L. (1975). Physical attractiveness and assertiveness. *Journal of Social Psychology, 96,* 79–84.

Jackson, R. M. (1977). Social structure and process

in friendship choice. In C. S. Fischer, R. M. Jackson, C. A. Stueve, K. Gerson, & L. M. Jones with M. Baldassare. *Networks and places* (pp. 59–78). New York: Free Press.

Jacobson, G. F. (1987). Family type, visiting patterns and children's behavior in the stepfamily: A linked family system. In K. Pasley & M. Ihingerp-Tallman (Eds.), *Remarriage and step-parenting*. New York: Guilford.

Jacobson, N. S., Follette, W. C., & McDonald, D. W. (1982). Reactivity to positive and negative behavior in distressed and nondistressed married couples. *Journal of Consulting and Clinical Psychology, 50,* 706–714.

Jacobson, N. S., McDonald, D. W., Follette, W. C., & Berley, R. A. (1985). Attributional processes in distressed and nondistressed married couples. *Cognitive Therapy and Research, 9,* 35–59.

Jankowiak, W. R., & Fischer, E. F. (1992). A cross-cultural perspective on romantic love. *Ethnology, 31,* 149–155.

Jeffries, V. (1993). Virtue and attraction: Validation of a measure of love. *Journal of Social and Personal Relationships, 10,* 99–117.

Jenks, R. J. (1985). Swinging: A test of two theories and a proposed new model. *Archives of Sexual Behavior, 14,* 517–527.

Jerrome, D. (1981). The significance of friendship for women in later life. *Aging and Society, 1,* 175–197.

Johnson, D. F., & Pittinger, J. B. (1984). Attribution, the attractiveness stereotype, and the elderly. *Developmental Psychology, 20,* 1168–1172.

Johnson, D. J., & Rusbult, C. E. (1989). Resisting temptation: Devaluation of alternative partners as a means of maintaining commitment in close relationships. *Journal of Personality and Social Psychology, 57,* 967–980.

Johnson, F. L., & Aries, E. J. (1983a). The talk of women friends. *Women's Studies International Forum, 6,* 353–361.

Johnson, F. L., & Aries, E. J. (1983b). Conversational patterns among same-sex pairs in late-adolescent close friends. *The Journal of Genetic Psychology, 142,* 225–238.

Johnson, M. P. (1982). Social and cognitive features of the dissolution of commitment to relationships. In S. Duck (Ed.), *Personal relation-ships 4: Dissolving personal relationships.* London: Academic.

Johnson, M. P. (1985). *Commitment, cohesion, investment, barriers, alternatives constraint: Why people stay together when they really don't want to.* Paper presented at the Theory Construction and Research Methodology Workshop, National Council on Family Relations, Dallas, Texas.

Johnson, M. P. (1991). Commitment to personal relationships. In W. H. Jones & D. Perlman (Eds.), *Advances in personal relationships* (Vol. 3). London: Kingsley.

Johnson, M. P., & Leslie, L. (1982). Couple involvement and network structure: A test of the dyadic withdrawal hypothesis. *Social Psychology Quarterly, 45,* 34–43.

Johnson, P. (1976). Women and power: Toward a theory of effectiveness. *Journal of Social Issues, 32,* 99–110.

Johnson-George, C., & Swap, W. C. (1982). Measurement of specific interpersonal trust: Construction and validation of a scale to assess trust in a specific other. *Journal of Personality and Social Psychology, 43,* 1306–1317.

Jones, E. E., & Archer, R. L. (1976). Are there special effects of personalistic self-disclosure? *Journal of Experimental Social Psychology, 12,* 180–193.

Jones, E. E., Farina, A. H., Hastorf, A. H., Markus, H., Miller, D. T., Scott, R. A., & French, R. D. (1984). *Social stigma: The psychology of marked relationships.* New York: W. H. Freeman.

Jones, R. A. (1970). Volunteering to help: The effects of choice, dependence, and anticipated departure. *Journal of Personality and Social Psychology, 14,* 121–129.

Jones, S. C. (1973). Self and interpersonal evaluations: Esteem theories versus consistency theories. *Psychological Bulletin, 79,* 185–199.

Jones, W. H. (1981). Loneliness and social contact. *Journal of Social Psychology, 113,* 295–296.

Jones, W. H. (1982). Loneliness and social behavior. In L. A. Peplau & D. Perlman (Eds.), *Loneliness: A sourcebook of theory, research and therapy.* New York: Wiley.

Jones, W. H. (1985). The psychology of loneliness: Some personality issues in the study of social support. In I. G. Sarason & B. R. Sarason

(Eds.), *Social support: Theory, research and application* (pp. 225–241). The Hague: Martinus Nijhoff.

Jones, W. H., Freeman, J. R., & Goswick, R. A. (1981). The persistence of loneliness: Self and other determinants. *Journal of Personality, 49,* 27–48.

Jones, W. H., Hansson, R. O., & Cutrona, C. E. (1984). Helping the lonely: Issues of intervention with young and older adults. In S. W. Duck (Ed.), *Personal relationships 5: Repairing personal relationships.* London: Academic.

Jones, W. H., Hansson, R. O., & Smith, T. G. (1980). *Loneliness and love: Implications for psychological and interpersonal functioning.* Unpublished manuscript, University of Tulsa, cited in Jones, W. H. (1982).

Jones, W. H., Hobbs, S. A., & Hockenbury, D. (1982). Loneliness and social skills deficits. *Journal of Personality and Social Psychology, 42,* 682–689.

Kahn, A., Hottes, J., & Davis, W. L. (1971). Cooperation and optimal responding in the prisoner's dilemma game: Effects of sex and physical attractiveness. *Journal of Personality and Social Psychology, 17,* 267–279.

Kalick. S. M., & Hamilton, T. E. (1986). The matching hypothesis reexamined. *Journal of Personality and Social Psychology, 51,* 673–682.

Kamo, Y. (1993). Determinants of marital satisfaction: A comparison of the United States and Japan. *Journal of Social and Personal Relationships, 10,* 551–568.

Kandel, D. B. (1978a). Homophily, selection and socialization in adolescent friendships. *American Journal of Sociology, 84,* 427–436.

Kandel, D. B. (1978b). Similarity in real-life adolescent friendship pairs. *Journal of Personality and Social Psychology, 36,* 306–312.

Kandel, D. B. (1985). On processes of peer influences in adolescent drug use: A developmental perspective. In J. Brook, D. Lettieri, & D. Brook (Eds.), *Advances in alcohol and substance abuse, 4,* 139–163.

Kandel, D. B., & Andrews, K. (1987). Processes of adolescent socialization by parents and peers. *International Journal of Addictions, 22,* 319–342.

Kantor, R. M. (1972). *Commitment and community: Communes and utopias in sociological perspective.* Cambridge, MA: Harvard University Press.

Kaplan, R. M. (1985). Behavioral epidemiology, health promotion, and health services. *Medical Care, 23,* 564–683.

Kaplan, R. M., & Toshima, M. T. (1990). The functional effects of social relationships on chronic illness and disability. In I. G. Sarason, B. R. Sarason, & G. R. Pierce (Eds.), *Social supports, an interactional perspective* (pp. 427–453). New York: Wiley.

Kaplan, S. L. (1975). *The exercise of power in dating couples.* Unpublished doctoral dissertation, Harvard University, as cited in Peplau, L. A., & Gordon, S. L. (1985).

Karasek, R. A., Baker, D., Marxer, R. Ahlbom, A., & Theorell, T. (1981). Job decision latitude, job demands, and cardiovascular disease: A prospective study of Swedish men. *American Journal of Public Health, 71,* 694–705.

Karweit, N. (1983). Extracurricular activities and friendship selection. In J. L. Epstein & N. Karweit (Eds.), *Friends in school: Patterns of selection and influence in secondary schools* (pp. 131–139). New York: Academic.

Katz, I. (1981). *Stigma: A social-psychological perspective.* Hillsdale, NJ: Erlbaum.

Keith, P. M., Hill, K., Goudy, W. J., & Powers, E. A. (1984). Confidants and well-being: A note on male friendship in old age. *The Gerontologist, 24,* 318–320.

Kelley, H. H. (1979). *Personal relationships: Their structure and processes.* Hillsdale, NJ: Erlbaum.

Kelley, H. H. (1983). Love and commitment. In H. H. Kelley et al., *Close relationships* (pp. 265–314). New York: W. H. Freeman.

Kelley, H. H. (1984). Affect in interpersonal relations. In P. Shaver (Ed.), *Review of personality and social psychology* (Vol. 5, pp. 89–115). Beverly Hills, CA: Sage.

Kelley, H. H., Berscheid, E., Christensen, A., Harvey, J. H., Huston, T. L., Levinger, G., McClintock, E., Peplau, L. A., & Peterson, D. R. (1983). *Close relationships.* New York: W. H. Freeman.

Kelley, H. H., Cunningham, J., & Braiker-Stambul, H. (1973). Unpublished data, cited in Kelley, H. H. (1979).

Kelly, C., Huston, T. L., & Cate, R. M. (1985).

Premarital relationship correlates of the erosion of satisfaction in marriage. *Journal of Social and Personal Relationships, 2,* 167–178.

Kendrick, D. T., & Trost, M. R. (1989). A reproductive exchange model of heterosexual relationships: Putting proximate economics in ultimate perspective. In C. Hendrick (Ed.), *Review of personality and social psychology: Vol. 10. Close Relationships* (pp. 92–118). Newbury Park, CA: Sage.

Kennedy, J. K., Kiecolt-Glaser, J. K., & Glaser, R. (1988). Immunological consequences of acute and chronic stressors, mediating role of interpersonal relationships. *British Journal of Medical Psychology, 61,* 77.

Kenny, M. (1962). *A Spanish tapestry: Town and country in Castile.* Bloomington, IN: University of Indiana Press.

Kepart, W. M. (1967). Some correlates of romantic love. *Journal of Marriage and the Family, 29,* 470–479.

Kerckhoff, A. C., & Davis, K. E. (1962). Value consensus and need complementarity in mate selection. *American Sociological Review, 27,* 295–303.

Kiecolt-Glaser, J. K. (1993). *Stress, health and immune function in older adults.* Paper presented at the annual convention of the American Psychological Association, Toronto.

Kiecolt-Glaser, J. K., Fisher, L. D., Ogrocki, P., Stout, J. C., Speicher, C. E., & Glaser, R. (1987). Marital quality, marital disruption and immune function. *Psychosomatic Medicine, 49,* 13–34.

Kiecolt-Glaser, J. K., Garner, W., Speicher, C., Penn, G. M., Holiday, J., & Glaser, R. (1984). Psychosocial modifiers of immunocompetence in medical students. *Psychosomatic Medicine, 46,* 7–14.

Kiecolt-Glaser, J. K., Kennedy, S., Malkoff, S., Fisher, L., Spreicher, C. E., & Glaser, R. (1988). Marital discord and immunity in males. *Psychosomatic Medicine, 50,* 213–229.

Kiesler, C. A. (1971). *The psychology of commitment: Experiments linking behavior to belief.* New York: Academic.

Kinney, D. A. (1993). From "nerds" to "normals": Adolescent identity recovery within a changing social system. *Sociology of Education, 66,* 21–40.

Kleck, R. E. (1968). Self-disclosure patterns of the nonobviously stigmatized. *Psychological Reports, 23,* 1239–1248.

Kleck, R., Ono, H., & Hastorf, A. H. (1966). The effects of physical deviance upon face-to-face interaction. *Human Relations, 19,* 425–436.

Klein, R., & Milardo, R. (1995). *The social context of pair conflict.* Paper presented at the conference of the International Network on Personal Relationships, College of William and Mary, Williamsburg, Virginia.

Klinger, E. (1977). *Meaning and void: Inner experience and the incentives in people's lives.* Minneapolis, MN: University of Minnesota Press.

Koestner, R., & Wheeler, L. (1988). Self presentation in personal advertisements: The influence of implicit notions of attraction and role expectations. *Journal of Social and Personal Relationships, 5,* 149–160.

Kohlberg, L. (1969). Stage and sequence: The cognitive-developmental approach in socialization. In D. Goslin (Ed.), *The handbook of socialization theory and research.* Chicago: Rand McNally.

Kojetin, B. A. (1993). *Adult attachment styles with romantic partners, friends and partners.* Ph.D. thesis. University of Minnesota, Minneapolis, as cited in Berscheid, E. (1994).

Kolata, G. (1992, November 24). After kinship and marriage, anthropology discovers love. *New York Times,* p. B9.

Kollock, P., Blumstein, P., & Schwartz, P. (1985). Sex and power in interaction: Conversational privileges and duties. *American Sociological Review, 50,* 34–46.

Komarovsky, M. (1971). *The unemployed male and his family.* New York: Octagon Books.

Kon, I. S. (1981). Adolescent friendship: Some unanswered questions for future research. In S. Duck & R. Gilmour (Eds.), *Personal relationships 2.* New York: Academic.

Kon, I. S., & Losenkov, V. A. (1978). Friendship in adolescence: Values and behavior. *Journal of Marriage and the Family 40,* 143–155.

Kopera, A. A., Maier, R. A., & Johnson, J. E. (1971). Perception of physical attractiveness: The influence of group interaction and group coaction on ratings of the attraction of photographs of women. *Proceedings of the 79th Annual Convention of the American Psychological Association, 6,* 317–318.

Korn, S. J., Chess, S., & Fernandez, P. (1978).

The impact of children's physical handicaps on marital quality and family interactions. In R. M. Lerner & G. B. Spanier (Eds.), *Child influences on marital and family interaction: A life-span perspective.* New York: Academic.

Krain, M. (1977). A definition of dyadic boundaries and an empirical study of boundary establishment in courtship. *International Journal of Sociology of the Family, 7,* 107–123.

Kraus, A. S., & Lilienfeld, A. M. (1959). Some epidemiological aspects of the high mortality rate in the young widowed group. *Journal of Chronic Diseases, 10,* 207–217.

Krebs, D., & Adinolfi, A. A. (1975). Physical attractiveness, social relations and personality style. *Journal of Personality and Social Psychology, 31,* 245–253.

Kummer, H. (1968). *Social organization of Hamadryas baboons: A field study.* Chicago: University of Chicago Press.

Kupersmidt, J. B., Coie, J. D., & Dodge, K. A. (1990). Predicting disorder from peer social problems. In S. R. Asher & J. D. Coie (Eds.), *Peer rejection in childhood.* New York: Cambridge University Press.

Kupersmidt, J. B., DeRosier, M. E., & Patterson, C. P. (1995). Similarity as the basis for children's friendships: The role of sociometric status and withdrawn behavior, academic achievement and demographic characteristics. *Journal of Social and Personal Relationships, 12,* 439–452.

Kurdek, L. A. (1993). Predicting marital dissolution: A 5-year prospective longitudinal study of newlywed couples. *Journal of Personality and Social Psychology, 64,* 221–242.

Kurdek, L. A., & Schmitt, J. P. (1986). Relationship quality of partners in heterosexual married, heterosexual cohabiting, and gay and lesbian relationships. *Journal of Personality and Social Psychology, 51,* 711–720.

Kurth, S. B. (1970). Friendship and friendly relations. In G. J. McCall, M. M. McCall, N. K. Denzin, G. D. Suttles, & S. B. Kurth, *Social relationships* (pp. 136–170). Chicago: Aldine.

Ladd, G. W. (1985). Documenting the effects of social skills training with children: Process and outcomes assessment. In B. H. Schneider, K. H. Rubin, & J. E. Ledingham (Eds.), *Children's peer relations: Issues in assessment and inter-*

*vention* (pp. 243–271). New York: Springer-Verlag.

Ladd, G. W., & Emerson, E. S. (1984). Shared knowledge in children's friendships. *Developmental Psychology, 20,* 932–940.

La Gaipa, J. J. (1981). A systems approach to personal relationships. In S. Duck & R. Gilmour (Eds.), *Personal relationships, I: Studying personal relationships.* New York: Academic.

Lambert, M. J., & Bergin, A. E. (1994). The effectiveness of psychotherapy. In A. E. Bergin & S. L. Garfield (Eds.), *Handbook of psychotherapy and behavior change* (4th ed., pp. 143–189). New York: Wiley.

Landy, D., & Sigall, H. (1974). Beauty is talent: Task evaluation as a function of the performer's physical attractiveness. *Journal of Personality and Social Psychology, 29,* 299–304.

Langford, M. (1962). *Community aspects of housing for the aged.* Cornell University Center for Housing and Environmental Studies, Ithaca, New York, as cited in Chown, S. M. (1981).

Langlois, J. H., & Roggman, L. A. (1990). Attractive faces are only average. *Psychological Science, 1,* 115–121.

Langlois, J. H., Roggman, L. A., Casey, R. J., Riesner-Danner, L. A., & Jenkins, V. Y. (1987). Infant preferences for attractive faces: Rudiments of a stereotype? *Developmental Psychology, 23,* 363–369.

Larkin, R. W. (1979). *Suburban youth in cultural crisis.* New York: Oxford University Press.

Larson, K. (1997, August 10). A month in Shaker country. *New York Times, Arts and Leisure,* pp. 31, 33.

Larson, R., Csikszentmihalyi, M., & Graef, R. (1982). Time alone in daily experience: Loneliness or renewal. In L. A. Peplau & D. Perlman (Eds.), *Loneliness: A sourcebook of theory, research and therapy* (pp. 40–53). New York: Wiley.

Larson, R., Zuzenek, J., & Mannell, R. (1985). Being alone versus being with people: Disengagement in the daily experience of older people. *Journal of Gerontology, 40,* 375–381.

Larzelere, R. E., & Huston, T. L. (1980). The dyads trust scale: Toward understanding interpersonal trust in close relationships. *Journal of Marriage and the Family, 42,* 595–604.

Latty-Mann, H., & Davis, K. E. (1996). Attachment theory and partner choice: Preference and actuality. *Journal of Social and Personal Relationships, 13,* 5–23.

Lawrence, D. H., & Festinger, L. (1962). *Deterrents and reinforcement.* Stanford, CA: Stanford University Press.

Lawton, M. P. (1977). Environmental and health influences on aging and behavior. In J. E. Birren & K. W. Schaie (Eds.), *Handbook of psychology of aging.* New York: Van Nostrand Reinhold.

Lazarus, R. S. (1993). From psychological stress to the emotions: A history of changing outlooks. In L. W. Porter & M. R. Rosenzweig (Eds.), *Annual review of psychology, 44,* 1–21.

Lea, M. (1989). Factors underlying friendship: An analysis of responses on the acquaintance description form in relation to Wright's friendship model. *Journal of Social and Personal Relationships, 6,* 275–292.

Lecky, P. (1945). *Self consistency: A theory of personality.* New York: Island Press.

Lee, J. A. (1973). *The colors of love: An exploration of the ways of loving.* Don Mills, Ontario: New Press.

Lee, J. A. (1977). A typology of styles of loving. *Personality and Social Psychology Bulletin, 3,* 173–182.

Lee, J. A. (1988). Love styles. In R. J. Sternberg & M. L. Barnes (Eds.), *The psychology of love.* New Haven, CT: Yale University Press.

Legge, N. J., & Rawlins, W. K. (1992). Managing disputes in young adult friendships: Modes of convenience, cooperation and commitment. *Western Journal of Communication, 56,* 226–247.

Lesko, N. (1988). *Symbolizing society: Stories, rites, and structure in a Catholic high school.* Philadelphia: Falmer.

Leslie, G. R. (1976). *The family in social context* (3rd ed.). New York: Oxford University Press.

Leslie, L. A. (1989). Stress in the dual-income couple: Do social relationships help or hinder? *Journal of Social and Personal Relationships, 6,* 451–461.

Leslie, L. A., Johnson, M. P., & Huston, T. L. (1986). Parental reactions to dating relationships: Do they make a difference? *Journal of Marriage and the Family, 48,* 57–66.

Levine, N. (1988). *The dynamics of polyandry: Kinship, domesticity, and population of the Tibetan border.* Chicago: University of Chicago Press.

Levinger, G. (1983). Development and change. In H. H. Kelley et al., *Close relationships.* San Francisco: W. H. Freeman.

Levinger, G. (1988). Can we picture "love"? In R. J. Sternberg & M. L. Barnes (Eds.), *The psychology of love* (pp. 139–158). New Haven, CT: Yale University Press.

Levinger, G., Rands, M., & Talaber, R. (1977). *The assessment of involvement and rewardingness in close and casual pair relationships.* National Science Foundation Technical Report. Amherst, MA: University of Massachusetts.

Levinger, G., & Snoek, J. D. (1972). *Attraction in relationships: A new look at interpersonal attraction.* Morristown, NJ: General Learning Press.

Levinson, D. J. (1978). *The seasons of a man's life.* New York: Knopf.

Levy, M. B., & Davis, K. E. (1988). Love styles and attachment styles compared: Their relation to each other and to the various relationship characteristics. *Journal of Social and Personal Relationships, 5,* 439–471.

Lewis, R. A. (1973). A longitudinal test of a developmental framework for premarital dyadic formation. *Journal of Marriage and the Family, 35,* 16–25.

Lewis, R. A. (1975). Social influences on marital choice. In S. Dragastin & G. H. Elder, Jr. (Eds.), *Adolescence in the life cycle.* New York: Wiley.

Lewis, R. A., & Spanier, G. B. (1979). Theorizing about the quality and stability of marriage. In W. Burr, R. Hill, F. Nye, & I. Reiss (Eds.), *Contemporary theories of the family* (Vol. I, pp. 268–294). New York: Free Press.

Lewittes, H. (1989). Just being friendly means a lot—women, friendship and aging. In L. Grau & I. Susser (Eds.), *Women in the later years: Health, social and cultural perspective.* New York: Harrington Park Press.

Little, R. (1990). Friendship in the military community. In H. Z. Lopata & D. Maines (Eds.), *Friendship in context.* Greenwich, CT: JAI Press.

Litwak, E. (1989). Forms of friendship among older people in an industrial society. In R. G. Adams & R. Blieszner (Eds.), *Older adult friendship: Structure and process.* Newbury Park, CA: Sage.

Lively, W. J., & Bromley, D. B. (1973). *Person perception in childhood and adolescence.* New York: Wiley.

Lloyd, S. A. (1987). Conflict in premarital relationships: Differential perceptions of males and females. *Family Relations, 36,* 290–294.

Lloyd, S. A. (1990). A behavioral self-report technique for assessing conflict in close relationships. *Journal of Social and Personal Relationships, 7,* 265–272.

Lloyd, S. A., & Cate, R. M. (1985). The developmental course of conflict in premarital relationship dissolution. *Journal of Social and Personal Relationships, 2,* 179–194.

Lloyd, S. A., Cate, R. M., & Henton, J. M. (1982). Equity and rewards as predictors of satisfaction in casual and intimate relationships. *Journal of Psychology, 110,* 43–48.

Lloyd, S. A., Cate, R. M., & Henton, J. M. (1984). Predicting premarital relationship stability: A methodological refinement. *Journal of Marriage and the Family, 46,* 71–76.

Lobdell, J., & Perlman, D. (1986). The intergenerational transmission of loneliness: A study of college females and their parents. *Journal of Marriage and the Family, 48,* 589–596.

Locke, K. D., & Horowitz, L. M. (1990). Satisfaction in interpersonal interactions as a function of similarity in level of dysphoria. *Journal of Personality and Social Psychology, 58,* 823–831.

Lopata, H. Z. (1969). Loneliness, forms and components. *Social Problems, 17,* 248–261.

Lopata, H. Z. (1979). *Women as widows.* New York: Elsevier.

Lowenthal, M. F., Thurnher, M., & Chiriboga, D. (1975). *Four stages of life: A comparative study of women and men facing transition.* San Francisco: Jossey-Bass.

Luborsky, L., Singer, R., & Luborsky, L. (1975). Comparative studies of psychotherapies: Is it true that "everyone has won and all must have prizes"? *Archives of General Psychiatry, 32,* 995–1007.

Luce, R. D., & Raiffa, H. (1957). *Games and decisions.* New York: Wiley.

Lucker, G. W., Beane, W. E., & Guire, K. (1981). The strength of the halo effect in physical attractiveness research. *Journal of Psychology, 107,* 57–67.

Lynch, J. J. (1977). *The broken heart: The medical consequences of loneliness.* New York: Basic.

Lyon, K., & Zucker, R. (1974). Environmental supports and post-hospital adjustment. *Journal of Clinical Psychology, 30,* 460–465.

Lyons, L. C., & Woods, P. J. (1991). The efficacy of rational-emotive therapy: A quantitative review of the outcome research. *Clinical Psychology Review, 11,* 357–369.

Lyons, R. F. (1986). The impact of chronic illness on activity patterns and friendship. *Research Report.* Ottawa: Fitness & Lifestyle Research Institute.

Lyons, R. F. (1987). Leisure adjustment to chronic illness and disability. *Journal of Leisurability, 14,* 4–10.

Lyons, R. F. (1991). Effects of acquired illness and disability on friendships. In W. H. Jones & D. Perlman (Eds.), *Advances in personal relationships: A research annual* (Vol. 3, pp. 233–276). London: Kingsley.

Lyons, R. F., Sullivan, M. J. L., Ritvo, P. G., & Coyne, J. C. (1995). *Relationships in chronic illness and disability.* Thousand Oaks, CA: Sage.

Maccoby, E. E. (1990). Gender and relationships: A developmental account. *American Psychologist, 45,* 513–520.

MacDonald, K., & Parke, R. D. (1984). Bridging the gap: Parent-child play interaction and peer interactive competence. *Child Development, 55,* 1265–1277.

MacDonald, K. B. (1988). *Social and personality development: An evolutionary synthesis.* New York: Plenum.

Macgregor, F. C., Abel, T. M., Bryt, A., Lauer, E., & Weissmann, S. (1953). *Facial deformities and plastic surgery: A psychosocial study.* Springfield, IL: Charles C. Thomas.

Macklin, E. D. (1972). Heterosexual cohabitation among unmarried college students. *The Family Coordinator, 21,* 463–472.

Madden, M. E., & Janoff-Bulman, R. (1981). Blame, control and marital satisfaction: Wives attributions for conflict in marriage. *Journal of Marriage and the Family, 43,* 663–674.

Maddison, D. C., & Walker, W. L. (1967). Factors affecting the outcome of conjugal bereavement. *British Journal of Psychiatry, 113,* 1057–1067.

Mahaffey, K. R., Annest, J. L., Roberts, J., & Murphy, R. S. (1982). National estimates of blood lead levels: United States, 1976-1980: Association with selected demographic and socioeconomic factors. *New England Journal of Medicine, 307,* 573–579.

Major, B., & Forcey, B. (1985). Social comparisons and pay evaluations: Preferences for same-sex and same-job wage comparisons. *Journal of Experimental Social Psychology, 21,* 393–405.

Main, M., Kaplan, N., & Cassidy, J. (1985). Security in infancy, childhood, and adulthood: A move to the level of representation. *Monographs of the Society for Research in Child Development, 50,* 66–104.

Malinowski, B. (1932). *Crime and custom in savage society.* London: Paul Trench Trubner.

Mannarino, A. P. (1976). Friendship patterns and altruistic behavior in preadolescent males. *Developmental Psychology, 12,* 555–556.

Mannarino, A. P. (1978). Friendship patterns and self-concept development in preadolescent males. *Journal of Genetic Psychology, 133,* 105–110.

Manuck, S. B., Kaplan, J. R., Adams, M. R., & Clarkson, T. B. (1988). Studies of psychosocial influences on coronary artery atherogenesis in cynomolgus monkeys. *Health Psychology, 7,* 113–124.

Maracek, J., & Mattee, D. R. (1972). Avoidance of continued success as a function of self-esteem, level of esteem certainty and responsibility for success. *Journal of Personality and Social Psychology, 22,* 90–107.

Marangoni, C., & Ickes, W. (1989). Loneliness: A theoretical review with implications for measurement. *Journal of Social and Personal Relationships, 6,* 93–128.

Marinelli, R. P., & Dell Orto, A. E. (1984). *The psychological and social impact of physical disability.* New York: Springer.

Markman, H. (1981). Prediction of marital distress: a 5-year follow-up. *Journal of Consulting and Clinical Psychology, 49,* 760–762.

Markman, H. J., Floyd, F. J., Stanley, S. M., & Storasli, R. D. (1988). Prevention of marital distress: A longitudinal investigation. *Journal*

of *Personality and Social Psychology, 56,* 210–217.

Markus, H. R., & Kitayama, S. (1991). Culture and the self: Implications for cognition, emotion, and motivation. *Psychological Review, 98,* 224–253.

Markus, H. R., & Nurious, P. (1986). Possible selves. *American Psychologist, 41,* 954–969.

Marmar, C. R., Horowitz, M. J., Weiss, D. S., & Marziali, E. (1986). The development of the Therapeutic Alliance Rating System. In L. S. Greenberg & W. M. Pinsof (Eds.), *The psychotherapeutic process: A research handbook* (pp. 325–366). New York: Guilford.

Martin, J. C., Carkhuff, R. R., & Berenson, G. B. (1966). Process variables in counseling and psychotherapy: A study of counseling and friendship. *Journal of Counseling Psychology, 13,* 356–359.

Masciuch, S., & Kienapple, K. (1993). The emergence of jealousy in children 4 months to 7 years. *Journal of Social and Personal Relationships, 10,* 421–435.

Mason, A., & Blankenship, V. (1987). Power and affiliation motivation, stress, and abuse in intimate relationships. *Journal of Personality and Social Psychology, 52,* 203–210.

Matarazzo, J. D. (1979). A good friend: One of mankind's most effective and inexpensive psychotherapists. *Journal of Clinical Psychology, 35,* 231–232.

Mathes, E. W. (1986). Jealousy and romantic love: A longitudinal study. *Psychological Reports, 58,* 885–886.

Mathes, E. W. (1992). *Jealousy: The psychological data.* Lanham, MD: University Press of America.

Mathes, E. W., Adams, H. E., & Davis, R. M. (1985). Jealousy: Loss of relationship rewards, loss of self-esteem, depression, anxiety, and anger. *Journal of Personality and Social Psychology, 48,* 1552–1561.

Mathes, E. W., & Severa, N. (1981). Jealousy, romantic love, and liking: Theoretical considerations and preliminary scale development. *Psychological Reports, 49,* 23–31.

Matute-Bianchi, M. E. (1986). Ethnic identities and patterns of school success and failure among Mexican-descent and Japanese-American students in a California high school: An ethnographic analysis. *American Journal of Education, 95,* 233–255.

McAdams, D. P. (1988). Personal needs and personal relationships. In S. W. Duck (Ed.), *Handbook of personal relationships: Theory, research and interventions* (pp. 7–22). New York: Wiley.

McAndrew, I. (1979). Adolescents and young people with spina bifida. *Developmental Medicine and Child Neurology, 21,* 619–629.

McCall, G. J., & Simmons, J. L. (1966). *Identities and interactions: An examination of human associations in everyday life.* New York: Free Press.

McCandless, B. R. (1970). Socialization. In H. W. Reese & L. P. Lipsitt (Eds.), *Experimental child psychology.* New York: Academic.

McCandless, B. R., & Marshall, H. R. (1957). A picture sociometric technique for preschool children and its relation to teacher judgments of friendship. *Child Development, 28,* 139–148.

McCarthy, B. (1986). Friendship behaviours and perceptions. In R. Gilmour and S. Duck (Eds.) (1986). *The emerging field of personal relationships.* Hillsdale, NJ: Erlbaum.

McCarthy, H. (1983). Understanding the motives of youth in transition to work: A taxonomy for rehabilitation counselors and educators. *Journal of Applied Rehabilitation Counseling, 14,* 52–61.

McClintock, C. G., Kramer, R. M., & Keil, L. J. (1984). Equity and social exchange in human relationships. In L. Berkowitz (Ed.), *Advances in experimental social psychology,* (Vol. 17, pp. 183–228). New York: Academic.

McCord, J., McCord, W., & Thurber, E. (1962). Some effects of paternal absence on male children. *Journal of Abnormal and Social Psychology, 54,* 258–262.

McCoy, J. K., Brody, G. H., & Stoneman, Z. (1994). A longitudinal analysis of sibling relationships as mediators of the link between family processes and youths' best friendships. *Family Relations, 43,* 400–408.

McGonagle, K. A., Kessler, R. C., & Gotlib, I. H. (1993). The effects of marital disagreement style, frequency, and outcome on marital disruption. *Journal of Social and Personal Relationships, 10,* 385–404.

McGuire, K. D., & Weisz, J. R. (1982). Social cognition and behavior correlations of preadolescent chumship. *Child Development, 53,* 1483–1484.

McNulty, S. E., & Swann, W. B., Jr. (1994). Identity negotiation in roommate relationships: The self as architect and consequence of social reality. *Journal of Personality and Social Psychology, 67,* 1012–1023.

McWhirter, D. P., & Mattison, A. M. (1984). *The male couple.* Englewood Cliffs, NJ: Prentice-Hall.

Mead, G. H. (1934). *Mind, self and society.* Chicago: University of Chicago Press.

Mead, M. (1931/1977). Jealousy: Primitive and civilized. In S. Schmalhausen & V. F. Calverton (Eds.), *Women's coming of age.* New York: Liveright. Reprinted in G. Clanton & L. G. Smith (Eds.), *Jealousy.* Lanham, MD: University Press of America.

Mech, L. D. (1970). *The wolf: The ecology and behavior of an endangered species.* New York: Natural History Press.

Mehrabian, A., & Ksionsky, S. (1974). *A theory of affiliation.* Lexington, MA: Lexington Books.

Mellen, S. L. W. (1981). *The evolution of love.* Oxford: W. H. Freeman.

Menesini, E. (1997). Behavioural correlates of friendship status among Italian school children. *Journal of Social and Personal Relationships, 14,* 109–121.

Mettee, D. R., & Aronson, E. (1974). Affective reactions to appraisals of others. In T. L. Huston (Ed.), *Foundations of interpersonal attraction.* New York: Academic.

Michaels, J. W., Adcock, A. C., & Edwards, J. N. (1986). Social exchange and equity determinants of relationship commitment. *Journal of Social and Personal Relationships, 3,* 161–175.

Miell, D., & Duck, S. W. (1986). Strategies in developing friendships. In V. Derlega & B. A. Winstead (Eds.), *Friendship and social interaction* (pp. 129–143). New York: Springer-Verlag.

Miell, D. E., Duck, S. W., & La Gaipa, J. J. (1979). Interactive effects of sex and timing of self-disclosure. *British Journal of Social and Clinical Psychology, 18,* 355–362.

Milardo, R. M. (1982). Friendship networks in developing relationships: Converging and diverging social environments. *Social Psychology Quarterly, 45,* 162–172.

Milardo, R. M. (1983). Social networks and pair relationships: A review of substantive and measurement issues. *Sociology and Social Research, 68,* 1–18.

Milardo, R. M. (1986). Personal choice and social constraint in close relationships: Application of network analysis. In V. J. Derlega & B. A. Winstead (Eds.), *Friendship and social interaction* (pp. 146–166). New York: Springer-Verlag.

Milardo, R. M., Johnson, M. P., & Huston, T. L. (1983). Developing relationships: Changing patterns of interactions between pair members and social networks. *Journal of Personality and Social Psychology, 44,* 964–976.

Milardo, R. M., & Lewis, R. A. (1985). Social networks, families and mate selection: A transactional analysis. In L. L'Abate (Ed.), *Handbook of family psychology and therapy* (Vol. 1). Homewood, IL: Dorsey Press.

Miller, C. T., Rothblum, E. D., Barbour, L., Brand, P. A., & Felicio, D. (1990). Social interaction of obese and nonobese women. *Journal of Personality, 58,* 365–380.

Miller, L. C., & Berg, J. H. (1984). Selectivity and urgency in interpersonal exchange. In V. J. Derlega (Ed.), *Communication and intimacy in close relationships.* Orlando, FL: Academic.

Miller, M. D. (1982). Friendship, power and the language of compliance-gaining. *Journal of Language and Social Psychology, 1,* 111–121.

Miller, P., & Ingham, J. (1976). Friends, confidants and symptoms. *Social Psychiatry, 11,* 51–58.

Mills, J., & Clark, M. S. (1982). Exchange and communal relationships. In L. Wheeler (Ed.), *Review of personality and social psychology* (Vol. 3, pp. 121–144). Beverly Hills, CA: Sage.

Mongeau, P. A., Hale, J. L., Johnson, K. L., & Hills, J. D. (1993). Who's wooing whom? An investigation of female initiated dating. In P. J. Kalbfleisch (Ed.), *Interpersonal communication: Evolving interpersonal relationships.* Hillsdale, NJ: Erlbaum.

Moreland, R. L., & Beach, S. R. (1992). Exposure effects in the classroom: The development of affinity among students. *Journal of Experimental Social Psychology, 28,* 255–276.

Morton, T. L. (1978). Intimacy and reciprocity of exchange: A comparison of spouses and strangers. *Journal of Personality and Social Psychology, 36,* 72–81.

Morton, T. L., Alexander, J. F., & Altman, I. (1976). Communication and relationship definition. In G. R. Miller (Ed.), *Explorations in interpersonal communication.* Beverly Hills, CA: Sage.

Mory, M. S. (1992). *"Love the ones you're with." Conflict and consensus in adolescent peer group stereotypes.* Paper presented at the biennial meetings of the Society for Research on Adolescence, Washington, DC, as cited in Brown, B. B., et al. (1994).

Moustakas, C. (1961). *Loneliness.* New York: Prentice-Hall.

Mullen, P. E. (1996). Editorial: Jealousy and the emergence of violent and intimidating behaviours. *Criminal behaviour and mental health, 6,* 199–205.

Mullen, P. E., & Martin, J. (1994). Jealousy: A community study. *British Journal of Psychiatry, 164,* 35–43.

Murphy, K., & Schneider, B. H. (1994). Coaching socially rejected early adolescents regarding behaviors used by peers to infer liking: A dyad-specific intervention. *Journal of Early Adolescence, 14,* 82–94.

Murstein, B. I. (1970). Stimulus-value-role theory: A theory of marital choice. *Journal of Marriage and the Family, 32,* 465–481.

Murstein, B. (1972). Physical attractiveness and marital choice. *Journal of Personality and Social Psychology, 22,* 8–12.

Murstein, B. (1976a). The stimulus-value-role theory of marital choice. In H. Grunebaum & J. Christ (Eds.), *Contemporary marriage: Structures, dynamics and therapy.* Boston: Little Brown.

Murstein, B. (1976b). *Who will marry whom: Theories and research in marital choice.* New York: Springer.

Murstein, B. (1986). *Paths to marriage.* Beverly Hills, CA: Sage.

Murstein, B. (1987). A clarification and extension

of SVR theory of dyadic pairing. *Journal of Marriage and the Family, 49,* 929–933.

Nahemow, L., & Lawton, M. P. (1975). Similarity and propinquity in friendship formation. *Journal of Personality and Social Psychology, 32,* 204–213.

Narayan, S. (1995, May 4). When life's partner comes pre-chosen. *New York Times,* pp. C1, C8.

Nardi, P. M. (Ed.). (1992). *Men's friendships.* Newbury Park, CA: Sage.

National Center for Health Statistics. (1970). Mortality from selected causes by marital status. *Vital and Health Statistics,* Series 20, no. 8.

Neese, R. M. (1990). Evolutionary explanations of emotion. *Human Nature, 1,* 261–289.

Neese, R. M., & Lloyd, A. T. (1992). The evolution of psychodynamic mechanisms. In J. H. Barkow, L. Cosmides, & J. Tooby (Eds.), *The adapted mind.* New York: Oxford University Press.

Neugarten, B. L. (Ed.). (1968). *Middle age and aging: A reader in social psychology.* Chicago: University of Chicago Press.

Newcomb, A. F., & Bukowski, W. M. (1983). Social impact and social preference as determinants of children's peer group status. *Developmental Psychology, 19,* 856–867.

Newcomb, A. F., Bukowski, W. M., & Pattee, L. (1993). Children's peer relations: A meta-analytic review of popular, rejected, neglected, controversial and average sociometric status. *Psychological Bulletin, 113,* 99–128.

Newcomb, T. M. (1961). *The acquaintance process.* New York: Holt, Rinehart & Winston.

Newman, B. M., & Newman, P. R. (1975). *Development through life: A psychological approach.* Homewood, IL: Dorsey Press.

Newman, J. (1994). Conflict and friendship in sibling relationships: A review. *Child Study Journal, 24,* 119–152.

Noller, P., Feeney, J. A., Bonnell, D., & Callan, V. J. (1994). A longitudinal study of conflict in early marriage. *Journal of Social and Personal Relationships, 11,* 233–252.

Noller, P., & White, A. (1990). The validity of the Communication Patterns Questionnaire. *Psychological Assessment: A Journal of Consulting and Clinical Psychology, 2,* 478–482.

Notarius, C. I., & Vanzetti, N. A. (1983). The marital agenda's protocol. In E. E. Filsinger (Ed.), *Marriage and family assessment* (pp. 209–227). Newbury Park, CA: Sage.

Nuckolls, K. B., Cassel, J., & Kaplan, B. H. (1972). Psychosocial assets, life crisis and the prognosis of pregnancy. *American Journal of Epidemiology, 95,* 431–441.

Oden, S., & Asher, S. R. (1977). Coaching children in social skills for friendship making. *Child Development, 48,* 495–506.

Oliker, S. J. (1989). *Best friends and marriage.* Berkeley, CA: University of California Press.

Orth-Gomer, K., Rosengren, A., & Wilhelmsen, L. (1993). Lack of social support and incidence of coronary heart disease in middle-aged Swedish men. *Psychosomatic Medicine, 55,* 37–43.

Osherson, S. (1992). *Wrestling with love: How men struggle with intimacy with women, children, parents and each other.* New York: Ballantine.

Otten, C. A., Penner, L. A., & Waugh, G. (1988). That's what friends are for: The determinants of psychological helping: *Journal of Social and Clinical Psychology, 7,* 34–41.

Packer, C. (1977). Reciprocal altruism in *papio anubis. Nature, 265,* 441–443.

Paloutzian, R. F., & Ellison, C. W. (1979). Emotional, behavioral and physical correlates of loneliness. Paper presented at the UCLA Research Conference on Loneliness, Los Angeles, California, as cited in Check, J. V. P., et al. (1985).

Parker, J. G., & Asher, S. R. (1987). Peer relations and later personal adjustment: Are low-accepted children at risk? *Psychological Bulletin, 102,* 357–389.

Parker, J. G., & Asher, S. R. (1993). Friendship and friendship quality in middle childhood: Links with peer group acceptance and feelings of loneliness and social dissatisfaction. *Developmental Psychology, 29,* 611–621.

Parkes, C. M. (1964a). Recent bereavement as a cause of mental illness. *British Journal of Psychiatry, 110,* 198–204.

Parkes, C. M. (1964b). The effects of bereavement on physical and mental health: A study of the medical records of widows. *British Medical Journal, 2,* 274–279.

Parkes, C. M., Benjamin, B., & Fitzgerald, R. G. (1969). Broken heart: A statistical study of increased mortality among widows. *British Medical Journal, 1,* 740–743.

Parks, M. R., & Adelman, M. B. (1983). Communication networks and the development of romantic relationships: An expansion of uncertainty reduction theory. *Human Communication Research, 10,* 55–79.

Parks, M. R., & Eggert, L. L. (1991). The role of social context in the dynamics of personal relationships. In W. H. Jones & D. Perlman (Eds.), *Advances in personal relationships* (Vol. 2, pp. 1–34). London: Kingsley.

Parks, M. R., Stan, C. M., & Eggert, L. L. (1983). Romantic involvement and social network involvement. *Social Psychology Quarterly, 46,* 116–131.

Parlee, M. B. (1979, October). The friendship bond. *Psychology Today,* pp. 43–54, 113.

Parrott, W. G. (1991). The emotional experiences of envy and jealousy. In P. Salovey (Ed.), *The psychology of jealousy and envy.* New York: Guilford.

Parsons, T., & Bales, R. F. (1955). *Family socialization and interaction processes.* New York: Free Press.

Patterson, C. J., Kupersmidt, J. B., & Griesler, P. C. (1990). Children's perception of self and relationships with others as a function of sociometric status. *Child Development, 61,* 1335–1349.

Patterson, G. R. (1982). *Coercive family process* (Vol. 3). Eugene, OR: Castalia Publishing.

Patterson, G. R., & Hops, H. (1972). Coercion, a game for two: Intervention techniques for marital conflict. In R. Ulrich & P. Mountjoy (Eds.), *The experimental analysis of social behavior.* New York: Appleton-Century-Crofts.

Patterson, G. R., & Reid, J. B. (1970). Reciprocity and coercion: Two facets of social systems. In C. Neuringer & J. L. Michael (Eds.), *Behavior modification in clinical psychology.* New York: Appleton-Century-Crofts.

Patterson, T. L., Kaplan, R. M., Sallis, J. F., & Nader, P. R. (1987). Aggregation of blood pressure in Anglo-American and Mexican-American families. *Preventive Medicine, 16,* 616–625.

Pelham, B., & Swann, W. B., Jr. (1987). *Self-esteem: Components and consequences.* Un-published manuscript, University of Texas, as cited in Swann, W. B., Jr. (1987).

Pennebaker, J. W. (1989). Confession, inhibition and disease. In L. Berkowitz (Ed.), *Advances in experimental social psychology, 22,* 211–244.

Pennebaker, J. W., Colder, M. L., & Sharp, L. K. (1988). *Accelerating the coping process.* Un-published manuscript, cited in Pennebaker, J. W. (1989).

Pennebaker, J. W., & Susman, J. R. (1988). Disclosure of traumas and psychosomatic processes. *Social Science and Medicine, 26,* 327–332.

Peplau, L. A. (1979). Power in dating relationships. In J. Freeman (Ed.), *Women: A feminist perspective* (2nd ed., pp. 107–121). Palo Alto, CA: Mayfield.

Peplau, L. A. (1983). Roles and gender. In H. H. Kelley et al., *Close relationships.* New York: W. H. Freeman.

Peplau, L. A. (1991). Lesbian and gay relationships. In J. C. Gonseorek & J. D. Weinrich (Eds.), *Homosexuality: Research implications for public policy.* Newbury Park, CA: Sage.

Peplau, L. A., & Gordon, S. L. (1985). Women and men in love: Gender differences in close heterosexual relationships. In V. E. O'Leary, R. K. Unger, and B. S. Wallston (Eds.), *Women, gender and social psychology.* Hillsdale, NJ: Erlbaum.

Peplau, L. A., Hill, C. T., & Rubin, Z. (1993). Sex role attitudes in dating and marriage: A 15-year follow-up of the Boston couples study. *Journal of Social Issues, 49,* 31–52.

Peplau, L. A., Padesky, C., & Hamilton, M. (1982). Satisfaction in lesbian relationships. *Journal of Homosexuality, 8,* 23–35.

Peplau, L. A., Rubin, Z., & Hill, C. T. (1977). Sexual intimacy and dating relationships. *Journal of Social Issues, 33,* 86–109.

Perlman, D. (1988). Loneliness: A life-span, family perspective. In R. M. Milardo (Ed.), *Families and social networks.* Newbury Park, CA: Sage.

Perlman, D., & Fehr, B. (1987). The development of intimate relationships. In D. Perlman & S. W. Duck (Eds.), *Intimate relations: Development, dynamics and deterioration.* Newbury Park, CA: Sage.

Perlman, D., Gerson, A., & Spinner, B. (1978). Loneliness among senior citizens. *Essence, 2,* 239–248.

Perrine, R. M. (1993). On being supportive: The emotional consequences of listening to another's distress. *Journal of Social and Personal Relationships, 10,* 371–384.

Pervin, L. A., & Rubin, D. B. (1967). Student dissatisfaction with college and the college dropout: A transactional approach. *Journal of Social Psychology, 72,* 285–295.

Peterson, D. R. (1979). Assessing interpersonal relationships by means of interaction records. *Behavioral Assessment, 1,* 221–236.

Peterson, D. R. (1983). Conflict. In H. H. Kelley et al., *Close relationships.* New York: W. H. Freeman.

Peterson, J. L., & Miller, C. (1980). Physical attractiveness and marriage adjustment in older American couples. *Journal of Psychology, 105,* 247–252.

Pfeiffer, E. (1977). Psychopathology and social pathology. In J. E. Birren & K. W. Schaie (Eds.), *Handbook of the psychology of aging.* New York: Van Nostrand.

Pfeiffer, S. M., & Wong, P. T. P. (1989). Multidimensional jealousy. *Journal of Social and Personal Relationships, 6,* 181–196.

Philliber, W. W., & Vannoy-Hiller, D. (1990). The effect of husband's occupational attainment on wife's achievement. *Journal of Marriage and the Family, 52,* 323–329.

Pilkington, C. J., Tesser, A., & Stephens, D. (1991). Complementarity in romantic relationships: A self-evaluation maintenance perspective. *Journal of Social and Personal Relationships, 8,* 481–504.

Pilkonis, P. A. (1977). The behavioral consequences of shyness. *Journal of Personality, 45,* 596–611.

Pilkonis, P. A., & Zimbardo, P. G. (1979). The personal and social dynamics of shyness. In C. E. Izard (Ed.), *Emotions in personality and psychopathology.* New York: Plenum.

Pines, A., & Aronson, E. (1981). Polyfidelity: An alternative lifestyle without jealousy? *Alternative Lifestyles, 4,* 373–392.

Pines, A., & Aronson, E. (1983). Antecedents, correlates and consequences of sexual jealousy. *Journal of Personality, 51,* 108–136.

Pitt-Rivers, J. (1954/1963). *The people of the sierra.* Chicago: Phoenix Books.

Pleban, R., & Tesser, A. (1981). The effects of relevance and quality of another's performance on interpersonal closeness. *Social Psychology Quarterly, 44,* 278–285.

Pope, B., Nudler, S., Vonkorff, R., & McGhee, J. P. (1974). The experienced professional interviewer versus the complete novice. *Journal of Consulting and Clinical Psychology, 42,* 680–690.

Poser, E. G. (1966). Group therapy in Canada: A national survey. *Canadian Psychiatric Association Journal, 11,* 20–25.

Powers, E. A., & Bultena, G. L. (1976). Sex differences in friendship in old age. *Journal of Marriage and the Family, 38,* 739–747.

Price, J. M., & Ladd, G. W. (1986). Assessment of children's friendships: Implications for social competence and social adjustment. In R. Prinz (Ed.), *Advances in behavioral assessment of children and families* (Vol. 2, pp. 121–149). Greenwich, CT: JAI Press.

Price, R. A., & Vandenberg, S. G. (1979). Matching for physical attractiveness in married couples. *Personality and Social Psychology Bulletin, 5,* 398–400.

Pringle, M. L. K., & Bossio, V. (1960). Early prolonged separation and emotional adjustment. *Journal of Child Psychology and Psychiatry, 1,* 37–48.

Prins, K. S., Buunk, B. P., & Van Yperen, N. W. (1993). Equity, normative disapproval and extramarital relationships. *Journal of Social and Personal Relationships, 10,* 39–53.

Pruitt, D. G., & Carnevale, P. J. (1982). The development of integrative agreements in social conflict. In V. J. Derlega & J. Grzelak (Eds.), *Living with other people.* New York: Academic.

Pruitt, D. G., & Lewis, S. A. (1977). The psychology of integrative bargaining. In D. Druckman (Ed.), *Negotiations: A social psychological perspective.* Beverly Hills, CA: Sage-Halstead.

Pryor, J. B., Reeder, G. D., & McManus, J. A. (1991). Fear and loathing in the workplace: Reactions to AIDS-infected co-workers. *Personality and Social Psychology Bulletin, 17,* 133–139.

Pryor, J. B., Reeder, G. D., Vinacco, R., & Kott, T. (1989). The instrumental and symbolic functions of attitudes towards persons with AIDS. *Journal of Applied Social Psychology, 19,* 377–404.

Pulakos, J. (1989). Young adult relationships: Siblings and friends. *The Journal of Psychology, 123,* 237–244.

Putallaz, M. (1987). Maternal behavior and children's sociometric status. *Child Development, 58,* 324–340.

Putallaz, M., & Gottman, J. M. (1981). Social skills and group acceptance. In S. R. Asher & J. M. Gottman (Eds.), *The development of children's friendships.* New York: Cambridge University Press.

Putallaz, M., & Heflin, A. H. (1990). Parent-child interaction. In S. R. Asher & J. D. Coie (Eds.), *Peer rejection in childhood* (pp. 189–216). New York: Cambridge University Press.

Quinton, D., & Rutter, M. (1976). Early hospital admission and later disturbances in behavior. An attempted replication of Douglas' findings. *Developmental Medicine and Child Neurology, 18,* 447–459.

Radecki-Bush, C., Farrell, A. D., & Bush, J. P. (1993). Predicting jealous responses: The influence of adult attachment and depression on threat appraisal. *Journal of Social and Personal Relationships, 10,* 569–588.

Raffaelli, M., & Duckett, E. (1989). "We were just talking . . .": Conversations in early adolescence. *Journal of Youth and Adolescence, 18,* 567–582.

Rajecki, D. W., Bledsoe, S. B., & Rasmussen, J. L. (1991). Successful personal ads: Gender differences and similarities in offers, stipulations and outcomes. *Basic and Applied Social Psychology, 12,* 457–469.

Rands, M., Levinger, G., & Mellinger, G. (1981). Patterns of conflict resolution and marital satisfaction. *Journal of Family Issues, 2,* 297–321.

Raush, H. L., Barry, W. A., Hertel, R. K., & Swain, M. A. (1974). *Communication, conflict and marriage.* San Francisco: Jossey-Bass.

Rawlins, W. (1983a). Negotiating close friendship: The dialectics of conjunctive freedoms. *Human Communication Research, 9,* 255–266.

Rawlins, W. (1983b). Openness as problematic in ongoing friendships: Two conversational dilemmas. *Communication Monographs, 50,* 1–13.

Ray, G. E., Cohen, R., Secrest, M. E., & Duncan, M. K. (1997). Relating aggressive and victimization behaviors to children's sociometric status and friendships. *Journal of Social and Personal Relationships, 14,* 95–108.

Reina, R. (1959). Two patterns of friendship in a Guatemalan community. *American Anthropologist, 61,* 44–50.

Reis, H. T. (1985). The role of the self in the initiation and course of social interaction. In W. Ickes (Ed.), *Compatible and incompatible relationships.* New York: Springer-Verlag.

Reis, H. T., Nezlek, J., & Wheeler, L. (1980). Physical attractiveness in social interaction. *Journal of Personality and Social Psychology, 38,* 604–617.

Reisman, J. M. (1979). *Anatomy of friendship.* New York: Irvington.

Reisman, J. M. (1981). Adult friendships. In S. W. Duck & R. Gilmour (Eds.), *Personal relationships, 2: Developing personal relationships.* New York: Academic.

Reisman, J. M. (1985). Friendship and its implications for mental health or social competence. *Journal of Early Adolescence, 5,* 383–391.

Reisman, J. M. (1990). Intimacy in same-sex friendships. *Sex Roles, 23,* 65–82.

Reisman, J. M., & Shorr, S. I. (1978). Friendship claims and expectations among children and adults. *Child Development, 49,* 913–916.

Reisman, J. M., & Yamokoski, T. (1974). Psychotherapy and friendship: An analysis of the communication of friends. *Journal of Counseling Psychology, 21,* 269–273.

Rempel, J. K., Holmes, J. G., & Zanna, M. P. (1985). Trust in close relationships. *Journal of Personality and Social Psychology, 49,* 95–112.

Repetti, R. L. (1989). Effects of daily workload on subsequent behavior during marital interaction: The roles of social withdrawal and spouse support. *Journal of Personality and Social Psychology, 57,* 651–659.

Retsinas, J., & Garrity, P. (1985). Nursing home friendships. *The Gerontologist, 25,* 376–381.

Reynolds, P., & Kaplan, G. A. (1990). Social connections and risk of cancer: Prospective evidence from the Alameda County Study. *Behavioral Medicine, 9,* 101–110.

Rhoads, J. M., & Feather, B. W. (1972). Transference and resistance observed in behaviour therapy. *British Journal of Medical Psychology, 45,* 99–103.

Richardson, J. L., Shelton, D. R., Krailo, M., & Levine, A. M. (1990). The effects of compliance with treatment on survival among patients with hemotologic malignancies. *Journal of Clinical Oncology, 8,* 356.

Richardson, S. A. (1971). Children's values and friendship: a study of physical disability. *Journal of Health and Social Behavior, 12,* 253–258.

Richardson, S. A. (1983). Children's values in regard to disabilities: A reply to Yuker. *Rehabilitation Psychology, 28,* 131–140.

Richardson, S. A., Ronald, L., & Kleck, R. E. (1974). The social status of handicapped and non-handicapped boys in a camp setting. *Journal of Special Education, 8,* 143–152.

Richey, M. H., & Richey, H. W. (1980). The significance of best friendships in adolescence. *Psychology in the Schools, 17,* 536–540.

Ridley, C. A., & Avery, A. W. (1979). Social network influence on the dyadic relationship. In R. L. Burgess & T. L. Huston (Eds.), *Social exchange in developing relationships.* New York: Academic.

Rindfuss, R. R., & Stephen, E. H. (1990). Marital noncohabitation: Separation does not make the heart grow fonder. *Journal of Marriage and the Family, 52,* 259–270.

Roberto, K. A., & Scott, J. (1986). Friendships of older men and women: Exchange patterns and satisfaction. *Psychology and Aging, 1,* 103–109.

Roberts, L. J., & Krokoff, L. L. (1990). A time-series analysis of withdrawal, hostility, and displeasure in satisfied and dissatisfied marriages. *Journal of Marriage and the Family, 52,* 95–105.

Robinson, J., & Godbey, G. (1997). *Time for Life.* University Park, PA: Penn State University Press.

Robinson, J. P. (1977). *How American's use time.* New York: Praeger.

Robinson, J. P., Yerby, J., Fieweger, M., & Somerick, N. (1977). Sex-role differences in time use. *Sex roles, 3,* 443–458.

Robinson, L. A., Berman, J. S., & Neimeyer, R. A. (1990). Psychotherapy for the treatment of depression: A comprehensive review of controlled outcome research. *Psychological Bulletin, 100,* 30–49.

Rodin, E. A., Shapiro, H. L., & Lennox, K. (1977). Epilepsy and life performance. *Rehabilitation Literature, 38,* 34–39.

Rodin, M. J. (1982). Non-engagement, failure to engage, and disengagement. In S. W. Duck (Ed.), *Personal relationships 4: Dissolving personal relationships* (pp. 31–50). London: Academic.

Rodin, M., & Price, J. (1995). Overcoming stigma: Credit for self-improvement or discredit for needing to improve? *Personality and Social Psychology Bulletin, 2,* 172–181.

Roff, M. (1961). Childhood social interactions and young adult bad conduct. *Journal of Abnormal and Social Psychology, 63,* 333–337.

Roff, M., Knight, R., & Wertheim, E. (1976). Disturbed preschizophrenics. *Journal of Nervous and Mental Disease, 162,* 274–279.

Roff, M., & Sells, S. B. (1967). The relation between the status of chooser and chosen in a sociometric situation at the grade school level. *Psychology in the Schools, 4,* 101–111.

Roff, M., Sells, S. B., & Golden, M. M. (1972). *Social adjustment and personality development in children.* Minneapolis, MN: University of Minnesota Press.

Rogers, C. (1957). The necessary and sufficient conditions of therapeutic personality change. *Journal of Consulting Psychology, 21,* 95–103.

Rogers, C. R. (1958a). The characteristics of a helping relationship. *Personnel and Guidance Journal, 37,* 6–15.

Rogers, C. R. (1958b). A process conception of psychotherapy. *American Psychologist, 13,* 142–149.

Roiger, J. F. (1993). Power in friendship and use of influence strategies. In P. J. Kalbfleisch (Ed.), *Interpersonal communication: Evolving interpersonal relationships.* Hillsdale, NJ: Erlbaum.

Rokeach, M. (1960). *The open and closed mind.* New York: Basic.

Rokeach, M. (1968). *Beliefs, attitudes and values: A theory of organization and change.* San Francisco: Jossey-Bass.

Rokeach, M., Smith, P. W., & Evans, R. I. (1960). Two kinds of prejudice or one? In M. Rokeach (Ed.), *The open and closed mind.* New York: Basic.

Roloff, M., & Cloven, D. H. (1990). The chilling effect in interpersonal relationships: The reluctance to speak one's mind. In D. Cahn (Ed.), *Intimates in conflict.* Hillsdale, NJ: Erlbaum.

Rook, K. S. (1987). Reciprocity of social exchange and social satisfaction among older women. *Journal of Personality and Social Psychology, 52,* 145–154.

Rook, K. S. (1988). Toward a more differentiated view of loneliness. In S. W. Duck (Ed.), *Handbook of personal relationships.* New York: Wiley.

Rosch, E. (1978). Principles of categorization. In E. Rosch & B. B. Lloyd (Eds.), *Cognition and categorization* (pp. 27–48). Hillsdale, NJ: Erlbaum.

Rose, S. M. (1985). Same and cross-sex friendships and the psychology of homosociality. *Sex Roles, 12,* 63–74.

Rosenblatt, P. (1977). Needed research on commitment in marriage. In G. Levinger & H. L. Raush (Eds.), *Close relationships: Perspectives on the meaning of intimacy.* Amherst, MA: University of Massachusetts Press.

Rosenblatt, P., & Cozby, P. C. (1972). Courtship patterns associated with freedom of choice of spouse. *Journal of Marriage and the Family, 34,* 689–695.

Rosenzweig, S. A. (1954). A trans-evaluation of psychotherapy—Reply to Hans Eysenck. *Journal of Abnormal and Social Psychology, 49,* 298–304.

Rosow, I. (1967). *Social integration of the aged.* New York: Free Press.

Rosow, I. (1968). Housing and local ties of the aged. In B. L. Neugarten (Ed.). *Middle age and aging.* Chicago: University of Chicago Press.

Rosow, I. (1974). *Socialization in old age.* Berkeley, CA: University of California Press.

Rosow, I. (1976). Status and role change through the life span. In R. H. Binstock & E. Shanas (Eds.), *Handbook of aging and the social sciences* (pp. 457–482). New York: Van Nostrand Reinhold.

Ross, E. A. (1921). *Principles of sociology.* New York: Century.

Rubenstein, C., & Shaver, P. (1974). *In search of intimacy.* New York: Delacorte Press.

Rubenstein, C., & Shaver, P. (1980). Loneliness in two northern cities. In J. Hartog, J. R. Audy, & Y. A. Cohen (Eds.), *The anatomy of loneliness.* New York: International Universities Press.

Rubenstein, C., & Shaver, P. (1982). The experience of loneliness. In L. A. Peplau & D. Perlman (Eds.), *Loneliness: A sourcebook of current theory, research and therapy* (pp. 206–224). New York: Wiley.

Rubenstein, C., Shaver, P., & Peplau, L. A. (1979, February). Loneliness. *Human Nature,* 58–65.

Rubermen, W., Weinblatt, E., Goldberg, J. D., & Chaudhary, B. S. (1984). Psychosocial influences on mortality after myocardial infarction. *The New England Journal of Medicine, 311,* 552–559.

Rubin, J. Z., Pruitt, D. G., & Kim, S. H. (1994). *Social conflict: Escalation, stalemate and settlement* (2nd ed.). New York: McGraw-Hill.

Rubin, K. H., & Krasnor, L. R. (1986). Social-cognitive and social behavioral perspectives on problem solving. In M. Perlmutter (Ed.), *Minnesota symposia on child psychology* (Vol. 18, pp. 1–68). Hillsdale, NJ: Erlbaum.

Rubin, L. B. (1985). *Just friends: The role of friendship in our everyday lives.* New York: Harper & Row.

Rubin, L. B. (1986). On men and friendship. *Psychoanalytic Review, 73,* 165–181.

Rubin, Z. (1970). Measurement of romantic love. *Journal of Personality and Social Psychology, 16,* 265–273.

Rubin, Z. (1973). *Liking and loving: An invitation to social psychology.* New York: Holt, Rinehart & Winston.

Rubin, Z. (1974). From liking to loving: Patterns of attraction in dating relationships. In T. Huston (Ed.), *Foundations of interpersonal attraction.* New York: Academic.

Rubin, Z. (1980). *Children's friendships.* Cambridge, MA: Harvard University Press.

Rubin, Z. (1982). Children without friends. In L. A. Peplau & D. Perlman (Eds.), *Loneliness: A sourcebook of theory, research and therapy* (pp. 255–268). New York: Wiley.

Rubin, Z., Hill, C. T., Peplau, L. A., & Dunkel-Schetter, C. (1980). Self-disclosure in dating couples: Sex roles and the ethic of openness. *Journal of Marriage and the Family, 42,* 305–317.

Rubin, Z., Peplau, L. A., & Hill, C. T. (1981). Loving and leaving: Sex differences in romantic attachments. *Sex Roles, 7,* 821–835.

Rumsey, N., Bull, R., & Gahagan, D. (1982). The effect of facial disfigurement on the proxemic behavior of the general public. *Journal of Applied Social Psychology, 12,* 137–150.

Rusbult, C. E. (1980a). Commitment and satisfaction in romantic associations: A test of the investment model. *Journal of Experimental Social Psychology, 16,* 172–186.

Rusbult, C. E. (1980b). Satisfaction and commitment in friendship. *Representative Research in Social Psychology, 11,* 96–105.

Rusbult, C. E. (1983). A longitudinal test of the investment model: The development (and deterioration) of satisfaction and commitment in heterosexual involvements. *Journal of Personality and Social Psychology, 45,* 101–117.

Rusbult, C. E., & Buunk, B. P. (1993). Commitment processes in close relationships: An interdependence analysis. *Journal of Social and Personal Relationships, 10,* 175–204.

Rusbult, C. E., & Farrell, D. (1983). A longitudinal test of the investment model: The impact on job satisfaction, job commitment and turnover of variations in rewards, costs, alternatives and investments. *Journal of Applied Psychology, 68,* 429–438.

Rusbult, C. E., Johnson, D. J., & Morrow, G. D. (1986a). Impact of couple patterns of problem solving on distress and nondistress in dating relationships. *Journal of Personality and Social Psychology, 50,* 744–753.

Rusbult, C. E., Johnson, D. J., & Morrow, G. D. (1986b). Predicting satisfaction and commitment in adult romantic involvements: An assessment of the generality of the investment model. *Social Psychology Quarterly, 49,* 81–89.

Rusbult, C. E., & Martz, J. (1995). Remaining in an abusive relationship: An investment model of nonvoluntary dependence. *Personality and Social Psychology Bulletin, 6,* 558–571.

Rusbult, C. E., Morrow, G. D., & Johnson, D. J. (1987). Self-esteem and problem-solving behavior in close relationships. *British Journal of Social Psychology, 26,* 293–303.

Rusbult, C. E., van Lange, P. A. M., & Verette, J. (forthcoming). *Perceived superiority of one's relationship as a relationship maintenance mechanism.* Manuscript in preparation, Dept. of Psychology, University of North Carolina at Chapel Hill.

Rusbult, C. E., Verette, J., Whitney, G. A., Slovik, L. F., & Lipkus, I. (1991). Accommodation processes in close relationships: Theory and preliminary empirical evidence. *Journal of Personality and Social Psychology, 60,* 53–78.

Rusbult, C. E., Yovetich, N. A., & Verette, J. (1996). An interdependence analysis of accommodation processes. In G. J. O. Fletcher & J. Fitness (Eds.), *Knowledge structures in close relationships: A social psychological approach.* Mahwah, NJ: Erlbaum.

Russell, D., Cutrona, C. E., Rose, J., & Yurko, K. (1984). Social and emotional loneliness: An examination of Weiss' typology of loneliness. *Journal of Personality and Social Psychology, 46,* 1313–1321.

Russell, D., Peplau, L. A., & Cutrona, C. E. (1980). The revised UCLA Loneliness Scale: Concurrent and discriminative validity evidence. *Journal of Personality and Social Psychology, 39,* 472–480.

Russell, D., Peplau, L. A., & Ferguson, M. L. (1978). Developing a measure of loneliness. *Journal of Personality Assessment, 42,* 290–294.

Russell, D., Steffen, M., Yurko, K., & Salih, F. A. (1981). *Testing a cognitive model of loneliness.* Paper presented at the American Psychological Association Convention, Los Angeles, as cited in Russell, D., et al. (1984).

Russell, D. W. (1996). UCLA Loneliness Scale (Version 3): Reliability, validity and factor structure. *Journal of Personality Assessment, 66,* 20–40.

Ryckman, R. M., Robbins, M. A., Thornton, B., Kaaczor, L. M., Gayton, S. L., & Anderson, C. V. (1991). Public self-consciousness and physique stereotyping. *Personality and Social Psychology Bulletin, 18,* 400–405.

Sabatelli, R. M., & Cecil-Pigo, E. F. (1985). Relational interdependence and commitment in marriage. *Journal of Marriage and the Family, 47,* 931–937.

Sadalla, E. K., Kenrick, D. T., & Vershure,

B. (1987). Dominance and heterosexual attraction. *Journal of Personality and Social Psychology, 52*, 730–738.

Sadava, S. W., & Matejcic, C. (1987). Generalized and specific loneliness in early marriage. *Canadian Journal of Behavioural Science, 19*, 56–66.

Safilios-Rothschild, C. (1976). A macro- and micro-examination of family power and love. An exchange model. *Journal of Marriage and the Family, 38*, 355–362.

Safilios-Rothschild, C. (1982). Social and psychological parameters of friendship and intimacy for disabled people. In M. G. Eisenberg, C. Griggins, & R. J. Duval (Eds.), *Disabled people as second class citizens* (pp. 40–51). New York: Springer Publications.

Sagrestano, L. M. (1992). Power strategies in interpersonal relationships: The effects of expertise and gender. *Psychology of Women Quarterly, 16*, 481–495.

Sallis, J. F., Grossman, R. M., Pinsky, R. B., Patterson, P. L., & Nader, P. R. (1987). The development of scales to measure social support for diet and exercise behaviors. *Preventive Medicine, 16*, 825–836.

Salzinger, L. L. (1982). The ties that bind: The effects of clustering on dyadic relationships. *Social Networks, 4*, 117–145.

Salzinger, L. L. (1985). Identities and self-identification. In B. R. Schlenker (Ed.), *The self and social life.* New York: McGraw-Hill.

Sapadin, L. A. (1988). Friendship and gender: Perspectives of professional men and women. *Journal of Social and Personal Relationships, 5*, 387–403.

Sarason, I. G. (1979). *Life stress, self-preoccupation and social supports.* Technical Report, SCS-LS-008, Office of Naval Research, Arlington, Virginia.

Sarason, I. G., & Sarason, B. R. (1984). Life changes, moderators of stress and health. In A. Baum, S. A. Taylor, J. E. Singer (Eds.), *Handbook of psychology and health Vol. IV: Social psychological aspects of health.* Hillsdale, NJ: Erlbaum.

Sartorius, N., Jablensky, A., Korten, A., Ernberg, G., Anker, M., Cooper, J. E., & Day, R. (1986). Early manifestations and first contact incidence of schizophrenia in different cultures. *Psychological Medicine, 16*, 909–928.

Savin-Williams, R. C. (1987). *Adolescence: An ethological perspective.* New York: Springer-Verlag.

Savin-Williams, R. C., & Berndt, T. J. (1990). Friendship and peer relationships. In S. S. Feldman & G. R. Elliott (Eds.), *At the threshold: The developing adolescent.* Cambridge, MA: Harvard University Press.

Schaap, C., Buunk, B. P., & Kerkstra, A. (1988). Marital conflict resolution. In P. Noller & M. Fitzpatrick (Eds.), *Perspectives on marital interaction* (pp. 203–244). Philadelphia: Multilingual.

Schafer, L. C., McCaul, K. D., & Glasgow, R. E. (1986). Supportive and non-supportive family behaviors: Relationships to adherence and metabolic control in persons with Type I diabetes. *Diabetes Care, 9*, 179–185.

Schafer, R. B., & Keith, P. M. (1980). Equity and depression among married couples. *Social Psychology Quarterly, 43*, 430–435.

Schleifer, S. J., Keller, S. E., Camerino, M. S., Thornton, J. C., & Stein, M. (1983). Suppression of lymphocyte stimulation following bereavement. *Journal of the American Medical Association, 250*, 374–377.

Schmidt, N., & Sermat, V. (1983). Measuring loneliness in different relationships. *Journal of Personality and Social Psychology, 44*, 1038–1047.

Schoenbach, V. J., Kaplan, B. H., Freedman, L., & Kleinbaum, D. G. (1986). Social ties and mortality in Evans County, Georgia. *American Journal of Epidemiology, 123*, 577–591.

Schofield, J. W. (1981). Complementary and conflicting identities: Images and interactions in an interracial school. In S. R. Asher & J. M. Gottman (Eds.), *The development of children's friendships* (pp. 53–90). Cambridge, UK: Cambridge University Press.

Schofield, W. (1964). *Psychotherapy: The purchase of friendship.* Englewood Cliffs, NJ: Prentice-Hall.

Schreiber, M., & Feeley, M. (1965). Siblings of the retarded: A guided group experience. *Children, 12*, 221–229.

Schultz, D. P., & Schultz, S. E. (1995). *A history of*

*modern psychology* (6th ed.). New York: Harcourt Brace Jovanovich.

Schultz, N. R., & Moore, D. (1988). Loneliness: Differences across three age levels. *Journal of Social and Personal Relationships, 5,* 275–284.

Schulz, C. G., & Decker, S. (1985). Long-term adjustment to physical disability: The role of social support, perceived control, and self-blame. *Journal of Personal and Social Psychology, 48,* 1162–1172.

Schwartz, C. G. (1957). Perspectives on deviance—wives' definitions of their husbands' mental illness. *Psychiatry, 20,* 275–291.

Schwartz, J. C., & Shaver, P. (1987). Emotions and emotion knowledge in interpersonal relationships. In W. H. Jones & D. Perlman (Eds.), *Advances in personal relationships* (Vol. 1, 197–241). London: Kingsley.

Schwartz, J. C., Shaver, P., & Kirson, D. (1987). Emotion knowledge: Further exploration of a prototype approach. *Journal of Personality and Social Psychology, 52,* 1061–1086.

Schwarzer, R., & Leppin, A. (1991). Social support and health: A theoretical and empirical overview. *Journal of Social and Personal Relationships, 8,* 99–127.

Seligman, C., Fazio, R. H., & Zanna, M. D. (1980). Effects of salience of extrinsic rewards on liking and loving. *Journal of Personality and Social Psychology, 38,* 453–460.

Selman, R. L. (1980). *The growth of interpersonal understanding: Developmental and clinical analyses.* New York: Academic.

Selman, R. L., & Jaquette, D. (1977a). Stability and oscillation in interpersonal awareness. *Nebraska Symposium on Motivation, 25,* 262–304.

Selman, R. L., & Jaquette, D. (1977b). *The development of interpersonal awareness.* Working draft of manual, Harvard-Judge Baker Social Reasoning Project, cited in Rubin, Z. (1980).

Selman, R. L., & Schultz, L. H. (1990). *Making a friend in youth: Developmental theory and pair therapy.* Chicago: University of Chicago Press.

Selman, R. L., & Selman, A. D. (1979). Children's ideas about friendship: A new theory. *Psychology Today, 114,* 71–80.

Sermat, V. (1980). Some situational and personality correlates of loneliness. In J. Hartog, J. R. Audy, & Y. A. Cohen (Eds.), *The anatomy of loneliness.* New York: International Universities Press.

Shapiro, A. K., Struening, E., Shapiro, E., & Barten, H. (1976). Prognostic correlates of psychotherapy in psychiatric outpatients. *American Journal of Psychiatry, 133,* 802–808.

Shapiro, D. A., & Shapiro, D. (1982). Meta-analysis of comparative outcome studies: A replication and refinement. *Psychological Bulletin, 92,* 581–604.

Shapiro, J. G., Krauss, H. H., & Truax, C. B. (1969). Therapeutic conditions and disclosure beyond the therapeutic encounter. *Journal of Consulting Psychology, 16,* 290–294.

Sharabany, R., Gershoni, R., & Hofman, J. E. (1981). Girlfriend, boyfriend: Age and sex differences in intimate friendships. *Developmental Psychology, 17,* 800–808.

Sharpsteen, D. J. (1991). The organization of jealousy knowledge: Romantic jealousy as a blended emotion. In P. Salovey (Ed.), *The psychology of jealousy and envy.* New York: Guilford.

Sharpsteen, D. J. (1993). Romantic jealousy as an emotion concept: A prototype analysis. *Journal of Social and Personal Relationships, 10,* 69–82.

Sharpsteen, D. J., & Kirkpatrick, L. A. (1997). Romantic jealousy and adult romantic attachment. *Journal of Personality and Social Psychology, 72,* 627–640.

Sharpsteen, D. J., & Schmalz, C. M. (1988). *Romantic jealousy as a blended emotion.* Paper presented at the meeting of the Colorado Psychological Association, Fort Collins, as cited in Sharpsteen, D. J. (1991).

Shaver, K. G. (1970). Defensive attribution: Effects of severity and relevance on the responsibility assigned for an accident. *Journal of Personality and Social Psychology, 14,* 101–113.

Shaver, P., & Buhrmester, D. (1983). Loneliness, sex-role orientation and group life: A social needs perspective. In P. B. Paulus (Ed.), *Basic group processes.* New York: Springer-Verlag.

Shaver, P., Furman, W., & Buhrmester, D. (1985). Transition to college: Network changes, social skills and loneliness. In S. Duck & D. Perlman (Eds.), *Understanding personal relationships:*

*An interdisciplinary approach* (pp. 193–219). London: Sage.

Shaver, P., & Hazan, C. (1988). A biased overview of the study of love. *Journal of Social and Personal Relationships, 5,* 473–501.

Shaver, P. R., & Hazan, C. (1993). Adult romantic attachment: Theory and evidence. In D. Perlman & W. H. Jones (Eds.), *Advances in personal relationships* (Vol. 4). London: Kingsley.

Shaver, P., Hazan, C., & Bradshaw, D. (1988). Love as attachment: The integration of three behavioral systems. In R. J. Sternberg & M. L. Barnes (Eds.), *The psychology of love.* New Haven, CT: Yale University Press.

Shaver, P., Schwartz, J., Kirson, D., & O'Connon, D. (1987). Emotion knowledge: Further explorations of a prototype approach. *Journal of Personality and Social Psychology, 52,* 1061–1086.

Shea, L., Thompson, L., & Blieszner, R. (1988). Resources in older adults' old and new friendships. *Journal of Social and Personal Relationships, 5,* 83–96.

Shea, M. T., Elkin, I., Imber, S. D., & Sotsky, S. M. (1992). Course of depressive symptoms over follow-up: Findings about the National Institute of Mental Health Treatment of Depression Collaborative Research Program. *Archives of General Psychiatry, 49,* 782–787.

Shechtman, Z., Vurembrand, N., & Hertz-Lazarowitz, R. (1994). A dyadic and gender-specific analysis of close friendships of preadolescents receiving group psychotherapy. *Journal of Social and Personal Relationships, 11,* 443–448.

Shepard, J. A., & Strathman, A. J. (1989). Attractiveness and height: The role of stature in dating preference, frequency of dating, and perceptions of attractiveness. *Personality and Social Psychology Bulletin, 15,* 617–627.

Shontz, F. C. (1971). Physical disability and personality: Theory and recent research. In W. S. Neff (Ed.), *Rehabilitation psychology.* Proceedings of the National Conference on the Psychological Aspects of Disability, Monterey, California, October 1970 (pp. 33–73). Washington, DC: American Psychological Association.

Shrauger, J. S. (1975). Responses to evaluation as a function of initial self-perceptions. *Psychological Bulletin, 82,* 581–596.

Shrum, W., & Cheek, N. H. (1987). Social structure during the school years: onset of the degrouping process. *American Sociological Review, 52,* 218–223.

Shrum, W., Cheek, N. H., & Hunter, S. M. (1988). Friendship in school: Gender and racial homophily. *Sociology of Education, 61,* 227–239.

Shubik, M. (1971). The dollar auction game: A paradox in noncooperative behavior and escalation. *Journal of Conflict Resolution, 15,* 109–111.

Shweder, R. A., Mahapatra, M., & Miller, J. G. (1990). Culture and moral development. In J. W. Stigler, R. A. Shweder, & G. Herdt (Eds.), *Cultural psychology.* New York: Cambridge University Press.

Sigall, H., & Landy, D. (1973). Radiating beauty: The effects of having a physically attractive partner on person perception. *Journal of Personality and Social Psychology, 28,* 218–224.

Sigall, H., & Ostrove, N. (1975). Beautiful but dangerous: Effects of offender attractiveness and nature of the crime in juridic judgment. *Journal of Personality and Social Psychology, 31,* 410–414.

Sigelman, C. K., & Singleton, L. C. (1986). Stigmatization in childhood: A survey of developmental trends and issues. In S. C. Ainlay, G. Becker, & L. M. Coleman (Eds.), *The dilemma of difference.* New York: Plenum.

Sillars, D. A. (1980). Attributions and communication in roommate conflicts. *Communication Monographs, 47,* 180–200.

Sillars, D. A., & Weisberg, J. (1987). Conflict as a social skill. In M. E. Roloff & G. R. Miller (Eds.), *Interpersonal processes: New directions in communication research.* Newbury Park, CA: Sage.

Silverman, I. (1971). Physical attractiveness and courtship. *Sexual Behavior, 3,* 22–25.

Silverstein, C. (1981). *Man to man: Gay couples in America.* New York: William Morrow.

Simpson, J. A. (1990). Influence of attachment style on romantic relationships. *Journal of Personality and Social Psychology, 59,* 971–980.

Simpson, J. A., Campbell, B., & Berscheid, E. (1986). The association between romantic love and marriage: Kepart (1967) twice revisited. *Personality and Social Psychology Bulletin, 12,* 363–372.

Simpson, J. A., Gangestad, S. W., & Lerma, M. (1990). Perception of physical attractiveness: Mechanisms involved in the maintenance of romantic relationships. *Journal of Personality and Social Psychology, 59,* 1192–1201.

Singleton, L. C., & Asher, S. R. (1979). Racial integration and children's peer preference: An investigation of developmental and cohort differences. *Child Development, 50,* 936–941.

Skipper, J. K., Fink, S. L., & Hallenbeck, P. N. (1968). Physical disability among married women. *Journal of Rehabilitation, 34,* 16–19.

Slamecka, N. J., & Graf, P. (1978). The generation effect: Delineation of a phenomenon. *Journal of Experimental Psychology: Human Learning and Memory, 4,* 592–604.

Smith, D. A., Vivian, D., & O'Leary, K. D. (1990). Longitudinal prediction of marital discord from premarital expression of affect. *Journal of Consulting and Clinical Psychology, 58,* 790–797.

Smith, M. L., Glass, G. V., & Miller, T. I. (1980). *The benefits of psychotherapy.* Baltimore: Johns Hopkins University Press.

Smuts, B. (1985). *Sex and friendship in baboons.* New York: Aldine de Gruyter.

Snyder, M., Tanke, E. D., & Berscheid, E. (1977). Social perception and interpersonal behavior: On the self-fulfilling nature of social stereotypes. *Journal of Personality and Social Psychology, 35,* 656–666.

Solano, C. H., & Batten, P. G. (1979). Loneliness and objective self-disclosure in an acquaintance exercise. Unpublished manuscript, Wake Forest University, cited in Derlega, V. J., & Margulis, S. T. (1982).

Solano, C. H., Batten, P. G., & Parish, E. A. (1982). Loneliness and patterns of self-disclosure. *Journal of Personality and Social Psychology, 43,* 524–531.

Solano, C. H., & Koester, N. H. (1989). Loneliness and communication problems: Subjective anxiety or objective skills. *Personality and Social Psychology Bulletin, 15,* 126–133.

South, S. J., & Lloyd, K. M. (1995). Social alternatives and marital dissolution. *American Sociological Review, 60,* 21–35.

Spence, J. T., & Helmreich, R. L. (1978). *Masculinity and femininity: Their psychological dimensions, correlates and antecedents.* Austin, TX: University of Texas Press.

Sperling, M. B. (1985). Discriminant measures for desperate love. *Journal of Personality Assessment, 49,* 324–328.

Spiegel, D. (1991). Mind matters: Effects of group support on cancer patients. *Journal of NIH Research, 3,* 61–63.

Spiegel, D., Bloom, J. R., Kraemer, H. C., & Gottheil, E. (1989). Psychological support for cancer patients. *Lancet, ii,* 1447.

Spitzberg, B. H., & Canary, D. (1985). Loneliness and relationship competent communication. *Journal of Social and Personal Relationships, 2,* 387–402.

Sprecher, S. (1985). Sex differences in bases of power in dating relationships. *Sex Roles, 12,* 449–462.

Sprecher, S. (1986). The relation between inequity and emotions in close relationships. *Social Psychology Quarterly, 49,* 309–321.

Sprecher, S. (1989). The importance to males and females of physical attractiveness, earning potential and expressiveness in initial attraction. *Sex Roles, 21,* 591–607.

Sprecher, S., & Felmlee, D. (1995). *The balance of power, decision making, and control in romantic couples.* Poster session presented at the International Conference on Personal Relationships, College of William & Mary, Williamsburg, Virginia.

Sprecher, S., & Metts, S. (1989). Development of the "Romantic Beliefs Scale" and examination of the effects of gender and gender-role orientation. *Journal of Social and Personal Relationships, 6,* 387–411.

Sprecher, S., Sullivan, Q., & Hatfield, E. (1994). Mate selection preferences: Gender differences examined in a national sample. *Journal of Personality and Social Psychology, 66,* 1074–1080.

Stafford, L., & Canary, D. J. (1991). Maintenance strategies and romantic relationship type, gender and relational characteristics. *Journal of Social and Personal Relationships, 8,* 217–242.

Staples, R. (1981). Black singles in America. In P. J. Stein (Ed.), *Single life: Unmarried adults in social context.* New York: St. Martin's.

Staples, R., & Johnson, L. B. (1993). *Black families at the crossroads.* San Francisco: Jossey-Bass.

Starker, J. E., Morgan, D. L., & March, S. (1993). Analyzing change in networks of personal relationships. In D. Perlman & W. H. Jones (Eds.), *Advances in personal relationships* (Vol. 4). London: Kingsley.

Steck, R., Levitan, D., McLane, D., & Kelley, H. H. (1982). Care, need and conceptions of love. *Journal of Personality and Social Psychology, 43,* 481–491.

Steil, J. M., & Weltman, K. (1991). Marital inequality: The importance of resources, personal attributes, and social norms on career valuing and the allocation of domestic responsibilities. *Sex Roles, 24,* 161–179.

Steil, J. M., & Weltman, K. (1992). Influence strategies at home and work: A study of sixty dual career couples. *Journal of Social and Personal Relationships, 9,* 65–88.

Stein, D. M., & Lambert, M. J. (1984). On the relationship between therapist experience and psychotherapy outcome. *Clinical Psychology Review, 4,* 1–16.

Steinberg, L. (1985). *Adolescence.* New York: Knopf.

Steinberg, L. (1987). Single parents, step-parents and the susceptibility of adolescents to antisocial peer pressure. *Child Development, 57,* 269–275.

Stern, L. A. (1995). *Grievance accounts between friends.* Paper presented at the conference of the International Network on Personal Relationships, College of William & Mary, Williamsburg, Virginia.

Sternberg, R. J. (1986). A triangular theory of love. *Psychological Review, 93,* 119–135.

Sternberg, R. J. (1987). Liking versus loving: A comparative evaluation of theories. *Psychological Bulletin, 102,* 331–345.

Sternberg, R. J. (1988a). Triangulating love. In R. J. Sternberg & M. Barnes (Eds.), *The psychology of love.* New Haven, CT: Yale University Press.

Sternberg, R. J. (1988b). *The triangle of love: Intimacy, passion, commitment.* New York: Basic.

Sternberg, R. J., & Barnes, M. (1985). Real and ideal others in romantic relationships: Is four a crowd? *Journal of Personality and Social Psychology, 49,* 1586–1608.

Sternberg, R. J., & Grajek, S. (1984). The nature of love. *Journal of Personality and Social Psychology, 47,* 312–329.

Stewart, A. J., & Rubin, Z. (1976). The power mo-

tive in the dating couple. *Journal of Personality and Social Psychology, 34,* 305–309.

Stocker, C. M., Lanthier, R. P., & Furman, W. (1997). Sibling relationships in early adulthood. *Journal of Family Psychology, 11,* 210–221.

Stokes, J. P. (1985). The relation of social network and individual difference variables to loneliness. *Journal of Personality and Social Psychology, 48,* 981–990.

Strauss, H. M. (1968). Reference group and social comparison among the totally blind. In H. H. Hyman & E. Singer (Eds.), *Readings in reference group theory and research* (pp. 222–237). New York: Free Press.

Stroebe, W. (1977). Self-esteem and interpersonal attraction. In S. W. Duck (Ed.), *Theory and practice of interpersonal attraction.* London: Academic.

Stroebe, W., & Stroebe, M. S. (1986). Beyond marriage: The impact of partner loss on health. In R. Gilmour and S. Duck (Eds.), *The emerging field of personal relationships* (pp. 203–224). Hillsdale, NJ: Erlbaum.

Stroebe, W., & Stroebe, M. S. (1987). *Bereavement and Health: The psychological and physical consequences of partner loss.* New York: Cambridge University Press.

Stroebe, W., & Stroebe, M. S. (1992). Bereavement and health: Processes of adjusting to the loss of partner. In L. Montada, S. Filipp, & M. J. Lerner (Eds.), *Life crises and experiences of loss in adulthood.* Hillsdale, NJ: Erlbaum.

Stroebe, W., Stroebe, M. S., Gergen, K. J., & Gergen, M. (1982). The effects of bereavement on mortality: A social psychological analysis. In J. R. Eiser (Ed.), *Social Psychology and Behavioral Medicine.* Chichester, UK: Wiley.

Strong, B., & DeVault, C. (1995). *The marriage and family experience* (6th ed.). Minneapolis, MN: West.

Strong, S. R., Hills, J. J., Kilmartin, C. T., DeVries, H., Lanier, K., Nelson, B. N., Strickland, D., & Meyer, C. W., III. (1988). The dynamic relations among interpersonal behaviors: A test of complementarity and anti-complementarity. *Journal of Personality and Social Psychology, 54,* 798–810.

Strube, M. J. (1988). The decision to leave an abusive relationship: Empirical evidence and theoretical issues. *Psychological Bulletin, 104,* 236–250.

Strum, S. C. (1987). *Almost human: A journey into the world of baboons.* New York: Norton.

Strupp, H. H., & Binder, J. L. (1984). *Psychotherapy in a new key: A guide to time limited dynamic psychotherapy.* New York: Basic.

Strupp, H. H., & Hadley, S. W. (1979). Specific vs. nonspecific factors in psychotherapy. *Archives of General Psychiatry, 36,* 1125–1136.

Suitor, J. J. (1987). Friendship networks in transition: Married mothers return to school. *Journal of Social and Personal Relationships, 4,* 445–461.

Sullivan, H. S. (1953). *The interpersonal theory of psychiatry.* New York: Norton.

Suls, J. M., & Miller, R. L. (Eds.). (1977). *Social comparison processes: Theoretical and empirical perspectives.* Washington, DC: Halsted-Wiley.

Sunby, H. S., & Kreyberg, P. C. (1968). *Prognosis in child psychiatry.* Baltimore: Williams & Wilkins.

Sunnafrank, M. (1992). On debunking the attitude similarity myth. *Communication Monographs, 59,* 164–179.

Sunnafrank, M., & Miller, G. R. (1981). The role of initial conversations in determining attraction to similar and dissimilar strangers. *Human Communication Research, 8,* 16–25.

Surra, C. A. (1985). Courtship types: Variations in interdependence between partners and social networks. *Journal of Personality and Social Psychology, 49,* 357–375.

Surra, C. A., & Huston, T. (1987). Mate selection as a social transition. In D. Perlman & S. Duck (Eds.), *Intimate relationships: Development, dynamics and deterioration.* Newbury Park, CA: Sage.

Surra, C. A., & Longstreth, M. (1990). Similarity of outcomes, interdependence, and conflict in dating relationships. *Journal of Personality and Social Psychology, 59,* 501–516.

Surra, C. A., & Milardo, R. M. (1991). The social psychological context of developing relationships: Interactive and psychological networks. In W. H. Jones & D. Perlman (Eds.), *Advances in personal relationships* (Vol. 3, pp. 1–36). London: Kingsley.

Swann, W. B., Jr. (1983). Self-verification: Bringing social reality into harmony with the self. In J. Suls & A. G. Greenwald (Eds.), *Psychological perspectives on the self* (Vol. 2, pp. 33–66). Hillsdale, NJ: Erlbaum.

Swann, W. B., Jr. (1984). Quest for accuracy in person perception: A matter of pragmatics. *Psychological Review, 91,* 457–477.

Swann, W. B., Jr. (1987). Identity negotiation: Where two roads meet. *Journal of Personality and Social Psychology, 53,* 1038–1051.

Swann, W. B., Jr. (1992). Seeking truth, finding despair: Some unhappy consequences of negative self-concept. *Current Directions in Psychological Science, 1,* 15–18.

Swann, W. B., Jr. (1996). *Self-traps: The elusive quest for higher self-esteem.* New York: W. H. Freeman.

Swann, W. B., Jr., De La Ronda, C., & Hixon, J. G. (1994). Authenticity and positivity strivings in marriage and courtship. *Journal of Personality and Social Psychology, 66,* 857–869.

Swann, W. B., Jr., & Ely, R. J. (1984). A battle of wills: Self-verification versus behavioral confirmation. *Journal of Personality and Social Psychology, 46,* 1287–1302.

Swann, W. B., Jr., & Hill, C. A. (1982). When our identities are mistaken: Reaffirming self-conceptions through social interaction. *Journal of Personality and Social Psychology, 43,* 59–66.

Swann, W. B., Jr., Hixon, J. G., & De La Ronda, C. (1992). Embracing the bitter "truth": Negative self-concepts and marital commitment. *Psychological Science, 3,* 118–121.

Swann, W. B., Jr., & Pelham, B. W. (1987). The social construction of identity: Self-verification among people with negative self-concept. Unpublished manuscript, cited in Swann, W. B., Jr. (1987).

Swann, W. B., Jr., Pelham, B. W., & Krull, D. S. (1989). Agreeable fancy or disagreeable truth? Reconciling self-enhancement and self-verification. *Journal of Personality and Social Psychology, 57,* 782–791.

Swann, W. B., Jr., & Predmore, S. C. (1985). Intimates as agents of social support: Sources of consolation or despair? *Journal of Personality and Social Psychology, 49,* 1609–1617.

Swann, W. B., Jr., & Read, S. J. (1981a). Acquiring self-knowledge: The search for feedback that fits. *Journal of Personality and Social Psychology, 41,* 1119–1128.

Swann, W. B., Jr., & Read, S. J. (1981b). Self-verification processes: How we sustain our self-conceptions. *Journal of Experimental Social Psychology, 17,* 351–372.

Swindler, D. R. (1980). A synopsis of primate phylogeny. In J. S. Lockard (Ed.), *The evolution of human social behavior.* New York: Elsevier.

Tannen, D. (1990). *You just don't understand: Women and men in conversation.* New York: Ballantine.

Taylor, D. A. (1968). Some aspects of the development of interpersonal relationships. Social penetration processes. *Journal of Social Psychology, 75,* 79–90.

Taylor, D. A., Altman, I., & Sorrentino, R. (1969). Interpersonal exchange as a function of rewards and costs and situational factors: Expectancy confirmation-disconfirmation. *Journal of Personality and Social Psychology, 5,* 324–339.

Tedeschi, J. T. (1974). Attributions, liking and power. In T. Huston (Ed.), *Foundations of interpersonal attraction.* New York: Academic.

Teismann, M. W., & Mosher, D. L. (1978). Jealous conflict in dating couples. *Psychological Reports, 42,* 1211–1216.

Tennov, D. (1979). *Love and limerance: The experience of being in love.* New York: Stein & Day.

Tesser, A. (1980). Self-esteem maintenance in family dynamics. *Journal of Personality and Social Psychology, 38,* 77–91.

Tesser, A. (1984). Self-evaluation maintenance processes: Implications for relationships and development. In J. C. Masters & K. Yarkin-Levin (Eds.), *Boundary areas in social developmental psychology.* New York: Academic.

Tesser, A. (1988). Toward a self-evaluation maintenance model of social behavior. In L. Berkowitz (Ed.), *Advances in experimental social psychology* (Vol. 21, 181–227). San Diego, CA: Academic.

Tesser, A., & Campbell, J. (1980). Self-definition: The impact of the relative performance and similarity of others. *Social Psychology Quarterly, 43,* 341–347.

Tesser, A., Campbell, J., & Smith, M. (1984). Friendship choice and performance: Self-eval-uation maintenance in children. *Journal of Personality and Social Psychology, 46,* 561–574.

Tesser, A., & Smith, J. (1980). Some effects of friendship and task relevance on helping: You don't always help the one you like. *Journal of Experimental Social Psychology, 16,* 582–590.

Thibaut, J. W., & Kelley, H. H. (1959). *The social psychology of groups.* New York: Wiley.

Thompson, L. W., Breckenridge, J. N., Gallagher, D., & Peterson, J. (1984). Effects of bereavement on self-perception of physical health in elderly widows and widowers. *Journal of Gerontology, 39,* 309–314.

Thompson, T. L. (1981). The impact of physical handicap on communicative characteristics of the marital dyad. *Western Journal of Speech Communication, 45,* 227–240.

Thorne, B., & Luria, Z. (1986). Sexuality and gender in children's daily worlds. *Social Problems, 33,* 176–190.

Thornhill, R., & Gangestad, S. W. (1994). Human fluctuating asymmetry and sexual behavior. *Psychological Science, 5,* 297–302.

Thornton, A. (1989). Changing attitudes toward family issues in the United States. *Journal of Marriage and the Family, 51,* 873–893.

Timmerman, K., & Hewitt, J. (1980). Examining the halo effect of physical attractiveness. *Perceptual and Motor Skills, 51,* 607–612.

Tizard, B. (1978). *Adoption: A second chance.* New York: Free Press.

Tornstam, L. (1992). Loneliness in marriage. *Journal of Social and Personal Relationships, 9,* 197–217.

Torrey, E. F. (1987). Prevalence studies in schizophrenia. *British Journal of Psychiatry, 150,* 598–608.

Tov-Ruach, L. (1980). Jealousy, attention, and loss. In A. O. Rorty (Ed.), *Explaining emotions* (pp. 465–488). Berkeley, CA: University of California Press.

Townsend, J. M., & Levy, G. D. (1990a). Effects of potential partner costume and physical attractiveness on sexuality and partner selection. *Journal of Psychology, 124,* 371–389.

Townsend, J. M., & Levy, G. D. (1990b). Effects of potential partner physical attractiveness and socioeconomic status on sexuality and partner selection. *Archives of Sexual Behavior, 19,* 149–164.

Tracey, J. (1994). An examination of complementarity in interpersonal behavior. *Journal of Personality and Social Psychology, 67,* 864–878.

Triandis, H. C. (1994). *Culture and social behavior.* New York: McGraw-Hill.

Trivers, R. I. (1971). The evolution of reciprocal altruism. *Quarterly Review of Biology, 46,* 35–57.

Trivers, R. I. (1972). Parental investment and sexual selection. In B. Campbell (Ed.), *Sexual selection and the descent of man 1871–1971.* Chicago: Aldine.

Trivers, R. (1985). *Social evolution.* Menlo Park, CA: Benjamin/Cummings.

Truax, C. B., & Carkhuff, R. R. (1967). *Toward effective counseling and psychotherapy.* Chicago: Aldine.

Tuma, N., & Hallinan, M. T. (1979). The effects of sex, race and achievement in school children's friendships. *Social Forces, 57,* 1265–1285.

Turner, F. (1884). *Samoa.* London: Macmillan.

Tutin, C. E. G. (1979). Mating patterns and reproductive strategies in a community of wild chimpanzees. *Behavioral Ecology and Sociobiology, 6,* 39–48.

Ullmann, C. A. (1957). Teachers, peers, and tests as predictions of adjustment. *Journal of Educational Psychology, 48,* 257–267.

Utne, M. K., Hatfield, E., Traupmann, J., & Greenberger, D. (1984). Equity, marital satisfaction, and stability. *Journal of Social and Personal Relationships, 1,* 323–332.

Van Hasselt, V. B., Hersen, M., & Kazdin, A. E. (1985). Assessment of social skills in visually handicapped adolescents. *Behaviour Research and Therapy, 23,* 53–63.

van Lange, P. A. M., Rusbult, C. E., & Drigotas, S. M. (1992). *Willingness to sacrifice in close relationships.* Unpublished manuscript, Free University, Amsterdam, as cited in Rusbult, C. E., & Buunk, B. P. (1993).

van Lange, P. A. M., Rusbult, C. E., Drigotas, S. M., Arriga, X. B., Witcher, B. S., & Cox, C. L. (1997). Willingness to sacrifice in close relationships. *Journal of Personality and Social Psychology, 72,* 1373–1395.

van Rooijen, L. (1979). Widow's bereavement: Stress and depression after 1 1/2 years. In I. G. Sarason & C. D. Spielberger (Eds.), *Stress and anxiety* (Vol. 6). Washington, DC: Hemisphere.

Van Yperen, N. W., & Buunk, B. P. (1990). A longitudinal study of equity and satisfaction in intimate relationships. *European Journal of Social Psychology, 20,* 287–309.

Varni, C. A. (1974). An exploratory study of spouse swapping. In J. R. Smith & L. G. Smith (Eds.), *Beyond monogamy* (pp. 214–229). Baltimore: Johns Hopkins University Press.

Venzor, E., Gillis, J. S., & Beal, D. G. (1976). Preference for counselor response styles. *Journal of Counseling Psychology, 23,* 538–542.

Verbrugge, L. M. (1977). The structure of adult friendship choices. *Social Forces, 56,* 576–597.

Verbrugge, L. M. (1979). Marital status and health. *Journal of Marriage and the Family, 41,* 267–285.

Verbrugge, L. M. (1983). A research note on adult friendship contact: A dyadic perspective. *Social Forces, 62,* 78–83.

Vitkus, J., & Horowitz, L. M. (1987). Poor social performance of lonely people: Lacking a skill or adopting a role? *Journal of Personality and Social Psychology, 52,* 1266–1273.

Vogt, T., Mullooly, J., Ernst, D., Pope, C., & Hollis, J. (1992). Social networks as predictors of ischemic heart disease, cancer, stroke and hypertension: incidence, survival and mortality. *Journal of Clinical Epidemiology, 45,* 659–666.

Walker, K. N., MacBride, A., & Vachon, M. L. S. (1977). Social support networks and the crisis of bereavement. *Social Science and Medicine, 11,* 35–41.

Waller, W. (1938). *The family: A dynamic interpretation.* New York: Dryden.

Waln, V. G. (1982). Interpersonal conflict interaction: An examination of verbal defense of self. *Central States Speech Journal, 33,* 557–566.

Walster, E., Aronson, V., Abrahams, D., & Rottmann, L. (1966). Importance of physical attractiveness in dating behavior. *Journal of Personality and Social Psychology, 4,* 508–516.

Walster, E., & Walster, G. W. (1978). *A new look at love.* Reading, MA: Addison-Wesley.

Walster, E., Walster, G. W., & Berscheid, E. (1971). The efficacy of playing hard-to-get. *Journal of Experimental Education, 39,* 73–77.

Walster, E., Walster, G. W., & Berscheid, E.

(1978). *Equity: Theory and research.* Boston: Allyn & Bacon.

Wedell, D. H., Parducci, A., & Geiselman, R. E. (1987). A formal analysis of ratings of physical attractiveness: Successive contrast and simultaneous assimilation. *Journal of Experimental Social Psychology, 23,* 230–249.

Wegner, D. M. (1986). Transactive memory: A contemporary analysis of the group mind. In B. Mullen & G. R. Goethals (Eds.), *Theories of group behavior* (pp. 185–208). New York: Springer-Verlag.

Wegner, D. M., Erber, R., & Raymond, P. (1991). Transactive memory in close relationships. *Journal of Personality and Social Psychology, 61,* 923–929.

Wegner, D. M., Giuliano, T., & Hertel, P. (1985). Cognitive interdependence in close relationships. W. J. Ickes (Ed.), *Compatible and incompatible relationships* (pp. 253–276). New York: Springer-Verlag.

Weis, N. S. (1973). Marital status and risk factors for coronary heart disease. *British Journal of Preventive Medicine, 27,* 41–43.

Weiss, L., & Lowenthal, M. F. (1975). Life-course perspectives on friendship. In M. F. Lowenthal, M. Thurnher, & D. Chiriboga (Eds.), *Four stages of life* (pp. 48–61). San Francisco: Jossey-Bass.

Weiss, R. L., & Dehle, C. (1994). Cognitive behavioral perspectives on marital conflict. In D. D. Cahn (Ed.), *Conflict in personal relationships.* Hillsdale, NJ: Erlbaum.

Weiss, R. S. (1969). The fund of sociability. *Transaction/Society, 6,* 36–43.

Weiss, R. S. (1973). *Loneliness: The experience of emotional and social isolation.* Cambridge, MA: MIT Press.

Weiss, R. S. (1991). The attachment bond in childhood and adulthood. In C. M. Parkes, J. Stevenson-Hinde, & P. Marris (Eds.), *Attachment across the life cycle.* London: Tavistock/Routledge.

Weiss, S. A., Fishman, S., & Krause, F. (1971). Severity of disability as related to personality and prosthetic adjustment of amputees. *Psychological Aspects of Disability, 18,* 67–75.

Weisz, J. R., Weiss, B., Alicke, M. D., & Klotz, M. L. (1987). Effectiveness of psychotherapy with children and adolescents. A meta-analysis

for clinicians. *Journal of Consulting and Clinical Psychology, 55,* 542–549.

Weltfish, G. (1965). *The lost universe.* New York: Basic.

Werner, C., & Parmelee, P. (1979). Similarity of activity preferences among friends: Those who play together stay together. *Social Psychology Quarterly, 42,* 62–66.

Westermark, E. (1922). *The history of human marriage* (Vol. 1). New York: Allerton.

Wheeler, L., Reis, H. T., & Bond, M. H. (1989). Collectivism-individualism in everyday social life: The middle kingdom and the melting pot. *Journal of Personality and Social Psychology, 57,* 79–86.

Wheeler, L., Reis, H. T., & Nezlek, J. (1983). Loneliness, social interaction and sex roles. *Journal of Personality and Social Psychology, 45,* 943–953.

White, G. L. (1980). Physical attractiveness and courtship progress. *Journal of Personality and Social Psychology, 39,* 660–668.

White, G. L. (1981a). Jealousy and partner's perceived motives for attraction to a rival. *Social Psychology Quarterly, 44,* 24–30.

White, G. L. (1981b). A model of romantic jealousy. *Motivation and Emotion, 5,* 295–310.

White, G. L. (1981c). Relative involvement, inadequacy, and jealousy: A test of a causal model. *Alternative Lifestyles, 4,* 291–309.

White, G. L., & Mullen, P. E. (1989). *Jealousy: Theory, research and clinical strategies.* New York: Guilford.

White, L. K., & Booth, A. (1991). Divorce over the life course: The role of marital happiness. *Journal of Family Issues, 12,* 5–21.

Wiederman, M. W., & Allgeier, E. R. (1992). Gender differences in mate selection criteria: Sociobiological or socioeconomic explanations. *Ethology and Sociobiology, 13,* 115–124.

Williams, J., & Solano, C. H. (1983). The social reality of feeling lonely: Friendship and reciprocation. *Personality and Social Psychology Bulletin, 9,* 237–242.

Wills, T. A. (1981). Downward comparison principles in social psychology. *Psychological Bulletin, 90,* 245–271.

Wilson, E. O. (1975). *Sociobiology: The new synthesis.* Cambridge, MA: Belknap Press.

Winstead, B. A., Derlega, V. J., Lewis, R. J., &

Margulis, S. T. (1988). Understanding the therapeutic relationship as a personal relationship. *Journal of Social and Personal Relationships, 5,* 109–125.

Winstead, B. A., Derlega, V. J., Montgomery, M. J., & Pilkington, C. (1995). The quality of friendships at work and job satisfaction. *Journal of Social and Personal Relationships, 12,* 199–215.

Winter, D. G. (1988). The power motive in women—and men. *Journal of Personality and Social Psychology, 54,* 510–519.

Winter, D. G., & Barenbaum, N. B. (1985). Responsibility and the power motive in women and men. *Journal of Personality, 53,* 335–355.

Winter, D. G., Stewart, A. J., & McClelland, D. C. (1977). Husband's motives and wife's career level. *Journal of Personality and Social Psychology, 35,* 159–166.

Witteman, H., & Fitzpatrick, M. A. (1986). Compliance-gaining in marital interactions: Power bases, processes, and outcomes. *Communication Monographs, 53,* 130–143.

Wittenberg, M. T., & Reis, H. T. (1986). Loneliness, social skills and social perception. *Personality and Social Psychology Bulletin, 12,* 121–130.

Wolf, A. P. (1966). Childhood association, sexual attraction and incest taboo: A Chinese case. *American Anthropologist, 68,* 883–898.

Wolf, A. P. (1968). Adopt a daughter-in-law, marry a sister. *American Anthropologist, 70,* 864–874.

Wolf, A. P. (1970). Childhood association and sexual attraction: A further test of the Westermark hypothesis. *American Anthropologist, 72,* 503–515.

Wolf, E. (1966). Kinship, friendship, and patron-client relations in complex societies. In M. Banton (Ed.), *The social anthropology of complex societies.* London: Tavistock.

Wolf, M. (1972). *Women and the family in rural Taiwan.* Palo Alto, CA: Stanford University Press.

Wolf, S. (1992). Predictors of myocardial infarction over a span of 30 years in Roseto, Pennsylvania. *Integrative Physiological and Behavioral Science, 27,* 246–257.

Wolf, S., & Bruhn, J. G. (1993). *The power of the clan: The influence of human relationships on heart disease.* New Brunswick, NJ: Transaction.

Wolins, M. (1970). Young children in institutions. *Developmental Psychology, 2,* 99–109.

Won-Doornik, M. J. (1979). On getting to know you: The association between the stage of a relationship and reciprocity of self-disclosure. *Journal of Experimental Social Psychology, 15,* 229–241.

Wong, M. M., & Csikszentmihalyi, M. (1991). Affiliation motivation and daily experience: Some issues on gender differences. *Journal of Personality and Social Psychology, 60,* 154–164.

Woodward, J. C., Zabel, J., & Decosta, C. (1980). Loneliness and divorce. *Journal of Divorce, 4,* 73–82.

Woody, E. Z., & Costanzo, P. R. (1990). Does marital agony precede marital ecstasy? A comment on Gottman and Krokoff's "Marital Interaction and Satisfaction: A Longitudinal View." *Journal of Consulting and Clinical Psychology, 58,* 499–501.

Wortman, C. B., & Dunkle-Schetter, C. (1979). Interpersonal relationships and cancer: A theoretical analysis. *Journal of Social Issues, 35,* 120–155.

Wright, B. (1983). *Physical disability: A psychosocial approach* (2nd ed.). New York: Harper & Row.

Wright, P. H. (1982). Men's friendships, women's friendships and the alleged inferiority of the latter. *Sex Roles, 8,* 1–20.

Wright, P. H. (1984). Self-referent motivation and the intrinsic quality of friendship. *Journal of Social and Personal Relationships, 1,* 115–130.

Wright, P. H. (1988). Interpreting research on gender differences in friendship: A case for moderation and a plea for caution. *Journal of Social and Personal Relationships, 5,* 367–373.

Wright, P. H. (1989). Gender differences in adults' same- and cross-gender friendships. In R. G. Adams & R. Blieszner (Eds.), *Older adult friendship* (pp. 197–221). Newbury Park, CA: Sage.

Wright, R. A., & Contrada, R. J. (1986). Dating selectivity and interpersonal attractiveness: Toward a better understanding of the "elusive phenomenon." *Journal of Social and Personal Relationships, 3,* 131–148.

Yinon, Y., Bizman, A., & Yagil, D. (1989). Self-evaluation maintenance and the motivation to interact. *Journal of Social and Personal Relationships, 6,* 475–486.

Young, M., Benjamin, B., & Wallis, C. (1963). Mortality of widowers. *Lancet, 2,* 254–256.

Youniss, J. (1980). *Parents and peers in social development.* Chicago: University of Chicago Press.

Youniss, J. (1986). Development in reciprocity through friendship. In C. Zahn-Waxler, E. Cummings, & R. Iannottee (Eds.), *Altruism and aggression.* New York: Cambridge University Press.

Youniss, J., & Smollar, J. (1985). *Adolescent relations with mothers, fathers and friends.* Chicago: University of Chicago Press.

Zahn, M. A. (1973). Incapacity, impotence and invisible impairment: Their effects upon interpersonal relations. *Journal of Health and Social Behavior, 34,* 115–123.

Zaragoza, N., Vaughn, S., & McIntosh, R. (1991). Social skills intervention and children with behavior problems. *Behavioral Disorders, 16,* 260–275.

Zillmann, D., Weaver, J. B., Mundorf, H. N., & Aust, C. F. (1986). Effects of an opposite-gender companion's affect to horror on distress, delight and attraction. *Journal of Personality and Social Psychology, 51,* 586–594.

Zimbardo, P. G. (1977). *Shyness: What is it, what to do about it.* Reading, MA: Addison-Wesley.

Zimmerman, D. H., & West, C. (1975). Sex roles, interruptions and silences in conversations. In B. Thorne & N. Heley (Eds.), *Language and sex: Difference and dominance* (pp. 105–129). Rawley, MA: Newbury House.

Zvonkovic, A. M., Pennington, D. C., & Schmiege, C. J. (1994). Work and courtship: How college workload and perceptions of work environment relate to romantic relationships among men and women. *Journal of Social and Personal Relationships, 11,* 63–76.

# Credits

**Text**

**Chapter 1: page 13,** Fig. 1-1 Reprinted by permission of the publisher from *Peacemaking Among Primates* by Frans B. M. de Waal, Cambridge, MA: Harvard University Press. Copyright © 1989 by Frans B. M. de Waal. **page 20,** Fig. 1-2 From Neese, R. M., 1990. "Evolutionary explanations of emotions," *Human Nature* 1(3), 275, Aldine de Gruyter. Copyright © 1990 Walter de Gruyter, Inc. Adapted with permission.

**Chapter 2: page 26,** With permission from Mary Frances Picciano. **page 27,** Fig. 2-1 From Murstein, B. I., 1977, "The stimulus-value-role (S-V-R) theory of dyadic relationships," in S. Duck, ed., *Theory and Practice in Interpersonal Attraction*, London: Academic Press. Reprinted by permission of publisher and author. **page 30,** Fig. 2-2 From Altman, I., 1974, "The communication of interpersonal attitudes: An ecological approach," in T. Huston, ed., *Foundations of Interpersonal Attraction*, New York: Academic Press. Adapted with permission of publisher and author.

**Chapter 4: page 66,** From Matarazzo, J. D., 1979, "A Good Friend: One of Mankind's Most Effective and Inexpensive Psychotherapists," *Journal of Clinical Psychology, 35,* 231–232. Reprinted by permission of John Wiley & Sons, Inc. **page 68,** Fig. 4-1 From Berkman, L. F., and Syme, S. L., 1979, "Social networks, host resistance, and mortality: A nine-year follow-up of Alameda County residence," *American Journal of Epidemiology, 103,* 186–204. Reprinted with permission from Johns Hopkins University School of Hygiene and Public Health and the authors. **page 70,** Fig. 4-2 Reprinted by permission of Transaction Publishers. From Wolf, S., 1992, "Predictors of myocardial infarction over a span of 30 years in Roseto, Pennsylvania," *Integrative Physiology and Behavioral Science, 27,* 249. Copyright © 1992 Transaction Publishers. All rights reserved. **page 75,** Fig. 4-3 From Pennebaker, J. W., 1989, "Confession, inhibition and disease," in L. Berkowitz, ed., *Advances in Experimental Social Psychology, 22,* 211–244, New York: Academic Press. Reprinted with permission from the publisher and the author.

**Chapter 5: page 88,** Table 5-1 Courtesy of Daniel W. Russell. Used by permission. **page 92,** Fig. 5-1 From Rubinstein, C., Shaver, P., and Peplau, L. A., 1979, "Loneliness." *Human Nature,* February, 58–65. Used by permission of the authors. **page 93,** Fig. 5-2 Reprinted by permission of Sage Publications Ltd. and the author from Tornstam, L., 1992, "Loneliness in Marriage," *Journal of Social and Personal Relationships,* Vol. 9, p. 205. Copyright © 1992 Sage Publications Ltd.

**Chapter 6: page 104,** From *The Interpersonal Theory of Psychiatry* by Henry Stack Sullivan. Copyright © 1953 by the William Alanson White Psychiatric Foundation. Reprinted by permission of W. W. Norton & Company, Inc.

**Chapter 7: page 129,** Fig. 7-1 Adapted from Brown, B. B., Mory, M. S., and Kinney, D., 1994, "Casting Adolescent Crowds in Relational Perspective: Caricature, channel, and context," in R. Montemayer, G. R.

Adams, and T. P. Gullota, eds., *Personal Relationships During Adolescence,* Sage Publications Inc. Copyright © 1994 Sage Publications Inc. Adapted by permission of the publisher.

**Chapter 10: page 177,** Table 10-1 Used by permission of Zick Rubin. **page 179,** Table 10-2 From Hatfield, E., and Sprecher, S., 1986, "Measuring Passionate Love in Intimate Relationships," *Journal of Adolescence, 9,* 383–410. Reprinted by permission of the publisher and the authors. **page 185,** Table 10-3 From Sternberg, R. J., 1988, *The Triangle of Love: Intimacy, Passion, Commitment,* Basic Books. Reprinted by permission of the author. **page 187,** Table 10-4 Adapted from Sternberg, R. J., 1986, "A Triangular Theory of Love," *Psychological Review, 93,* 119–135. Copyright © 1986 by the American Psychological Association. Adapted with permission. **page 188,** Table 10-5 From Fehr, B., 1988, "Prototype Analysis of the Concepts of Love and Commitment," *Journal of Personality and Social Psychology, 55,* 557–579. Copyright © 1988 American Psychological Association. Reprinted with permission.

**Chapter 12: page 228,** Fig. 12-1 From Wegner, D. M., Erber, R., and Raymond, P., 1991, "Transactive Memory in Close Relationships," *Journal of Personality and Social Psychology, 61,* 926. Copyright © 1991 American Psychological Association. Reprinted with permission.

**Chapter 15: page 271,** Table 15-1 From Sharpsteen, D. J., 1993, "Romantic Jealousy as an Emotion Concept: A Prototype Analysis," *Journal of Social and Personal Relationships, 10,* 74–75. Copyright © 1993 Sage Publications Ltd. Reprinted by permission of the publisher. **page 276,** Table 15-2 From Pfeiffer, S. M., and Wong, P. T. P., "Multidimensional jealousy," *Journal of Social and Personal Relationships, 6,* 181–196. Copyright © 1989 Sage Publications Ltd. Reprinted by permission of the publisher and the authors.

**Chapter 16: page 291,** Fig. 16-1 From Braiker, H. B., and Kelley, H. H., 1979, "Conflict in Development of Close Relationships," in R. L. Burgess and T. L. Huston, eds., *Social Exchange in Developing Relationships,* Academic Press. Used by permission of the publisher and authors. **page 292,** Table 16-1 From Lloyd, S. A., and Cate, R. M., 1985, "The developmental course of conflict in premarital relationship dissolution," *Journal of Social and Personal Relationships, 2,* 179–194. Copyright © 1985 Sage Publications Ltd. Reprinted by permission of the publisher. **page 297,** Fig. 16-2 From Fincham, F. D., Beach, S. R., and

Baucom, D. H., 1987. Attribution processes in distressed and nondistressed couples: 4. Self-partner attribution differences. *Journal of Personality and Social Psychology, 53,* 739–748. Copyright © 1986 by the American Psychological Association. Adapted with permission.

**Photography**

**Chapter 1: page 11,** © Harlow Primate Laboratory, University of Wisconsin; **page 14,** © Steve McCurry/Magnum Photos; **page 16,** © Elizabeth Crews

**Chapter 2: page 29,** © Tony Savino/The Image Works; **page 34,** © Joel Gordon; **page 37,** © Gary Conner/PhotoEdit

**Chapter 3: page 48,** © John Boykin/PhotoEdit; **page 53,** © Robert Brenner/PhotoEdit; **page 57,** © Dagmar Fabricius/Stock Boston

**Chapter 4: page 67,** © Deborah Richards/PhotoEdit; **page 71,** © Hazel Hankin/Stock Boston; **page 77,** © Alan Carey/The Image Works

**Chapter 5: page 86,** © Nancy Richmond/The Image Works; **page 89,** © Elizabeth Crews; **page 99,** © Joel Gordon

**Chapter 6: page 106,** © Erika Stone; **page 108,** © Skjold Photographs; **page 118,** © Michael Newman/PhotoEdit

**Chapter 7: page 124,** © Michael Newman/PhotoEdit; **page 125,** © Bob Daemmrich/Stock Boston; **page 132,** © McLaughlin/The Image Works

**Chapter 8: page 143,** © Frank Siteman/Stock Boston; **page 149,** © Jeff Greenberg/PhotoEdit; **page 155,** © David Wells/The Image Works

**Chapter 10: page 180L,** © Willie Hill, Jr./The Image Works; **page 180R,** © Lionel Delevingne/Stock Boston; **page 184,** © Felicia Martinez/PhotoEdit; **page 193,** © Myrleen Ferguson Cate/PhotoEdit

**Chapter 11: page 198,** © Peter Weimann/Animals Animals; **page 201L,** © Paul Conklin/PhotoEdit; **page 201R,** © P. Rouchon/Explorer/Photo Researchers, Inc.; **page 208,** © Bobby Kingsley/Photo Researchers, Inc.; **page 211,** © Joel Gordon

**Chapter 12: page 217,** © Robert Brenner/PhotoEdit; **page 220,** © Joseph Nettis/Photo Researchers, Inc.; **page 224,** © Comstock, Inc.

**Chapter 13: page 236,** © Joseph Nettis/Stock Boston; **page 239,** © David R. Frazier/Photo Researchers, Inc.; **page 244,** © Steven D. Starr/Stock Boston

# Index

adolescent friendships, 4, 122–139
  cliques and crowds and, 125–131
  conflict in, 133
  correlates of, 133–139
  gender differences in, 135–136
  of girls, 123–124
  opposite-sex, 136–137
  peer pressure and, 138
  popularity and, 137
  race and, 137
  significance of, 123
  similarity as basis of, 134–135
  social adjustment and, 138–139
  socioeconomic status and, 133–134
  stability of, 131–133
adolescents
  adjustment in, and early hospitalization, 15
  loneliness in, 90–91, 94–95, 96–97, 99
  stigmatized, 167–169
  *See also* adolescent friendships
adopted children, adjustment of, and early
    attachment, 15
adult friendships, 4, 141–158
  among older adults, 153–157
  among young adults, 149–151
  culture and, 145
  defining and measuring, 142
  of disabled people, 169–170
  during maturity and middle age, 151–153
  gender differences in, 144–146, 152, 154
  life transitions and, 148

  marriage and, 6, 150, 152–153
  negative effect of, 157–158
  similarity/proximity in, 154–155
  types of, 142–144
  in workplace, 147–148
adults
  loneliness in, 91–92
  stigmatized, 169–170
  *See also* adult friendships
affiliation, 2, 9–11
  advantages of, 10–11
  vs. attachment, 11
  disadvantages of, 9–10
affinity seeking, 35
affinity testing, 34–36
agape, as love style, 183, 194
age, loneliness in adults and, 92
aggression
  power in friendships and, 253–254
  *See also* violence
AIDS, as stigma, 163
alternative relationships
  derogation of, and commitment, 245
  power and, 254–256
  satisfaction vs. commitment and, 240–244
Altman, I., social penetration theory of, 28–33
altruism, 9, 16–22
  in children's friendships, 116
  costs of, 17
  defined, 17
  emotions and, 19–22

altruism *(continued)*
  kin selection and, 17
  reciprocal, 2, 18–19, 49
ambivalence
  commitment and, 238–240
  in interacting with stigmatized people, 165
  in romantic relationship development, 290,
    291–292
Amish societies, shunning in, 96
androgyny, loneliness and, 94
anger, cooperation in relationships and, 20–21
animals, nonhuman
  affiliation among, 9–10
  attachment among, 11–13, 15–16
  reciprocal altruism in, 18–19
  sexual relationship patterns among, 22–23
anxiety, as preserving relationship, 21
Aron, Arthur, on "inclusion of other in self," 221
Aron, Claire, on "inclusion of other in self," 221
attachment, 2, 9, 11–16
  vs. affiliation, 11
  disruption of normal, 12–13
  early, and later adjustment, 13–15, 193–195
  as foundation for peer socialization, 15–16
  hospitalization and, 15
  infant/childhood, and adult love relationships,
    192–195
  jealousy and, 278
  loneliness in children and, 90
  love as, 192–195
  orphanage rearing and, 15
attribution
  causal vs. responsibility, 297–298
  commitment and, 245–247
  in conflict in romantic relationships, 295–298
  exchange theory and, 52–53
  jealousy and, 283–284
  with physical attractiveness, 203–206
authenticity, 56–58

beauty
  radiation of, 202–203
  universal agreement on, 200, 201
  *See also* physical attractiveness
bereavement
  cancer and, 78
  causes of death and, 77–78
  depression and, 75–76
  health and, 75–78
  immune function and, 76, 81

Berkman, Lisa, study of social connections and
    mortality rates, 67–69
betrayal, 20
Boston Couples Study, 209, 257–258, 264
boys. *See* males
Brazelton, T. Berry, on attachment and
    adjustment, 14
Brickman, Philip, on commitment, 235, 238–239

cancer
  bereavement and, 78
  social support and, 72–73
caretakers, bereaved, 76
caricatures, adolescent crowds as, 126–127
catastrophe theory, on ambivalence, 238
causal attribution, 297–298
ceiling effect, on wife's accomplishments, 261
channeling, by adolescent crowds, 127–128
cheating, 18–19, 20
children
  attachment of, to mother, 11–16
  early separation of, from mothers, 12–13,
    14–15
  friendships of parents of, 150–151
  loneliness in, 89–90
  physical attractiveness and, 206–207
  sibling relationships of, 110–111
  stigmatized, 167
  *See also* children's friendships
children at risk, 116–120
  defined, 116
  intervention with, 118–120
  problems in later life for, 116–118
children's friendships, 3–4, 104–121
  arranged, 119
  change in friendship concept in, 104–106
  consequences of peer rejection, 116–120
  gender and, 111–112
  parenting styles and, 120
  popularity and, 113, 115–116
  race and, 112
  reciprocity in, 107–110
  similarity as basis of, 111
  sociometric status and, 112–115
  stability in, 112
church attendance, and health, 72
cliques
  adolescent identity and, 125–129
  defined, 125
  importance of, 131

male vs. female, 136

*See also* crowds

close friends, among adults, 142

closeness, in self-evaluation maintenance, 225, 226

cognitive dissonance, commitment and, 235–238

commitment, 2, 5, 233–249

ambivalence and, 238–240

among lesbians and gay males, 243

attribution and, 245–247

cognitive dissonance and, 235–238

as component of love, 184, 186–187, 190

expression of, and culture, 248

individual differences in, 247–248

investment model of, 240–244

personal and structural, 234–235

prototype analysis of, 188–189

relationship maintenance strategies and, 244–245

sacrifice and, 245

satisfaction vs., 240–244

testing of, 247

community cohesiveness, heart disease and, 69–71

companionate love, 178, 180, 186, 187

companionship, as type of support, 65

comparison, in self-evaluation maintenance, 224, 226

comparison level (CL)

in exchange theory, 46

in investment model, 240

comparison level for alternatives (CLalt), in exchange theory, 46–47

complementarity, 221–231

inclusion of other in self, 221

interpersonal theory, 223

self-evaluation maintenance (SEM), 223–227

similarity, 222–223

transactive memory, 227–231

conciliation, for conflict resolution, 302

confidants

coping with traumatic events and, 73–74, 75

loneliness in adults and, 95

*See also* friendships

conflict, 5, 288–304

areas of, 289–290

attribution in, 295–298

aversion to, and power, 265

and career orientation, 263

confronting vs. avoiding, 293–295

couples who never fight, 300

demand-withdraw pattern and, 298, 302

and duration of marriage, 299–300

in friendships, 133, 288–289

normative, 296

over values, beliefs, and goals, 298–299

precipitating events for, 290

relationship development and, 290–293

conflict resolution, 300–303

conciliation, 302

escalation, 301

integrative agreements, 302–303

negotiation, 300–301

context

relational, 56

social, 58–60

control

mutuality of, 55

power as, 251

controversial children, children's friendships and, 113, 114–115

Cooley, Charles Horton, "looking-glass" self concept of, 215

cooling-off signals, in relationship development, 36

cooperation

emotions and, 19–22

*See also* altruism

costs

in exchange theory, 46

immediate vs. ultimate, of altruism, 17

couples, transactive memory in, 227–231

crowds

adolescent identity and, 125–129

as caricatures (prototypes), 126–127

channeling by, 127–128

as context for friendships, 129–131

defined, 125

desirability of, 129

importance of, 131

permeability of, 128

culture

adolescent, 125–131

commitment and, 248

effect of celibacy requirement of, 23

friendships and, 41, 49, 119, 132, 145

jealousy and, 274, 279, 280, 281

marriage and, 183, 262, 280, 301

mental illness and, 63, 74

norms and, 6

physical attractiveness and, 200, 201

Darwin, Charles, 7–8
dating
    commitment in, investment model on, 242
    equity in, 51–52
    exchange in, 49
    physical attractiveness and, 207–209
    *See also* romantic relationships
decision, as component of love, 184, 186–187
depression
    bereavement and, 75–76
    risk of, with early loss of mother, 14
    in separated/divorced women, 81
derogation of attractive alternatives, commitment
    and, 245
desperate love, 194
Differential Loneliness Scale (DLS), 87
differential reproduction, 8
disabilities
    acquired, and friendships/family, 170, 172–173
    degree of impairment from, and social
        adjustment, 171–173
    effects of, 161–165
    interacting with people with, 165–166
    *See also* stigma
diversity. *See* culture
divorce
    attachment style and, 194
    health and, 78–79, 81–82
    loneliness and, 90, 91–92, 97
"dollar auction game," 237
dominance
    male, preference for, 260–261
    power as, 251
dyadic realignment, 59–60
dyadic withdrawal hypothesis, 59

ecological niche, 217
emotional bonding, 2
emotional loneliness, 86, 87
emotional support, 65
emotions, cooperation and, 19–22
entrapment, 238, 240
epidemiology
    on church attendance and health, 72
    on community cohesiveness and heart disease,
        69–71
    on confidants and coping with trauma, 73–74,
        75
    defined, 66

on rehabilitation/recovery and social support,
    73, 74
on social connectedness and health, 66–69,
    72–73
on social support, stress and pregnancy
    complications, 71–72
equity theory, 50–52
    assumptions of, 51
    jealousy and, 284–285
    on overbenefited and underbenefited, 51–52
Eros, as "color" of love, 182, 183, 194
escalation, conflict, 301
*Essay on the Principle of Population* (Malthus), 7
ethnopsychiatry, 74
evolutionary theory, 2–3, 7–24
    affiliation and, 9–11
    altruism and, 9, 16–22
    attachment and, 9, 11–16
    jealousy and, 279
    origin of, 7–8
    on physical attractiveness, 201–202
    sexuality and, 9, 22–23
    on social behavior origins, 8–9
exchange theory, 45–53
    attribution and, 52–53
    basic concepts of, 45–47
    critique of, 47–48
    equity theory variation of, 50–52
    in friendships, dating, and marriage, 48–50
    norms in relationships and, 50
Extramarital Behavioral Intention Scale, 284

fairness, 50
fait accompli jealousy, 269
fathers
    absence of, and adolescent girls' behavior,
        134
    *See also* parents
Fehr, Beverley, on love as prototype, 187–192
females
    abused, commitment to marriage of, 242–244
    adolescent, and absence of father, 134
    friendships of, 123–124, 145
    lesbian, 168, 242, 243, 259
    need for power in, 264–265
    *See also* gender
financial support, 64–65
friendly relationships, among adults, 142–144,
    147

friendships, 3–4
  conflict in, 133, 288–289
  culture and, 41, 49, 119, 132, 145
  development of, 36–38, 39, 40
  as element of love, 180–181, 187
  emotional bonding in, 2
  exchange in, 48–49
  gender and, 111–112, 135–137, 144–146, 152, 154
  intimacy in, 105, 136
  mutuality of control in, 55
  physical attractiveness and, 210–211
  popularity and, 113, 115–116, 137
  power and, 253–254
  race and, 112, 137
  reciprocity in, 48–49, 107–110
  as result of cooperation, 20
  self-verification in, 219–221
  similarity as basis of, 111, 134–135, 154–155
  social context of, 58–60
  social support from, 66
  stability of, 112, 131–133
  stigma and, 164–165
  types of, and culture, 41
  *See also* adolescent friendships; adult friendships; children's friendships; confidants

Galton, Francis, on affiliation, 10
gay males
  adolescent, relationship development among, 168
  commitment among, 242, 243
  power in relationships of, 259
  *See also* homosexuality
gender
  career orientation and conflict and, 263
  division of household labor and, 263–264
  friendships and, 111–112, 135–137, 144–147, 152, 154
  jealousy and, 279–281
  liking/loving and, 177
  loneliness and, 93–94
  physical attractiveness and, 200–203, 206, 212–213
  power and, 256–265
  skills training for children and, 120
  *See also* females; males

generation effect, with memory, 230
guilt, as preserving relationship, 21

Hamilton, William, on kin selection, 17
Harlow, Harry, attachment experiments of, 11–12, 15–16
health
  church attendance and, 72
  community cohesiveness and, 69–71
  partner loss and, 75–79
  separation/divorce and, 78–79, 81–82
  social connectedness and, 72–73
  social support and, 66–75, 79–82
  of widowed people, 75–78
heart disease
  as cause of death among widowed people, 77–78
  social support and, 69–71, 73
hedging, in prototypes, 191
HIV positive, as stigma, 163
homosexuality
  as normal premarital activity, 6
  *See also* gay males; lesbians
hospitalization, attachment and, 15
*How to Win Friends and Influence People* (Carnegie), 252
Hutterites, mental illness among, 63

identity
  adolescent, cliques/crowds and, 125–129
  social support and, 66
identity negotiation, through self-verification, 215–221
immune function
  in bereaved, 76, 81
  in separated/divorced people, 81–82
infants. *See* children
influence, power as, 250–251
influence potential, consensus on, 55–56
instrumental support, 64
integrative agreements, 302–303
interdependence, 1
  conflict and, 295–296
interpersonal theory, 223
intimacy
  acquired disabilities and, 172–173
  as component of love, 184, 186–187
  in friendships, 105, 136
investment model of commitment, 240–244

jealousy, 5, 268–287
  attachment style and, 278
  attribution and, 283–284
  components of, 273–275
  culture and, 274, 279, 280, 281
  equity theory and, 284–285
  gender differences in, 279–281
  individual differences in, 275–279
  measuring, 275–277
  open/group marriage and, 285–286
  permissive attitudes and, 285
  as prototype, 270–273
  relationship status and, 282–283
  self-concept and, 277
  self-esteem and, 277–278
  self-evaluation maintenance (SEM) and, 279
  situations provoking, 269–275
  types of, 268–269
  violence and, 281–282

Kelley, Harold, exchange theory of, 45–46
kin selection, 17
known-about-ness, of stigmas, 161, 163

Lambo, Thomas Adeoye, 74
law of personal exploitation, 254
Lee, John, on love styles, 181–183, 194
lesbians
  adolescent, relationship development among, 168
  commitment among, 242, 243
  power in relationships of, 259
life transitions, adult friendships and, 148
liking
  defined, 175–176
  as source of power, 252–253
  as type of love, 186, 187
  *See also* love
Liking Scale, 176–177
limerence, as style of love, 194
limitations, due to stigma, 161, 164
loneliness, 3, 84–102
  in adolescence, 90–91, 94–95, 96–97, 99
  in adults, 91–92
  in children, 89–90
  defined, 84
  descriptions of, 85
  due to sanctions, 96
  gender differences in, 93–94
  increasing concern with, 85

  intervention for, 101–102
  marriage and, 88, 91–92, 93
  measuring, 87, 88
  personality and, 97–101
  prevalence of, 87–89
  separation/divorce and, 91–92, 97
  social interactions and, 94–97
  types of, 85–87
  in widowed people, 97
lonely people, others' perceptions of, 100–101
"looking-glass" self, 215
love, 4, 175–196
  as attachment, 192–195
  defined, 175
  friendship as element of, 180–181, 187
  Lee's styles of, 181–183, 194
  as prototype, 187–192
  as result of cooperation, 20
  Sternberg's triangular theory of, 184–187, 195
  types of, 177–181, 186–187
Love Attitude Scale, 183
Love Scale, 176–177
*ludus,* as "color" of love, 182, 194

males
  adolescent friendships of, 132
  childhood dependency of, and commitment, 248
  gay, 168, 242, 243, 259
  need for power in, 247–248, 264
  *See also* fathers; gender
Malthus, Thomas, 7
mania, as love style, 182, 183, 194
marriage
  acquired disabilities and, 172–173
  adult friendships and, 6, 150, 152–153
  arranged, 183
  asymmetry in, 261–262
  conflict and, 299–300, 301
  consensus on influence potential in, 56
  culture and, 183, 262, 280, 301
  exchange in, and happiness, 49–50
  loneliness and, 88, 91–92, 93
  open/group, and jealousy, 285–286
  physical attractiveness and, 210, 211–212
  polyandry, 280
  self-verification in, 217
  stability of, and mortality rates, 67
  *See also* romantic relationships

Matarazzo, Thomas, on importance of support from friends, 66
matching hypothesis, of physical attractiveness, 208–209
Mead, George Herbert, on "significant others," 215
measurement
    of adult friendships, 142
    of jealousy, 275–277
    of liking/loving, 176–177, 179, 183, 185–186
    of loneliness, 87, 88
    of physical attractiveness, 199–200
men. *See* males
mental health
    bereavement and, 75–76
    children's peer relationships and, 116–117
    physical attractiveness and, 205
    of separated/divorced people, 78–79
mental illness
    among Hutterites, 63
    interacting with people with history of, 165
    "passing" with, 164
    social support and, 63, 73, 74
monogamy, in primate sexual behavior, 22
mortality rates
    social connectedness and, 66–69, 72
    for widowed people, 76–77
mothers
    attachment to, 11–16
    early separation from, 12–13, 14–15
    importance of, and culture, 6
    substitute, and peer socialization, 15–16
    *See also* parents
Multidimensional Jealousy Scale, 275, 276
Murstein, Bernard, stimulus-value-role theory of, 27–28

National Center for Health Statistics
    on causes of death and marital status, 78
    on divorce/health relationship, 79
natural selection, 7–8
    kin selection and, 17
negative nominations, children's sociometric status and, 113
neglected children, children's friendships and, 113, 114
negotiation
    for conflict resolution, 300–301
    identity, 215–221
Nevada, vs. Utah, health statistics, 66–67

New York University Loneliness Scale, 87
norm ambiguity, in interacting with stigmatized people, 165
normative conflict, 296
norms, 50

obesity, as stigma, 160, 162
obtrusiveness, of stigmas, 161
*On the Origin of Species* (Darwin), 7–8
opportunity structures, 217
orphanage rearing, attachment and, 15
outcomes, in exchange theory, 46

parenting styles, children's friendships and, 120
parents
    adult friendships of, 150–151
    single, loneliness and, 90, 91–92
    *See also* fathers; mothers
partner loss
    health and, 75–79
    immune function and, 81–82
    social support and, 64–66
    transactive memory and, 230–231
    *See also* divorce; widowed people
passing
    defined, 162
    by people with stigma, 161–164
passion, as component of love, 184, 186–187
passionate love, 178, 179, 180
Passionate Love Scale (PLS), 178, 179
peers
    adolescent, 125–131, 138
    effects of stigma on, 167–169
    rejection by, among children, 116–120
    socialization by, 15–16
permeability, of adolescent crowds/cliques, 128
permissiveness, jealousy and, 285
personal commitment, 234–235
personality
    commitment and, 247–248
    jealousy and, 275, 277
    loneliness and, 97–101
    physical attractiveness and, 205–206
    power and, 264–266
personal relationships
    affiliation in, 9–11
    altruism in, 9, 16–22
    attachment in, 9, 11–16
    defining characteristics of, 1–2

personal relationships *(continued)*
  sexuality in, 9, 22–23
  voluntary, focus on, 2
  *See also* friendships; romantic relationships
physical attractiveness, 4, 197–213
  attributions accompanying, 203, 205–206
  children and, 206–207
  defined, 197
  friendships and, 210–211
  gender and, 200–203, 206, 212–213
  genetic advantage of, 198–199
  marriage and, 210, 211–212
  matching hypothesis of, 208–209
  measuring, 199–200
  negative associations with, 212–213
  romantic relationships and, 207–209
  social interactions and, 204–206
  social mobility and, 209–210
  universal agreement on, 200
play, in peer relationships, 16
polyandry, 280
popularity, friendships and, 113, 115–116, 137
positive disregard, in relationship development,
    40
positive nominations, children's sociometric status
    and, 112–113
power, 5, 250–266
  availability of alternative relationships and,
    254–256
  defined, 250–251
  friendships and, 253–254
  gender and, 256–265
  individual differences and, 264–266
  in lesbian/gay male relationships, 259
  liking as source of, 252–253
  marriage asymmetry and, 261–262
  need for, 247–248, 264–265
  principle of least interest and, 254
  short- vs. long-term effects of, 251–252
pragma, as love style, 182–183
pregnancy, complications of, and social support
    and stress, 71–72
pride, as preserving relationship, 21–22
primates. *See* animals, nonhuman
principle of least interest, 254
prisoner's dilemma game, 19–20
promiscuity, in primate sexual behavior, 22
prototype
  adolescent crowd as, 126–127
  hedging in, 190–191

jealousy as, 270–273
love as, 187–192

race, friendships and, 112, 137
receptivity signals, in early relationship
    development, 33–34
reciprocal altruism, 2, 18–19, 49
reciprocity
  in friendships, 48–49, 107–110
  practice vs. principle of, 108–109
  of self-disclosure, 39
  stability of adolescent friendships and, 131
reference groups, defined, 125
reflection, in self-evaluation maintenance, 224,
    225
rejected children, children's friendships and,
    113–114
relational context, 56
relationship definition, 54–55
relationship development, 3, 26–41
  affinity testing in, 34–36
  cooling-off signals in, 36
  decisions made early in, 36–40
  incremental theories of, 28–33
  positive disregard in, 40
  receptivity signals in, 33–34
  social penetration theory of, 28–33
  stage theories of, 26–28
  uncertainty reduction in, 33
relationship maintenance, 3, 44–61
  authenticity for, 56–58
  consensus on influence potential and, 55–56
  equity theory on, 50–52
  exchange theory on, 45–53
  mutual agreements needed for, 53–56
  mutuality of control and, 55
  relationship definition and, 53–55
  social context of personal relationships and,
    58–60
Relationship Rating Form, 181
relevance, in self-evaluation maintenance, 225,
    226
responsibility attribution, 297–298
retirement, adult friendships and, 155–156
rewards
  in exchange theory, 46
  in friendships, dating, and marriage, 48–50
romantic relationships
  authenticity in, 56–58
  career orientation and, 254, 263

closeness and relevance in, 226
commitment in, investment model on, 242–244
conflict in, 289–303
development of, 38–39, 39–40
emotional bonding in, 2
jealousy in, 268–287
physical attractiveness and, 207–209
playing hard to get in, 256
social context of, 58–60
strategies for maintaining, 244–245
turning points in, 35–36
*See also* dating; marriage
roommates
  self-disclosure among, 31, 32
  self-verification with, 217, 219
Roseto, Pennsylvania, community cohesiveness of, 69–71
Rusbult, Caryl, on investment model of commitment, 240–244

sacrifice, commitment and, 245
satisfaction, vs. commitment, 240–244
schizophrenia
  passing with, 164
  social support and rehabilitation with, 73
self, inclusion of other in, 221
self-concept
  jealousy and, 277
  negative, 218, 220–221
self-disclosure, in relationship development, 31, 39
self-esteem
  jealousy and, 277–278
  loneliness and, 98–99
self-evaluation maintenance (SEM), 223–227, 279
self-interest, cooperation and, 22
self-verification, 216–221
  from friends, 219–221
  interactions for, 217–219
  opportunity structures for, 217
separation (marital)
  attachment style and, 194
  health and, 78–79, 81–82
  loneliness and, 90, 91–92, 97
sexuality, 3, 9, 22–23
Shakers, 23
shunning, in Amish societies, 96
shyness, loneliness and, 98
sibling relationships, of children, 110
"significant others," 215

similarity
  as basis of friendships, 111, 134–135, 154–155
  complementarity and, 222–223
social adjustment
  adolescent friendship and, 138–139
  and early attachment, 13–15, 193–194
  impairment from disability and, 171–173
social behavior, origins of, 8
social connectedness
  cancer and, 72–73
  health and, 72–73
  mortality rates and, 66–69, 72
social context, of romantic relationships and friendships, 58–60
Social and Emotional Loneliness Scale for Adults (SELSA), 87
social interactions
  of adults vs. adolescents, 141
  loneliness and, 94–97
  self-verification in, 217–219
  with stimatized people, 165–166
social loneliness, 86
social mobility, physical attractiveness and, 209–210
social penetration theory of relationship development, 28–33
social skills
  loneliness and, 99–100, 101
  training in, for children at risk, 118–120
social support
  from adult friendships, 146–147
  cancer and, 72–73
  coping with traumatic events and, 73–75
  defined, 64
  health and, 66–75, 79–82
  heart disease and, 69–71, 73
  mental illness and, 63, 73, 74
  mortality rates and, 66–69, 72
  pregnancy complications and, 71–72
  rehabilitation/recovery and, 73, 74
  types of, 64–66
socioeconomic status
  adolescent friendships and, 133–134
  social support and health and, 79–80
sociometric status
  children's friendship and, 112–115
  stability of, 115
special-interest friendships, among adults, 144
stability
  of attachment styles, 193–194

stability *(continued)*
    of children's sociometric status, 115
    of conflict level in romantic relationships, 294
    of friendships, 112, 131–133
stage theories
    of children's friendships, 105–106
    of relationship development, 26–28
state loneliness, 85
Sternberg, Robert, triangular theory of love of, 184–187, 195
stigma, 4, 160–173
    adolescents with, 167–169
    adults with, 169–170
    AIDS/HIV positive as, 163
    children with, 167
    choice of friends and, 164–165
    disavowing limitations of, 164
    effects of, 161–165
    interacting with people with, 165–166
    "marked" vs. "markable," 161
    obesity as, 160, 162
    origin of term, 160
    passing with, 161–164
    *See also* disabilities
stimulus-value-role (S-V-R) theory of relationship development, 27–28
*storge,* as "color" of love, 182, 183
stress
    among bereaved, 80
    immune function and, 81–82
    pregnancy complications and social support and, 71–72
    social networks and, 146–147
structural commitment, 234–235
suicide
    among bereaved, 80
    by widowed people, 78
suspicious jealousy, 269

Swann, William, on identity negotiation, 215–221
Syme, Leonard, study of social connectedness and mortality rates, 67–69

Tesser, Abraham, on self-evaluation maintenance (SEM), 223–227
Thematic Apperception Test (TAT), 219
Thibaut, John, exchange theory of, 45–46
trait loneliness, 85
transactive memory, 227–231
    generation effect with, 230
    implications of, 230–231
traumatic events, confidants and, 73–74, 75
Triangular Love Scale, 185–186
trust, 20, 57–58
turning points, in early relationship development, 35–36

UCLA Loneliness Scale, 87, 88
uncertainty reduction, in early relationship development, 33
Utah, vs. Nevada, health statistics, 66–67

validational support, 65
violence
    jealousy and, 281–282
    *See also* aggression

Wegner, Daniel, on transactive memory, 227–231
widowed people
    adult friendships of, 156–157
    causes of death of, 77–78
    health of, 75–78
    loneliness in, 97
    mortality rates for, 76–77
women. *See* females
workplace, adult friendships in, 147–148